Y0-CDF-234

SILVER BURDETT music

TEACHER'S EDITION / 3

ELIZABETH CROOK
BENNETT REIMER
DAVID S. WALKER

SILVER BURDETT COMPANY
MORRISTOWN, NEW JERSEY • GLENVIEW, ILLINOIS
PALO ALTO • DALLAS • ATLANTA

SPECIAL CONTRIBUTORS

William M. Anderson (non-Western music), Aurora, Ohio

Kojo Fosu Baiden (music of Africa), Silver Springs, Maryland

Dulce B. Bohn (recorder), Wilmington, Delaware

Charles L. Boilès (music of Mexico), Bloomington, Indiana

Ian L. Bradley (Canadian music), Victoria, British Columbia, Canada

Gerald Burakoff (recorder), Levittown, New York

Henry Burnett (music of Japan), Flushing, Long Island, New York

Richard J. Colwell (testing and evaluation), Urbana, Illinois

Marilyn C. Davidson (music for Orff instruments), Bergenfield, New Jersey

Joan Davies (music of Canada and Japan), Charlottetown, P.E.I., Canada

Kay Hardesty (special education), Chautaugua, New York

James M. Harris (music in early childhood), San Francisco, California

Doris E. Hays (avant-garde music), New York City

Nazir A. Jairazbhoy (music of India), Windsor, Ontario, Canada

Maria Jordan (music of Greece), Hicksville, Long Island, New York

Robert A. Kauffman (music of Africa), Seattle, Washington

Edna Knock (music of Canada), Brandon, Manitoba, Canada

John Lidstone (visual arts), Brooklyn, New York

David McHugh (youth music), New York City

Alan P. Merriam (music of the North American Indians), Bloomington, Indiana

Lucille Mitchell (American folk songs), Alexandria, Virginia

María Luisa Muñoz (music of Puerto Rico), Houston, Texas

Lynn Freeman Olson (listening program), New York City

Mary E. Perrin (music in the inner city), Chicago, Illinois

Carmino Ravosa (children's song literature), Briarcliff Manor, New York

Joyce Bogusky Reimer (avant-garde music), Wilmette, Illinois

Geraldine Slaughter (music of Africa), Washington, D.C.

Mark Slobin (music of the Near East), Middletown, Connecticut

Ruth Marie Stone (music of Africa), New York City

Leona B. Wilkins (music in the inner city), Evanston, Illinois

©1981 SILVER BURDETT COMPANY. All Rights Reserved. Printed in the United States of America. Published simultaneously in Canada. This publication, or parts thereof, may not be reproduced in any form by photographic, electrostatic, mechanical, or any other method, for any use, including information storage and retrieval, without written permission from the publisher.   74 363 00   ISBN 0-382-05779-1

CONSULTANTS

Lynn Arizzi (levels 1 and 2), Reston, Virginia

Joy Browne (levels 5 and 6), Kansas City, Missouri

Nancy Crump, classroom teacher, Alexandria, Louisiana

Lyla Evans, classroom teacher, South Euclid, Ohio

Catherine Gallas, classroom teacher, Bridgeton, Missouri

Linda Haselton, classroom teacher, Westminster, California

Ruth A. Held, classroom teacher, Lancaster, Pennsylvania

Judy F. Jackson, classroom teacher, Franklin, Tennessee

Mary E. Justice, Auburn University, Auburn, Alabama

Jean Lembke (levels 3 and 4), Tonawanda, New York

Barbara Nelson, classroom teacher, Baytown, Texas

Terry Philips (youth music), New York City

Ruth Red, Director of Music Education, Houston, Texas

Mary Ann Shealy (levels 1 and 2), Florence, South Carolina

Beatrice Schattschneider (levels 1–6), Morristown, New Jersey

Paulette Schmalz, classroom teacher, Phoenix, Arizona

Sister Helen C. Schneider, Clarke College, Dubuque, Iowa

Merril Staton (recordings), Alpine, New Jersey

ACKNOWLEDGMENTS

The authors and editors of SILVER BURDETT MUSIC acknowledge with gratitude the contributions of the following persons.

Marjorie Hahn, New York

Yoriko Kozumi, Japan

Ruth Merrill, Texas

Bennie Mae Oliver, Texas

Joanne Ryan, New York

Helen Spiers, Virginia

Mary Ann Nelson, Texas

Shirley Ventrone, Rhode Island

Avonelle Walker, New York

Credit and appreciation are due publishers and copyright owners for use of the following.

"April Fool's Day" by Marnie Pomeroy from POEMS FOR SEASONS AND CELEBRATIONS, edited by William Cole. © 1961 World Publishing Company, Cleveland, Ohio

"Blum" reprinted by permission of G. P. Putnam's Sons from Here, There and Everywhere by Dorothy Aldis. Copyright © 1928, 1956 by Dorothy Aldis.

"But You Are Mine" ("Lullaby") used by permission of Institute of African Studies, University of Ghana, Legon, Ghana.

"Cat" Copyright, 1938 by Eleanor Farjeon, Renewal, ©, 1966 by Gervase Farjeon. From the book Poems for Children by Eleanor Farjeon, Copyright, 1951, by Eleanor Farjeon, and from Silver Sand & Snow by Eleanor Farjeon, published by Michael Joseph Ltd. Used by permission of J. B. Lippincott Company and David Higham Associates, Ltd.

"Lewis Has A Trumpet" from In the Middle of the Trees by Karla Kuskin. Copyright ©, 1968 by Karla Kuskin. Reprinted by permission of Harper & Row, Publishers, Inc.

"Paper I" from THE COMPLETE POEMS OF CARL SANDBURG, copyright 1950 by Carl Sandburg; renewed 1978 by Margaret Sandburg, Helga Sandburg Crile and Janet Sandburg. Reprinted (or recorded) by permission of Harcourt Brace Jovanovich, Inc.

"Rain Sizes" from the book The Reason for the Pelican by John Ciardi. Copyright, ©, 1959 by John Ciardi. Reprinted by permission of J. B. Lippincott Company.

"What the Wind Said" reprinted from The Pedaling Man by Russell Hoban. Text copyright © 1968 by Russell Hoban. By permission of the publishers, Grosset & Dunlap, Inc. and World's Work Ltd., The Windmill Press, Kingswood, Tadworth, Surrey.

"Wind" from Runny Days, Sunny Days by Aileen Fisher Abelard-Schuman. N.Y. 1958. Reprinted by permission of the author.

CONTENTS

Also available from the publisher are
• Student Response spirit masters for the *What Do You Hear?* lessons
• Competency Tests, three for each level, 1–6

INTRODUCTION

The first edition of SILVER BURDETT MUSIC heralded a new age for music education. SILVER BURDETT MUSIC was based firmly in the long history and strong traditions of school music; its organization reflected newly gained understanding of how children can best be helped to learn; and its philosophy captured the emerging focus on aesthetic education. The first edition was accepted enthusiastically and used successfully by teachers and students in all sections of the country.

Those responsible for SILVER BURDETT MUSIC, however, were determined that it not be allowed to rest on its success, but that it be studied conscientiously for ways to improve it. A major effort was launched to study scientifically what was being learned by children using the materials, what levels of success they were achieving, what tasks in the materials were too easy or too difficult, what examples were effective in enhancing musical perception and what examples were less so, what lessons needed reorganization, what possible changes would make every learning event as powerful as

MODULE
The module is the organizing unit of the program. A module is a single lesson or a cluster of lessons that can stand alone as an entity.

OBJECTIVES
Beginning on page xi, objectives for the modules are presented in chart form.

SUBJECT
...the subject of the module and the number of the lesson.

MATERIALS
...a list of the records, pupils' pages, instruments, and equipment needed to teach the lesson.

VOCABULARY
...a list of the terms used in this lesson.

IDEAS FOR TEACHING
...ideas for introducing the material and presenting it effectively.

ESSENTIAL ACTIVITY
The heavy black line identifies the Essential Activity in the lesson. If time permits, use of the additional suggestions is recommended.

ACCOMPANIMENT
...indicates the page number of the accompaniment. Accompaniments are for piano. Some songs have Orff-Instrument accompaniments also.

RECORDING
...indicates the location of the selection in the record package.

MODULE 4

OBJECTIVES, p. xi

METER • Lesson 1

MATERIALS
Record 3, "New Year's Song"; Pupil's Book, pp. 60 and 61; percussion instruments, recorder, balls

VOCABULARY
beats in sets of two, meter in 2, bar lines, measure, quarter notes, eighth notes, half notes, meter signature

IDEAS FOR TEACHING
1. Play the recording of "New Year's Song" and ask children to keep the steady beat by bouncing and catching a ball. Note: Using the bounce-catch, bounce-catch motions, children will feel beats in sets of two. (Just as the bounce motion is stronger than the catch motion, the first beat in a set of two is stronger than the second beat.)

2. You may want to review other motions in sets of two:
• Marching motions (left-right) in "Marching to Pretoria," p. 4
• Rocking motions in "Old Joe Clark," p. 8

3. When children are able to feel beats in sets of two through movement, have them play beats in sets of two on a percussion instrument throughout "New Year's Song."

When you bounce and catch a ball, you make motions in sets of two.

In music, these sets are called **meter.**

NEW YEAR'S SONG   Kazoe-uta   FOLK SONG FROM JAPAN   ENGLISH VERSION BY ROSEMARY JACQUES

Orff acc. p. 278

1. On the eve of New Year's,   Bus - y peo - ple, hap - py peo - ple,
   Hi - to - tsu to ya,   Hi - to - yo a - ku - re - ba,

   Run - ning here and there,   Run - ning here and there,
   Ni - gi - ya - ka de,   Ni - gi - ya - ka de,

   Dec - o - rate the bam-boo trees to cel - e - brate the day,
   O - ka - za - ri ta - te - ta - ru ma - tsu - ka - za - ri,

   Cel - e - brate the day.
   Ma - tsu - ka - za - ri.

2. On the eve of New Year's,
   Paper streamers, fresh plum blossoms
   Hang above the door,
   Hang above the door,
   Telling all who pass by
       to have a happy day,
   Have a happy day.

3. On the day of New Year's,
   Games are played and songs are sung
   To celebrate the day,
   Celebrate the day.
   People come to wish each other
       Happy New Year's Day,
   Happy New Year's Day.

60   MODULE 4: Meter

TEACHER INFORMATION

New Year's Eve has been called the most important of all Japanese holidays. Bells are rung to celebrate at midnight on New Year's Eve.

"New Year's Song" is sung by children as a ball-bouncing chant.

Mainstreaming: "New Year's Song" can be used to strengthen lateral perception by having children move their head, hands, or legs—left-right, right-left, or left to right and right to left, emphasizing the first movement. When beats are in sets of two, slower reacting children may perform only the first of each set of beats.

60 · Meter · Lesson 1

iv

experience and research could lead it to be. This research effort is described in more detail on page *ix*, "Testing Musical Competencies."

The result of all this work is the present edition of SILVER BURDETT MUSIC. It contains many of the improvements the studies suggested could be made, including more songs in each grade, greatly revised teachers' editions giving highly detailed suggestions for teaching, a clearer format (see below), more effective graphics, and reorganization of certain learning sequences. Virtually every change was based on hard evidence

that the change would indeed improve children's learning. SILVER BURDETT MUSIC offers the flexibility of being usable as a coherent curriculum in and of itself, or serving as a source of materials for use within an alternative curriculum. However used, the materials of SILVER BURDETT MUSIC embody "state of the art" principles from education in general combined with the best available knowledge about effective music education in particular. The authors and editors believe the series provides a model for what a good music curriculum should be. (Continued on p. *vi*.)

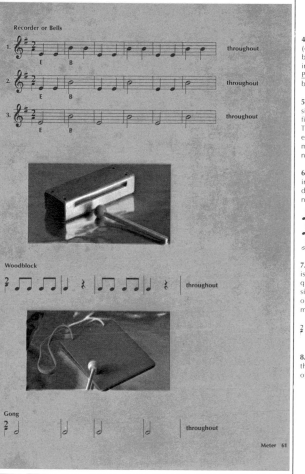

4. Ask children to find the lines (called *bar lines*) that separate the beats into sets of two in the instrumental parts on p. 61.
Point out: The space between the bar lines is called a *measure*.

5. Call attention to the meter signature (²) that appears before the first note of the instrumental parts. The 2 means that there are two beats each measure. The *quarter note* (♩) means that in this song a quarter note lasts for one beat.

6. Before children try playing the instrumental parts, review the relative duration of quarter notes, eighth notes, and half notes.

7. Point out the quarter rest (𝄽) that is used in the woodblock part. The quarter rest symbolizes a beat of silence. Use the quarter rest to focus on the first strong beat in each measure.

play, rest play, rest

8. When children are ready, have them play the instrumental parts as others sing "New Year's Song."

Meter · Lesson 1 · 61

TEACHER INFORMATION

Japanese folk songs often have simple rhythms and only a few notes in the melody, and they are not meant to have harmony. The people especially enjoy nature, not only in landscapes or large scenic views, but in small things such as a few flowers, leaves, branches, and pebbles. There are many Japanese songs that show the enjoyment of nature—songs about rain and snow, about twilight, about the moon, and about animals and insects.

Singing a melody with only one or two accompanying instruments and no harmony is perhaps like making a flower arrangement with only three flowers, or with a few flowering branches. For other Japanese folk songs, see "Hana ichi momme," p. 128, and "Imagination of Grand Sea," p. 129.

BLUE PANEL MATERIAL
Various kinds of materials are presented in the blue panel.

• Dance Directions

• Instrumental Parts

• Orff-instrument accompaniments; short ostinatos are notated on page. Longer arrangements are in the accompaniment section.

• Music Reading: Suggestions for developing music reading skills are frequently independent of the main emphasis of the lesson.

• Try This: The suggestions under this heading represent a wide variety of materials and approaches to teaching. Often they provide a challenge for gifted students. They are optional.

• Teacher Information: This historical, biographical, or procedural information enhances or expands upon the subject of the lesson. It may be shared with the students at your discretion.

• Mainstreaming: Suggestions for adapting the materials for mainstreamed classes are given, as well as references to adaptations in *Silver Burdett Music for Special Education.*

• Competency Tests: When the appropriate amount of material has been covered, a note reminds you that a certain test should be given at that time.

• Language Arts and Social Studies Correlation: Suggestions for language arts and social studies correlation are made when appropriate.

In addition to the teaching aids found on page, other helps are provided in the back of the Teacher's Edition.

• The Kodály Guide categorizes the song material in terms of the basic melody patterns used in the Kodály approach.

• The Note Reading Index categorizes the songs according to note values, rhythm patterns, and pitches.

• Classified Index

• Instructions for tuning the Autoharp

THE ORGANIZATION OF SILVER BURDETT MUSIC

MODULES AND LESSONS. In SILVER BURDETT MUSIC, the organizing unit is the module. A module is a single lesson or a cluster of lessons that can stand alone as an entity. The modules are the building blocks from which the teacher structures the curriculum. They are interchangeable and can be arranged in a great variety of sequences depending on particular circumstances.

A lesson is a single teaching-learning event that involves children in music through a variety of activities. Each lesson is designed to serve a twofold function:

1. A complete learning episode in itself

2. One of a set of lessons making up a module

The final lesson in many of the modules is called *What Do You Hear?* This kind of lesson requires the children to demonstrate what they have learned by responding to the instructions on the recording. These lessons give the children and the teacher a concrete assessment of progress toward increased musical discernment.

Each book in the series is part of a cyclical movement from obvious to subtle that extends from early childhood through Grade 8. From lesson, to module, to book, to series of nine books, each level is both complete in itself and a structural part of a larger whole. This cyclical, or "spiral," organization ensures a high level of consistency and a maximum of efficiency. It takes the child through a nine-year period of progressively deeper experiences with music. At the same time, it allows a newcomer to the program to begin at any point and be drawn into the spiral from that point on.

The spiral mode of organization is consistent with learning theory. The developmental nature of human learning has been well established. SILVER BURDETT MUSIC provides opportunities for gradual, progressive, consistent growth— constantly building upon and widening previous learnings, consistently challenging each musical behavior while providing a high level of success, and focusing activities in a specific direction while allowing for and encouraging individual freedom of movement within the general organization.

USING SILVER BURDETT MUSIC

THE BASIC PROGRAM. The quantity of materials provided in SILVER BURDETT MUSIC is so great that it is unlikely that any particular class could cover the complete contents of a given book in a year's time. For this reason, the lessons constituting the Basic Program have been identified. These lessons form the basis for a year's work. The Basic Program includes the material evaluated in the *Silver Burdett Music Competency Tests,* available from the publisher.

THE ENTENDED PROGRAM. The lessons in the Extended Program reinforce or extend the learning provided in the basic lessons. In many instances, a specific extended lesson can be substituted for a basic lesson if the song or listening selection in the extended lesson is more appropriate for a particular teaching situation, and if the concept taught is the same.

Identification of whether a lesson is part of the Basic Program or the Extended Program is provided in the Progress Chart, page xvi.

PROGRESSING THROUGH THE PROGRAM. A simple and effective way to progress through SILVER BURDETT MUSIC is consecutively from beginning to end. The sequence of lessons and modules has been arranged so that a majority of children will be likely to encounter a maximum of unity and diversity as they move from page to page. The teacher using a book for the first time may well find it advantageous to follow the book's outline progressively.

However, a high level of choice is built into the books. The lessons in each module can be taken in sequence until the module is finished. Depending upon the response of the children, a switch can be made at any time to a new module or to a previously unfinished module. The rule to follow is that in switching from module to module *the lessons within each module be covered in numerical sequence.* This procedure applies whether all lessons in a module are used or only the lessons in the Basic Program. In choosing lesson sequences, the teacher will be sensitive to

(1) the amount of time available,
(2) the children's attention span,
(3) a spontaneous interest in a new concept,
(4) the desire to explore a particular concept further, and
(5) the need to explore a wide variety of concepts.

The progression of learnings can be tailored to each situation with full confidence. The cyclical organization of the lessons ensures that learnings will not be diffuse or unrelated. Freedom and structure are basic and compatible features of SILVER BURDETT MUSIC.

PROGRESS CHART. The Progress Chart on p. xvi is provided to help teachers plan their program and to record class progress through the materials. When a lesson is completed, it can be checked off on the chart.

THE PHILOSOPHY OF SILVER BURDETT MUSIC

The SILVER BURDETT MUSIC program is aesthetic education in action. Its major goal is to increase the sensitivity of all children to the power of music as an art—to develop their abilities to perceive the art of music keenly and respond to it deeply. Nonartistic values—the social, psychological, physical, and other benefits of involvement in music—are recognized and included. They are treated as contributory to the main purpose.

Musical aesthetic experience consists of the following:
(1) Perceiving the expressive qualities in a piece of music;
(2) Responding to those qualities in a feelingful way. Each such musical experience has two important values: it is satisfying for its own, immediate sake; and it whets the appetite for more of such experience in the future. Opportunities for immediate aesthetic satisfaction and future aesthetic growth are built into every learning episode.

If musical experience is to be powerful, it must involve both the mind and feelings. Materials that overemphasize intellectual learnings can lead to a bloodless, clinical atmosphere, which leaves the whole person untouched. On the other hand, materials that cater only to immediate pleasure can lead to superficiality and a stagnation of growth. To balance musical challenges with musical satisfactions is a delicate task. Every effort has been made to do so in SILVER BURDETT MUSIC.

Challenges to understanding and perception are present in abundance. But equally abundant are opportunities for success and pleasure. Each lesson includes both perceptual problems to be grappled with and musical experiences to be enjoyed, one reinforcing the other. As perception deepens, enjoyment deepens. And as children's feelings are moved by the power of music, their ability and desire to perceive increase. Thinking and feeling become inseparable as both are exercised in the experience of music.

To be effective, aesthetic education must be active education. Passive learning will not generate the intellectual and emotional excitement that helps bring people and art together. In SILVER BURDETT MUSIC children are involved wholeheartedly in a variety of activities designed to make music come alive for them. But activities for the simple sake of keeping children busy are avoided. Involvement must never be mindless and unfocused. SILVER BURDETT MUSIC requires energy—of students and of teachers. But it carefully channels this energy toward a larger goal—the ever-increasing ability to share the aesthetic power of music.

THE REPERTORY OF
SILVER BURDETT MUSIC

MUSIC LITERATURE. The music in SILVER BURDETT MUSIC offers a wide variety of styles, types, and mediums. At most grade levels, music is included that may seem quite adventurous for children of that age. In regard to the introduction of unfamiliar music, the general principle guiding this program is "better sooner than later."

A great deal of evidence points to the receptivity of young children to musical experiences of great diversity. If musical tastes are to be broadened rather than narrowed, the wide world of music must be sampled and enjoyed at every step of the way. If an attitude of adventure is adopted, if no one assumes that every piece must be immediately "liked," and if the commitment of the music educator is to be honest as to what music really consists of in the world outside the classroom, then at every grade level the materials presented will contain as wide a variety of music as is feasible.

When teaching for deeper perception of a particular musical quality, one should present examples of that quality as it appears in music of many different types and levels of complexity. The quality must be obvious enough to be perceived by most children studying it, yet subtle enough to expand their perceptivity. These conditions are present in each module. By focusing on a particular musical quality, examples can be chosen from many segments of music literature. This broadens the familiarity of children with many kinds of music while helping them become involved in the pieces as much as they can for their present level of development.

SONGS. The songs in SILVER BURDETT MUSIC are
(1) of high musical quality,
(2) attractive to children,
(3) notated in vocal ranges appropriate for particular age groups, according to current research,
(4) representative of a wide variety of types, styles, and ethnic origins, and

(5) helpful in developing musical perception.

Songs are used in the modules to illustrate concepts. They have also been chosen because each of the other conditions has been met.

THE ARTS. While the basic purpose of SILVER BURDETT MUSIC is to offer an aesthetic education in the art of music, children should recognize that music is a member of a larger community that includes all the arts. Developing sensitivity to other modes of aesthetic expression is valuable in and of itself, and it also gives children a broad view of music as one of several ways to explore and understand feeling.

Each book contains several lessons on the arts. Each lesson explores a particular aesthetic quality or process that exists in several arts. The purpose of the lesson is to show how that quality or process operates distinctively in each art. The focus is always on the unique way each art uses that particular aesthetic quality. The impression that "all arts are the same" is avoided. Indeed, it is the *differences* among arts—the characteristics that make them unique—that are explored. The more sensitive a child becomes to the expressiveness of painting *as* painting, of poetry *as* poetry, of dance *as* dance, of music *as* music, the more deeply can that child share the characteristic way each fulfills its goal of capturing and displaying a sense of human subjectivity. At the same time, the child comes to recognize that all the arts share that same goal.

MUSIC STYLES. The style lessons in each book are integrative experiences. They pull together previous learnings and focus them on the characteristic musical style of a specific composition. Children can respond to style characteristics with great success even in the primary grades. It is essential that style-expectations be cultivated from the very start of music education so that children can develop the ability to share and enjoy a rich variety of music styles.

MUSIC READING IN
SILVER BURDETT MUSIC

The ability to read music notation is considered an important means for exploring music and participating in its creation. Every child should be helped to learn to read music.

Most modules include an involvement with notation as an essential part of the learnings. Music reading is integrated in a variety of ways as an important means for perceiving, performing, analyzing, and conceptualizing. Reading skills are developed gradually but consistently, moving from simplified notation to traditional notation and to exploration of nontraditional notation. These learnings are fostered in the context of a rich involvement with musical experience itself, the notation being one of many means toward closer contact with the expressiveness of music.

To master the skill of sight-singing requires many hours of practice. However, in many situations, too little time is alloted in general music classes for students to acquire the kind of mastery that makes sight-singing truly functional. On the other hand, the ability to read music with the aid of a simple instrument is a practical goal for general music classes. For this reason, beginning in *Book 1*, notation is also studied in conjunction with instruments available in the classroom.

KODALY GUIDE and NOTE READING INDEX. The Kodály Guide indexes the songs in this volume according to basic melody patterns used in the Kodály approach to the teaching of sight-singing. In the Note Reading Index, the songs are indexed according to the note values, rhythm patterns, and pitches that are contained in the songs. This Guide and Index precede the Classified Index.

THE INDIVIDUAL AND
SILVER BURDETT MUSIC

This program may be used in a large-group situation, or in a small-group situation, or it may be used by individual children. Used in conjunction with the accompanying recordings and classroom instruments, the Pupil's Book provides the materials the students need to gain considerable insight on their own. In an "open" classroom, small groups of children may be working on different parts of a learning module. In addition to saving time, such a plan allows for choice and for more concentration on specific details. Moreover, some parts of a module can be done by one or two children working independently or by several children, one of whom is given the responsibility of leadership.

As the students progress through the program, they will be given more and more opportunity to develop the skills needed to sing, to play an instrument, to read notation, and to create their own compositions. It is not necessary for every student to take part in all the options SILVER BURDETT MUSIC provides. Each individual should be encouraged to follow his or her own bent, but should also be encouraged to "stick with" a particular activity until a reasonable skill is developed.

When books, recordings, and classroom instruments are made available to each child through a media center, students can learn at home as well as in school. When students prepare assignments or performances outside the large-group situation, they should be given an opportunity to share their achievements with their classmates. Such sharing among members of a peer group is a powerful motivating force.

MAINSTREAMING AND
SILVER BURDETT MUSIC

The needs of children in mainstreamed classes are as varied as the children themselves. SILVER BURDETT MUSIC helps to meet these needs by (1) providing lessons that encompass a range of learnings, from very simple to more complex; (2) suggesting ways that lesson materials can be adapted to special needs; (3) providing references to *Silver Burdett Music for Special Education* for further ideas about helping special children.

The following is a summary of some basic approaches to teaching that are *essential* in dealing with children who have been designated as requiring special education.

- Always communicate acceptance and respect for all students.
- Be consistent in rules and in dealing with groups and individuals.
- Stress positive rather than negative things about children; this will help forestall inappropriate behavior.

- Communicate openly with students concerning their feelings, expectations, and needs.
- Take time to talk with students, parents, and other teachers to promote a better understanding of disabilities and individual differences.
- Recognize and accept the fears and frustrations of your students, and help them find acceptable means of dealing with them.
- Avoid overprotecting special students. Do not lower your expectations for reasonable behavior.
- Offer assistance to disabled students, but never do things for them that they can do for themselves.
- Give students the opportunity to make choices and decisions, and to assume leadership roles.
- Evaluate *with* students rather than *for* them.
- Teach for transfer. Remind students of opportunities to use previously learned skills in new contexts.
- Avoid over-verbalizing. Involve students in activities *before* giving extensive directions or explanations.
- Allow adequate time for individuals to respond. Be patient.
- Be sensitive to those students for whom reading and writing tasks are difficult or impossible.
- Plan lessons that are socially appropriate. All children are quick to resent materials they consider "baby stuff."
- In teaching for concepts, use as many concrete means (teaching aids, manipulative materials, charts) as you possibly can.
- Use more than words to communicate—touch, show, move, manipulate, gesture, demonstrate.

THE RECORDINGS FOR
SILVER BURDETT MUSIC

The recordings for SILVER BURDETT MUSIC are carefully coordinated with the text material in every module. In each module there is a variety of activities. In addition to providing for singing and listening, the recordings include music for improvising, dramatizing, echo clapping. Among the recorded materials are poems, direct teaching materials, evaluation tools, and play-along/sing-along accompaniments. (The songs in this book are recorded in the key of the printed version. However, the recording does not necessarily follow the same chord structure as the piano accompaniment.)

When played on a stereo phonograph, the *Pick-a-Track* recordings enable the teacher to highlight either the voices or the song accompaniments. When the voices are highlighted, the children can (1) focus on vocal quality and style, (2) learn parts quickly, and (3) perfect the pronunciation of foreign and English lyrics. When the instrumental accompaniments are highlighted, the children can (1) focus on identifying instrumental tone colors and (2) sing to professional accompaniments in the classroom and assembly or for special performances.

Sometimes a song has been recorded to serve as a listening experience only. This occurs when children can readily grasp and understand the musical intent, but because of limited vocal skill are unable to reproduce the correct sound and vocal style.

Musicians will readily agree that the music score is only a "skeleton of intent" for the performer. At best, a score is a mere approximation of the composer's musical ideas. Notated tempo, rhythm patterns, dynamics, and all the rest must, in performance, be made flexible in order to "bend" into a musical statement while still remaining true to the composer's wishes. The "bending of the notation" results in an artistic performance. In the SILVER BURDETT MUSIC recordings, the intent of the performances is not necessarily to duplicate the exact notation in all cases, but rather to create as powerful a musical experience as possible for children to hear and share. The teacher must bear this fact in mind when comparing the performances on the recordings with the notation in the book.

The recordings of the *What Do You Hear?* lessons give children an opportunity to make active choices about the qualities of music they are learning to perceive. These lessons use focused listening as a means to

(1) reinforce perception of a particular quality in familiar music,
(2) widen perception of a particular quality in unfamiliar music,
(3) develop habits of perceptive listening to music.

Each *What Do You Hear?* lesson, therefore, is an integral part of its module, bringing the varied activities in the module to a musical culmination. It should be used for its educational function rather than as a formal test. Even if all the lessons in a particular module are not used, the *What Do You Hear?* material should be included. If children are uncertain about the terms or instructions on the *What Do You Hear?* recording, explain them more fully. Work out an item or two at the chalkboard while the class watches. With familiarity, these lessons will become quite easily understood. (Spirit masters for these lessons are available from the publisher.)

ILLUSTRATIONS/ PHOTOGRAPHS

Throughout the series, photographs are used as a means of acquainting students immediately with the concepts and vocabulary presented within the lessons. Usually these visuals make use of environmental scenes, home, school, and playground activities, as well as common objects known to children. These visuals will help children progress from the known to the unknown and will provide a means for relating particular visual concepts with similar music concepts. Other visuals that teach show particular activities such as movement, correct playing positions for classroom instruments, and specific illustrations of orchestral, folk, and ethnic instruments. Each book shows photographs of children at the appropriate age level.

The *Silver Burdett Sound/Color Filmstrips,* available from the publisher, are a series of six experiences that expand on the concepts presented in the text materials. The filmstrips are cross-referenced in the Teacher's Notes when germane to the lesson.

TESTING MUSICAL COMPETENCIES

Throughout the long history of music education it has been assumed that involvement in musical activities—singing, playing, listening, moving, etc.—would improve children's abilities to discern what the sounds are actually doing in a piece of music. There was a lack of hard evidence as to precisely what children at each grade level were capable of perceiving. In planning SILVER BURDETT MUSIC, the authors and editors were determined to improve on the timeworn practice of teaching "by hunch and by hope."

The philosophy of SILVER BURDETT MUSIC suggests that aesthetic learnings occur when specific behaviors are cultivated—the behaviors discussed below under the heading "Objectives of SILVER BURDETT MUSIC." The central behavior—musical perception—is capable of being measured with a high degree of accuracy when children are asked to analyze and conceptualize what they notice as they listen to a musical example. This fact was the guideline for a history-making project to (1) assess the musical perceptual abilities of children at each grade level, 1 to 6, (2) develop a series of tests that could be used to measure students' musical perception at each grade level, and (3) produce teaching materials reflecting not just *opinion* as to what children are capable of learning in music, but *factual evidence* of what they can and cannot perceive.

Under the direction of Dr. Richard Colwell, data were collected from several thousand children in a carefully planned, step-by-step series of initial pilot testings. *What Do You Hear?* listening lessons from the first edition of SILVER BURDETT MUSIC were given extensive field trials. Then initial prototype tests were given in 30 school systems in 21 states; later, random-sample testing was administered in 54 communities representing all sections of the country. In all, some 26,000 children were involved in the study, representing small, medium, and large communities and diverse socioeconomic and cultural groupings in the United States. This project accumulated more information about how and what children learn about music than has ever before been available.

The results of this unprecedented project are the *Silver Burdett Music Competency Tests* and this edition of the SILVER BURDETT MUSIC text materials. Revision of the textbooks and recordings has been extensive. Effects of the massive research project on the instructional program include (1) a more gradual, step-by-step learning sequence for concepts that take more time to develop, (2) increased review and reinforcement of some concepts, and (3) additions and substitutions in the listening program.

Together, the SILVER BURDETT MUSIC text materials and the *Competency Tests* provide the most carefully researched and therefore the most realistic, most effective musical learning opportunities ever available to all children in the schools.

OBJECTIVES OF SILVER BURDETT MUSIC

The major goal of SILVER BURDETT MUSIC, as stated in the philosophy, is to increase the sensitivity of all children to the power of music as an art. This goal is fulfilled through the accomplishment of objectives stated in terms of seven behaviors:

(1) Perceiving
(2) Reacting
(3) Producing
(4) Conceptualizing

(5) Analyzing
(6) Evaluating
(7) Valuing

The first two of these behaviors—perceiving and reacting—are "ends." They constitute musical aesthetic experience. The next four behaviors—producing, conceptualizing, analyzing, and evaluating—are "means" to those ends. The seventh behavior—valuing—is an "outcome." It occurs as a result of effective development of the other six behaviors.

PERCEIVING. To perceive music aesthetically, one must notice or discern those qualities that make sound expressive. Works of art present conditions or qualities that must be perceived in order to be enjoyed. Most, if not all, works of art present a complex set of such qualities, requiring far more than casual attention if they are to be more fully perceived.

Silver Burdett Music is devoted to the cultivation of musical perception. The materials carefully, systematically, and progressively involve children in opportunities to perceive music more precisely. Each child demonstrates his or her perception through a variety of overt responses, ranging from simple body movements to written responses.

REACTING. Whereas perceiving requires *thinking*, reacting requires *feeling*. Aesthetic education has often been called the "education of feeling." For aesthetic experience to take place, one must *respond* to the expressive qualities one *perceives*.

Reaction is an intensely personal, subjective behavior. Silver Burdett Music never tells children what their individual feelings should be, nor does it invade their privacy by asking them to describe what they feel. The materials often suggest, however, that what is *heard* should also be *felt*.

Musical perception and musical reaction together equal musical experience. Such experience occurs through listening. Silver Burdett Music provides opportunities for active listening unprecedented in the history of music education. Whatever the particular activity of the moment—singing, playing, composing, and so forth—listening is present as an essential, active ingredient. And special, imaginative devices are used to help develop listening skills directly.

PRODUCING. In Silver Burdett Music, the term *producing* denotes singing, playing, composing, conducting, moving, and so forth. In the general music program, producing is a major means of experiencing musical sounds and how they work. Silver Burdett Music relies heavily on production activities to bring children and music together. Production activities are both means and ends. As ends, they need no discussion, for they have found an honored place in the music education curriculum for many years. As means, the production activities are powerful tools to aid in heightening musical perception, intensifying musical reaction, and encouraging musical creativity. Since the production activities are all observable behaviors, they can serve as a valuable means for assessing student progress.

CONCEPTUALIZING. A child conceptualizes about music when describing
(1) the inner workings of music (melody, rhythm, texture, form, tone color),

(2) the roles of music in human life,
(3) styles of music, or
(4) the relationship of music to the other arts.

Although these four concept categories form the organizational basis of Silver Burdett Music, they are not treated as ends in themselves. Conceptual development is a means for fostering deeper perception of the actual sounds being described. So verbal descriptions are always kept in direct contact with the experience of musical sounds.

ANALYZING. To analyze music is to explore its inner workings. Silver Burdett Music includes analysis in every learning event as a means of heightening musical discrimination. But a sterile kind of analysis, in which the examination of musical sounds is separated from actual involvement with those sounds, is useless for aesthetic education and is carefully avoided in Silver Burdett Music.

EVALUATING. As a basic objective, Silver Burdett Music seeks to help the child

(1) appraise the musical quality of a wide variety of pieces,
(2) recognize that appraisal is a tentative process, subject to change,
(3) become aware of the many problems inherent in judging the arts, and
(4) learn about his or her own tastes and preferences in the context of the tastes and preferences of others.

The materials avoid giving the impression that judging is the major thing one should do with music, or that one can judge a work immediately, or that one is always qualified to do so. Nevertheless, thoughtful evaluation is an important means toward the development of musical discrimination.

VALUING. As children are successful in developing the other six behaviors, it is hoped that they will come to value music and the arts as important, fulfilling aspects of their world. The materials openly show that music is valued highly by others, without imposing on the child any particular set of values about music or even asking the child to "like" the music. Rather, Silver Burdett Music shows the child that music can be valued by all who are willing to become involved with it.

The seven behaviors described above are cultivated at every grade level. They differ from grade to grade only in degree of sophistication, cyclically growing in breadth and depth throughout the program. At every level, the specific objectives, as stated in terms of the seven behaviors, serve a larger, more general goal—to increase each child's ability to participate in the aesthetic experience of music.

SCOPE AND SEQUENCE CHART

On the pages following, the objectives for this level of Silver Burdett Music are presented in chart form. Scanning the chart horizontally provides a review of the behaviors that are covered in a particular module. Scanning the chart vertically provides a survey of the cyclical development of particular behaviors. Thus the chart illustrates both the scope of the musical learnings and the sequence of learning events.

OBJECTIVES: SCOPE AND SEQUENCE

	Perceiving and Reacting	Producing	Conceptualizing	Analyzing	Evaluating	Integrative Learning
MODULE 1 pages 40–47	Fast and slow tempos, getting faster and slower, holding	Chanting, singing, playing instruments, moving, playing a game—to sharpen discernment of tempo	The speed of musical movement is called "tempo" • Some pieces have a single tempo; others change by getting faster or slower or holding (stopping) the movement • Tempo is a basic way for music to create a sense of feeling.	Recognizing and discussing different tempos and tempo changes in a wide variety of musical settings • Associating tempos with words and musical settings	Judging the musical effects of different tempos for the same piece	Two musicians may conceive of a piece of music as having two different tempos; each is "correct," yet each produces a different musical effect.
MODULE 2 pages 48–58	Upward and downward movement of melody	Producing sounds vocally and on instruments, playing instruments, creating melodies, singing, moving	Tones move upward and downward, creating a sense of direction • Melodic direction is an important way for music to arouse an experience of feeling.	Discriminating between upward and downward direction in melodies with conventional and unconventional pitch organizations • Using line drawings and notation to clarify direction • Discerning form through direction characteristics		One quality of a melody is direction—the movement upward and downward of its tones. Some melodies have many changes of direction and also places where a particular direction is prominent.
MODULE 3 pages 58–59	The variety of devices that shape a musical composition		Working with rhythm, melody, form, texture, tone color, and dynamics, the composer can generate many musical possibilities. Judgment must be made as to how to organize all these possibilities into an effective whole.	Comparing a variety of musical elements and devices used by the composer to make his or her composition effective		In creating a musical composition, the composer uses all or most of the elements of music in ways suitable to the desired musical effect.
MODULE 4 pages 60–69	Metrical and nonmetrical organization	Playing games, moving, playing instruments, chanting, singing, creating accompaniments—to show duple and triple meters	Musical movement is often organized into beats • Beats can be organized into sets of two and three • Some pieces use just one or the other; others use both • Some pieces have no beat at all or just a hint of a beat • Each kind of movement has its own way of feeling.	Discriminating metrical organizations in various pieces • Associating beats and meters with musical notation • Recognizing absence of beat and ambiguous beat	Assessing the appropriateness of self-created accompaniments for a metrical song	One quality of movement is an organization of beats into meter. Music need not always be metrical, however. Movement (rhythm) can exist even if no beat is present.
MODULE 5 pages 70–79	Dynamic levels and changes of dynamics	Experimenting with speech sounds, singing, creating interpretations and original ideas, manipulating phonograph equipment, playing instruments, moving—to employ a variety of dynamic possibilities	Musical sounds can be soft or loud, or gradually get softer or louder • This quality of sound is called dynamics • Many pieces use several of these possibilities • Each level or change of dynamics adds to the effect of a piece.	Recognizing and comparing dynamic levels and changes in a variety of compositions, poems, and self-created pieces • Using notation and descriptive words for dynamics	Judging effectiveness of various dynamics in accompaniments, performances, and original compositions	Different dynamics can be used with the same piece, each usage adding a different expressive value to the piece, which remains "the same" in other respects.
MODULE 6 pages 80–81	Stylistic characteristics of American Indian music		Music is an important part of American Indian life and has its own stylistic qualities.	Identifying melodic, harmonic, timbral, and formal elements of several American Indian songs		While music is its own reason for being, it also serves its culture by filling many societal needs.

	Perceiving and Reacting	Producing	Conceptualizing	Analyzing	Evaluating	Integrative Learning
MODULE 7 pages 82–93	Formal structure	Exploring the environment, moving, playing instruments, singing, creating accompaniments and original music—to clarify the concept of formal sound structures	Music can be structured (organized) by repeating and contrasting. • The overall structure of a piece, with its repetitions and contrasts, is the piece's "form."	Exploring repetitions and contrasts of several musical qualities in a variety of contexts • Using letters and shapes to notate form • Following contemporary notation to create a formed piece	Judging effectiveness of tone color choices and self-created events in producing musical contrasts	Several musical qualities may function as structuring agents that form a larger whole from related parts.
MODULE 8 pages 94–95	Formal organization in the arts	Exploring the environment, playing a game, painting and drawing—to develop perception of repetition and contrast	Repetition and contrast give art unity and variety • Music, painting, and poetry all use repetition and contrast, but each uses these qualities in ways determined by its different artistic modes.	Discovering repeated and contrasted qualities in the environment, musical sounds, a painting, a poem		Works of art are organized by events that are repeated and contrasted. We recognize organization by hearing, by seeing, by reading.
MODULE 9 pages 96–105	Use of register	Playing instruments, using natural sound producers, moving, creating accompaniments, singing, experimenting with speaking voices—to focus perception on register	Faster vibrations cause higher sounds, slower vibrations cause lower sounds • High sounds and low sounds are basic qualities of music • Two notes are an octave apart if they fall on "one" and "eight" when the lines and spaces from one to the other are counted. Even though one is low and the other high, they have the same apparent pitch.	Discovering high and low sounds on several instruments and in several musical contexts • Notation to indicate high and low and to identify the octave • Some music has parts that are mostly high or mostly low • Some music has both, as well as parts where high and low occur together.		
MODULE 10 pages 106–107	Stylistic characteristics of two eras		Music from different historical periods can be compared on the basis of stylistic elements.	Noticing that when the qualities of music are put together in a characteristic way, the result is a "style"	Comparing specific musical qualities and general stylistic sounds of several pieces from two historical eras	
MODULE 11 pages 108–123	Durational values	Using vocal sounds; reciting; singing; creating sound pieces, rhythm patterns, and movement routines; using motions to reflect rhythm patterns, accents, and rests; playing instruments; dancing—to enhance understanding of durations and patterns	Words (as in poems) and music can use short sounds and long sounds to create expressive events • Short and long sounds combined in recognizable ways are rhythm patterns • Such patterns can be expressive in themselves and can help form the ongoing experience of music • Several patterns of short and long sounds can occur together • Silence and accent are often used as parts of rhythm patterns.	Recognizing long and short sounds separately and as they function in rhythm patterns • Notation for several patterns, accents, and rests (silences)	Assessing effects of short and long durations as appropriate for certain words in songs • Judging the effectiveness of patterns as accompaniment figures for a song	Rhythm patterns, accents, and tone color can be combined to form an appropriate accompaniment for a story.

	Perceiving and Reacting	Producing	Conceptualizing	Analyzing	Evaluating	Integrative Learning
MODULE 12 pages 124–125	Use of pattern in the arts		Visual patterns (repeated configurations of lines, colors, shapes) are found in natural objects and paintings • Aural patterns (repeated groupings of sounds) are used in music • In paintings, patterns are seen all at once • In music, patterns are heard over a span of time.	Discerning differences in visual and musical patterns		Patterns are used in several arts. We perceive pattern in different ways depending on the particular senses employed by each art.
MODULE 13 pages 126–141	Tone color characteristics	Making vocal sounds, reciting poems, singing, accompanying songs, playing a game, moving	The voice and instruments can produce many identifiable sound qualities, or "tone colors" • Some tone colors are produced by blowing; some by bowing, strumming, and plucking; some by striking, shaking, or scraping; and some by electronic machines • Each tone color adds to the experience of feeling that music can provide.	Discerning differences in the quality of a wide variety of sound producers • Associating particular sounds with pictures and names of the instruments that produce them and with the physical methods by which the sounds are made		
MODULE 14 pages 142–143	Stylistic characteristics of Modern music		Things in Modern style have a general look, or style, that tells that they did not exist until recently • Modern music has a general style that sounds new • Not all modern pieces sound the same • Within modern music there are many different styles to hear and feel.	Recognizing and comparing the styles of several modern pieces		An overall style, such as Modern, can have several different substyles within it.
MODULE 15 pages 144–155	Phrase construction and organization	Using motions to reflect phrasing; dancing; singing; experimenting with accompaniments; playing instruments; composing sound pieces; playing a game—to clarify the concept of phrases	Musical phrases can help give a feeling of organization • Phrases can be of different lengths; can have strong or weak endings (cadences), can have silence as well as sound.	Discerning the organization of a variety of phrases • Notating phrase length • Recognizing strong and weak cadences	Assessing the effect of phrases and cadences in organizing a poem, songs, self-created pieces	Phrase organization is a major factor in the overall structure—the form—of a piece.
MODULE 16 pages 156–157	Use of variation in the arts		A visual and musical idea can be varied by changing some of its parts • Shapes, lines, colors may be used to create variations in painting • Dynamics, rhythm patterns, tempos, additional notes may be used to create variations in music.	Examining variation in visual and aural modes • Using musical notation for a subject that is to be varied • Describing specific qualities that are varied in each of several movements of a piece		

Module	Perceiving and Reacting	Producing	Conceptualizing	Analyzing	Evaluating	Integrative Learning
MODULE 17 pages 158–161	Presence and absence of focus in the arts		Both music and painting can use focus and no focus as ways of organizing experience • In music, *focus* and *no focus* refer to sounds; in painting they refer to the presence or absence of a place to which one's eyes are drawn—a *center of interest.*	Inspecting paintings for center of interest • Discerning pitch organizations in music • Comparing the phenomenon of focus and of no focus as it exists in painting and music		
MODULE 18 pages 162–167	Tonal or atonal pitch organization	Singing, playing instruments, creating accompaniments—to emphasize tonal and atonal settings	When pitches are organized so that one of them is more important than the others, giving a focal point to the sounds, the music is *tonal* • When no one pitch is more important than any other, the sounds lack a pitch focus—the music is *atonal* • Each pitch organization has a particular expressive quality.	Differentiating among the pitch organizations of several tonal and atonal pieces and of one piece presented in both tonal and atonal organizations • Recognizing tonality and atonality from notational representations	Judging the effect of accompaniments in heightening a sense of tonality	Notation can give clues to the overall sound of a piece, showing whether it is likely to be, for example, tonal or atonal.
MODULE 19 pages 168–177	Patterns of rhythmic movement	Playing instruments, singing, moving, chanting, creating a dance and a percussion piece—to demonstrate recognition of rhythm patterns	Short and long sounds combined in recognizable ways are rhythm patterns • Such patterns can be expressive in themselves and help form the ongoing experience of music • Several patterns of short and long sounds can occur together • Notes, rests, dotted notes, and fermatas are used to represent the duration of sounds and silences.	Recognizing duration in relation to the beat • Notating several rhythm patterns and the durations of sounds and silences	Judging the effectiveness of several rhythm patterns as accompaniment figures for a song	Rhythm pattern, tempo, dynamics, and tone color can be combined to heighten the effectiveness of the dramatization of a story.
MODULE 20 pages 178–179	Stylistic characteristics of Modern music	Creating a sound piece with vocal or instrumental sounds—to demonstrate perception of Modern style	Things in Modern style have a general look, or style, that tells that they did not exist until recently • Modern music has a general style that sounds new • But not all modern pieces sound the same • Within modern music there are many different styles to hear and feel.	Recognizing and comparing the styles of several different modern pieces		An overall style, such as Modern, can have several different substyles within it.
MODULE 21 pages 180–195	Intervallic relations and melodic contour	Singing, playing instruments, dancing, composing—to clarify interval functions and contour possibilities	Tones can move from one to another by steps, by leaps, or by being repeated • Some melodies move mostly by steps, or by leaps, or by repeated tones; many combine them • The set of intervals used in a melody gives it an overall shape, or contour • Each melodic contour has its own expressiveness.	Examining a variety of pieces to discover the kinds of intervals used • Associating intervals and contour with traditional and nontraditional notations • Comparing melodic contours by their notational representations	Judging the effectiveness of self-created pieces that follow notational suggestions of contour	When separate sound events (intervals) are combined, a whole is produced (melodic contour) that gives a higher level of musical organization. Music is made of smaller parts combined into larger wholes.

	Perceiving and Reacting	Producing	Conceptualizing	Analyzing	Evaluating	Integrative Learning
MODULE 22 pages 196–197	Contour	Moving, singing, drawing, improvising a melody, exploring the environment, playing a game, creating a score—to experience a sense of contour	Both aural and visual events can have a contour, or general shape.	Associating contour lines with the appropriate sounds and pictures		
MODULE 23 pages 198–214	Use of harmony, no harmony, countermelody	Singing, playing chordal and melodic accompaniments to change texture of a variety of pieces	Music can have a melody alone, a melody with chords, or several melodies together • Each organization (texture) has its particular expressiveness • A piece can be changed from one texture to another • When parts are added to music the density moves from thinner to thicker, giving still another way for music to be expressive.	Discerning differences in several textures and experimenting with changes of texture • Using notational representation of different textures	Noticing the effects of adding various accompaniments that change the texture and density of a piece	A piece can have several "layers" of sound-events, the experience differing when the texture differs.
MODULE 24 pages 215–217	Stylistic differences in the music of different periods		Musical style has changed with time • Many styles had an instrument or group of instruments associated with them.	Using a time line and well-known historical events to clarify the idea that music exists in history and changes just as other things in the world change		

SILVER BURDETT MUSIC TEACHER'S
PROGRESS CHART

The PROGRESS CHART shows the Module/Lesson organization of this book—a module being a sequence of lessons, or a single lesson, that can stand alone as an entity. Although progressing through the modules consecutively from beginning to end is a simple and effective way to approach the material, it is possible to switch from one module (before finishing all of its lessons) to another module. It is important, however, that the lessons within a module be covered in numerical sequence. This procedure applies whether all lessons in a module are used or a selection of lessons. When a lesson is completed it can be checked off on the chart. Teachers with more than one class may duplicate this chart.

CONTENTS	PAGES	LESSONS											
Beginning Experiences	2–35												
The Arts: Active—Still	36–37	**1** (36)											
Listening to Music	38–39	**1** (38)											
MODULES		Lessons identified by boldface numerals constitute the Basic Program. The Basic Program covers all the material evaluated in the *Silver Burdett Music Competency Tests*. The Basic Program can be extended by adding lessons identified by lightface numerals. Numerals in parentheses are page numbers.											
1. Tempo	40–47	**1** (40)	**2** (42)	**3** (43)	4 (44)	5 (45)	6 (46)	**7** (47)					
2. Melody	48–57	**1** (48)	2 (50)	3 (51)	**4** (52)	5 (54)	**6** (55)	7 (56)	**8** (57)				
3. Things People Do With Music	58–59	1 (58)											
4. Meter	60–69	**1** (60)	**2** (62)	3 (63)	**4** (64)	**5** (65)	**6** (66)	7 (67)	8 (68)	**9** (69)			
5. Dynamics	70–79	1 (70)	**2** (71)	**3** (72)	**4** (73)	5 (74)	6 (75)	7 (76)	8 (77)	9 (78)	**10** (79)		
6. Style: American Indian	80–81	**1** (80)											
7. Form	82–93	1 (82)	**2** (84)	3 (86)	4 (87)	**5** (88)	**6** (90)	**7** (92)	**8** (93)				
8. The Arts: Repetition/Contrast	94–95	1 (94)	*Silver Burdett Music Competency Test 1**										
9. Register	96–105	**1** (96)	2 (98)	3 (100)	4 (102)	**5** (103)	6 (104)						
10. Style: Renaissance/Romantic	106–107	**1** (106)											
11. Duration	108–123	1 (108)	**2** (110)	**3** (112)	4 (114)	5 (115)	**6** (116)	**7** (118)	8 (120)	**9** (122)			
12. The Arts: Pattern	124–125	**1** (124)											
13. Tone Color	126–141	1 (126)	**2** (127)	3 (128)	**4** (130)	5 (132)	**6** (134)	**7** (136)	**8** (138)	9 (140)	**10** (141)		
14. Style: Classic/Rock	142–143	**1** (142)											
15. Phrases	144–155	1 (144)	**2** (146)	**3** (147)	4 (148)	5 (150)	**6** (151)	**7** (152)	8 (153)	**9** (154)	**10** (155)		
16. The Arts: Varying a Subject	156–157	1 (156)	*Silver Burdett Music Competency Test 2*										
17. The Arts: Focus/No Focus	158–161	**1** (158)											
18. Tonality	162–167	1 (162)	**2** (164)	**3** (166)	4 (167)								
19. Rhythm Patterns	168–177	**1** (168)	2 (170)	3 (172)	**4** (174)	5 (176)	6 (177)						
20. Style: Modern	178–179	**1** (178)											
21. Intervals	180–195	1 (180)	**2** (181)	**3** (182)	4 (183)	5 (184)	**6** (186)	**7** (188)	**8** (190)	**9** (191)	10 (192)		
										11 (194)	12 (195)		
22. The Arts: Contour	196–197	1 (196)											
23. Texture	198–214	**1** (198)	2 (199)	**3** (200)	**4** (202)	5 (204)	**6** (206)	**7** (208)	**8** (210)	**9** (211)	10 (212)		
											11 (214)		
24. Style: Time Lines	214–217	1 (214)	*Silver Burdett Music Competency Test 3*										

*The *Silver Burdett Music Competency Tests* are criterion-referenced to the series, and are available from the publisher. Test 1 should be administered after the completion of Module 8; Test 2 after completion of Module 15; and Test 3 after completion of Module 24. Use of the *Competency Tests* is optional.

WHAT THE WIND SAID

"Far away is where I've come from," said the wind.
"Guess what I've brought you."

"What?" I asked.

"Shadows dancing on a brown road by an old
Stone fence," the wind said. "Do you like that?"

"Yes," I said. "What else?"

"Daisies nodding, and the drone of one small airplane
In a sleepy sky," the wind continued.

"I like the airplane, and the daisies too," I said.
"What else?"

"That's not enough?" the wind complained.

"No," I said. "I want the song that you were singing.
Give me that."

"That's mine," the wind said. "Find your own." And left.

Russell Hoban

BEGINNING EXPERIENCES: Rhythm

MATERIALS
Record 1, "I Clap My Hands"; Pupil's Book, p. 2

VOCABULARY
steady beat

IDEAS FOR TEACHING
1. Have children look at the pictures on p. 2. They show three ways to keep time to the steady beat in music—jumping rope, snapping fingers, swaying from side to side. Question: Can you think of other ways to keep time to the beat? (Clap hands, tap feet, pat lap, etc.)

2. Play the recording of the song and let children keep time to the steady beat any way they choose. (On the recording, steady beats are clapped in the introduction.) Suggestion: If space is limited, small groups can take turns moving while others try singing some of the words. When working in a large room, take time for children to explore the area. Each child should find his or her own "space" for moving.

• Ev'ry time I hear some music playin' in time,/ I clap my hands./ Ev'ry time I notice that the weather is fine,/ I clap my hands./ Clap your hands. (4 times)

• Ev'ry time I see somebody winnin' a race,/ I clap my hands./ Ev'ry time a puppy comes alickin' my face,/ I clap my hands./ Clap your hands. (4 times)

• Ev'ry time I see somebody smilin' at me,/ I clap my hands./ Ev'ry time I think about how good life can be,/ I clap my hands./ Clap your hands. (4 times)

"I Clap My Hands"
Piano acc. p. 234

2 Beginning Experiences

TEACHER INFORMATION

The procedure suggested in Ideas for Teaching can be varied to suit individual needs. However, the activity indicated by a black line should always be done, since it highlights a specific music learning.

The Beginning Experiences (pp. 2–39) are designed for children's immediate participation in singing, listening, moving, and playing instruments. For some children, the materials will serve as a review; for others, they will introduce the concepts for the first time.

Use as many of the Beginning Experiences as necessary for your class. However, be sure to cover the material on pp. 36–39, since this material is included in Test 1 of *Silver Burdett Music Competency Tests* for Book 3.

Show rhythm by playing.

If you can move
to the steady beat,
you are ready to play
the steady beat.

Which way will you choose?

Which part will you play?

steady beat

quarter notes

eighth notes

eighth notes and quarter notes

MATERIALS
Record 1, "I Clap My Hands"; Pupil's Book, p. 3; percussion instruments

VOCABULARY
steady beat, quarter notes, eighth notes

IDEAS FOR TEACHING

1. Direct attention to the photograph (p. 3) of the child playing the steady beat on a drum. Ask children to think of other ways to play the steady beat. (Play a percussion instrument, tap pencil, rap door, scrape blinds, etc.)

2. Play the recording and have children take turns playing the steady beat while others sing along.

3. Direct attention to the lines and quarter notes in the Pupil's Book. Point out: The steady beat can be written using vertical lines (|||) or quarter notes (♩♩).

4. When children can play a steady beat to keep time to the music, ask them to play two sounds for each beat. They will be playing eighth notes (♫). (On the recording, eighth notes are played on a cowbell in the introduction.)

5. Ask children to find the row of eighth notes in their book. Point out: Two eighth notes can take the place of one quarter note.

6. Some children may be able to combine quarter notes with eighth notes to form a pattern. Let them take turns playing the pattern at the bottom of p. 3. (On the recording, this pattern is played on the woodblock in verse 3.

TRY THIS

Children can make up other patterns of long and short sounds to play, using quarter notes and eighth notes. Encourage them to notate their patterns, using line notation or quarter notes and eighth notes. To get them started, write a few patterns on the chalkboard. For example:

TEACHER INFORMATION

It is important to repeat the activities in this lesson from time to time so that all children will have beginning experiences in playing, writing, and reading notation. It takes time for an individual child to develop skill in accompanying on an instrument, making up a rhythm pattern, and writing notation.

BEGINNING EXPERIENCES: Melody

MATERIALS
Record 1, "Marching to Pretoria";
Pupil's Book, pp. 4 and 5

VOCABULARY
upward direction, downward
direction, staff

IDEAS FOR TEACHING
1. Ask children to listen for the
words in the song that will tell them
when to march "to Pretoria." When
the music is played, children will get
ready during the first section (verse)
and will march throughout the
second section (refrain). Suggestion:
If space is limited, individual
children or small groups can take
turns marching during the refrain.
The purpose of this activity is to call
attention to the second section.

2. Children, in groups, can take turns
singing the second section of the
song along with the recording as
others march.

3. Ask children to listen to the
melody to hear whether the ending
("-to-ri-a, hur rah!") moves upward
or downward. (Downward)

4. Direct attention to the notes at
the end of the song on p. 5.
Children should observe how the
notes look on a staff. Ask them to
follow those notes when they sing
the end of the song. Do the children
see what they *hear?* Point out: The
group of five lines and the spaces
between, on which notes are written,
is called a *staff.*

Show direction in melody by singing.

MARCHING TO PRETORIA
DUTCH FOLK SONG FROM SOUTH AFRICA

ENGLISH WORDS BY JOSEF MARAIS
FROM SONGS FROM THE VELD. © 1942. G. SCHIRMER, INC. USED BY PERMISSION.

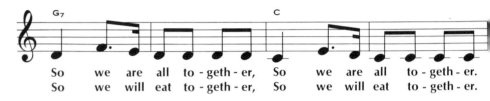

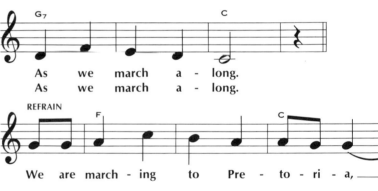

4   Beginning Experiences

TRY THIS

1. As others march, children can take turns playing this
pattern on a drum during the second section of the song.

It will be necessary for children to start playing on the first
strong beat, or on the first syllable of the word *marching*
("We are MARCH-ing").

2. Children can play other patterns of long and short
sounds during the second section. For example:

We are march - ing to Pre - to - ri - a, _____

Pre - to - ri - a, hur - rah! _____

Show direction in melody by playing.

Start on G and play down to C.

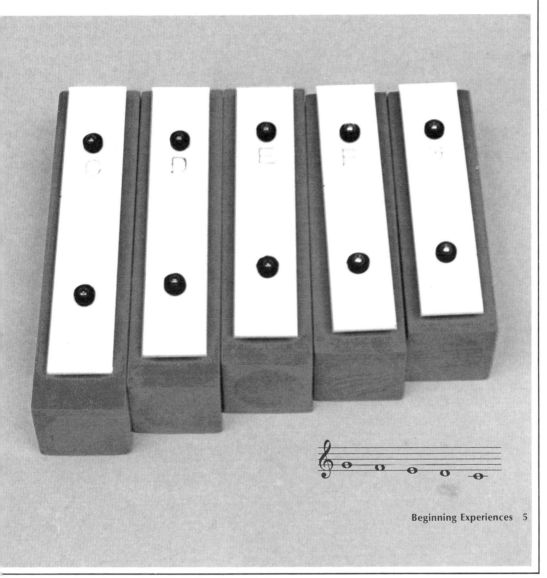

BEGINNING EXPERIENCES: Melody

MATERIALS
Record 1, "Marching to Pretoria"; Pupil's Book, pp. 4 and 5; bells

VOCABULARY
upward direction, downward direction, staff

IDEAS FOR TEACHING
1. Ask children to look on p. 5 in their book to see which bells will be needed for this experience. Have someone line up the bells on a desk or on a table so they match the picture—the longest bell, C, at the left and the shortest bell, G, at the right.

Note: Through experimentation, help children become aware that the longer the bell, the lower the tone; the shorter the bell, the higher the tone. Holding the bells upright in the box with short bells at the top will help reinforce this concept.

2. Children can take turns playing the bells downward from G to C. They will be playing the ending of "Marching to Pretoria." Note: While one child plays the bells the others in the class can use the bell diagram at the back of their book and "play" along, using the eraser end of a pencil as a mallet.

3. As soon as the children have the concept of downward direction, let them take turns playing the ending of "Marching to Pretoria" without the recording.

4. Even though many children will play the part by ear (because they know the song), it is important to call attention to the notation of what they play. Direct attention to the notation at the bottom of p. 5.

TEACHER INFORMATION

In this initial experience with playing bells, it is important that children understand that when they play from left to right, they are playing tones that move from lower to higher; when they play from right to left, they are playing tones that move from higher to lower.

Mainstreaming: Suggestions for using "Marching to Pretoria" appear in the song list in *Silver Burdett Music for Special Education.*

TRY THIS

Children will become aware of the function of lines and spaces by drawing high and low notes on a staff. Have them practice using both quarter notes and eighth notes. (You may want to review quarter notes and eighth notes as they are presented on p. 3.)

BEGINNING EXPERIENCES: Melody

MATERIALS
Record 1, "Brother Noah"; Pupil's Book, p. 6

VOCABULARY
upward direction, downward direction, staff

IDEAS FOR TEACHING

1. Ask children to look at the ending of the last line in the song "Brother Noah." Help them discover there are no notes to tell whether the ending moves in an upward direction or a downward direction.

2. Direct attention to the two patterns at the bottom of p. 6. One of the patterns is the correct notation for the ending of the song.

3. Play the recording and help children discover that the ending is shown in pattern 1—the tones move in a downward direction.

4. Play the recording again and ask children to follow the notes in pattern 1 when they come·in the song. <u>Point out</u>: The group of five lines and the spaces between, on which notes are written, is called a *staff*.

5. Have children take turns singing the ending of "Brother Noah" along with the recording. When they are familiar with the song, have them take turns singing the ending without the recording. Eliminate that part of the song by turning down the volume control on the record player. <u>Note</u>: All children should have the experience of singing alone.

Show direction in melody by singing.

Listen to a melody to discover whether the ending moves

upward,

or downward

BROTHER NOAH

Orff acc. p. 290

AMERICAN SEA SONG

REPRINTED FROM AMERICAN SEA SONGS AND CHANTEYS. COMPILED BY FRANK SHAY AND ILLUSTRATED BY EDWARD A. WILSON. BY PERMISSION OF W. W. NORTON & COMPANY, INC. COPYRIGHT 1948 BY FRANK SHAY AND EDWARD A. WILSON. COPYRIGHT RENEWED 1976.

1. Broth - er No - ah, Broth - er No - ah,
2. No, you can't, sir, No, you can't, sir,

May I come in - to the Ark of the Lord,
You can't come in - to the Ark of the Lord,

For it's grow - ing ver - y dark and it's rain - ing ver - y hard?
Though it's grow - ing ver - y dark and it's rain - ing ver - y hard.

REFRAIN

Hal - le - loo, hal - le - loo, hal - le - loo - oo - oo - oo - ia!

Follow the notes as you sing.

Find the notes that show the missing part.

Do you see what you hear?

TEACHER INFORMATION

<u>Mainstreaming</u>: For sight-impaired children, a tactile staff can be constructed as follows: Draw a large staff with a G clef on a piece of cardboard 8½" x 11". Squeeze a thin line of glue on the lines and sprinkle with sand before the glue dries. Notes cut from thicker cardboard may be manipulated on the staff. This equipment may be used throughout the year.

6 · Beginning Experiences: Melody

Show direction in melody by playing.

Play the ending of a song you know on the bells.

Start on high D and play down to G.

Which bells play _high_ tones?

Which bells play _low_ tones?

Draw notes for _high_ tones on a staff.

Draw notes for _low_ tones on a staff.

MATERIALS
Pupil's Book, p. 7; bells

VOCABULARY
upward direction, downward direction, staff

IDEAS FOR TEACHING
1. Have someone line up the bells on a desk or on a table so they match the picture on p. 7—the longest bell, G, at the left; the shortest bell, D, at the right.

2. Children can take turns playing the downward-moving pattern at the bottom of p. 7 on the bells. The pattern starts on high D and moves downward to G. They will discover that it is the ending of "Brother Noah." Point out: When playing the bells, the mallet is used to pull sound "out" of the bells. It is not used to bang sound "in." Note: While one child plays the bells the others in the class can use the bell diagram at the back of their book and "play" along, using the eraser end of a pencil as a mallet.

3. Children can take turns playing the ending of "Brother Noah" as others sing. Questions: Which bell plays the highest sound? (The one on the right) Which bell plays the lowest sound? (The one on the left) Some children will remember that the longer the bell, the lower the tone; the shorter the bell, the higher the tone. (See Teacher Information, p. 5.)

TRY THIS

If children have had previous experience playing the bells, they may be able to play this additional part at the end of the song. They will need the low-D, E, F#, and G bells. (Call attention to the repeated D at the beginning of the pattern.)

Help children discover that the part notated in their book moves downward and that the additional part moves upward; that one part starts high and the other starts low.

Some children will hear the harmony made by the parts when they are played together.

Encourage children to try singing the additional part along with the bells when the class sings the song.

BEGINNING EXPERIENCES: Melody

MATERIALS
Record 1, "Old Joe Clark"; Pupil's Book, p. 8

VOCABULARY
upward direction, downward direction, upward and downward direction

IDEAS FOR TEACHING
1. Review the listening (getting ready) and marching activities in "Marching to Pretoria," p. 4.

2. Play the recording of "Old Joe Clark" and ask children to listen for the two sections of the song. Questions: In which section did you hear the word *rock*? (Second section—refrain) Can you think of different ways to rock to the music in the second section? (Forward and back, from side to side, from one foot to the other)

3. After children have rocked to the music in their own way, ask them to stop and listen to the melody in the first section (verse). Question: Does the melody in the first section move upward, downward, or does each phrase move both upward and downward? (Both upward and downward)

4. To reinforce the concept of both upward and downward direction, play the recording of "Old Joe Clark" and ask children to move an arm in the air, following the upward and downward direction of each phrase in the first section. This will serve as an ear-training game. Note: Activities such as this help children to become aware of how the tones in a melody move.

Listen to upward and downward direction.

OLD JOE CLARK
AMERICAN FOLK SONG   WORDS BY RAYMOND MATTHEWS
Piano acc. p. 238

1. Old Joe Clark, he built a house, Took him 'bout a week,

He built the floors a-bove his head, The ceil-ings un-der his feet

REFRAIN

Rock - a - rock, Old Joe Clark, Rock - a - rock, I'm gone;

Rock - a - rock, Old Joe Clark, Good - by, Lu - cy Long.

2. Old Joe Clark, he had a dog
Like none you've ever seen;
With floppy ears and curly tail,
And six feet in between. *Refrain*

3. Old Joe Clark, he had a wife,
Her name was Betty Sue;
She had two great big brown eye
The other two were blue. *Refrai*

8 Beginning Experiences

TRY THIS

The ear-training activity suggested in item 4 above can be used with other songs children know. If stereo equipment is available, use the Pick-a-Track technique to highlight the voices (melody), which are recorded on one track. The song accompaniment is recorded on the other track. Adjusting the balance control knob on the record player will isolate the voices. Most of the songs in this program are recorded this way.

TEACHER INFORMATION

Mainstreaming: Suggestions for using "Old Joe Clark" appear in the song list in *Silver Burdett Music for Special Education*.

ITY THE POOR PATAT

WORDS AND MUSIC BY JOSEF MARAIS. (ASCAP)

...ODY BASED ON AN AFRICAN FOLK TUNE
...RIGHT 1946, 1956 FIDEREE MUSIC CO. USED BY PERMISSION.

Piano acc. p. 246

1. The tree, he has a bark,
A bark that's thick or thin.
Pit-y ____ the poor pa-tat,
He's on-ly got a skin.

The tree, he has his trunk,
He stares up in the sky.
Pity the poor patat,
He can't see with his eye.

The tree, he has his leaves,
They're waving all around.
Pity the poor patat,
For he lives in the ground.

4. Although the tree is proud,
He only gives us wood,
But from the poor patat
We get our daily food.

Patat (pah-táht) is Afrikaans for "sweet potato."

Bells

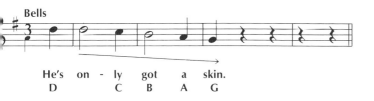

He's on-ly got a skin.
D   C   B   A   G

Beginning Experiences 9

BEGINNING EXPERIENCES: Melody

MATERIALS
Record 1, "Pity the Poor Patat";
Pupil's Book, p. 9; bells

VOCABULARY
downward direction, staff

IDEAS FOR TEACHING

1. Play the recording of "Pity the Poor Patat" and ask children to follow the notes of the song as they listen. Question: How do the tones move at the end of the song? (In a downward direction)

2. Have someone line up the bells on a desk or on a table so they match the picture on p. 7—the longest bell, G, at the left; the shortest bell, D, at the right.

3. Children can take turns playing the downward-moving pattern at the end of the song on the bells as others sing. Note: The repeated phrase in verses 1–3 (*Pity the poor patat*) and the rhyming phrases in the song (phrases 2 and 4 in each verse) will help children "catch" the words as they sing.

4. Direct attention to the pattern at the bottom of p. 9. Question: Do the notes on the staff show that the ending of the song moves in a downward direction? (With the exception of the repeated note on the first syllable of *only*, the notes move downward.) This experience will help children understand the function of notation.

5. Have children compare the ending of "Brother Noah," p. 6, with the ending of "Pity the Poor Patat." Some children may recognize that although the same ending tones are used, they are organized differently in each song.

TRY THIS

Some children may be able to play this additional part at the end of the song. They will need the low-D, E, F♯, and G bells.

D   D   D E   F♯ G

Help children discover that the part notated in their book moves downward and that the additional part moves upward; that one part starts high and the other starts low. Some children will hear the harmony made by the parts when they are played together.

Encourage children to try singing the additional part along with the bells when the class sings the song.

BEGINNING EXPERIENCES: Melody

MATERIALS
Record 1, "The Tree in the Wood";
Pupil's Book, pp. 10 and 11; bells

VOCABULARY
upward direction, repeated tones

IDEAS FOR TEACHING

1. Play the recording and ask children to listen for the part that gets longer as each verse is sung. (One more phrase is added in line 3 in each verse.)

2. This song can be sung as a game: Assign each cumulative line to a different solo singer. Whoever makes a mistake in the order of accumulation is out of the game. This activity will help children learn the song.

3. Play the recording again and ask children to follow the notation to find two lines of music in which the notes move in an upward direction. (With the exception of a few repeated notes, the notes in the first two lines move in an upward direction.)

4. Direct attention to the melody pattern on p. 11. To play that part, children will need six bells—low C, D, E, F, G, and A. Have someone line up the bells—the longest bell, C, at the left; the shortest bell, A, at the right.

5. Before children try playing the bell part, have them sing the first two staffs, tracing the direction of the melody in the air as they sing. Note: To help children know where tones repeat, write this diagram on the chalkboard.

— — — — —
— — —

THE TREE IN THE WOOD

FOLK SONG FROM ENGLAND

Orff acc. p. 284

1. All in a wood there grew a tree,
2. And on this tree there grew a limb,

The fin - est tree you ev - er did see;
The fin - est limb you ev - er did see;

The tree was in the wood,
The limb was on the tree, The tree was in the wood,

And the green leaves grew all a-round, a-round, a-round,

And the green leaves grew all a-round.

Repeat for additional lines in verses 3-8.

3. And on this limb there was a branch,

The finest branch you ever did see;

The branch was on the limb,

The limb was on the tree,

The tree was in the wood,

And the green leaves grew . . .

4. And on this branch there was a nest, .

5. And in this nest there was an egg, . . .

6. And in this egg there was a bird, . . .

10 Beginning Experiences

TRY THIS

Children might enjoy assigning a different percussion sound (tap woodblock, crash cymbal, etc.) to each item of the song—wood, tree, limb, etc. The sound is played each time the word is sung.

TEACHER INFORMATION

One kind of fun-and-game song that may be found among the oldest folk songs is the cumulative song, which adds new words in each successive verse. "Old MacDonald Had a Farm" and "The Twelve Days of Christmas" are familiar examples of cumulative songs.

Mainstreaming: You may reinforce language and visual sequencing skills by making visual cards to illustrate the items in any cumulative song. Avoid using too much color in order to keep lines distinct for children with perceptual problems and neurological impairments.

And on this bird there was a wing, . . .

And on this wing there was a feather, . . .

⊃IN INTO THE GAME
WORDS AND MUSIC BY PAUL CAMPBELL 🔘 Piano acc. p. 262

ME ON AND! JOIN INTO THE GAME" TRO—© COPYRIGHT 1951 FOLKWAYS MUSIC PUBLISHERS, INC. NEW YORK, N.Y. USED BY PERMISSION.

1. Let ev - 'ry - one clap hands like me. *(clap hands)*
2. Let ev - 'ry - one whis - tle like me. *(whistle)*

Let ev - 'ry - one clap hands like me. *(clap hands)*
Let ev - 'ry - one whis - tle like me. *(whistle)*

Come on and join in - to the game;____
Come on and join in - to the game;____

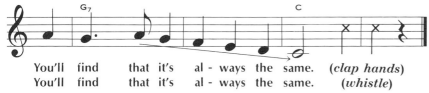

You'll find that it's al - ways the same. *(clap hands)*
You'll find that it's al - ways the same. *(whistle)*

Let ev'ryone laugh like me, *(laugh)*   5. Let ev'ryone yawn like me, *(yawn)*

Let ev'ryone sneeze like me, *(sneeze)*   6. Let ev'ryone do what he wants,

                                                  (various sounds)

Beginning Experiences 11

BEGINNING EXPERIENCES: Melody

MATERIALS
Record 1, "Join into the Game";
Pupil's Book, p. 11; bells

VOCABULARY
downward direction, upward
direction, strong cadence, weak
cadence

IDEAS FOR TEACHING
1. Ask children to look at the last
phrase (line) of "Join into the
Game." Questions: Do the notes
move mostly in a downward
direction or mostly in an upward
direction? (Mostly downward) How
many other phrases look like the last
phrase? (Phrases 1 and 2) Are they
the same length? (Yes)

2. Play the recording and ask
children to follow the notation in
their book.

3. To play the three phrases that
move in a downward direction,
children will need six bells—low C,
D, E, F, G, and A. (Have someone
line up the bells—the longest bell, C,
at the left; the shortest bell, A, at the
right.) These are the same bells
children used to play the part in
"The Tree in the Wood." (See
Teacher Information below.)

4. Let children take turns playing the
phrase every time it comes in the
song (phrases 1, 2, and 4). Point out:
There is a strong cadence (a strong
feeling of coming to a resting place)
at the end of those phrases.

5. Play the recording and ask
children to listen especially for the
ending of phrase 3. Question: Does
phrase 3 have a strong ending? (No.
Emphasize the "unfinished" feeling
that this weak cadence gives.)

TEACHER INFORMATION

Point out that in "The Tree in the Wood" they played
mostly in an upward direction; in "Join into the Game"
they will play mostly in a downward direction.

TRY THIS

1. Encourage children to make up new verses for "Join
into the Game." For example:
Let ev'ryone tap sticks like me. (tap tap)
Let ev'ryone stamp feet like me. (stamp stamp)
Let ev'ryone pound fists like me. (pound pound)

2. Children can replace words *clap hands, whistle,* etc.,
with just the actions whenever they occur in the song.

MATERIALS
Record 1, "Roll an' Rock"; Pupil's Book, pp. 12 and 13

VOCABULARY
contrasting sections, section A, section B

IDEAS FOR TEACHING

1. In the song "Marching to Pretoria" (p. 4) children are asked to stand still during the first section of the song and to march during the second section. In "Old Joe Clark" (p. 8), children are asked to listen to the melody in the first section and to rock during the second section. This is a good time to review contrasting sections in those two songs.

2. Ask children to look at the pictures on pp. 12 and 13 in their book. Question: How do the pictures show that the form of "Roll an' Rock" has two different sections? (Children are taking part in two different activities—in one picture, singing; in the other picture, moving.)

3. Call attention to the letter A in a circle above the notation at the beginning of the first section (verse) and the letter B in a square above the notation at the beginning of the second section (refrain).

4. Play the recording and ask children to listen for the two sections, A and contrasting B. (Some children may discover that section A is sung as a solo, section B is sung by a group; section A is sung freely, section B is sung with a steady beat; section A is sung one time, section B is sung several times. $\longrightarrow$

How do the pictures show different sections?

ROLL AN' ROCK BLACK SPIRITUAL Piano acc. p. 250

Oh, tell me,___ Mar-tha,___ Mar-tha, won't you tell me,

Where have___ you been so long?

Been a-roll-in' an' a-rock-in' at the old church gate,

An' my soul wants to go home to glo-ry.

12 Beginning Experiences

TEACHER INFORMATION

<u>Mainstreaming</u>: For non-ambulatory children, suggest (or have them suggest) alternative contrasting movements that they can perform.

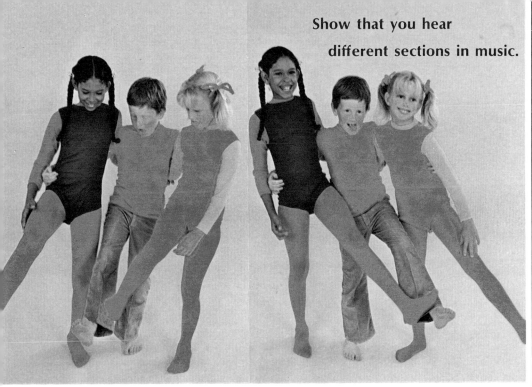

Show that you hear different sections in music.

5. When children can hear the difference between section A and section B, have them make up a clapping pattern to use during section B, using quarter notes and eighth notes. For example:

<u>Note</u>: You may want to review patterns that use quarter notes and eighth notes in the activities suggested on pp. 3 and 4.

Roll an' rock,____ come a - long,____

Roll an' rock ____ all day long.____

Roll an' rock,____ come a - long,____

My soul wants to go home____ to glo - ry.

Beginning Experiences 13

TRY THIS

1. Children can make up a rocking and clapping pattern to use throughout section B, such as one phrase (two measures) of rocking, followed by one phrase of clapping.

2. Children can make up different ways to rock with a partner: forward, backward, sideways, etc.

3. Have children bring in sets of photographs and pictures that show contrasting things. They may want to use photographs they have taken of their pets (one cat sleeping, another cat stretching), their friends (one friend tall, another friend short), etc. A collection of these visuals would make an attractive bulletin-board display.

BEGINNING EXPERIENCES: Form

MATERIALS
Record 1, "Marching to Pretoria";
Pupil's Book, p. 14; Autoharp, drum

VOCABULARY
contrasting sections, section A,
section B, AB form

IDEAS FOR TEACHING

1. Play the recording of "Marching to Pretoria" (music on p. 4) to review contrasting sections. There are two different sections in the song, A (verse) and B (refrain), making the form AB.

2. Ask children to look at the pictures on p. 14 in their book. Question: How do the pictures show a contrast between sections? (A in a circle and the Autoharp picture show that an Autoharp part will be played throughout section A. B in a square and the drum picture show that a drum part will be played during section B.)

3. (Since playing the Autoharp will be a new experience for many children, focus attention on the drum part in order to involve children immediately.) Play the recording and ask children to follow the notation of the drum part in their book. This part will reinforce the use of quarter notes and eighth notes. Point out: Two eighth notes (two sounds for a beat) will take the place of one quarter note.

4. Play the recording and have children take turns playing the drum part as others sing. Note: Before children play, they must be aware that they will start playing on the first strong beat, or on the first syllable of the word *marching* ("We are | MARCH-ing").

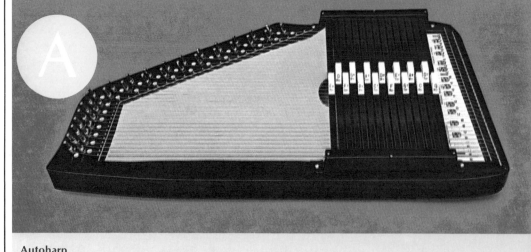

Autoharp

Show form by playing.

Drum

14   Beginning Experiences

TRY THIS

Some children will be able to make up and notate their own drum patterns, using quarter notes and eighth notes. For example:

TEACHER INFORMATION

Take time to introduce the Autoharp as an instrument for accompanying. Children will then be able to practice on their own. (The A section of "Marching to Pretoria" uses two chords, C and G₇. Children should get in the habit of using the left index finger to press the C button. Then the left middle finger will fall naturally on the G₇ button. With the right hand, the player strums on every beat, or quarter note, strumming away from the body—from the low strings to the high strings. The C and G₇ chord symbols in the Autoharp part will tell the player when to play each chord.

LD DAN TUCKER

AMERICAN FOLK SONG — Piano acc. p. 224

Old Dan Tuck-er was a might-y man,

He washed his face in the fry - ing pan,

Combed his hair with a wag - on wheel,

Had a tooth-ache in his heel;

So get out the way, Old Dan Tuck - er;

Get out the way, Old Dan Tuck - er;

Get out the way, Old Dan Tuck - er,

You're too late to get your sup - per.

15

BEGINNING EXPERIENCES: Form

MATERIALS
Record 1, "Old Dan Tucker"; Pupil's Book, p. 15

VOCABULARY
section A, section B, AB form

IDEAS FOR TEACHING

1. Play the recording and ask children to listen for the two sections, A and B. Have them follow the notation as they listen.

2. Call attention to the A in a circle at the beginning of the first section and the B in a square at the beginning of the second section.

3. Before playing the recording again, ask "What do you hear that makes section B different from section A?" (The melody is different, the rhythm is different, the words are different; a man sings in section A and a group sings in section B.)

4. Children can show the AB form through movement. Encourage them to make up a movement for section A and a contrasting movement for section B. For example: clap, or tap steady beat on knees for section A; walk forward, backward, or around in a circle for section B. Note: Use the dance (directions below) to reinforce the concept of AB form.

TRY THIS

Children can make up new verses for "Old Dan Tucker." For example:
Old Dan Tucker had a pair of shoes,/
The one was green and the other blue;/
He could tell which one was which—/
The left one made his big toe itch!

DANCE DIRECTIONS

Designate one child to be Old Dan Tucker. Other children choose partners. Partners stand facing each other, making two lines eight to ten steps apart.

Section A: While children in the lines clap the steady beat, Old Dan Tucker moves up and down between the lines, pantomiming the words of the song. At the end of section A, Old Dan Tucker "gets out of the way," moving to another part of the room.

Section B:
• Phrase 1: Partners take 4 steps toward each other (4 beats).
• Phrase 2: Partners take 4 steps backward to original place (4 beats).
• Phrases 3 and 4: Partners take 7 steps forward, passing right shoulders, then turn to face their partner on step 8 (8 beats).

The lines of children are now reversed. Old Dan Tucker chooses a new Dan Tucker and takes the new Dan Tucker's place in line. The dance begins anew.

BEGINNING EXPERIENCES: Form

MATERIALS
Record 1, "Old Tante Koba"; Pupil's Book, pp. 16 and 17; percussion instruments

VOCABULARY
contrasting sections, section A, section B, AB form

IDEAS FOR TEACHING

1. This song has two sections, A and B. Play the recording and ask children to listen for the rhythm of "Old Tante Koba."

Old Tan - te Ko - ba

Question: In which section did you hear the "Old Tante Koba" pattern? (Section A uses the pattern as part of the accompaniment—it is played on a drum.) Suggestions: If stereo equipment is available, use the Pick-a-Track technique to highlight the instrumental track.

2. Play the recording again and ask children to listen for the drum part in section B. (In section B the drum plays the steady beat (♩♩♩♩).

3. Direct children's attention to the patterns at the bottom of p. 17 in their book. Point out: The pattern next to the A in a circle is the "Old Tante Koba" pattern; the pattern next to the B in a square shows steady beats. Also, call attention to the quarter rest (𝄽) in the A pattern. The quarter rest replaces the beat with silence.

4. Children can take turns playing the "Old Tante Koba" pattern on a percussion instrument throughout

→

Show form by playing and singing.

OLD TANTE KOBA

WORDS AND MUSIC BY JOSEF MARAIS, (ASCAP)

COPYRIGHT 1946, 1956 FIDEREE MUSIC CO. USED BY PERMISSION

Piano acc. p. 275

(A) VERSE

1. Old Tan - te Ko - ba she ought to know,
2. Old Tan - te Ko - ba she loves to eat,

She stirs her cof - fee with her own big toe.
She got so fat___ she can't see her feet.

Old Tan - te Ko - ba she is so dumb,
Old Tan - te Ko - ba she eats a - lone,

She thinks it's bet - ter than to use her thumb.
So no one knows___ that she nibbles the bone.

B REFRAIN

'Tis - n't my af - fair,___ 'tis - n't your af - fair,___

16 Beginning Experiences

TEACHER INFORMATION

Joseph Marais wrote the words and music for "Old Tante Koba." Marais and his wife, Miranda, delighted concert audiences all over the world, singing and playing songs they collected. You will find other songs from the Marais collection in this book: "Marching to Pretoria" (p. 4), "Pity the Poor Patat" (p. 9), and "But the Cat Came Back" (p. 20).

It's Tan - te Ko - ba's trou - bles so we need - n't care.

'Tis - n't my af - fair,___ 'tis - n't your af - fair,___

It's Tan - te Ko - ba's trou-bles so we need - n't care.

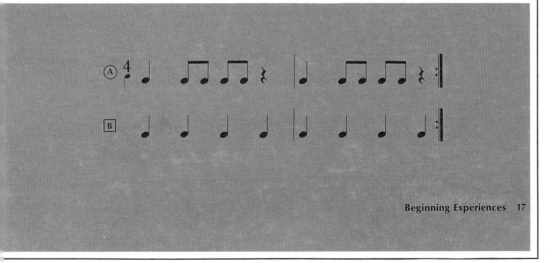

section A; they can play the steady beat during section B. Have children follow the notation of the patterns as they play.

5. When children know the song, have individuals or small groups sing the verses (section A); have everyone sing the refrain (section B).

6. Children learned to play the C and G_7 chords on the Autoharp to accompany "Marching to Pretoria" (p. 14). They can use the C and G_7 chords to accompany section A of "Old Tante Koba." Write the chord pattern on the chalkboard so that children can practice the Autoharp part. They will strum half notes, or two strums in each measure.

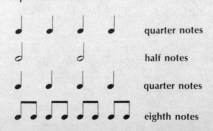

TEACHER INFORMATION

Mainstreaming: Sight-impaired children can play the Autoharp with little difficulty. Their fingers must be placed on the chord bars at first. After considerable experience, some children will memorize the chord-bar "keyboard."

REVIEW/REINFORCEMENT

Call attention to the two-to-one relationship between quarter notes and half notes; between eighth notes and quarter notes.

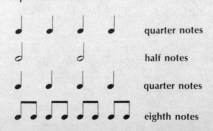

quarter notes

half notes

quarter notes

eighth notes

MATERIALS
Record 1, *Instrumental Parts for Mama Paquita;* "Mama Paquita"; Pupil's Book, pp. 18 and 19; drum, maracas, cowbell, bells, claves

VOCABULARY
tone color

IDEAS FOR TEACHING
1. Ask children to look at the pictures of instruments on p. 18 in their book. How many instruments can they identify?

2. Play the recording of *Instrumental Parts for Mama Paquita.* When children hear an instrument they know, ask them to point to its picture. Note: The instruments play their parts in this order on the recording: claves, cowbell, drum, guitar, maracas. These tone colors are appropriate for the style of this Latin-American song.

3. Play the recording of "Mama Paquita" and ask children to listen for what has been added to the tone color of the instruments. (Voices are added.) Note: When children listen again, ask them to follow the notes in their book and add the tone color of their voices (when they can). This is a way to make children consistently aware of the music score—how sounds are shown on the staff.

4. While some children sing, let others experiment with tone color by playing their own accompaniment on claves, maracas, cowbell, or drum. (They will start playing on the first strong beat, or on the second →

Instruments have tone color. When you hear an instrument you know, point to its picture.

claves

drum

guitar

cowbell

maracas

Each instrument has its own special sound, or *tone color*, that you can hear.

Instrumental Parts for "Mama Paquita" 🔘

Piano acc. p. 260   "Mama Paquita" 🔘

MAMA PAQUITA   CARNIVAL SONG FROM BRAZIL   ENGLISH WORDS BY MARGARET MARKS

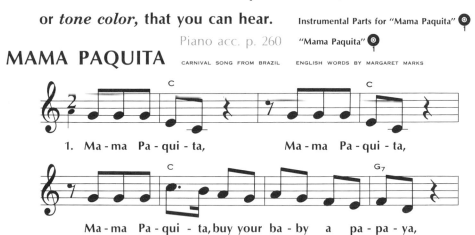

1. Ma - ma Pa - qui - ta,   Ma - ma Pa - qui - ta,

Ma - ma Pa - qui - ta, buy your ba - by a pa - pa - ya,

18 Beginning Experiences

TRY THIS

1. Children can play an ear-training game, using instruments they have played. Line up these instruments on a table, or on the floor, where they cannot be seen. One child chooses an instrument and plays it for others to identify.

2. Play another ear-training game, using voices. Several children hide. One of them pretends to call an unhidden child on the telephone. If the unhidden child recognizes the caller's voice, he or she becomes the caller. If the unhidden child does not recognize the caller's voice, he or she is out of the game. A new group of children hide and the game begins again.

A ripe pa-pa-ya and a ba-na-na,

A ripe ba-na-na that your ba-by will en-joy, ma-ma-ma-ma,

Ma-ma Pa-qui-ta, Ma-ma Pa-qui-ta,

Ma-ma Pa-qui-ta says, "I have-n't an-y mon-ey

To buy pa-pa-yas and ripe ba-na-nas,

Let's go to Car-ni-val and dance the night a-way!"

Mama Paquita, Mama Paquita,

Mama Paquita, buy your baby some pajamas,

Some new pajamas, and a sombrero,

A new sombrero that your baby will enjoy, ma-ma-ma-ma,

Mama Paquita, Mama Paquita,

Mama Paquita says, "I haven't any money

To buy pajamas and a sombrero,

Let's go to Carnival and dance the night away!"

Voices have tone color.

Add the tone color of your own voice as you follow the notes.

Beginning Experiences 19

syllable of *Paquita*—"Ma-ma Pa | QUI-ta.") <u>Suggestion</u>: If children have difficulty making up an accompaniment part, they might start with these. Write the patterns on a chart or on the chalkboard. (These parts will help reinforce the concept of duration introduced on p. 3 and reviewed on pp. 4, 13, and 14.)

REVIEW/REINFORCEMENT

1. You can use this song to review the concept of melody direction, which is introduced on p. 4 and continued on pp. 6–11. Play the recording of "Mama Paquita" and ask children to follow the notation to find two places in the song where the notes move in a downward direction. (These are identified by arrows in the music.)

2. Some children will be able to play the downward-moving part on the bells. It starts on high D and moves downward to low C.

TRY THIS

Some children learned to play the C and G₇ chords on the Autoharp to accompany "Marching to Pretoria" (p. 14). These chords can also be used to accompany "Mama Paquita." Write the chord pattern on the chalkboard, or on a chart, so that children can practice the Autoharp on their own. They will start strumming on the first strong beat, or

on the second syllable of *Paquita*—"Ma-ma Pa | QUI-ta."

BEGINNING EXPERIENCES: Tone Color

MATERIALS
Record 1, "Michie Banjo"; Pupil's Book, p. 20; percussion instruments

VOCABULARY
tone color

IDEAS FOR TEACHING

1. Play the recording and ask children to listen for the tone color of the percussion instruments that are used in the accompaniment. (In addition to percussion instruments—tambourine and woodblock—xylophones and glockenspiels are used in the accompaniment.)

2. Play the recording again and let children take turns improvising a pattern of short sounds, a pattern of long sounds, a pattern of long and short sounds on a percussion instrument. <u>Note</u>: This is a good time to reinforce the concept of rhythm pattern, using the activities suggested on one or two of the following pages: 3, 4, 14, 16, 19.

3. Encourage children to make up their own pattern of long and short sounds to accompany the singing of "Michie Banjo." Help them notate what they play, using line notation, or quarter notes, eighth notes, and half notes. <u>Suggestion</u>: Children can extract a pattern from the song itself and repeat it throughout the song.

1.   (measure 1)

2.   (measure 6)

3.   (measure 11)

MICHIE BANJO
CREOLE BAMBOULA   ENGLISH WORDS BY MARGARET MARKS

Orff acc. p. 282

Look at Mich-ie Ban-jo, Fan-cy Mich-ie Ban-jo,
Strut-tin'___ down the street.

1. *Cha-peau* ___ cocked on one
2. *Dia-mond* ___ pin in his

side, Mich-ie Ban-jo, High but-ton shoes that squeak,
tie, Mich-ie Ban-jo, Bright yel-low gloves so neat,

Walk-in' stick a-swing-in' wide, Mich-ie Ban-jo,
Trou-sers pleat-ed way up high, Mich-ie Ban-jo,

D.C. al Fine

Ev-'ry-thing's all com-plete.
Ev-'ry-thing's all com-plete.

BUT THE CAT CAME BACK
WORDS AND MUSIC BY JOSEF MARAIS. (ASCAP)

COPYRIGHT 1956. FIDEREE MUSIC CO. USED BY PERMISSION.

Piano acc. p. 226

(A) VERSE

1. Fred-die Wil-son had a cat that he did-n't want to keep.

He of-fered him for free and he tried to sell him cheap.

20 Beginning Experiences

TEACHER INFORMATION

1. The repetition of section A is indicated by *D.C. al Fine* (*Da Capo al Fine*—Dah Kah'-poh ahl Fee'-nay), which means repeat from the beginning and continue to the word *Fine*.

2. In the early days, the blending of the African, French, and Spanish cultures resulted in one that was unique in this hemisphere—the Creole culture. "Michie Banjo" is a Creole bamboula.

One of the most popular Creole dances, the bamboula, was named after one of two drums that were used to accompany the dance. The bamboula, the smaller drum, was made from a section of thick bamboo and was played at a fast tempo. The larger drum was played by two people. It was laid flat on the ground and one player, astride, played on the drum head with both hands and feet while another player behind him tapped a complex rhythm on the body of the drum with drumsticks.

He called up - on the preach - er one Sun - day for ad - vice;

The preach - er said, "Yes, leave him here, it would be so nice!"

B REFRAIN

But the cat came back, he would - n't stay a - way,

He was sit - ting on the porch on the ver - y next day.

The cat came back, he did - n't want to roam,

The ver - y next day it was "Home, Sweet Home."

Freddie put him on a ship and they headed for Ceylon.

The ship was overloaded more than twenty thousand ton.

Not far away from shore the cargo ship went down,

There wasn't any doubt about it, everybody drowned. *Refrain*

Then he put the cat aboard with a man in a balloon,

Who would give the cat away to the man in the moon.

The balloon it didn't rise, it burst in bits instead,

And ten miles from the spot, they found the man stone dead. *Refrain*

Beginning Experiences 21

BEGINNING EXPERIENCES: Tone Color

MATERIALS

Record 1, "But the Cat Came Back"; Pupil's Book, p. 20; percussion instruments

VOCABULARY

tone color, steady beat, AB form

IDEAS FOR TEACHING

1. As children listen to the recording, have them follow the notation of the song and clap the steady beat. Help them observe that the beat "stops and holds" at the note marked with a *fermata*—⌒ (fehr-mah'-tah). The fermata occurs on the first note of the refrain.

2. Have individual children choose a percussion instrument to play along with the recording. They may play the steady beat or make up a pattern of their own. For the fermata, encourage them to find a way to make each instrument stop and hold the sound (shake a tambourine, scrape a mallet back and forth on a woodblock, use both hands or two mallets to play a "roll" on a drum).

3. Another way to focus on the tone color of percussion instruments is to have individual children line up four different percussion instruments (for example, drum, cowbell, woodblock, gong) and play the instruments one after the other on the steady beat.

drum   cowbell   woodblock   gong

4. When children know the song, encourage solo singing on the verses (section A) contrasted with group singing on the refrain (section B).

TEACHER INFORMATION

Fermata is an Italian word meaning "stop" and indicates that the note is to be held beyond its designated time value.

TRY THIS

1. The class chooses four different mouth sounds—for example, "meow," "cluck," "pop," "ugh." As the song is sung, a small group keeps the steady beat by repeatedly performing the four sounds one after the other.

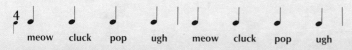

meow   cluck   pop   ugh   meow   cluck   pop   ugh

2. Four children or groups of children are each assigned one of the sounds from the pattern in Try This 1. As the song is sung, they perform the pattern, making their sound each time it occurs. The teacher or a child might act as conductor.

3. Help children plan a series of sound effects to use with the song—the sound of the sea, the boat sinking, the balloon bursting, the cat meowing, etc. The words of the song will direct the action.

BEGINNING EXPERIENCES: Tone Color

MATERIALS
Record 1, "Lady, Come"; Pupil's Book, p. 22; Autoharp

VOCABULARY
tone color, harmony, half notes

IDEAS FOR TEACHING

1. Direct attention to the picture (p. 22) of the child playing the Autoharp.

2. Play the recording and ask children to listen for the Autoharp part. The Autoharp plays half notes (♩), two strums per measure the first time the song is sung on the recording.

3. Call attention to the notation of half notes at the bottom of p. 22.

4. Let children take turns pressing the button for the G chord with the index finger of the left hand. With the right hand, the player strums so that each strum lasts for two beats (♩). Suggestion: Children can try strumming from the low strings to the middle ones on the first half note of the pattern and from the middle to the high strings for the second half note.

5. When children know the song, let them take turns accompanying "Lady, Come" as others sing. Suggestion: So that children can develop skill in playing the Autoharp, encourage them to practice on their own—at recess, or at other times outside a formal classroom setting.

LADY, COME FOLK SONG FROM ENGLAND

La - dy, come, Can't you see?

John fell off the white oak tree.

Add harmony to melody by playing the Autoharp.

With the index finger of your left hand, press the G button.

With your right hand, play half notes. Strum the strings every two beats.

22 Beginning Experiences

REVIEW/REINFORCEMENT

1. Other Beginning Experiences involving the Autoharp are found on pp. 14 and 19.

2. Play the recording of "Lady, Come" and ask children to follow the notation as they listen. Question. How do the notes move in the first line of the song? In the second line? (Some children may notice that the notes in the first line move upward, while in the second line the notes move downward.)

TRY THIS

1. "Lady, Come" can be sung as a two-part round. (However, before children attempt to sing it as a round, they should be very familiar with the melody.) One group will start to sing at entrance I and when they reach entrance II, a second group will start the song.

2. Change the tone color by having the Autoharp part played on bells. Children will play low G on the first half note and high G on the second half note.

Listen to a sound piece for Autoharp.

Then, make up a sound piece of your own.

◉ *Autoharp Sound Piece*

SOUND PIECE 1: Autoharp Design
DAVID S. WALKER

Explore ways of making new sounds on the Autoharp.

TRY
- Plucking strings
- Strumming strings
- Playing with hard mallet
- Playing with soft mallet
- Playing with plastic pick
- Playing with felt pick
- Sliding a comb along strings
- Sliding a ruler along strings
- Tapping wood case
- Rubbing strings with fingertips

PLAY
- High sounds
- Low sounds
- Sounds from high to low
- Sounds from low to high
- Several high sounds together
- Several low sounds together
- Loud sounds
- Soft sounds
- Long sounds
- Short sounds

Can you play this notation on the Autoharp?

1. ↑ ↑ ↑

2. • • • •

3. • • • •

4. ↑ ↓ ↑

23

BEGINNING EXPERIENCES: Tone Color

MATERIALS
Record 1, Eddleman: *Autoharp Sound Piece;* Pupil's Book, p. 23; Autoharp

VOCABULARY
tone color, high and low sounds, loud and soft sounds, long and short sounds

IDEAS FOR TEACHING
Play the recording of *Autoharp Sound Piece.* This piece can serve as a model for student experimentation.

The experience of creating a sound piece for Autoharp will extend over a period of time.

Interpretation of symbols:
1. Three swoops from low to high, each encompassing more strings

2. Pluck individual strings from left (low) to right (high).

3. Pluck one string four times, sweep the strings, following the contour of the arrows.

4. Three swoops—upward, downward, upward

Encourage children to invent their own symbols for the sounds they play. Suggestion: Have children make a selection from the sounds they have discovered and decide in which order they will play them.

Give children an opportunity to practice their composition, then let them perform for the class.

TEACHER INFORMATION

David Eddleman (American, 1936–) *Autoharp Sound Piece:* Eddleman's music has received performances all over the world. While known in many music circles in the United States and Europe for his serious avant-garde works, he has devoted the major part of his output to the creation of attractive, contemporary music capable of being performed by nonprofessional groups, especially school choruses and bands. Eddleman composed *Autoharp Sound Piece* especially for SILVER BURDETT MUSIC and performed it on the recording.

The composer used the following techniques for playing *Autoharp Sound Piece:*
- Running paper through the strings
- Caressing the strings with chamois cloth
- Running a comb across the strings
- Depressing more than one chord button at a time
- Plucking individual strings with the fingernails
- Rubbing the strings with the soft part of the fingers

BEGINNING EXPERIENCES: Tone Color

MATERIALS
Record 1, "Ain't Gonna Rain"; Pupil's Book, pp. 24 and 25; Autoharp

VOCABULARY
tone color, harmony, steady beat, strong beat, quarter notes, half notes

IDEAS FOR TEACHING

1. Play the recording and ask children to pretend to strum an Autoharp on each beat as they listen. They will strum two beats in each measure and will begin strumming on the first strong beat, or on the first syllable of the word *woodchuck*—"The | WOOD-chuck." Note: This activity can be used as preparation for playing the Autoharp part notated on p. 25 in the Pupil's Book.

2. Children will need to play two chords (G and D_7) to accompany "Ain't Gonna Rain." For songs that use these two chords, children should get in the habit of using the left index finger to press the G button. Then the left middle finger will fall naturally on the D_7 button.

3. Call attention to the notation of the Autoharp part at the top of p. 25. Question: What kind of notes do you see in the Autoharp part? (Quarter notes and half notes)

4. This may be a good time to review the relative duration of quarter notes and half notes.

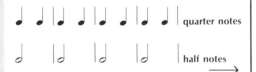

Add harmony to this song by playing chords on the Autoharp.

AIN'T GONNA RAIN

AMERICAN FOLK SONG   Piano acc. p. 266

1. The wood-chuck, he's a-chop-pin' wood,

The pos-sum, he's a-haul-in'.

My poor old dog fell off a log And killed him-self a-bawl-in'.

REFRAIN

It ain't gon-na rain, it ain't gon-na rain, It ain't gon-na rain no more.

Come on down, ev-'ry-bod-y sing. It ain't gon-na rain no more.

2. Just bake them biscuits good and brown,
   It ain't gonna rain no more.
   Swing your ladies round and round,
   It ain't gonna rain no more. *Refrain*

3. I'll tune the fiddle, you get the bow,
   It ain't gonna rain no more.
   The weatherman just told me so,
   It ain't gonna rain no more. *Refrain*

4. Oh, what did the blackbird say to the crow?
   "It ain't gonna rain no more.
   It ain't gonna hail, it ain't gonna snow,
   It ain't gonna rain no more." *Refrain*

24 Beginning Experiences

TEACHER INFORMATION

<u>Mainstreaming</u>: Children who have difficulty with a great many music activities can sometimes strum the Autoharp strings if another student depresses the chord buttons.

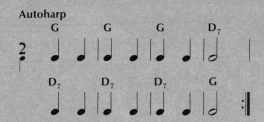

This song uses the G and D₇ chords.

Follow the letter names in the music.

SWEETLY SINGS THE DONKEY ROUND

Sweet-ly sings the don-key   at   the break of day;

If   you do not feed   him,   this   is what he'll say,

"Hee-haw!   Hee-haw!   Hee-haw! Hee-haw! Hee-haw!"

5. Children can take turns playing the strumming pattern. They will strum the steady beat (quarter notes) in the first three measures of each line and strum a sound that lasts for two beats for the half note at the end of each line.

6. When children know the song, let them take turns accompanying "Ain't Gonna Rain" as others sing.

MATERIALS
Record 1, "Sweetly Sings the Donkey"; Pupil's Book, p. 25; Autoharp

VOCABULARY
chords

IDEAS FOR TEACHING
1. Play the recording of "Sweetly Sings the Donkey" and ask children to listen for the Autoharp part as they follow the chord letters in the music. (The Autoharp plays two strums per measure.) Question: What chords will you use to accompany the song? (G and D₇)

2. Play the recording again and have children follow the chord letters to see when they will play the G chord and when they will play the D₇ chord.

3. Children can take turns accompanying the song. Remind them to use the left index finger to press the G button and the left middle finger to press the D₇ button.

TRY THIS

When children are familiar with the melody of "Sweetly Sings the Donkey," let them try singing the song as a two-part round. One group will start to sing at entrance I and when they reach entrance II, a second group will start the song.

BEGINNING EXPERIENCES: Tone Color

MATERIALS
Record 1, Anonymous: *Dadme Albricias, Hijos d'Eva;* Pupil's Book, pp. 26–31; recorder

VOCABULARY
tone color, recorder, G-clef sign, countermelody, staff

IDEAS FOR TEACHING
1. Direct attention to the photograph on p. 26. The men, in their many-colored hats and heavy ponchos, are playing "flutes" in a musical procession during fiesta in Puno, Peru.

2. Play the recording of *Dadme Albricias, Hijos d'Eva* ("Give me Joy, Sons of Eva"). <u>Point out</u>: This piece is played by a group of four recorders called a *consort.* For other pieces featuring recorders, play the following:
• Roussel: *Pipe in D Major,* p. 51
• Bull: *In Nomine,* p. 106
• Anonymous: *Coranto,* p. 124

3. Take time to give all children the initial experiences suggested on pp. 26–31. Working with three or four children at a time, you can spread these experiences over a long period of time.

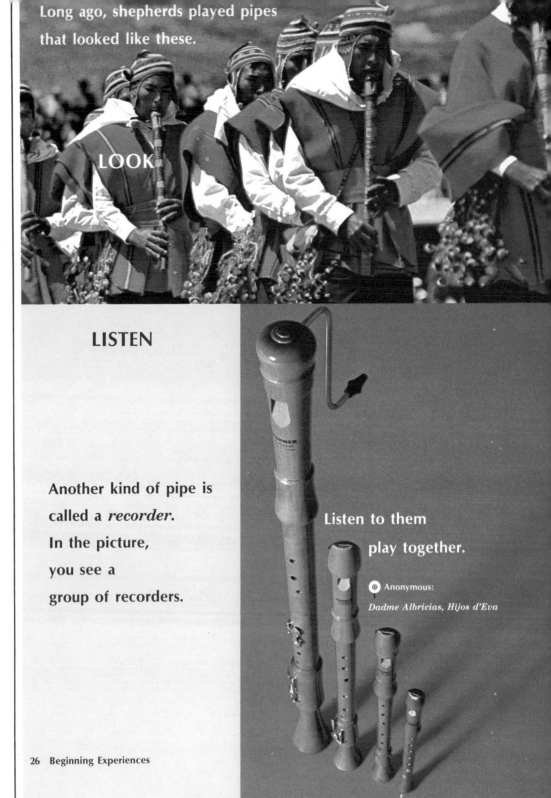

Long ago, shepherds played pipes that looked like these.

LOOK

LISTEN

Another kind of pipe is called a *recorder.* In the picture, you see a group of recorders.

Listen to them play together.

◉ Anonymous:
Dadme Albricias, Hijos d'Eva

26 Beginning Experiences

TEACHER INFORMATION

After all children have been introduced to the recorder, some of them may want to play the recorder parts that are included throughout the book. Other children can play the same parts on bells or on keyboard instruments (e.g., piano or xylophones). <u>Note</u>: As in other areas of the curriculum, a music program should provide for individual and small-group work in addition to regular class instruction.

You can play a pipe
called a
soprano recorder.

Hold the recorder
with both hands,
with the left hand
on top.

Cover-the-Hole Test
Press just hard enough
so the hole will make
a light mark on each
finger of your
left hand.

Making a Sound
Cover the tip of
the mouthpiece
with your lips.
Blow gently through
the recorder,
starting to blow with
a "daah."

IDEAS FOR TEACHING

1. Have children practice playing each note pictured on pp. 28 and 29. They should look at the note on the staff as they play the sound of that note. Children should keep a steady beat as they play the quarter notes: "daah, daah, daah, daah," take a breath, and repeat the four-note pattern several times—a breath after each group of four notes. Have them practice playing the tone B in this way, then A, then G.

2. Before children try playing the countermelody (a second melody sounding simultaneously with another melody) for "Ain't Gonna Rain," notated on p. 29 (song on p. 24), review the function of the staff (the group of five lines and the spaces between, on which notes are written). Also, call attention to the G-clef sign (ξ), the sign that shows the line G on the staff.

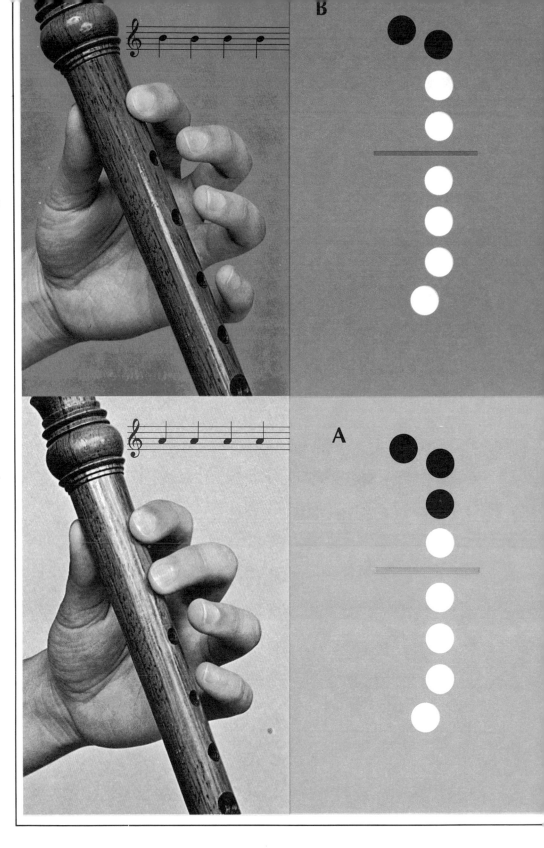

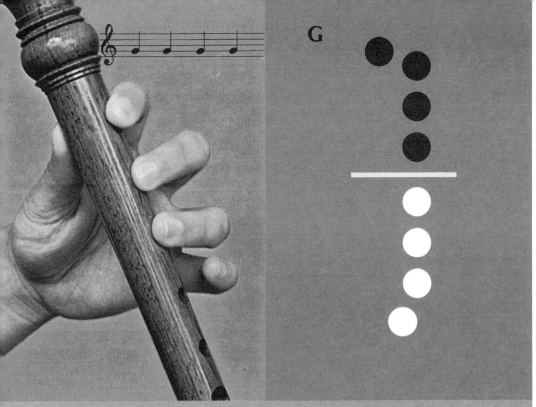

G

Look at the pictures to see which fingers you use
to play the tones B, A, and G.

Cover the holes with your fingers.
Now blow gently four times for each tone.
Start each blow with a "daah."

Can you find a sign that tells you where
the line G is on the staff?

Now you are ready to play
a part with the melody of
"Ain't Gonna Rain."
Your part is
a countermelody.

Recorder

IDEAS FOR TEACHING

1. Before children try playing the countermelody for "Brother Noah" (notated at the bottom of p. 30), you may need to point out that in $\frac{4}{4}$ meter, a half rest equals two beats, a quarter rest equals one beat, and a dotted half note is held for three beats.

2. Tips for playing the recorder:
• Rest mouthpiece lightly on lower lip.
• Press upper lip against mouthpiece with just enough pressure to keep the breath from escaping through the sides of the mouth—don't touch the mouthpiece with tongue or teeth.
• Cover holes with fleshy pad of fingers rather than with the fingertips—this allows an easier finger motion.
• Fingers covering holes should be fairly flat, not arched.

Use B A G with songs you know.

1. Fill in the silences in "Mama Paquita," p. 12

playing

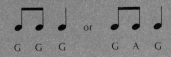

G   G   G   G   A   G

2. Play this pattern throughout "Lady, Come." p. 22

3. Play G throughout the first section of "Marching to Pretoria," p. 4

using

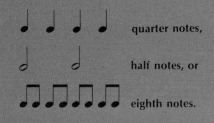

4. Play a countermelody with "Brother Noah." p. 6

Use **B A G** to play these melodies.

LULLABY   FRENCH FOLK MELODY

HOP, OLD SQUIRREL   BLACK-AMERICAN SINGING GAME

Beginning Experiences   31

BEGINNING EXPERIENCES:
Harmony/No Harmony

MATERIALS
Record 1, "Sing Together"; Pupil's Book, p. 32; Autoharp

VOCABULARY
harmony, no harmony, chords

IDEAS FOR TEACHING

1. Play the recording of "Sing Together" and ask children to listen for the Autoharp part as they follow the chord letters in the music. (The Autoharp plays one strum per measure except in measures 3, 7, and 11—in these measures the Autoharp plays two strums.) Question: What chords will you use when you accompany the song? (G and D_7)

2. Play the recording again and have children follow the chord letters to see when they will play the G chord and when they will play the D_7 chord.

3. Children can take turns accompanying the song. Remind them to use the left index finger to press the G button and the left middle finger to press the D_7 button.

4. When children are familiar with the melody, let them try singing the song as a two-part round. One group will start to sing at entrance I and when they reach entrance II, a second group will start the song.

SING TOGETHER OLD ENGLISH ROUND

Sing, sing to-geth - er, Mer - ri - ly, mer - ri - ly sing;

Sing, sing to-geth - er, Mer - ri - ly, mer - ri - ly sing;

Sing, sing, sing, sing.

1. A melody sung alone has no harmony.

2. A melody with chords has harmony.

3. A melody sung as a round has harmony.

32 Beginning Experiences

TEACHER INFORMATION

The diagrams at the bottom of p. 32 help clarify the concept of harmony/no harmony. When children are able to sing a round with ease and are able to play the Autoharp chords to accompany the song, use the diagrams to reinforce the concept.

1. Choose a round ("Lady, Come," p. 22; "Sweetly Sings the Donkey," p. 25; "Sing Together," p. 32) and have children sing the melody. Then call attention to the first diagram. Point out that the single wavy line shows a melody sung with no harmony added.

2. Ask a child to play the Autoharp chords while the class sings the melody. Call attention to the second diagram. Point out that the single wavy line plus the short horizontal lines represents a melody with chords—a melody with chords has harmony.

3. Have children sing the song as a two-part round. Call attention to the third diagram. Point out that sometimes two groups sing the same melody, but don't begin at the same time (a round). A melody sung as a round has harmony.

Sing "A Ram Sam Sam" with *no* harmony.

Add Autoharp chords for harmony.

RAM SAM SAM FOLK SONG FROM MOROCCO

Which of these pieces of music has harmony?

Which has no harmony?

Smith: *Three Brevities for Solo Flute*

Sor: *Variations on a Theme by Mozart*

Beginning Experiences 33

MATERIALS
Record 2, "A Ram Sam Sam," Versions 1, 2, and 3; Smith: *Three Brevities for Solo Flute*; Sor: *Variations on a Theme by Mozart*; Pupil's Book, pp. 32 and 33; Autoharp

VOCABULARY
harmony, no harmony, chords, round

IDEAS FOR TEACHING

1. Direct attention to the diagrams on p. 32. Make sure children understand that No. 1 represents a melody alone; No. 2 represents a melody with chords; No. 3 represents two melodies, each starting at a different time.

2. Play the recording of "A Ram Sam Sam," Version 1, and ask children to decide which diagram shows what they hear. (No. 1—the song is sung as a melody alone.)

3. Play Version 2. Ask children to decide which diagram shows what they hear. (No. 2—a melody with chords) Question: Which chords will you use to accompany the song? (F and C_7) Children can accompany the song, following the chord letters in the music.

4. Play Version 3. Ask children to decide which diagram shows what they hear. (No. 3—a melody sung as a round) When children are familiar with the song, let them try singing it as a two-part round.

5. Play the instrumental pieces listed in Materials. Note: The Smith piece has no harmony; the Sor piece has harmony.

TRY THIS

In music, sudden loud sounds are called *accents* (>). Play Version 1 of "A Ram Sam Sam" and ask children to listen for the words that are accented. (The word *Ram* is accented each time it comes in the song.)

Ask children to find accent marks in the music. Play Version 1 and ask children to follow the music and clap on the accents. Children can take turns playing the accents on a percussion instrument as others sing.

TEACHER INFORMATION

Hale Smith (American, 1925–) *Three Brevities for Solo Flute*, No. 1: This free-lance composer and arranger is also a performer and lecturer. His music for television dramas, for documentary films, and for concerts has earned him numerous awards and commissions. A photograph of Hale Smith appears on p. 58, lower left.

Fernando Sor (Spanish, 1778–1839) *Variations on a Theme by Mozart* (excerpt): This composer was also a virtuoso guitarist. He had much to do with stimulating interest in the guitar.

BEGINNING EXPERIENCES: Phrases

MATERIALS
Record 1, "Che che koolay"; Pupil's Book, pp. 34 and 35

VOCABULARY
melody alone, melody with harmony, phrases

IDEAS FOR TEACHING
1. Play the recording and ask children whether they hear a melody alone, or a melody with harmony. (A melody alone)

2. Play the recording again and have children imitate the motions they see pictured in their book.

3. Call attention to the length of the phrase lines (⌢) in the leader's part and in the group's part. The leader's part is on p. 34; the group's part is on p. 35. Children will have to look at the two pages in turn. Question: Are the phrases the same length, or different lengths? (The same length)

4. Play the recording again and have children trace the phrase lines in the air. This will help them feel the phrase length. Children can also draw the phrase lines on the chalkboard as they listen.

5. When they can, have children sing the group's part along with the recording, following the phrase lines in their book.

6. Children can play a game with "Che che koolay." (Directions below)

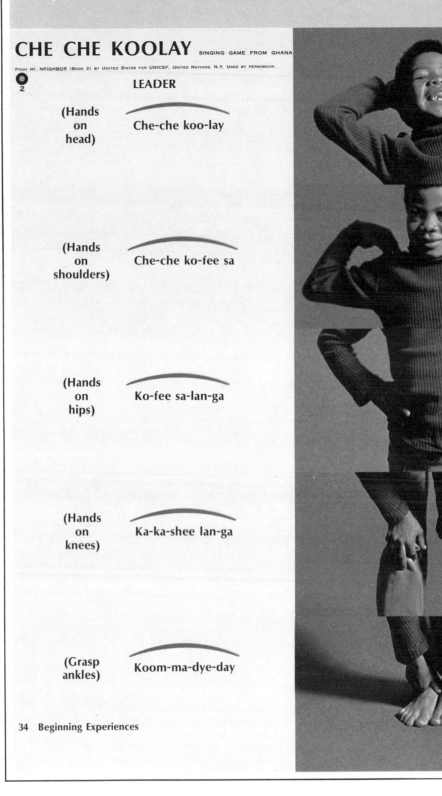

Do you hear harmony, or no harmony, in this song?

CHE CHE KOOLAY SINGING GAME FROM GHANA

From HI, NEIGHBOR (Book 2) by United States for UNICEF, United Nations, N.Y. Used by permission.

⊚ 2

LEADER

(Hands on head)   Che-che koo-lay

(Hands on shoulders)   Che-che ko-fee sa

(Hands on hips)   Ko-fee sa-lan-ga

(Hands on knees)   Ka-ka-shee lan-ga

(Grasp ankles)   Koom-ma-dye-day

34 Beginning Experiences

GAME

One child, the leader, stands in the middle of a circle of children. While singing the leader's part, the child makes motions, which the other children then imitate as they sing the group's part. (For the motions, see the photographs on pp. 34 and 35 in the Pupil's Book.) When the game is over, the leader chooses another child to be the leader and the game begins again.

Suggestion: If the game is used on the playground or in a gym (where there is room to run), this ending can be used.

At the end of the song, the leader falls to the ground. All the children do the same. Suddenly the leader jumps up and tries to catch one of the children, who all jump to their feet and try to get away. The child who is caught becomes the new leader and the game begins again.

Follow the phrases as you sing. Are they the same length, or different?

As you play the game, feel the length of each phrase.

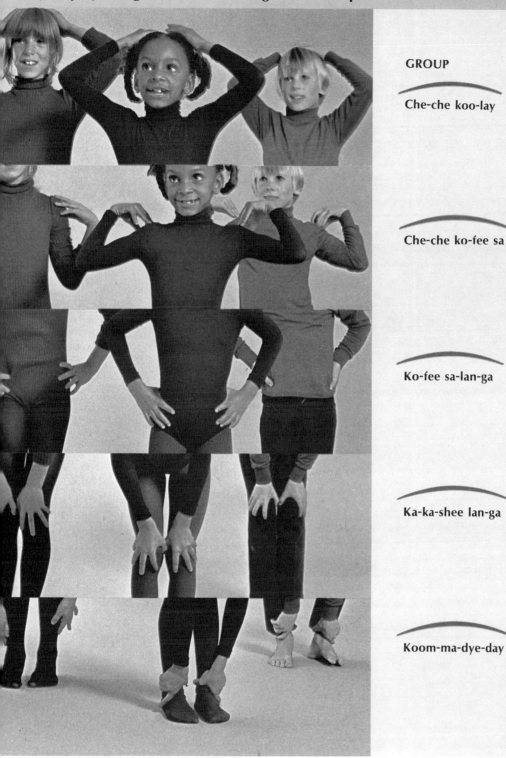

GROUP

Che-che koo-lay

Che-che ko-fee sa

Ko-fee sa-lan-ga

Ka-ka-shee lan-ga

Koom-ma-dye-day

35

REVIEW/REINFORCEMENT

1. Children can use a drum to accompany the "Che che koolay" game. Encourage them to make up their own drum patterns. Help them notate what they play, using long and shorter lines (line notation) or quarter notes and eighth notes. To get them started, write a few patterns on the chalkboard. For example:

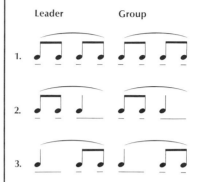

2. When children can play their patterns to accompany the game, have them play accents on some of the notes. (Accents are introduced on p. 33.) For example:

TEACHER INFORMATION

Mainstreaming: Rhythm call-and-response games can be played and enjoyed by the majority of special students. Hearing-impaired children can echo patterns that they see or that are performed by touching.

EAR-TRAINING GAME

Children can work in pairs to play an ear-training game. One child (leader) plays a pattern on a drum; the other child echos the leader's pattern on another drum.

Leader   Echo

BEGINNING EXPERIENCES: THE ARTS, Active-Still

MATERIALS
Record 2, Stravinsky: *A Soldier's Tale Suite,* "The Royal March" and "Music to Scene II"; Pupil's Book, pp. 36 and 37

VOCABULARY
phrases, active, still

IDEAS FOR TEACHING
1. As children sing "Join into the Game" (p. 11) or "Che che koolay" (p. 34), have them trace each phrase in the air. <u>Point out</u>: Music takes *time* to happen—their hands are showing *time passing* as they sing.

2. Ask children to look at Mathieu's *Painting.* Help children understand that we see the painting all at once—not, as in music, waiting for time to pass as each thing happens. <u>Questions</u>: Which part of the painting seems more active—the colored lines, or the dark background? (The colored lines. They seem to dash about in all directions with much energy and action and movement.) Which part seems "still," not active? (The dark background. It is an almost solid mass of flat color, spread evenly all over the canvas.)

3. Help children become aware that we can experience the still and active parts working together. Each has its own quality, but together they give the painting a special feeling of active *with* still.

4. Have children listen to the Stravinsky pieces listed in Materials. <u>Questions</u>: Which piece gives a more active, quick feeling? (The first—"The Royal March") Which gives a more →

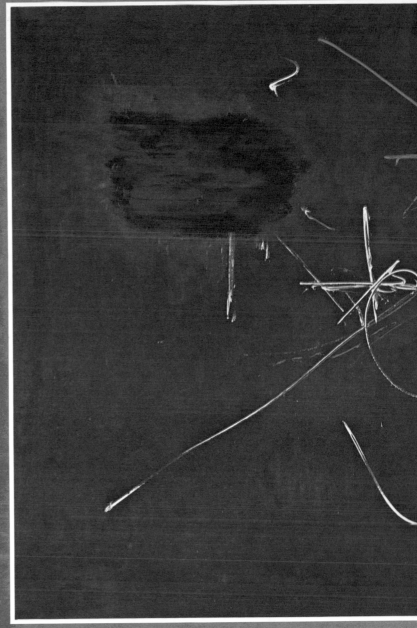

What part of this painting seems to be lively and active? What part seems to have little or no movement?

Listen to these two pieces of music. In one, the music is mostly still. In the other, it is active.

36   The Arts: Movement

TEACHER INFORMATION

Georges Mathieu (French, 1921-   ) *Painting:* This "action painting" is like visual jazz—it emphasizes the spontaneous, the intuitive. Mathieu applies paint right out of the tube, in quick, impulsive movements. But, as in good jazz, the quick actions are guided by the sensitive control of the artist. One gets an impression of great energy but also of meaningful order and structure.

Igor Stravinsky (Russian born, 1882–1971) *A Soldier's Tale Suite,* "The Royal March" and "Music to Scene II" (excerpts): Stravinsky was one of the greatest composers of the 20th century. His music was once thought to be so "far out" as to be an affront to the ear. But by the end of his life his acceptance as a mainstream composer was total. This ballet music has a typical Stravinsky sound—lean, lively, moderately dissonant, and rhythmically complex.

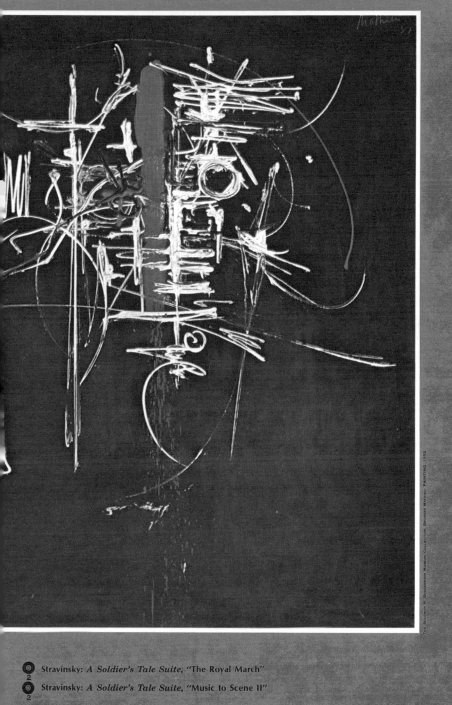

Stravinsky: *A Soldier's Tale Suite*, "The Royal March"

Stravinsky: *A Soldier's Tale Suite*, "Music to Scene II"

You *see* things in a painting all at once.

You *hear* things in music over a span of time.

still feeling? (The second—"Music to Scene II") <u>Point out</u>: Music can give a sense of action and of stillness. Painting can give a sense of action and stillness, too. Music takes place over time, while paintings are seen all at once.

TRY THIS

1. Children can change a song from still to active or from active to still by (a) changing tempo (speed) from slow to fast or from fast to slow; (b) using instruments and adding an active accompaniment (fast notes) or a still accompaniment (long notes).

2. Children can move their bodies in a still way (long, slow, controlled motions) or in an active way (fast, short, jerky motions).

3. Children can draw or paint "still" and "active" pictures, using nonobjective shapes. They can experiment with combinations of still and active in the same picture, using one still and one active, or in various groupings. <u>Suggestion</u>: A series of children's active and still pictures will make an attractive bulletin-board display.

37

REINFORCEMENT FOR ACTIVE-STILL

Songs
Active: Old Joe Clark, p. 8; Old Dan Tucker, p. 15
Still: Shepherd, Shepherd, p. 75; Hawaiian Rainbows, p. 146

Visuals
Active: Pollock, p. 160; Balla, p. 161
Still: O'Keeffe, pp. 94 and 95

Listening Selections
Active: Bartók, *Roumanian Dance No. 6*, p. 119; Brahms, *Hungarian Dance No. 6*, p. 106

Still: Roussel, *Pipe in D Major*, p. 51; Mendelssohn, *A Midsummer Night's Dream*, "Nocturne," p. 75

BEGINNING EXPERIENCES: Listening

MATERIALS
Record 2, *Kites Are Fun*; Pupil's
Book, pp. 38 and 39

VOCABULARY
steady beat, long sounds, short
sounds

IDEAS FOR TEACHING
1. <u>Note</u>: This picture-sound essay
focuses on the process of listening
to music. Pictures, words, and
sounds lead children to become
aware of the body, the mind, and
the feelings as components of music
listening.

2. Direct attention to the
photographs in the Pupil's Book.
<u>Point out</u>: In three of the
photographs, children are listening to
recorded music; in the others, people
(p. 38) and a child (p. 39) are
listening to live music.

3. Play the recording of *Kites Are
Fun* and have children listen for one
thing at a time:
• Who sings the song? (A group,
both men and women)
• Who plays the accompaniment?
(Instrumentalists, playing a variety of
instruments—guitars, electric bass
guitar, recorder, tambourine, drums,
and cymbals)
• Listen for the steady beat.
• Listen for long and short sounds.
→

What are these children hearing?

TEACHER INFORMATION

Chris Dedrick (American, c. 1943–   ) *Kites Are Fun:* On
this recording, *Kites Are Fun* is performed by The Free
Design, a family quartet—Chris, Bruce, Ellen, and Sandy
Dedrick. They have been singing together since they were
small children and now these well-trained musicians are
like a professional basketball team, passing melodies and
accompanying lines around with astonishing ease. Chris
Dedrick writes and arranges most of their songs, with an
occasional helping hand from the others.

For other songs by Chris Dedrick, see "I Clap My Hands,"
p. 2, and "What Is Love?" p. 109. The Free Design recorded
the songs *Love You* (see *What Do You Hear? 13,* p. 211)
and *California Dreamin',* p. 143.

(Long sounds on the words *kites* and *fun;* short sounds on the words *and we run along together through the field behind my house . . . away from everyone*)

4. Play the recording as many times as children's attention span allows.

TRY THIS
This picture-sound essay may be repeated at another time, using music that children select.

They are hearing the *sounds.*

How do you hear sounds?

You hear sounds with your *ears.*

Think of what you hear in "Kites Are Fun."

⊙ Dedrick, Chris: *Kites Are Fun*
2

A group sings the song. There are both

men's and women's voices in the group.

The voices are accompanied by a variety of

instruments.

The music has a steady beat. | | | | | |

The music has both long and short sounds.

       The more sounds your ears hear—

       The more sounds you think about—

       The more sounds you feel.

Listening to Music   39

TEACHER INFORMATION

The Beginning Experiences, pp. 2–39, are designed for children's immediate involvement with music through singing, listening, moving, creating, reading, and playing instruments. In addition, children have been led to think about the qualities (concepts) of music—rhythm, melody, tone color, form, dynamics, and harmony.

If children seem ready, move on to the learning modules that follow. If they need more Beginning Experiences, review specific ones on pp. 2–39, or select similar experiences from the modules.

MODULE 1

OBJECTIVES, p. xi

TEMPO • Lesson 1

MATERIALS
Record 2, "Oh, What a Beautiful
City," Versions 1 and 2; Handel:
Water Music, "Air," Versions 1 and 2;
Pupil's Book, pp. 40 and 41

VOCABULARY
fast tempo, slow tempo

IDEAS FOR TEACHNG
1. Call attention to the photograph
in the Pupil's Book. Question: Do
you think the horse is moving fast,
or slow?

2. To introduce the concept of
tempo (speed), let children take
turns saying their names, days of the
week, months of the year, or the
multiplication tables at a fast tempo;
at a slow tempo.

3. Play the recording of "Oh, What a
Beautiful City," Versions 1 and 2, and
ask children to listen for the tempo
in each version. Question: Which
version (performance) is in a fast
tempo? Which is in a slow tempo?
(Version 1 is fast; Version 2 is slow.)

4. Help children understand that the
speed, or tempo, of music is one
thing that makes music feel the way
it does. Fast music can feel very
different from slow music.

5. Play the two versions of the song
again and have children sing along
when they can. Use the Pick-a-Track
technique to highlight the voices.
Note: Children may have different
→

Listen to two recordings of this song.

Which is *fast?* Which is *slow?*

OH, WHAT A BEAUTIFUL CITY   BLACK SPIRITUAL

Piano acc. p. 226

Oh,   what   a beau - ti - ful   cit - y,——

Oh,   what   a beau - ti - ful   cit - y,——

40   MODULE 1: Tempo

TEACHER INFORMATION

George Frideric Handel (German born, 1685–1759)   *Water
Music,* "Air" (excerpts): Handel (along with Johann
Sebastian Bach) was the greatest composer of his time.
Among his enormous number of compositions is this
"outdoor music" intended for the king's court to enjoy
during leisurely excursions on huge barges on the river
Thames.

Mainstreaming: Hearing-impaired children can grasp the
concept of slow and fast tempo through movement
and touch.

Sing the song both ways.

Which *tempo* feels right to you?

Which conductor chooses a *faster tempo* for this piece?

Handel: *Water Music,* "Air"

Oh, what a beau - ti - ful cit - y,____

Twelve gates - a to the cit - y,____ Hal - le - lu - jah!

ideas of which tempo feels right for them. No one tempo is necessarily correct.

6. Play the recording of Handel's "Air," Versions 1 and 2, and ask children to listen to music played by two different orchestras, led by two different conductors. Question: Which performance has the faster tempo? (Version 2)

7. Point out that the same music can be sung or played at different tempos. A conductor is guided by the composer's indication of tempo, which gives a general idea. Within that idea, the conductor takes the music as fast or as slowly as feels right. Note: Help children discover that while the same music can be played faster or slower and that neither is necessarily correct, a tempo that is too fast or too slow can distort the composer's intent.

8. Play the two versions of "Air" again and have children tap the beat as they listen. This will help them feel the difference in the tempo of the two performances.

TRY THIS

1. Choose a group of children and lead them in singing a familiar song at too fast a tempo, at too slow a tempo, at a tempo that feels right. Encourage the class to evaluate each interpretation.

2. Have children bring in photographs and pictures illustrating people or things moving fast or slow to share with the class. This will help fix the concept of fast tempo and slow tempo.

MATERIALS
Record 2, "Hey Ho, Hey Lo"; Reimer:
Speed of the Beat; Pupil's Book,
p. 42; tambourine

VOCABULARY
beat getting faster, beat getting
slower, steady beat

IDEAS FOR TEACHING

1. Play the recording of "Hey Ho,
Hey Lo" and ask children to listen
for the tempo of the music. (The
beat gets faster. The music is
performed three times—vocal,
instrumental, vocal. The music starts
to get faster at the beginning of the
instrumental and gets faster and
faster to the end of the song.)

2. Play the recording again. To help
them feel the beat getting faster,
have children take turns playing the
beat on a tambourine as others sing
along with the recording.

3. Play the recording of *Speed of the
Beat* and ask children to think of
how they will move to the music.
Note: Help children discover that the
music starts at a moderate tempo
(the beat is steady), then it is played
again with many changes.

4. Play *Speed of the Beat* again and
let small groups of children take
turns moving to the beat. Note:
Children may need help before
creating their own fast and slow
movements. Have them move an arm
fast and then slow, or legs, feet,
head, etc.

In this song does the beat get slower, or faster, or stay the same?

HEY HO, HEY LO
SLOVAKIAN FOLK TUNE ENGLISH WORDS BY RAYMOND MATTHEWS

Piano acc. p. 226

Reimer: *Speed of the Beat*

42 Tempo

TRY THIS

1. Children can feel the beat getting faster by playing the
note A over and over on a recorder throughout "Hey Ho,
Hey Lo," using a quarter-note pattern (♩♩♩♩).

2. Call attention to the downward movement in parts of
the "Hey Ho, Hey Lo" melody. These are identified in the
music by arrows. Children can play these parts on bells.
They will start on the A bell and play downward (by step)
to the D bell.

TEACHER INFORMATION

Joyce Bogusky-Reimer (American, 1944–) *Speed of the
Beat:* This composer and music educator uses the tape
recorder and the electronic synthesizer as her basic
instruments for composing. *Speed of the Beat* was
composed especially for SILVER BURDETT MUSIC.

Does the beat get faster, or slower, in this song?

WIND UP THE APPLE TREE

AMERICAN SINGING GAME

FROM SINGING GAMES AND PLAYPARTY GAMES BY RICHARD CHASE. DOVER PUBLICATIONS, INC., NEW YORK, 1949, 1967.
REPRINTED THROUGH THE PERMISSION OF THE PUBLISHER.

Wind up the ap-ple tree! Hold on tight!

Wind it all__ day__ and wind it all__ night!

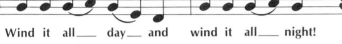

Faster

Stir up the dump-lings, the pot boils o - ver!

Can you hear the beat change in this music?

 Ibert: *Entr-acte*

MATERIALS
Record 2, "Wind Up the Apple Tree";
Ibert: *Entr'acte;* Pupil's Book, p. 43

VOCABULARY
changing tempo, beat getting faster, beat getting slower, steady beat

IDEAS FOR TEACHING
1. Play the recording of "Wind Up the Apple Tree" and ask children to listen for the tempo of the music. Question: Does the beat get faster, or slower? (Faster. The music starts getting faster after the cymbal crash.)

2. Play the recording again and have children clap the beat lightly to feel when the music gets faster.

3. Teach the singing game for "Wind Up the Apple Tree" (directions below).

4. Before playing the recording of *Entr'acte* (an interlude between the acts of a play or an opera), point out that you can feel the changes of tempo as you sing and as you move. The beat feels one way when it is slow and another way when it is fast.

5. Play the recording of *Entr'acte* and ask children to listen for the changes in tempo. (The music starts fast, gets slow, then ends at a fast tempo again.) Note: Some children may hear that the music is played on flute and guitar.

SINGING GAME

To play the game, children stand in a semicircle. The child at one end is the "tree," and stands still. At the other end is the leader, who starts to wind the circle around the tree as all sing the song. On the words *Hold on tight!* the children stamp their feet. As each player is wound up near the tree, he or she stops moving. When the leader stops, all hold on tight and jump up and down while singing the last two phrases (*Stir up the dumplings, . . .*). As the music gets faster and faster, all slide to the left as the leader pulls the line out straight.

TEACHER INFORMATION

Jacques Ibert (French, 1890-1962) *Entr'acte* (excerpt): The music of this composer has a charming, colorful quality. There is an element of humor in his lighter works as in his popular *Divertissements*. "Parade," a selection from *Divertissements,* is included in the lesson on p. 71.

MATERIALS

Record 2, "Carrot Stew"; Pupil's Book, p. 44; tambourine

VOCABULARY

steady beat, fermata (beat stops and holds)

IDEAS FOR TEACHING

1. Play the recording of "Carrot Stew" and ask children to listen for the place in the song where the beat stops and holds. (The beat stops and holds in measure 6 in section B on the word *two*.)

2. Play the recording again and have children follow the notation in their book as they listen. <u>Question</u>: Can you find the sign that tells you when the beat stops and holds? (The sign ⌒) This sign is called a *fermata*—fehr-mah'-tah—an Italian word meaning "pause." The sign indicates that the note is to be held beyond its designated time value.

3. When children are familiar with the song, have them take turns playing the steady beat on a tambourine as everyone sings. When the beat stops and holds, they shake the tambourine throughout the fermata.

<u>Note</u>: These diagrams relate to the dance (directions below).

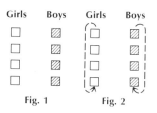

Girls	Boys	Girls	Boys
Fig. 1		Fig. 2	

Can you hear the beat stop and hold in this song? Can you find the sign that tells you when to stop and hold?

44 Tempo

DANCE DIRECTIONS

Partners stand side by side in longways formation—set of 6 or 8 couples (Fig. 1).

Section A: First boy and girl, turning away from each other, lead their lines around and back to place (Fig. 2).

Section B: (all short, 2-measure phrases)

Phrase 1: Both lines of children, facing each other, walk forward toward partner (4 steps).

Phrase 2: Partners walk backward to place (4 steps).

Phrase 3: Partners join both hands and turn halfway round, changing places (4 steps). Raise joined hands at the fermata (⌒) to make an arch.

Phrase 4: First boy and girl, with hands joined, slide quickly through the arch. They are now at the other end of the line. A new couple is in the lead and the dance begins again.

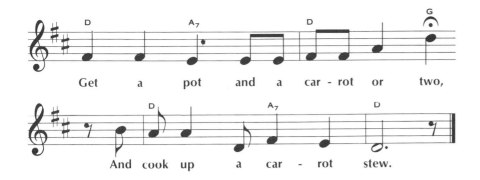

Get a pot and a car-rot or two,

And cook up a car-rot stew.

2. Nothing makes our tummies so full
   And keeps us happy too,
   As a great big pot or a little bitty bowl
   Or a spoonful of carrot stew. *Refrain*

3. So when you come to our little house,
   Bring a carrot if you have a few.
   We'll put it in a pot 'til it's nice and hot,
   And make some carrot stew. *Refrain*

Try these jump-rope chants at recess. Will you jump fast, or slow?

Hana, mana, mona, mike,

Barcelona, bona, strike,

Hare, ware, frown, venac,

Harrico, warrico, we, wo, wac.

Down by the ocean,

Down by the sea,

Johnnie broke a milk bottle

And blamed it on me.

I told Ma and Ma told Pa.

Johnnie got a licking

With a Ha! Ha! Ha!

How many licks did he get?

1, 2, 3, etc.

Tempo 45

TEMPO • Lesson 5

MATERIALS
Pupil's Book, p. 45

VOCABULARY
fast, slow, changing tempo

IDEAS FOR TEACHING

1. Choose one or two children to show changes of tempo while jumping rope.

2. Help children read the jump-rope chants on p. 45. Have them make up a series of motions for each chant, performing the motions as they chant the words.

THE WITCH GAME

Someone is chosen to be the witch. As they move slowly toward the witch, a group of children chant, "Hey, old witch, are you coming out tonight?" Witch answers, "No!" The group asks, "Why?" Witch makes up some silly answer like, "I'm haunting the house on the hill," or "My black cat is sick," or "I'm taking a bath in the stew."

The chanting continues until the group is close to the witch. Witch then answers "Yes!" to the first question instead of "No!" Witch tries to catch someone as she or he is running away. The one who is caught is the new witch and the game continues.

TRY THIS

1. Children can make up their own jump-rope chants in the rhythm of those on p. 45 in their book. For example:

Peánuts, popcorn, pumpkin pié,
Pumpernickel, purple tié.
Jump, pump, spell well:
Hop-along, shop-along,
Tip-toe, tell.

2. Children can accompany their chants on instruments—two bells, low C and G above, to be played simultaneously (a mallet held in each hand), woodblock, and finger cymbals. The bell part can use quarter notes, half notes, or a combination.

MATERIALS
Record 2, "Alouette";
Pupil's Book, p. 46; tambourine

VOCABULARY
fermata, steady beat

IDEAS FOR TEACHING
1. Play the recording and ask children to listen for the place in the song where the beat stops and holds. (The beat stops and holds each time the word *Oh* is sung.)

2. Play the recording again and have children follow the notation in their book as they listen. Question: Can you find the sign that tells you when to stop and hold? (The sign ⌒) This is called a *fermata*. The word is defined on p. 44 under item 2 in Ideas for Teaching.

3. Ask children to find different ways to play the tambourine—strike it with the hand; strike it on the knee, the head, the elbow, etc.

4. When children are familiar with the song, have them take turns playing the steady beat on a tambourine as everyone sings. (Most children will feel four beats in a measure.) When the beat stops and holds, they shake the tambourine throughout the fermata.

Literal translation: I shall pluck your feathers, gentle lark, from your head (*tête*); your beak (*bec*); your nose (*nez*); your back (*dos*); your claws (*pattes*); your neck (*cou*).

Play a tambourine on every beat.

Find the sign that tells you when to stop and hold.

ALOUETTE FOLK SONG FROM CANADA Piano acc. p. 227

REFRAIN

A - lou - et - te, gen - tille A - lou - et - te,

A - lou - et - te, je te plu - me - rai.

1. Je te plu - me - rai la tête, Je te plu - me - rai la tête,
2. Je te plu - me - rai la bec, Je te plu - me - rai la bec,

(No repeat first time)

1. Et la tête, et la tête.
2. Et la bec, et la bec. A - lou-ette, A - lou-ette. Oh!
   Et la tête, et la tête.

3. Le nez 4. Le dos 5. Les pattes 6. Le cou

46 Tempo

TRY THIS

Children can take turns accompanying "Alouette" on the Autoharp. They will use the F and C$_7$ chords. The chord names in the music will tell the Autoharp player when to play the F chord and when to play the C$_7$ chord.

Pronunciation guide

A-lou-et-te, gen-tille A-lou-et-te,
ah-loo-et-tuh zhan-tee ah-loo-et-tuh

A-lou-et-te, Je te plu-me-rai.
ah-loo-et-tuh zhuh tuh plew-muh-ray

Je te plu-me-rai la tete, . . .
zhuh tuh plew-muh-ray lah tet . . .

le nez; le bec; le dos; les pattes; le cou
luh nay; luh bek; luh doh; lay paht; luh koo

WHAT DO YOU HEAR? 1: TEMPO 🎵²

Listen to this music. Circle the word that best describes what is happening to the beat.

Is it fast, or slow? Is it getting faster, or getting slower?

1. FAST	*SLOW*	
2. *GETTING FASTER*	GETTING SLOWER	
3. *FAST*	SLOW	
4. FAST	*SLOW*	
5. GETTING FASTER	*GETTING SLOWER*	

Train Ride

Now listen to the music on this recording.

Circle the word that best describes the tempo.

Is it fast, or slow? Do you hear the beat stop and hold?

If you do, circle ⌢. If you do not, circle NO ⌢.

1. *FAST*	SLOW	*⌢*	NO ⌢
2. *FAST*	SLOW	⌢	NO ⌢
3. FAST	*SLOW*	⌢	*NO ⌢*
4. *FAST*	SLOW	⌢	NO ⌢

Beethoven: *Violin Concerto,* "Rondo"
Alouette

Chopin: *Sonata in B♭ Minor,* "Funeral March"
Haydn: *Quartet in D Minor,* Movement 4

Tempo   47

TEMPO • Lesson 7

MATERIALS
Record 2, *What Do You Hear? 1;
Tempo;* spirit master

VOCABULARY
fast, slow, getting faster, getting slower, fermata

TEACHER INFORMATION
The last part of many of the modules in this book will be a What Do You Hear? evaluation. The evaluations can be done with a large group in a classroom situation or with a small group using earphones. Spirit masters are available so that each child can respond individually.

Sometimes it may be feasible to write the items on the chalkboard so that the group can answer the questions together. Children can take turns circling the correct answers.

In *What Do You Hear? 1,* the evaluation could also be done through movement. Children move fast or slow as they hear the tempo of the music on the recording.

In the second part of *What Do You Hear? 1,* children are asked to listen for two things—fast or slow; fermata or no fermata. It is suggested that this part of the *What Do You Hear? 1* be given twice. The first time, let children listen for tempo only. The second time, have them listen for the presence or absence of fermatas. Children need much practice listening for one thing at a time.

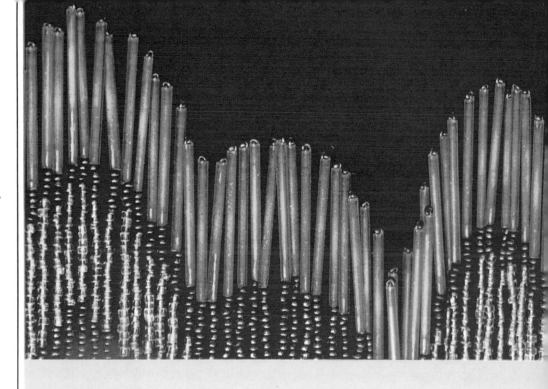

MODULE 2

OBJECTIVES, p. xi

MELODY • Lesson 1

MATERIALS
Record 2, *Electronic Sounds 1 and 2;*
Hearing Electronic Sounds; Record 3,
"All the Pretty Little Horses"; Pupil's
Book, pp. 48 and 49; bells

VOCABULARY
direction, upward, downward, staff,
phrase

IDEAS FOR TEACHING
1. Introduce the concept of upward
and downward direction by using
the photograph on p. 48 in the
Pupil's Book. Call attention to the
"up-and-down" outline of the
abstract design.

2. Have children experiment with
voice sounds that go in an upward
direction and then in a downward
direction. For example: imitate a
siren, sing syllables like "ah," "oh,"
"moo" in upward and downward
directions. Call someone's name over
and over, using a higher pitch each
time; using a lower pitch each time.

3. Let children experiment making
upward and downward swooping
sounds on bells or on the keyboard.
After they have experimented with
these sounds, call attention to the
upward and downward arrows on
p. 48 in their book.

4. To reinforce the relationship of
each arrow's direction to the
direction of the sound, have children
take turns following the arrows in
one of the boxes and showing the
direction by playing the bells. Other

Choose a box

and trace the arrows.

Play a swooping sound

on the bells or on the keyboard

in the same direction

as the arrows.

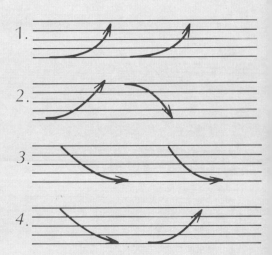

48   MODULE 2: Melody

ollow the lines as you hear
ie sound moving upward
id downward on the recording.

🎵 *Electronic Sounds 1 and 2*

o you see what you hear?
Vhich line shows
hat you hear next?

🎵 *Hearing Electronic Sounds*

ollow the notes to discover direction in this song. Does the
nding of each phrase move upward, or downward?

ano acc. p. 220

LL THE PRETTY LITTLE HORSES
FOLK SONG FROM SOUTHERN UNITED STATES 🎵₃

CTED, ADAPTED AND ARRANGED BY JOHN A. LOMAX & ALAN LOMAX TRO-© COPYRIGHT 1934 AND RENEWED 1962 LUDLOW MUSIC, INC., NEW YORK, N.Y. USED BY PERMISSION.

Hush-a-by, don't you cry, Go to sleep-y, lit-tle ba-by.

When you wake, you shall have All the pret-ty lit-tle hors-es:

Blacks and bays, dap-ples and grays, Coach and six-a lit-tle hors-es.

Hush-a-by, don't you cry, Go to sleep-y, lit-tle ba-by.

Melody 49

children will try to identify which box is being followed.

5. Play the recording of *Electronic Sounds 1 and 2* and have children follow the arrows on the first two staffs on p. 49 as they listen.

6. Direct attention to the second two staffs on p. 49. Then play the recording of *Hearing Electronic Sounds* and ask children to identify what they hear—staff 3 or staff 4. (Children should be able to hear that staff 4 is played. Each sound starts at the same high point and swoops lower and lower.)

7. Play the recording of "All the Pretty Little Horses" and ask children to listen (with books closed) for how the tones move at the end of each phrase. (Except for the repeated tone—last note—at the end of each phrase, the tones move downward by step—from line to space to line, etc.)

8. Help children make the transition from the use of lines and arrows on the staff to the use of notes on the staff. Have them find this pattern at the end of every phrase in the song:

D C B A G F♯ E

9. As others sing, let children take turns playing the downward melody on the bells when it comes in the song. They will need the high-D, C, B, A, G, F♯, and E bells.

TRY THIS

1. Children may be able to find other pictures or photographs that illustrate upward and downward direction.

2. Some children might enjoy making up their own upward and downward piece for voice or instrument. So that others can play it, they can use upward and downward arrows on a staff. For example:

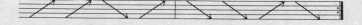

TEACHER INFORMATION

Mainstreaming: Allow students with sight impairments to experience upward and downward movement tactually by covering the outline for the notation for their compositions with glue, highlighting with grains of sand or a similar material.

MATERIALS
Record 3, "Clover"; Pupil's Book, p. 50; bells

VOCABULARY
downward melody pattern, repeated notes

IDEAS FOR TEACHING

1. Direct attention to the three-note pattern at the top of p. 50. Question: How do the notes move in the three-note pattern? (Downward, by step)

2. Let children take turns playing the three-note pattern on the bells.

3. Have children look at the five-note pattern on p. 50. Question: How is this pattern different from the three-note pattern? (Although it uses the same notes, the first two notes, A and B, are repeated before moving downward—B-B-A-A-G.)

4. Play the recording of "Clover" and have children follow the notation to find the five-note pattern in the song. It occurs three times (measures 1, 5, and 8).

5. After children have practiced playing the five-note pattern on bells, let them take turns playing the pattern along with the recording each time it comes in the song. Other will sing.

Play B A G on the bells.

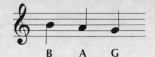

Play it fast. Play it slow.

Play it in this pattern.

CLOVER   FOLK SONG FROM CZECHOSLOVAKIA   ENGLISH WORDS BY RAYMOND MATTHEWS

Piano acc. p. 219

1. Clo - ver's grow - ing here;   Clo - ver's grow - ing there.

Now the win - ter's o - ver, Fields are green with clo - ver

Grow - ing ev - 'ry - where.   Now the win - ter's o - ver,

Fields are green with clo - ver Grow - ing ev - ry - where.

2. Clover smells so sweet. (*2 times*)

   When the day is fair,

   Its fragrance fills the air,   (*2 times*)

   The clover smells so sweet.

3. Clover has three leaves. (*2 times*)

   If a fourth one's there,

   You'll find it's very rare,   (*2 tim*

   For clover has three leaves.

50 Melody

TRY THIS

1. Children who have had the initial experiences on pp. 28 and 29 can play the five-note pattern on a recorder. Let them play the pattern each time it comes in "Clover" as others sing the song.

2. Some children may be able to find another downward pattern in the music that looks like the B-B-A-A-G pattern, but which starts higher on the staff—measure 2, D-D-C-C-B.

Follow the upward and downward direction of the notes in this melody as you listen to the recording.

PE IN D MAJOR   ALBERT ROUSSEL

RIGHT BY LOUISE B. M. DYER 1934 USED BY PERMISSION OF EDITIONS DE L'OISEAU-LYRE, MONACO

Melody   51

MATERIALS
Record 3, Roussel: *Pipe in D Major;*
Pupil's Book, p. 51.

VOCABULARY
upward, downward, repeated notes

IDEAS FOR TEACHING
1. Play the recording of *Pipe in D Major* and ask children to follow the notation to see where the notes move upward and downward, and where notes repeat.

REINFORCEMENT
This would be a good time for children to listen to the recordings and follow the melody direction of the notes in familiar songs. For example:
• Old Joe Clark, p. 8
• Join into the Game, p. 11
• Lady, Come, p. 22
• Sweetly Sings the Donkey, p. 25
• A Ram Sam Sam, p. 33
• Hey Ho, Hey Lo, p. 42

TEACHER INFORMATION

Although the concept in this module focuses on the upward and downward direction in music, *Pipe in D Major,* like other listening selections, should be re-heard from time to time so that children can discover its other qualities. For example:
• Dynamics—louder, softer, getting louder, getting softer
• Tempo—slow, getting slower

Albert Roussel (French, 1869–1937)   *Pipe in D Major:* The music of this composer includes songs, piano pieces, and symphonies. His *Symphony No. 3* was composed for the 50th anniversary of the Boston Symphony (1930).

MATERIALS

Record 3, "Skin and Bones"; Pupil's Book, pp. 52 and 53; bells, recorder

VOCABULARY

downward melody pattern, repeated notes

IDEAS FOR TEACHING

1. Play the recording of "Skin and Bones" and have children follow the notation as they listen.

2. This is a good song for individual singing. Have children take turns singing the *Oo-oo-oo-ooh!* parts when they come in the song.

3. Call attention to the four-note melody pattern on p. 52 in the Pupil's Book. <u>Question:</u> Do the notes in the pattern move in an upward, or a downward, direction? (Downward direction)

4. Ask children to find the pattern in the music. (The pattern occurs twice on the *Oo oo-oo-ooh!* parts.)

5. Ask children to look in their book to discover which bells will be needed to play the pattern. (B, A, G, and E)

6. Have someone line up the bells on a desk or on a table the longest bell, E, at the left and the shortest bell, B, at the right. Then let children take turns playing the pattern each time it comes in the song as others sing "Skin and Bones."

7. Direct attention to the bell or recorder part (see Teacher Information below) at the bottom of p. 53. Help children discover that the ⟶

SKIN AND BONES
FOLK SONG FROM KENTUCKY   COLLECTED BY JEAN RITCHIE

© 1952 JEAN RITCHIE GEORDIE MUSIC PUBLISHING INC

Orff acc. p. 283

1. There was an old wom-an all skin and bones, Oo - oo - oo-ooh!
2. One night __ she thought __ she'd take a walk, Oo - oo - oo-ooh!

She lived down by the old grave-yard, Oo - oo - oo-ooh! (*To verse 2*)
She walked down by the old grave-yard, Oo - oo - oo-ooh! (*To verse 3*)

She o-pened the door and BOO!!

3. She saw the bones a-layin' around,

Oo-oo-oo-ooh!

She went to the closet to get a broom,

Oo-oo-oo-ooh!   (*To coda*)

Play this pattern on the bells every time it comes in the song.

B   A   G   E

To play the pattern on the recorder, you need a new note, E. Look on page 53 to discover how to play it.

52 Melody

TEACHER INFORMATION

Those children who have had initial experiences with the recorder (pp. 28 and 29) can already play the notes B, A, and G. To play the four-note pattern (p. 53) on recorder, they will need a new note, E.

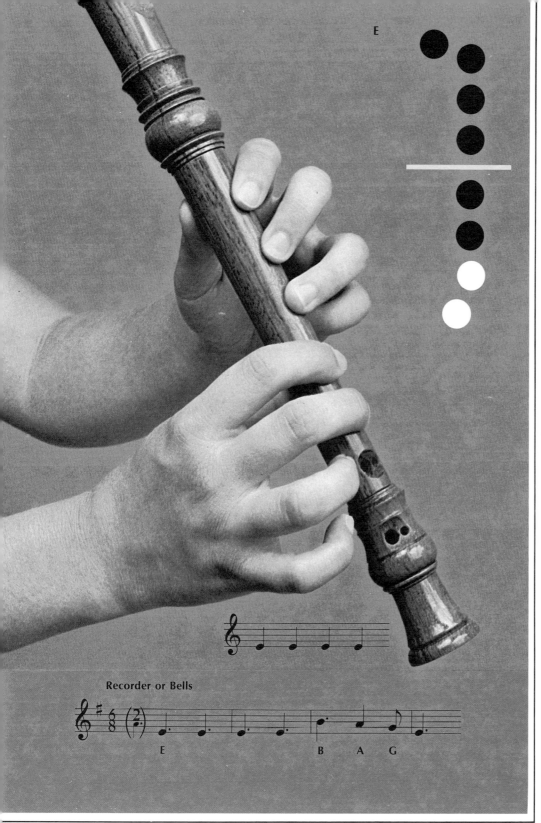

E

part starts with repeated notes (measures 1 and 2) followed by the four-note downward pattern notated on p. 52.

8. Some children may want to practice the bell or recorder part on their own. When they are ready, let them take turns playing the pattern as others sing the song.

Recorder or Bells

E   B   A   G

TRY THIS

1. Make a variety of percussion instruments available. Let children each choose an instrument and then take turns playing a sound after the *Oo-oo-oo-ooh*'s in "Skin and Bones." (Let children decide whether to play the sound soft or loud.) For example:

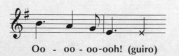

Oo - oo - oo-ooh! (guiro)

2. Working in groups of six (one child for each *Oo-oo-oo-ooh* pattern in the song), children can each choose a different accented sound to play. Encourage them to notate the sequence of sounds in their own way.

MATERIALS
Record 3, "Chicka Hanka"; Pupil's
Book, p. 54

VOCABULARY
downward melody pattern, repeated
notes, phrase

IDEAS FOR TEACHING

1. Play the recording and ask
children to think of a "train" sound
they can chant at the end of phrases
(lines) 1, 2, and 4. This will help
children focus on the length of the
phrases as they learn the song. For
example:

chick-a hank-a, chick-a hank-a, chick-a hank-a

2. Play the recording again and have
children follow the notation of each
phrase.

3. Help children to analyze how the
tones move. Have them look at the
first phrase (line) of the song.
Question: Can you find another
phrase in the song that looks like
phrase 1? (The last phrase, line 4, is
like phrase 1.) Being aware of
repetition in a song makes it easier
to learn.

4. Call attention to the first two
measures (*Number Three in line*) in
the third line of the song. With the
exception of the repeated note at
the beginning of the pattern, the
melody moves downward. Point out:
The notes in measures 1 and 2 of the
third phrase are repeated in
measures 3 and 4.

You can play this song on bells or recorder.

Follow the direction of the melody as you play.

CHICKA HANKA   AMERICAN FOLK SONG

FROM ECHOES OF AFRICA IN FOLK SONGS OF THE AMERICAS, BY BEATRICE LANDECK. COPYRIGHT © 1961, BY BEATRICE LANDECK. PUBLISHED BY DAVID McKAY COMPANY, INC. REPRINTED BY PERMISSION.

Here are parts of songs to play on bells.

Follow the direction of the melody as you play.

1. Brother Noah, p. 6

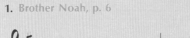

2. Marching to Pretoria, p. 4

TRY THIS

1. Some children may be able to play this four-note tune
on bells or recorder. It uses the same tones (E, G, A, and
B) as "Skin and Bones," p. 52. Encourage children to
practice on their own.

2. Have children experiment with the tone color of a
variety of percussion instruments. Then let them take turns
filling in the pauses at the end of phrases 1, 2, and 4 as
others sing the song.

3. One child can play the melody on recorder or bells;
others can fill in the pauses with percussion sounds.

4. "Chicka Hanka" is appropriate for movement. The
words suggest interaction between two lines of children
representing the cars of two trains, each on a different
track. Have each line work out a floor pattern, or "track,"
on which to move. Encourage children to add sounds to
go with the movement.

3. Ain't Gonna Rain, p. 24

It ain't gon-na rain no more.

4. Pity the Poor Patat, p. 9

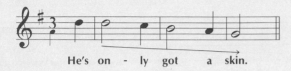

He's on - ly got a skin.

5. All the Pretty Little Horses, p. 49

Go to sleep-y lit-tle ba - by.

6. Lady, Come, p. 22

La - dy, come, Can't you see?

7. Skin and Bones, p. 52

Oo - oo - oo - ooh!

8. Mama Paquita, p. 18

Car - ni - val and dance the night a - way!

9. The Tree in the Wood, p. 10

All in___ a___ wood there grew a tree,

Melody 55

MATERIALS
Pupil's Book, p. 55; bells

VOCABULARY
upward, downward, repeated tones

IDEAS FOR TEACHING

1. After children have analyzed the direction of all the melody patterns notated on p. 55, have them choose one to play on the bells or other mallet instruments.
• Patterns 1, 2, 4, 5, 7, and 8 move in a downward direction.
• Patterns 3, 6, and 9 move in an upward direction.
• Patterns 2, 3, 4, 5, 6, and 9 have repeated tones.

2. Use p. 55 over a period of time, having each child play the pattern he or she chooses while others sing the whole song. <u>Note</u>: If possible, make the bells and the Pupil's Book available so that children can practice outside music class time.

TEACHER INFORMATION

To play the patterns on p. 55, children will need the following bells.

MATERIALS

Record 3, "On the First Thanksgiving Day"; Pupil's Book, p. 56;, bells

VOCABULARY

phrases, downward direction, repeated tones

IDEAS FOR TEACHING

1. Play the recording and ask children to trace the phrases in the air as they listen. This will help them feel the length of each phrase. Point out: All the phrases are the same length—two measures.

2. Play the recording again and have children follow the notation to find the phrases in which tones move in a downward direction. These are shown by an arrow in the notation—phrases 2, 4, and 8.

3. Before children take turns playing the downward phrases on the bells, take time to analyze how the tones move. (See notation below.)

4. Have someone line up the bells (C, D, E, F, G, A) on a desk—the longest bell, C, at the left; the shortest bell, A, at the right. Let children take turns playing the downward phrases when they come in the song.

5. Through questioning and discussion, help children discover that phrases 1 and 3 are alike; that phrases 2 and 4 are alike. Being aware of repetition in a song makes it easier to learn.

ON THE FIRST THANKSGIVING DAY

WORDS TRADITIONAL

MUSIC BY JAKOB HINTZE

On the first Thanks - giv - ing Day,

Pil - grims went to church to pray,

Thanked the Lord for sun and rain,

Thanked him for the fields of grain.

Now Thanks - giv - ing comes a - gain:

Praise the Lord as they did then.

Thank him for the sun and rain,

Thank him for the fields of grain.

56 Melody

TEACHER INFORMATION

Phrases 2 and 4 start on G, repeat it, then the notes move downward to C, repeating D.

G G F E D D C

The last phrase starts on A and moves stepwise downward to C, repeating D.

A G F E D D C

Mainstreaming: Suggestions for using "On the First Thanksgiving Day" appear in the song list in *Silver Burdett Music for Special Education.*

WHAT DO YOU HEAR? 2: MELODY ⊚₃

Listen to these pieces of music.

As each number is called, circle the word that best describes the direction the melody is moving. Is it moving *upward*, or *downward*, or both *upward* and *downward*?

1. UPWARD   DOWNWARD
   UPWARD AND DOWNWARD

2. UPWARD   DOWNWARD
   UPWARD AND DOWNWARD

3. UPWARD   DOWNWARD
   UPWARD AND DOWNWARD

Beethoven: *Concerto No. 5 in E♭ Major*, "Emperor," Movement 1

1. UPWARD   DOWNWARD

2. UPWARD   DOWNWARD

3. UPWARD   DOWNWARD

4. UPWARD   DOWNWARD

Gershwin: *Rhapsody in Blue*
Poncielli: *Dance of the Hours*
Rimsky-Korsakov: *Le Coq D'or*
Kuhlah: *Sonatina*

Melody 57

MATERIALS
Record 3, *What Do You Hear? 2; Melody*; spirit master

VOCABULARY
upward, downward, upward and downward

TEACHER INFORMATION
The last part of many of the modules in this book will be a What Do You Hear? evaluation. This activity requires the children to demonstrate what they have learned by responding to the instructions on the recording. It also gives the children and the teacher a concrete assessment of progress toward increased musical perception.

The What Do You Hear? evaluations can be done with a large group in a classroom situation or with a small group using earphones. Spirit masters are available so that each child can respond individually.

In *What Do You Hear? 2*, the evaluation can also be done through movement. A child makes an upward movement, a downward movement, or an upward and downward movement as she or he responds to the music on the recording.

MODULE 3

OBJECTIVES, p. xi

THINGS PEOPLE DO WITH MUSIC:
Compose

MATERIALS
Record 3, *Things People Do with Music*—"Rain Song"; Pupil's Book, pp. 58 and 59

VOCABULARY
loud-soft, fast-slow, high-low, long sounds-short sounds

IDEAS FOR TEACHING

1. <u>Note</u>: This is the first of a series of picture-sound essays on *What People Do with Music* in SILVER BURDETT MUSIC. Other essays in the program focus on the conductor, the performer, the teacher, and the listener. These recorded lessons help children become aware of vocational opportunities in music as well as how some people value music in their lives.

2. Direct attention to the photographs of four composers on p. 58 in the Pupil's Book. Through questioning and discussion, help children become aware that composers work in a variety of ways. Gershon Kingsley (upper left) and David McHugh (upper right) are working at a piano. Hale Smith (lower left) is working at a table. Doris Hays (lower right) is experimenting with an electronic sound instrument.

3. On the recording of *Things People Do with Music*—"Rain Song," David McHugh tells how he composed "Rain Song." Near the end of the recording, the composer ——→

TEACHER INFORMATION

David McHugh (American, c. 1941–) "Rain Song": This gifted composer is also an arranger and singer. Among other things, he has written several Broadway musicals, the music for numerous commercials, and the score for the television movie *Mr. Inside, Mr. Outside*. His *Symphonic Overture* was performed by the Louisville Orchestra in 1979 to dedicate the opening of their Center for the Performing Arts.

Hale Smith is the composer of *Three Brevities for Solo Flute*, No. 1 (see p. 33). Gershon Kingsley is the composer of *Piece in Two Meters* (see Call Chart 1, p. 64). Doris Hays is the composer of *Sound Piece 3* (p. 87) and *Ol' Clo'* (p. 165).

Here are four composers.

On the recording, you will hear one of them tell you

what a composer does.

🔘 *Things People Do with Music*
3

RAIN SONG

WORDS AND MUSIC BY DAVID McHUGH © 1972 DAVID McHUGH 🔘
3

Piano acc. p. 272

The rain just keeps on fall-ing, And the sky is col-ored grey;

The birds don't stop their sing-ing—— 'Cause it's just an-oth-er day;

And the clouds keep pass-ing o-ver, Bring-in' rain to flow'rs be-low;

While the sun keeps wait-ing pa-tient-ly To un-veil its gold-en glow;

Some-times sun shines, and oth-er times it rains;——

But to me it's all the same,——

To me it's all the same.——

MODULE 3: Things People Do with Music—Compose 59

Piano acc. p. 272

invites children to sing along with him. "Rain Song" is sung twice on the recording. Encourage children to sing as much as they can when the song is performed the second time.

4. Help children identify the instruments that accompany "Rain Song" on the recording—piano, electric piano, guitar, electric bass, drums.

5. Suggestion: If there are composers, (or college·students who are studying composition) in your community, invite them to discuss their work with the children.

MODULE 4

OBJECTIVES, p. xi

METER • Lesson 1

MATERIALS
Record 3, "New Year's Song"; Pupil's Book, pp. 60 and 61; percussion instruments, recorder, balls

VOCABULARY
beats in sets of two, meter in 2, bar lines, measure, quarter notes, eighth notes, half notes, meter signature

IDEAS FOR TEACHING

1. Play the recording of "New Year's Song" and ask children to keep the steady beat by bouncing and catching a ball. <u>Note</u>: Using the bounce-catch, bounce-catch motions, children will feel beats in sets of two. (Just as the bounce motion is stronger than the catch motion, the first beat in a set of two is stronger than the second beat.)

2. You may want to review other motions in sets of two:
• Marching motions (left-right) in "Marching to Pretoria," p. 4
• Rocking motions in "Old Joe Clark," p. 8

3. When children are able to feel beats in sets of two through movement, have them play beats in sets of two on a percussion instrument throughout "New Year's Song."

When you bounce and catch a ball, you make motions in sets of tw
In music, these sets are called *meter.*

Orff acc. p. 278

NEW YEAR'S SONG · *Kazoe-uta* · FOLK SONG FROM JAPAN · ENGLISH VERSION BY ROSEMARY JACQ

1. On the eve of New Year's,___ Bus-y peo-ple, hap-py peo-ple,
   Hi - to - tsu to ya,_____ Hi - to - yo a - ku - re - ba,

   Run - ning here and there, Run - ning here and there,
   Ni - gi - ya - ka de, Ni - gi - ya - ka de,

   Dec - o - rate the bam-boo trees to cel - e - brate the day,___
   O - ka - za - ri ta - te - ta - ru ma - tsu - ka - za - ri,___

   Cel - e - brate the day.
   Ma - tsu - ka - za - ri.

2. On the eve of New Year's,
   Paper streamers, fresh plum blossoms
   Hang above the door,
   Hang above the door,
   Telling all who pass by
     to have a happy day,
   Have a happy day.

3. On the day of New Year's,
   Games are played and songs are sung
   To celebrate the day,
   Celebrate the day.
   People come to wish each other
     Happy New Year's Day,
   Happy New Year's Day.

60 MODULE 4: Meter

TEACHER INFORMATION

New Year's Eve has been called the most important of all Japanese holidays. Bells are rung to celebrate at midnight on New Year's Eve.

"New Year's Song" is sung by children as a ball-bouncing chant.

Mainstreaming: "New Year's Song" can be used to strengthen lateral perception by having children move their head, hands, or legs—left-right, right-left, or left to right and right to left, emphasizing the first movement. When beats are in sets of two, slower reacting children may perform only the first of each set of beats.

Recorder or Bells

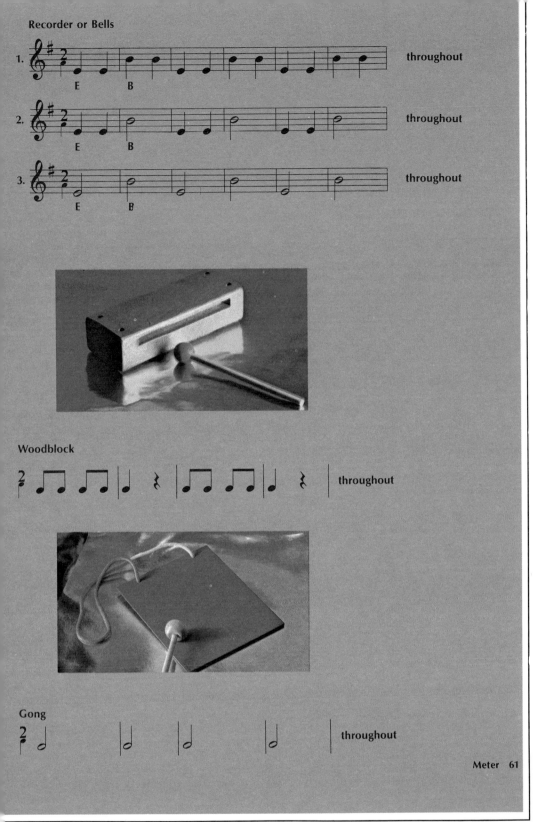

1. E B   throughout

2. E B   throughout

3. E B   throughout

Woodblock

throughout

Gong

throughout

Meter   61

4. Ask children to find the lines (called *bar lines*) that separate the beats into sets of two in the instrumental parts on p. 61. <u>Point out</u>: The space between the bar lines is called a *measure.*

5. Call attention to the meter signature (²₂) that appears before the first note of the instrumental parts. The 2 means that there are two beats each measure. The *quarter note* (♩) means that in this song a quarter note lasts for one beat.

6. Before children try playing the instrumental parts, review the relative duration of quarter notes, eighth notes, and half notes.

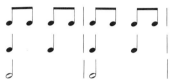

7. Point out the quarter rest (𝄽) that is used in the woodblock part. The quarter rest symbolizes a beat of silence. Use the quarter rest to focus on the first strong beat in each measure.

play, rest play, rest

8. When children are ready, have them play the instrumental parts as others sing "New Year's Song."

TEACHER INFORMATION

Japanese folk songs often have simple rhythms and only a few notes in the melody, and they are not meant to have harmony. The people especially enjoy nature, not only in landscapes or large scenic views, but in small things such as a few flowers, leaves, branches, and pebbles. There are many Japanese songs that show the enjoyment of nature—songs about rain and snow, about twilight, about the moon, and about animals and insects.

Singing a melody with only one or two accompanying instruments and no harmony is perhaps like making a flower arrangement with only three flowers, or with a few flowering branches. For other Japanese folk songs, see "Hana ichi momme," p. 128, and "Imagination of Grand Sea," p. 129.

MATERIALS

Record 3, "Find the Ring"; Pupil's Book, pp. 62 and 63; tambourine, finger cymbals

VOCABULARY

beats in sets of three, meter in 3, bar lines, quarter notes, half notes, meter signature

IDEAS FOR TEACHING

1. Play the recording of "Find the Ring" and ask children to feel the steady beat as they listen.

2. Play the recording again and have children keep the steady beat, using motions. <u>Note</u>: Using the following tapping motions (four-measure pattern for each phrase) will help children feel beats in sets of three and will help prepare them for the ring game (directions below).

Extend left hand (palm up) in front. Then, using right hand,
• tap to left three times;
• tap left hand three times;
• tap to right three times;
• tap left hand three times.

Tap   Tap   Tap   Tap
left   left   right   left
    hand   hand

3. To reinforce the concept that the first beat in each measure seems stronger than the other beats, have children use motions with "Find the Ring." <u>Point out</u>: The strong motion, like the strong beat, comes on the

When you play the "Find the Ring" game, you feel beats in sets of three.

Feel the meter without moving as you sing the song.

FIND THE RING

FOLK SONG FROM GREECE   ENGLISH WORDS BY MARIA JORDAN

Piano acc. p. 221

1. Find the ring, the ring that keeps mov - ing,
2. Find the ring, the ring that keeps mov - ing,

Find the ring, oh, where did it go?
Find the ring of sil - ver or gold.

The se - cret ring's in some - bod - y's hand, Some -
Pass it to me, I'll pass it to you, We

bod - y you know, come guess if you can!
must - n't get caught, what - ev - er we do!

Don't say a word if you are the one, Don't

give it a - way and spoil all the fun!

62 Meter

RING GAME

Children sit cross-legged in a circle (facing in) close enough to touch palms with those on either side—right hand against another's left; left hand against another's right; and so forth around the circle.

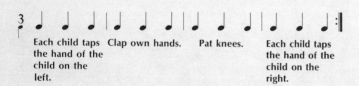

Each child taps   Clap own hands.   Pat knees.   Each child taps
the hand of the   the hand of the
child on the   child on the
left.   right.

Tambourine

Finger Cymbals

Find the lines that separate the beats in sets of three.

These are called *bar lines*.

SANDY McNAB ROUND

USED BY PERMISSION OF ANFOR MUSIC PUBLISHING COMPANY.

I

There was an old fel-low named San-dy Mc-Nab,

II

Who had for his sup-per a ver-y fine crab,

III

And had to be car-ried home in a cab.

Meter 63

---

first beat in each measure.
• Beat 1: Clap hands.
• Beats 2 and 3: Touch left elbow with right hand.

4. Ask children to find the lines (called *bar lines*) that separate the beats into sets of three in the instrumental parts on p. 63. Call attention to the meter signature ($\frac{3}{4}$). The 3 means that there are three beats in each measure. The *quarter note* (♩) means that in this song a quarter note lasts for one beat.

5. Have children try playing one percussion part at a time as others sing "Find the Ring."

METER • Lesson 3

MATERIALS
Record 3, "Sandy McNab"; Pupil's Book, pp. 62 and 63

VOCABULARY
meter in 3

IDEAS FOR TEACHING
1. Ask children to look at the meter signatures in "Find the Ring" (p. 62) and "Sandy McNab." Question: Are they the same, or are they different? (The same. Both songs use meter in 3.)

2. Play the recording of "Sandy McNab" and ask children to feel the steady beat moving in threes as they listen.

TRY THIS

1. To help children feel that "Find the Ring" starts on a strong beat and that "Sandy McNab" starts on a weaker beat, have them chant the words of the first four measures of each song, emphasizing the word or syllable that falls on the strong beat in each measure.

FIND the |RING, the |RING that keeps |MOV-ing
There |WAS an old |FEL-low named |SAN-dy Mc|NAB

2. To reinforce the concept of strong and weaker beats in music that uses meter in 3, have children play the steady beat on percussion instruments throughout "Sandy McNab." Then, working in pairs, one child will play beat 1 on a drum and the other will play beats 2 and 3 on a woodblock.

3. When children are very familiar with the melody of "Sandy McNab," let them try singing it as a two- or three-part round.

MATERIALS

Record 3, *Call Chart 1: Meter*; Pupil's Book, p. 64

VOCABULARY

meter in 2, meter in 3

TEACHER INFORMATION

Call Charts are instructional materials that direct children's attention to specific qualities in music. Numbers are called at those moments when specific qualities (such as meter in 2 and meter in 3) are to be perceived in the music.

Using the Call Chart on p. 64 in their book, children can hear the difference between meter in 2 and meter in 3.

Point out that when a number is called, children should find that number on the Call Chart. They will see drawings that show beats in sets of two or beats in sets of three, as well as the words that describe the meter.

You may want to review meter in 2 and meter in 3, using familiar songs.

Meter in 2
• Mama Paquita, p. 18
• Ain't Gonna Rain, p. 24
• All the Pretty Little Horses, p. 49
• New Year's Song, p. 60

Meter in 3
• Pity the Poor Patat, p. 9
• Join into the Game, p. 11
• Find the Ring, p. 62
• Sandy McNab, p. 63

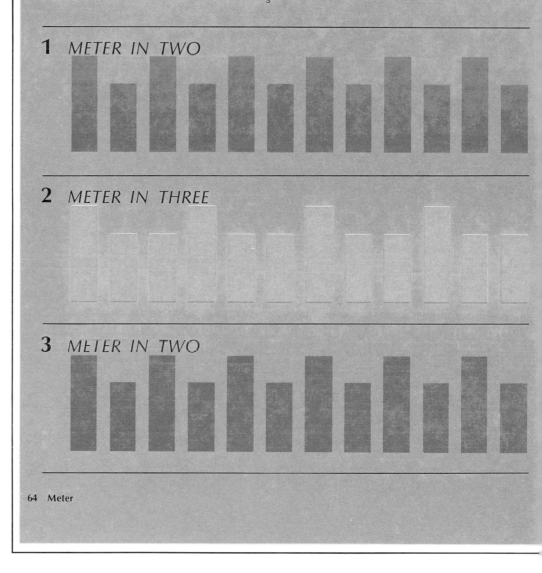

You have sung, played, and heard music in different meters.

Listen to the recording.

As each number is called, look at the chart. It will help you hear the meter in sets of two and sets of three.

Kingsley: *Piece in Two Meters*

CALL CHART 1: METER ⊙ 3

1 *METER IN TWO*

2 *METER IN THREE*

3 *METER IN TWO*

64 Meter

TEACHER INFORMATION

Gershon Kingsley (American, c. 1926–) *Piece in Two Meters:* This composer has created many works for the electronic synthesizer. He is the founder of the First Moog Quartet, which tours the United States. The composer performed *Piece in Two Meters* on a synthesizer. A photograph of Gershon Kingsley appears on p. 58, upper left.

Mainstreaming: For children who are sight-impaired or who are non-readers, an alternate method of using the Call Charts must be devised. Each non-reading child can be paired with a reader who can read or describe the events softly as the numbers are called. If the non-readers can be grouped without stigma, one reader can read the events for the group. The one advantage of the latter method is that it reduces the amount of speaking during the playing of the music.

Feel the beats moving in sets of three as you listen to this song.

Play a tambourine in section B.

Hit shake shake Hit shake shake

Which of the three beats is the strongest?

Make up a tambourine part of your own.

Piano acc. p. 249

BUYING FISH

YIDDISH FOLK SONG   ENGLISH WORDS BY ELIZABETH S. BACHMAN

"FISHELECH KOYFN" REPRINTED BY PERMISSION OF SCHOCKEN BOOKS INC. FROM A TREASURY OF JEWISH FOLKSONG EDITED BY RUTH RUBIN. COPYRIGHT ©1950 BY SCHOCKEN BOOKS INC.
COPYRIGHT RENEWED © 1978 RUTH RUBIN

VERSE

1. One day his moth - er sent him to mar - ket
2. Moth - er had said, "Go straight to the mar - ket;

To buy some fish_____ to fry. _____
Don't lin - ger on _____ the way." _____

But when he got there he could - n't re - mem - ber
But he stopped to watch a game in the park, And

What kind she want - ed him to buy. _____
now— oh, dear! what will Moth - er say?_____

REFRAIN

Day, day, day, day, day, day, Day, day, day, day, day, day,

Day, day, day, day, day, day, Day, day, day, day.

Meter 65

METER • Lesson 5

MATERIALS
Record 3, "Buying Fish"; Pupil's Book, p. 65, tambourine

VOCABULARY
meter in 3, meter signature, quarter notes, bar lines

IDEAS FOR TEACHING

1. Play the recording and ask children to listen for the meter. Point out that the first beat in each measure feels stronger. Question: Does the song use meter in 3, or meter in 2? (Meter in 3)

2. Help children analyze the tambourine part on p. 65. Ask children to find the bar lines that separate the beats into sets of three. Call attention to the meter signature (³₄). Questions: The notes in the tambourine part are quarter notes. How long will each quarter note last? (One beat) Which beat in each measure will be strongest? (The first beat)

3. Ask children to pretend to play a tambourine—hit palm of left hand with knuckles of right hand on beat 1; make shaking motions with right hand on beats 2 and 3. They can use the "hit-shake-shake" motions in the refrain of the song as they listen to the recording.

4. As others sing, let children take turns playing the tambourine during the refrain. They will hit the tambourine on beat 1 in each measure (strong beat) and shake the tambourine on beats 2 and 3 (weaker beats).

TEACHER INFORMATION

If necessary, help children feel the strong beat in music with meter in 3 by reviewing "Find the Ring" (see item 3 in Ideas for Teaching, p. 62) and "Sandy McNab" (see item 2 in Try This, p. 63).

TRY THIS

1. Children can stamp on beat 1 and clap on beats 2 and 3 throughout the refrain of "Buying Fish."

2. Recorder players can play low E on the first beat (strong beat) in each measure throughout the refrain.

3. Selected children can sing the verses as a solo; others can join in on the refrain.

MATERIALS

Record 3, "'Taters"; Pupil's Book, p. 66; tambourine

VOCABULARY

beats in sets of two, meter in 2, meter in 3

IDEAS FOR TEACHING

1. Before children open their books, play the recording of "'Taters" and ask them to listen for the meter. Point out that the first beat in each measure feels stronger. Question: Does the song use meter in 2, or meter in 3? (Meter in 2)

2. If necessary, help children feel the strong beat in meter in 2 by reviewing the motions for "New Year's Song," p. 60.

3. Have children experiment with the tambourine to find ways to play beats in sets of two. (Remind children that the first beat in each set is the strongest.) Suggestions: Tap tambourine on parts of the body; shake tambourine; strike it with hand.

4. Let children take turns playing beats in sets of two on the tambourine with the recording of "'Taters."

5. Review meter in instrumental music. Play the recordings and ask children to identify meter in 2 and meter in 3.
• Anonymous: *Dadme Albricias, Hijos d'Eva,* Record 1 (meter in 2)
• Roussel: *Pipe in D Major,* Record 3 (meter in 3)

'TATERS

YIDDISH FOLK SONG ENGLISH WORDS BY JACOB SLOAN

"ZUNTIG-BULBE" REPRINTED BY PERMISSION OF SCHOCKEN BOOKS INC. FROM A TREASURY OF JEWISH FOLKSONG EDITED BY RUTH RUBIN. COPYRIGHT © 1950 BY SCHOCKEN BOOKS INC. COPYRIGHT RENEWED © 1978 BY RUTH RUBIN.

Orff acc. p. 279

1. Sun - day, 'ta - ters, Mon - day, 'ta - ters,

Tues - day and Wednes - day,___ 'ta - ters,

Thurs - day and Fri - day,___ 'ta - ters,

Sab - bath, for a spe - cial treat, there's a 'ta - ter pud - ding!

Sun - day___ starts with___ 'ta - ters.

2. Bread and 'taters,

Meat and 'taters,

Lunch and dinner, 'taters.

Over and over, 'taters.

Once, for a special treat, there's a 'tater pudding!

Sunday starts with 'taters.

3. Still, 'taters,

Ever, 'taters,

Always, always, 'taters!

Today and tomorrow, 'taters!

After Sabbath pot roasts there's a 'tater pudding!

Sunday starts with 'taters.

66 Meter

TRY THIS

1. Using any percussion instrument, children can play a rhythm pattern in a meter of 2 or a meter of 3. They can make up a pattern, or they can choose a two-measure pattern from a familiar song. For example:

("All the Pretty Little Horses," p. 49)

("Clover," p. 50)

2. Have children play an ear-training game. They can take turns playing a tambourine pattern (using meter in 2 or meter in 3) over and over. Other children will listen and determine whether the pattern uses meter in 2 or meter in 3.

GING GONG GOOLI

FOLK SONG FROM BRITISH GUIANA

Piano acc. p. 238

Ging gong goo-li goo-li goo-li goo-li wat-cha,

Ging gong goo, ging gong goo.

Ging gong goo-li goo-li goo-li goo-li wat-cha,

Ging gong goo, ging gong goo.

Hai - la, _____ hai - la shai - la, _____

Shai - la hai - la shai - la ho - la - ho!

Hai - la, _____ hai - la shai - la, _____

Shai - la hai - la shai - la ho! _____

Meter 67

MATERIALS
Record 3, "Ging Gong Gooli"; Pupil's Book, p. 67; percussion instruments

VOCABULARY
meter in 2, sets of two

IDEAS FOR TEACHING
1. Play the recording of "Ging Gong Gooli" and ask children to listen for the meter. Question: Does the song use meter in 3, or meter in 2? (Meter in 2)

2. This is a good song for using motions in sets of two. Teach the dance (directions below).

3. Children can play three percussion parts to accompany "Ging Gong Gooli."

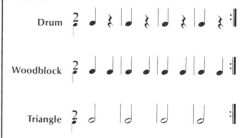

Call attention to the meter signature that appears at the beginning of each percussion part. The 2 means there are two beats in each measure. The *quarter note* means that a quarter note lasts for one beat. Point out that the quarter rest in the drum part symbolizes a beat of silence; that each half note in the triangle part lasts for two beats.

DANCE DIRECTIONS

SECTION A (lines 1–4): 2-measure pattern throughout
Measure 1: Move right hand out front as if pushing something (beat 1). Do same with left hand (beat 2).
Measure 2: Right hand hits right knee (beat 1). Left hand hits left knee (beat 2).

SECTION B (lines 5–8): 8-measure pattern, repeated
Measures 1–4: Stamp one foot after the other in measures with accents (1 and 3); stand still in measures with no accents (2 and 4).
Measures 5–8: Each child turns around in a single circle.

TEACHER INFORMATION

Mainstreaming: Suggestions for using "Ging Gong Gooli" appear in the song list in *Silver Burdett Music for Special Education.*

METER • Lesson 8

MATERIALS
Record 3, "Love"; Pupil's Book, p. 68; triangle

VOCABULARY
meter in 3, measure, tempo

IDEAS FOR TEACHING

1. Play the recording of "Love" and ask children to feel the strong beat in the music by making a big pushing motion with the right hand followed by a pushing motion with the left hand. Point out: When the tempo is fast, a song with meter in 3 has a feeling of one beat per measure.

2. Have children make up their own big motions to show meter in 3 in a fast tempo. Suggestions: Skating motions, one foot after the other; tracing circles in the air, first one arm then the other; swinging arms from side to side.

3. After they have felt the strong first beat in meter in 3, have children take turns playing a triangle on the first beat of each measure. Note: It is important for children to move with their whole body before trying small movements such as striking a triangle.

LOVE
WORDS AND MUSIC BY CARMINO RAVOSA © 1971 CARMINO RAVOSA
Piano acc. p. 228

1. Love can charm the birds___ right out of the trees,

   Love can take the hon - ey a - way from the bees;

   Love can make a li - on stand up and say, "Please."___

2. Love can turn a hurricane into a breeze,
   Love can get a hermit to smile and say, "Cheese";
   Love can make a dog learn to live with his fleas.

3. Love can bring a giant right down to his knees,
   Love can make the North and the South Poles unfreeze;
   Love can make a kid learn to eat all his peas.

Recorder or Bells

G   A

68 Meter

TRY THIS

Direct attention to the recorder/bell part in the Pupil's Book, p. 68. With one exception, the dotted half notes (𝅗𝅥.) show one sound for each beat. Ask children to find one measure that is not like the others. (The second measure from the end is different—it has a half note and a quarter note.)

When children are familiar with the song and when the recorder and bell players are ready, have them perform the song together.

TEACHER INFORMATION
Carmino Ravosa (1930–   ), composer of "Love," is Composer in Residence at the Dalton School in New York City. He regularly writes songs for the *Captain Kangaroo* television program. His musical, *Scarecrow*, won four awards at the International Light Opera Festival in Waterford, Ireland. Two of his musicals, *Aeverything's Aesop* and *Put On a Handicap* won New York State Regents' Exemplary Award. Invited to entertain at the White House in October 1978, he gave a one-man performance of his musical *Ghosts in the White House* for the President and his guests.

WHAT DO YOU HEAR? 3: METER

Each time a number is called, decide whether the beats are grouped in sets of two, or in sets of three.

If you think the beats are grouped in sets of two, draw a circle around METER IN 2.

If you think the beats are grouped in sets of three, draw a circle around METER IN 3.

Listen. Then circle what you hear.

1	(METER IN 2)	METER IN 3
2	METER IN 2	(METER IN 3)
3	(METER IN 2)	METER IN 3

Kingsley: *Piece in Two Meters*

1	METER IN 2	(METER IN 3)
2	(METER IN 2)	METER IN 3
3	METER IN 2	(METER IN 3)

Ton moulin

METER • Lesson 9

MATERIALS
Record 3, *What Do You Hear? 3: Meter;* spirit master

VOCABULARY
meter in 2, meter in 3

TEACHER INFORMATION
In *What Do You Hear? 3,* children are asked to identify meter in 2 and meter in 3.

Reminder for students: "When you are deciding about the meter of a piece of music, feel the beat, and listen especially for some beats that seem stronger than others. Call the strong beat 'one.' Then you can decide whether the beats are grouped in sets of two (ONE-two, ONE-two) or in sets of three (ONE-two-three, ONE-two-three)."

Suggestion: If necessary, review a few of the movement activities involving meter in 2 and meter in 3:
- New Year's Song, p. 60 (meter in 2)
- 'Taters, p. 66 (meter in 2)
- Ging Gong Gooli, p. 67 (meter in 2)
- Find the Ring, p. 62 (meter in 3)
- Buying Fish, p. 65 (meter in 3)

Play the pieces in *What Do You Hear? 3* more than once so that children can feel confident when they make their responses on paper.

TEACHER INFORMATION

Mainstreaming: Sight-impaired children can respond by arranging small objects into groups of two's and three's. Hearing-impaired children can identify meter by observing repeated motions that are grouped in two's and three's.

MODULE 5

OBJECTIVES, p. xi

DYNAMICS • Lesson 1

MATERIALS
Record 3, *Rain Sizes;* Pupil's Book,
p. 70

VOCABULARY
soft, loud, getting softer, getting
louder

IDEAS FOR TEACHING

1. Write the words *mist, crash,
tickles, twinkle, rattles,* and *roars*
on the chalkboard. If necessary,
discuss the meaning of each word.
Questions: Which of these words
would you say loud? Which would
you say soft? (Mist, tickles, twinkle—
soft; crash, rattles, roars—loud)

2. Encourage children to experiment
with the dynamics of vocal sound.
Have them say the words in any
order, changing the dynamics as they
go—for example: *mist, tickles,
twinkle* (soft, soft, soft) or *crash,
rattles, roars* (loud, loud, loud) or
*crash, mist, rattles, twinkle, roars,
tickles* (loud, soft, loud, soft, loud,
soft).

3. Play the recording of the poem
and ask children to listen for the
dynamics. Question: Did you hear
soft sounds? Loud sounds? Sounds
getting softer? Sounds getting
louder? (All these dynamics are
heard on the recording.)

**How would you read this poem?
Use loud and soft sounds to change
the dynamics.**

RAIN SIZES

Rain comes in various sizes.
Some rain is as small as a mist.
It tickles your face with surprises,
And tingles as if you'd been kissed.

Some rain is the size of a sprinkle
And doesn't put out all the sun.
You can see the drops sparkle and twinkle,
And a rainbow comes out when it's done.

Some rain is as big as a nickle
And comes with a crash and a hiss.
It comes down too heavy to tickle.
It's more like a splash than a kiss.

When it rains the right size and you're
   wrapped in
Your rainclothes, it's fun out of doors.
But run home before you get trapped in
The big rain that rattles and roars.

John Ciardi

70 MODULE 5: Dynamics

TRY THIS

1. Have children read the poem, adding their own ideas of
dynamics to enhance its meaning. Encourage them to use
sharp dynamic contrasts where appropriate.

2. Children can pick a soft subject and a loud subject and
make up their own contrasting rhymes. For example:
Soft: The little cat/Quietly sat.
Loud: The lion's roar/Made my ears sore.

3. Children can read the lyrics of a favorite song as if they
were a poem, using appropriate dynamics. This may lead
to a more expressive performance when they *sing* the
song.

To change the dynamics in the recording of this song, use the volume knob on the record or cassette player.

THE GHOST OF JOHN

WORDS AND MUSIC BY MARTHA GRUBB

"POOR TOM" FROM ROUNDS. USED THROUGH COURTESY OF COOPERATIVE RECREATION SERVICE, INC., DELAWARE, OHIO.

Piano acc. p. 222

Have you seen the ghost of John?

Long white bones with the skin all gone,

Oo, Oo,

Would-n't it be chil-ly with no skin on!

Ibert: "Parade"

Dynamics 71

MATERIALS

Record 3, "The Ghost of John"; Record 4, Ibert: *Divertissement,* "Parade"; Pupil's Book, p. 71

VOCABULARY

loud, soft, getting louder, getting softer, phrases

IDEAS FOR TEACHING

1. Play the recording of "The Ghost of John" and ask children to listen for the dynamics. Question: Did the music get softer, or louder, or did it sound the same all through the song? (Most children will hear no change in dynamics.)

2. Play the recording again and ask children to decide which parts they think should be loud and which should be soft.

3. Let children use the volume control on the record player and plan their own dynamics for the song. Before they begin, ask, "Will you start loud and get softer, or start soft and get louder? Will some phrases be louder or softer than others?"

4. Play the recording of Ibert's "Parade" and ask children to listen for the dynamics. (Children should hear that, after the first loud chord, the music starts soft, gets louder, and ends softer.)

TRY THIS

1. One way to plan a dynamic scheme for "The Ghost of John" is to use the four phrases of the song as a basis. (The music is performed three times on the recording—vocal, instrumental, vocal.) For example: *Vocal*—start soft and get louder on each successive phrase. *Instrumental*—loud throughout. *Vocal*—start loud and get softer on each successive phrase.

2. When children are familiar with the melody, they can sing "The Ghost of John" as a two-part round.

TEACHER INFORMATION

Jacques Ibert (French, 1890–1962) *Divertissement,* "Parade": The music of this composer has a charming, colorful quality. There is an element of humor in his popular orchestral *Divertissement.* For another example of Ibert's compositions, see *Entr'acte,* p. 43.

MATERIALS
Pupil's Book, p. 71; ringing instruments (triangle, finger cymbals, etc.)

VOCABULARY
dynamics, loud, soft, getting louder, getting softer

IDEAS FOR TEACHING
1. To direct children's attention to changes in dynamics, play an ear-training game. Game: Clap or tap a rhythm pattern loud or soft. Ask children to imitate the pattern but respond with the opposite dynamic level. If they hear the pattern loud, they repeat it soft, etc.

2. Direct attention to the three signs (dynamic marks) on p. 72. Through questioning and discussion, help children to discover that the first sign (<) shows getting louder—crescendo (kre-shen'-doh). The second sign (>) shows getting softer—decrescendo (day'-kre-shen-doh). The third sign (<>) shows getting louder, then getting softer.

3. Let children take turns playing one of the three patterns on a ringing instrument throughout "The Ghost of John" (p. 71) as others sing the song.

Add dynamics to a song you know.

Take turns playing a ringing instrument

to "The Ghost of John."

Which sign tells you to get louder? get softer?

Notice that two quarter notes can take the place of a half note.

How many quarter notes can take the place of a whole note? 4

How many half notes can take the place of a whole note? 2

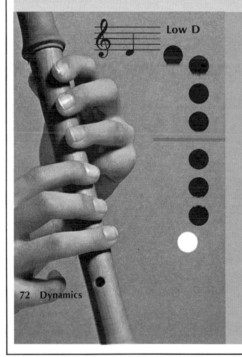

Low D

To play a recorder part for

"The Ghost of John," you need a

new note, low D.

When you can play low D,

try playing the bells or recorder

part at the top of page 73.

72 Dynamics

TRY THIS

Before children try playing the recorder and bell parts (notated on p. 73 in the Pupil's Book), take time to analyze each part.
• The rhythm pattern is the same for each part.

• The melody contour is the same for each part, but part 1 starts on low E; part 2 on high E; and part 3 on B.

While one or two children play bells or recorder, others can sing, or play the ringing instruments.

TEACHER INFORMATION

To introduce whole notes (𝅝) you may want to write the following on the chalkboard and call attention to the two-to-one relationship between quarter notes and half notes; between half notes and whole notes.

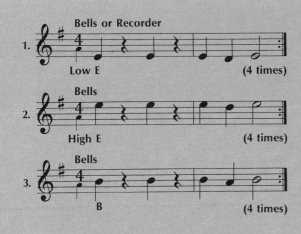

1. Bells or Recorder
Low E (4 times)

2. Bells
High E (4 times)

3. Bells
B (4 times)

Grieg: "In the Hall of the Mountain King"

In this piece you will hear many changes of dynamics.
As each number is called, decide what dynamics you hear.

CALL CHART 2: DYNAMICS

1. *LOUD*

2. *SOFT*

3. *LOUD*

4. *GETTING SOFTER*

5. *GETTING LOUDER*

6. *LOUD*

Locke: *Saraband*

Dynamics 73

DYNAMICS • Lesson 4

MATERIALS
Record 4, Grieg: *Peer Gynt Suite*
No. 1, "In the Hall of the Mountain
King"; *Call Chart 2: Dynamics;*
Pupil's Book, p. 73

VOCABULARY
dynamics

TEACHER INFORMATION

1. Henrik Ibsen, a famous Norwegian writer, wrote a play that includes an adventure with trolls. In one part of the play, Peer Gynt (the hero) is surrounded by ugly trolls in their magical palace.

The trolls are angry with Peer because he refuses to marry the Mountain King's daughter. From every nook and corner of the great hall, the trolls come to tease and bite Peer. They circle around him, growling and snarling. Peer tries to escape, but the trolls jump on him. Peer calls to his mother for help. Just then, the church bells ring in the valley and frighten the trolls away. The trolls shriek and shout as the hall falls to pieces and disappears.

2. Play the recording of "In the Hall of the Mountain King" and help children hear how the music becomes more exciting. The tempo becomes faster, the dynamics louder, and the sound of the orchestra richer as the music goes along.

3. The music in *Call Chart 2* is repeated as a What Do You Hear? evaluation on p. 79.

TEACHER INFORMATION

Edvard Grieg (Norwegian, 1843–1907) *Peer Gynt Suite* No. 1, "In the Hall of the Mountain King": By the time Grieg was twenty-five he had established himself as a major composer of his time. In 1874 he wrote incidental music for Ibsen's *Peer Gynt;* the two orchestral suites arranged from this music became extremely popular and remain so today.

Matthew Locke (English, 1632–1677) *Saraband:* This composer was a favorite of the court of King Charles II. His *Saraband* (a dance found in Europe at the beginning of the 16th century) is typical of the dances of such a court.

Mainstreaming: Suggestions for the use of Call Charts with children who are sight-impaired or who are non-readers, are provided on p. 64 in the Teacher's Edition.

MATERIALS

Record 4, "Polly Wolly Doodle";
"Shepherd, Shepherd"; Pupil's Book,
pp. 74 and 75

VOCABULARY

dynamics, loud, soft

IDEAS FOR TEACHING

1. Read the lyrics of "Polly Wolly
Doodle" and "Shepherd, Shepherd"
with the children. Point out: The
lyrics of a song sometimes give a
clue as to how loud or soft or how
fast or slow it should be sung.

2. Through questioning and
discussion, help children discover
that although several styles of
performance could possibly work for
these songs, "Polly Wolly Doodle"
seems more at home in the louder,
faster style and "Shepherd, Shepherd"
in the softer, slower style.

3. Play the recording of "Polly Wolly
Doodle" and "Shepherd, Shepherd"
and ask children to describe, in
musical terms, the performance of
each song. Note. Most children will
hear that the dynamic level of "Polly
Wolly Doodle" is fairly loud and that
the music bounces along at a fairly
fast clip. "Shepherd, Shepherd" is
softer (somewhat in the style of a
lullaby) and is performed in a
smooth manner. The contrast here is
"bouncy" and "smooth."

4. When they are familiar with "Polly
Wolly Doodle," let children take
turns singing the verses as solos; the
class can join in on the refrain. Ask
them to decide on a dynamic plan
before they begin.

POLLY WOLLY DOODLE

AMERICAN FOLK SONG · Piano acc. p. 252

1. Oh, I went down South for to see my Sal,
2. Oh, my Sal, she is a____ maid - en fair,

Sing - ing Pol - ly Wol - ly Doo - dle all the day;
Sing - ing Pol - ly Wol - ly Doo - dle all the day;

My____ Sal, she is a____ spunk - y gal,
With____ curl - y eyes and____ laugh - ing hair,

Sing - ing Pol - ly Wol - ly Doo - dle all the day.
Sing - ing Pol - ly Wol - ly Doo - dle all the day.

REFRAIN

Fare thee well,____ fare thee well, Fare thee well my fair - y fay,

For I'm goin' to Loui - si - an - a, For to see my Su - sy - an - na,

Sing - ing Pol - ly Wol - ly Doo - dle all the day.____

74 Dynamics

TRY THIS

1. Children can play an Autoharp part to accompany the
singing. The song uses two chords, F and C_7. You may
want to write the chord pattern on a chart or on the
chalkboard so that children can practice on their own.

2. Children might enjoy making up another verse for
"Polly Wolly Doodle." For example:

The June-bug he has golden wings,
The lightning bug totes a flame,
The caterpillar's got no wings at all,
But he gets there just the same!

The partridge is a pretty bird,

It has a speckled breast,

It steals away the farmer's grain,

And totes it to its nest! *Refrain*

4. The raccoon's tail is ringed around,

The 'possum's tail is bare,

The rabbit's got no tail at all,

Just a little bitty bunch of hair! *Refrain*

HEPHERD, SHEPHERD   BLACK SPIRITUAL   Piano acc. p. 239

FROM AMERICAN NEGRO SONGS AND SPIRITUALS BY JOHN W. WORK. © 1940 BY JOHN W. WORK. USED BY PERMISSION OF CROWN PUBLISHERS, INC.

1. Shep - herd, Shep - herd, where'd you lose your sheep?
2. Shep - herd, Shep - herd, where'd you leave your lambs?

Shep - herd, Shep - herd, where'd you lose your sheep?
Shep - herd, Shep - herd, where'd you leave your lambs?

Shep - herd, Shep - herd, where'd you lose your sheep?
Shep - herd, Shep - herd, where'd you leave your lambs?

O the sheep all gone a - stray,_____
O the sheep all gone a - stray,_____

The sheep all gone____ a - stray.
The sheep all gone____ a - stray.

Shostakovich: "Polka"

Mendelssohn: "Nocturne"

Dynamics 75

DYNAMICS • Lesson 6

MATERIALS
Record 4, "Shepherd, Shepherd";
Shostakovitch: *The Golden Age*,
"Polka"; Mendelssohn: *A Midsummer
Night's Dream*, "Nocturne"; Pupil's
Book, p. 75.

VOCABULARY
dynamics, loud, soft, getting louder,
getting softer, staccato, legato

IDEAS FOR TEACHING
1. Play the recording of "Shepherd,
Shepherd" and ask children to listen
for the dynamics. Question: Is the
music bouncy and fast, or smooth
and slow? (Smooth and slow)

2. After they know the song, let
children try singing it at a variety of
dynamic levels. For example: Line
1—soft; line 2—a little louder; line
3—louder; lines 4 and 5—getting
softer. Note: Whatever the dynamic
scheme however, encourage children
to sing the song in a smooth
manner.

3. Play the recording of "Polka" and
"Nocturne" (listed in Materials) and
have children listen to hear how the
pieces are different.

4. Through questioning and
discussion, help children to
articulate, in their own words, that in
"Polka" the notes are played
staccato—stah-kah'-toh (detached,
separated); that in "Nocturne," the
music is performed *legato*—leh-gah'-
toh (the notes smoothly connected).

TEACHER INFORMATION
Dmitri Shostakovitch (Russian, 1906–1975) *The Golden
Age*, "Polka": Except for Stravinsky, Shostakovitch has
probably been more highly honored throughout the world
than any other 20th-century composer.
Felix Mendelssohn (German, 1809–1847) *A Midsummer
Night's Dream*, "Nocturne": Mendelssohn never wrote an
opera, but his music for Shakespeare's *A Midsummer
Night's Dream* entitles him to a place among the
composers of dramatic music. This kind of composition is
called *incidental music*. For other incidental music, see
Peer Gynt Suite, p. 73.

MATERIALS

Pupil's Book, p. 76; classroom instruments

VOCABULARY

dynamics, loud, soft, getting louder, getting softer

IDEAS FOR TEACHING

1. IDEA A: Choose ringing instruments (triangle, bell, finger cymbals, gong). In this Idea, the dynamics (getting louder and softer) are shown in the traditional way. Have children practice the three separate items until they get the "feel" of time span. Do not attempt to keep a steady beat.

2. IDEA B: Two players are needed—a drum player and a claves player. In this Idea, the range of loud and soft is indicated at the left, before the instruments are listed. This is another way to show changes from loud to soft and from soft to loud. When the instrument lines go toward the top, the sound gets louder; when they go toward the bottom, the sound gets softer. Have children practice until they get the "feel" for Idea B. Do not attempt to keep a steady beat.

3. This Sound Piece may be performed in AB form, but encourage children to experiment with different ways of repeating sections A and B and changing the order in which the sections are played. For example, to change the form to ABA, Idea A will be repeated after Idea B is over.

SOUND PIECE 2: Dynamic Design   DAVID S. WALKER

Can you discover how to play one of the instruments in Idea A?

Follow the color line. It will tell you when to play louder or softer.

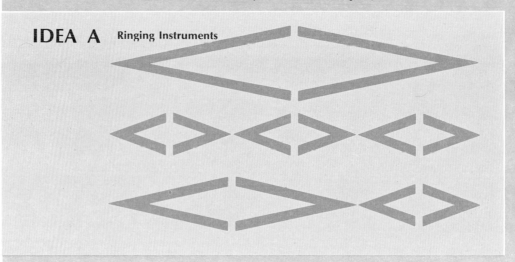

IDEA A   Ringing Instruments

Notice when you play loud and soft in Idea B.

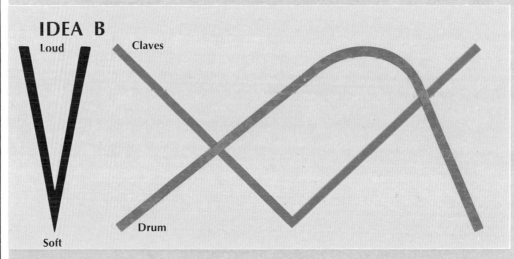

IDEA B

Loud

Claves

Drum

Soft

Play your part of the Sound Piece alone before playing it with others.

Make up your own Sound Piece using some of these ideas.

76   Dynamics

TRY THIS

Some children might want to create their own sound piece, using Sound Piece 2: Dynamic Design as a model. Help them draw a plan, or score, so others can play it.

WHAT YOU GONNA CALL YOUR PRETTY LITTLE BABY?

Orff acc. p. 286

BLACK SPIRITUAL

REFRAIN

What you gon - na call your pret - ty lit - tle ba - by,

What you gon - na call your pret - ty lit - tle ba - by,

What you gon - na call your pret - ty lit - tle ba - by,

Fine

Born, born in Beth - le - hem? ___

1. Some say one thing, I'll say Im - man - uel,

D.C.

Born, born in Beth - le - hem. ___

Some call Him one thing,
I'll call Him Jesus,
Born, born in Bethlehem.

3. Sweet little baby,
Born in a manger,
Born, born in Bethlehem.

Dynamics 77

DYNAMICS • Lesson 8

MATERIALS
Record 4, "What You Gonna Call Your Pretty Little Baby?"; Pupil's Book, p. 77

VOCABULARY
dynamics, loud, soft, getting louder, getting softer

IDEAS FOR TEACHING

1. Play the recording and ask children to listen for the dynamics. Question: Is the music loud and bouncy, or is it soft and smooth? (On the soft side and smooth)

2. Play the recording again and ask children to follow the notation as they listen. Question: Can you find any lines of music that are alike? (The melody in lines 1 and 3 is the same; the melody in lines 4 and 6 is the same.) Noticing similarities in the notation helps children learn a song more easily.

3. After they know the song, let children try singing it at a variety of dynamic levels. For example:
• Refrain—soft; Verse—louder
• Refrain—starting soft and getting gradually louder; Verse—starting loud and getting gradually softer

TRY THIS

1. Let children take turns singing the first two measures of the verses as a solo and have the class sing the next two measures ("Born, born in Bethlehem") as a response. The solo part may also be played on bells.

G E A

2. Before proceeding to the suggestion below, you may want to review the styles of performance (staccato and legato) in the two listening selections, "Polka" and "Nocturne," listed on p. 75.

Have children choose two songs they know and let them decide which one they will sing in a staccato style and which one they will sing in a legato style. For example, they may discover that singing "All the Pretty Little Horses" (p. 49) legato sounds right for that song; singing "The Ghost of John" (p. 71) staccato suits the mood of that song.

MATERIALS

Record 4, "Pray God Bless";
"Valentine Round"; Pupil's Book,
p. 78; percussion instruments

VOCABULARY

phrases, accents, loud, soft, getting
louder, getting softer

IDEAS FOR TEACHING

1. Play the recording of "Pray God
Bless" and have children listen for
the two short phrases and the one
long phrase in this round.

2. Use this activity to reinforce the
concept of short and long phrases.
Each child faces a partner.
• Phrase 1: Shake right hands twice.
• Phrase 2: Without dropping hands,
shake left hands twice.
• Phrase 3: Without uncrossing
hands, make an arch by raising arms
upward then downward, following
the direction of the melody.

3. Ask children to find the sign (>)
that shows accent in "Valentine
Round." (last three notes) Accents
are introduced on p. 33.

4. Play the recording of "Valentine
Round" and have children take turns
playing the accents on a percussion
instrument as others sing.

5. Encourage children to experiment
wih dynamics in "Pray God Bless"
and "Valentine Round." (For specific
suggestions, see Ideas for Teaching,
item 3, p. 71.)

PRAY GOD BLESS

Choose one of these parts to play on bells or recorder.

Play the part all through "Pray God Bless."

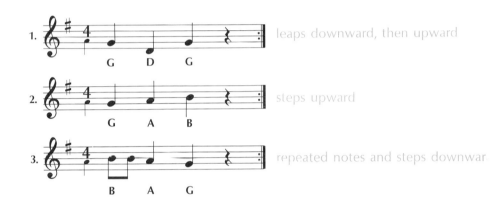

VALENTINE ROUND

78 Dynamics

TRY THIS

1. Children can play one of the parts notated on p. 78 on
bells or recorder to accompany "Pray God Bless." Before
they begin, help them analyze how the tones move in
each part.

2. Children can play one of these parts on a mallet
instrument as an ostinato throughout "Pray God Bless."

WHAT DO YOU HEAR? 4: DYNAMICS 4

Each time a number is called, decide what dynamics you hear and draw a circle around the correct word.

Listen. Then circle what you hear.

Locke: *Saraband*

(LOUD)	SOFT
LOUD	(SOFT)
(LOUD)	SOFT
GETTING LOUDER	(GETTING SOFTER)
(GETTING LOUDER)	GETTING SOFTER
(LOUD)	SOFT

DYNAMICS • Lesson 10

MATERIALS
Record 4, *What Do You Hear? 4: Dynamics;* spirit master

VOCABULARY
dynamics, loud, soft, getting louder, getting softer

TEACHER INFORMATION
In *What Do You Hear? 4,* children are asked to identify dynamics.

The What Do You Hear? evaluation can be done with a large group in a classroom situation or with a small group, using earphones. Spirit masters are available so that each child can respond individually.

Play the recording of *What Do You Hear? 4* more than once so that children can feel confident when they make their responses on paper.

MODULE 6

OBJECTIVES, p. xi

STYLE: American Indian

MATERIALS
Record 4, American Indian: *Navajo Night Chant; Sioux Rabbit Dance; Stomp Dance;* Pupil's Book, pp. 80 and 81

VOCABULARY
style

IDEAS FOR TEACHING

1. Direct attention to the photographs of instruments on pp. 80 and 81. (Top right, middle left, lower left—rattles; all others are drums.) Point out: These instruments are played by hitting (drums) or shaking (rattles).

2. Discuss the decoration of the instruments. The colorful designs often have meanings referring to worship, nature, and folk history. The Indians not only wanted their instruments to give musical sounds, they also wanted them to look beautiful.

3. Play the recording of the three Indian songs so that children can answer the questions on p. 81 in their book. *Navajo Night Chant* and *Stomp Dance* use rattles; *Sioux Rabbit Dance* uses drum.

4. Point out that a song leader is used in much American Indian music to set the tempo and decide how high or how low to pitch the music. Play *Stomp Dance* again so that children can hear the song leader at work. ⟶

There are many different styles of music among the tribes of Indians in America.

In all styles of Indian music, the voice is the most important instrument.

To accompany the singing and dancing, Indians use drums and rattles.

Each drum and rattle has a design of its own.

Through these designs, the Indian shows his feeling for things in Nature.

80

TEACHER INFORMATION

While this lesson concentrates on some common characteristics of American Indian music, it is imporant to remember that there are many different tribes in America and many different flavors of American Indian culture.

Music has played an important part in most tribal cultures, many tribes having special songs and pieces of their very own. Many Indians believed that songs were created by gods and given to humans through dreams and visions.

Scholars of American Indian music can tell a great deal about the culture of a tribe through its music, such as whether the tribe was primarily hunters or farmers, whether it was characterized by strong leaders, and what other tribe it might be related to.

The singers follow a song leader, who sets the tempo and decides how high or how low they will sing.

Listen to the accompaniment of these Indian songs.
Which ones use rattles?
Which ones use drums?

⦿ Navajo Night Chant
4

⦿ Sioux Rabbit Dance
4

⦿ Stomp Dance
4

You heard a special way of singing and playing found in much Indian music.

When you listen again, notice some other things to be found in the music of American Indians.

1. Much repetition of melodies and rhythm patterns
2. Very little or no harmony
3. Simple or no accompaniment
4. Tone colors of percussion instruments

Style: American Indian 81

5. Several other style characteristics of Indian music can be heard in these pieces. Depending on the interest shown by the class, you may want to explore the following questions with the children.
• Are melodies often repeated? (Yes)
• Are rhythm patterns repeated over and over? (Yes)
• Do you hear harmony (chords as accompaniment) in this music? (No. American Indian music uses little or no harmony.)
• In *Navajo Night Chant,* is the voice low and in a relaxed style, or high and in a tight, tense style? (High and in a tight, tense style)
• In *Sioux Rabbit Dance,* is there much change in dynamic level, or does it remain at the same level? (There is little or no change in dynamic level.)
• In *Stomp Dance,* does the tempo ever change, or does it stay the same? (It stays the same.)

6. Point out: High, tense voice style, little or no dynamic changes, and little or no tempo changes are typical of all three songs and of much American Indian music.

TRY THIS

1. Encourage children who might have authentic American Indian instruments available to them, or community members who might be involved with Indian music, to demonstrate and perform. Local museums often are good sources for Indian artifacts and musical instruments of local tribes. Try to arrange a field trip and, if possible, a demonstration by the museum staff.

2. Let children choose familiar songs and take turns being the song leader. The song leader will set the tempo and will decide how high or how low to sing. Encourage children to experiment to find ways of communicating how fast or how slow to sing.

MODULE 7

OBJECTIVES, p. xii

FORM • Lesson 1

MATERIALS
Record 4, "Oh, What a Beautiful City"; Pupil's Book, pp. 82 and 83

VOCABULARY
form, repetition, contrast, section A, section B, ABA form

IDEAS FOR TEACHING

1. Ask children to find things in the classroom that repeat. (Windows, chairs, desks, etc.) Ask them to find things that contrast. (Light and dark wall surfaces, colors and designs, etc.)

2. Direct attention to the photographs on p. 82. Ask children to point to things that repeat. (Dogs, barrels, eyes, noses, tongues, bottles) Ask children to point to things that are a contrast. (Colors of the dogs' legs; dogs and bottles)

3. Opposites provide contrast, too. Talk about the following words, which are some of the ones used to describe music.
• loud-soft
• high-low
• long-short
• upward-downward
• fast-slow

4. Before introducing ABA form in "Oh, What a Beautiful City," you might want to review AB form in one of the following songs that are found in the Beginning Experiences.

→

OH, WHAT A BEAUTIFUL CITY

BLACK SPIRITUAL

Piano acc. p. 266

(A) REFRAIN

Oh,   what   a beau - ti - ful   cit - y,____

Oh,   what   a beau - ti - ful   cit - y,____

82   MODULE 7: Form

Oh, what a beau - ti - ful cit - y,____

Twelve gates - a to the cit - y,____ Hal - le - lu - jah! *Fine*

B VERSE

Three gates____ to the East,

Three gates____ to the West,

Three gates____ to the North,____

Three gates____ to the South,

There's twelve gates - a to the cit - y,____ Hal - le - lu - jah! *D.C. al Fine*

Form 83

5. Play the recording of "Oh, What a Beautiful City" and ask children to follow the notation as they listen. Call attention to the letters and shapes that show the sections—Ⓐ and ☐B☐. Note: Most children will hear that section A repeats, making the form ABA. The repetition of section A is indicated by *D.C. al Fine* (*Da Capo al Fine*—Dah Kah'-poh ahl Fee'-nay), which means "repeat from the beginning and continue to the word *Fine*."

6. Have children show a contrast between the sections in "Oh, What a Beautiful City" by doing a stamp-clap pattern (stamp on one beat, clap on the next, etc.) during section A and stopping to listen during section B, ready to do the stamp-clap pattern on the repeat of A.

7. After children have discovered the ABA form of "Oh, What a Beautiful City" as suggested in item 5, help them to hear other contrasts between the two sections:
• different lyrics
• different melody
• different rhythm
• different tone color on the recording (group of singers in section A; man's voice in section B)
Note: Some children may notice that while section B is a contrast of section A, the last phrase is almost identical for both sections.

TRY THIS

1. Children can show contrast and repetition by using different dynamic levels. For example:
• A—soft, B—loud, A—soft
• A—loud, B—soft, A—loud

2. Ask children to bring in pictures of repeated things and things that show contrast. These would make an appropriate bulletin-board display. Also, children may have personal photographs that show repetition and contrast.

MATERIALS
Record 4, "Boil Them Cabbage Down"; Pupil's Book, pp. 84 and 85; Autoharp, percussion instruments

VOCABULARY
repetition, contrast, section A, section B, accents, AB form

IDEAS FOR TEACHING

1. Play the recording and ask children to follow the notation as they listen. Call attention to the two sections, Ⓐ and B̄, and encourage children to sing section B (refrain) when it comes in the song.

2. Direct attention to the photographs on p. 84. Question: Are the photographs the same, or are they different? (Different—the children shown in the picture at the left of the page are in a circle; the two children in the other picture are swinging arms.) Point out: The photograph at the left is a contrast to the one at the right.

3. Teach the dance for "Boil Them Cabbage Down" (directions below). The dance movements will help children to feel the contrast between sections. Also, clapping the hands in the dance points up the accents (sudden loud sounds) in the music.

4. Ask children to find the sign (>) in music that shows the accents. (There are four accent marks in the first line of section B.)

5. After children have shown a contrast between section A and section B through the dance, have them show a contrast between the sections through ⟶

This song has two sections, A and B.

Listen for the accents in section B.

Clap hands on each accent.

84   Form

DANCE DIRECTIONS

Partners stand side by side facing the center of a circle, leaders on the left.

Section A: All slide to the left.

Section B, Phrase 1: Still maintaining a single circle, partners face each other and clap each other's hands on the accented words *down, down.*

Section B, Phrase 2: Leaders pass partner's right shoulder while moving counterclockwise to the next person in the circle, clapping hands with this partner on the accented words *brown, brown.*

Section B, Phrase 3: Linking right arms, new partners circle once around, facing the center of the circle at the end of the section.

The dance continues.

ometimes one section of music is different from another.

is a *contrast*.

ow is section B a *contrast* of section Ⓐ in this song?

OIL THEM CABBAGE DOWN

AMERICAN PIONEER SONG

M MORE SONGS OF THE NEW WORLD BY DESMOND MACMAHON. PUBLISHED BY HOLMES MCDOUGALL LIMITED

Piano acc. p. 274

1. The rac-coon's got a fur-ry tail,

The pos-sum's tail is bare,___

The rab-bit ain't got no tail at all,

But a lit-tle bit o' bunch o' hair.

B REFRAIN

Boil them cab-bage down, down, Bake them bis-cuits brown, brown,

The on-ly tune I ev-er did learn is Boil them cab-bage down.

The June bug he has wings of gold,

The firefly wings of flame,

The bedbug's got no wings at all,

But he gets there just the same. *Refrain*

3. Oh, love it is a killing fit

When beauty hits a blossom,

And if you want your finger bit,

Just poke it at a possum. *Refrain*

e words "killing fit" in verse 3 mean "highly amusing activity."

(a) tone color and (b) playing instruments.
• (a) Choose children to sing the verses (section A) as a solo; others can join in on the refrain (section B).
• (b) Have children take turns accompanying the song on the Autoharp. Others can play percussion instruments on the accents in section B. <u>Note</u>: In this three-chord song, children should get in the habit of using the left index finger to press the G button, the left middle finger to press the D_7 button, and the left ring finger to press the C button.

6. Write the chord pattern on a chart or on the chalkboard so that children can practice on their own. Autoharp players should be aware that they will start strumming on the first strong beat, or on the first syllable of *raccoon's*—"The RAC-coon's."

85

TEACHER INFORMATION

Children have focused on the contrast of the two sections of "Boil Them Cabbage Down" by moving, singing, and playing instruments.

To help them answer the question on p. 85 in their book, take time to analyze what musical qualities make section B different from section A. For instance, the melody at the beginning of the section is different. The rhythm is different. Section B has accents. The words in section A change each time the section is sung; the words in section B remain the same.

Children will hear another contrast on the recording. Section A is sung by a man; section B is sung by a man and children.

Mainstreaming: An adaptation of "Boil Them Cabbage Down" appears in *Silver Burdett Music for Special Education*.

MATERIALS
Pupil's Book, p. 86; classroom instruments

VOCABULARY
repetition, contrast, AB form, ABA form

IDEAS FOR TEACHING
The photographs on p. 86 will remind children of the variety of tone colors they can use when creating a sound piece.

Suggestions: Children can form small groups. Each group will choose two or three sounds from those suggested by the photographs—or they can use sounds of their own—and create a sound piece to perform for the class.

Children should be sure to have sufficient contrast between sections. Their sound piece may have the form AB, or the form ABA.

When each group performs its sound piece, the class tries to identify the form.

Remind children that in addition to contrasting tone colors, the sections of their sound piece might show contrast in dynamics (loud-soft), tempo (fast-slow), register (high-low), duration (long sounds-short sounds), etc.

This small-group involvement may best be done at times other than the formal music class time.

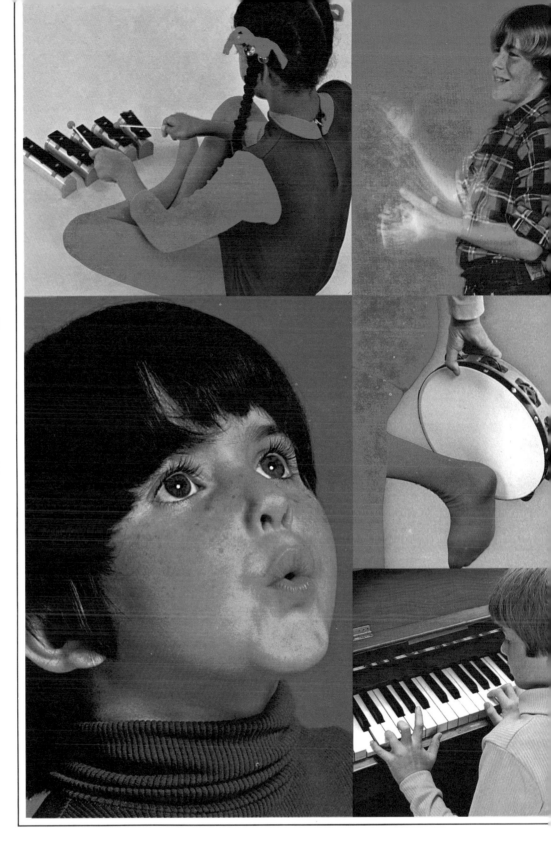

TEACHER INFORMATION

Although many of the qualities of music will be perceived in a large-group experience, it is most beneficial to a child's musical growth to have opportunities for small-group experiences.

Add contrasting sections of your own to those on the recording.

Look at the directions for section A.

SOUND PIECE 3: Sound on Sound

DORIS HAYS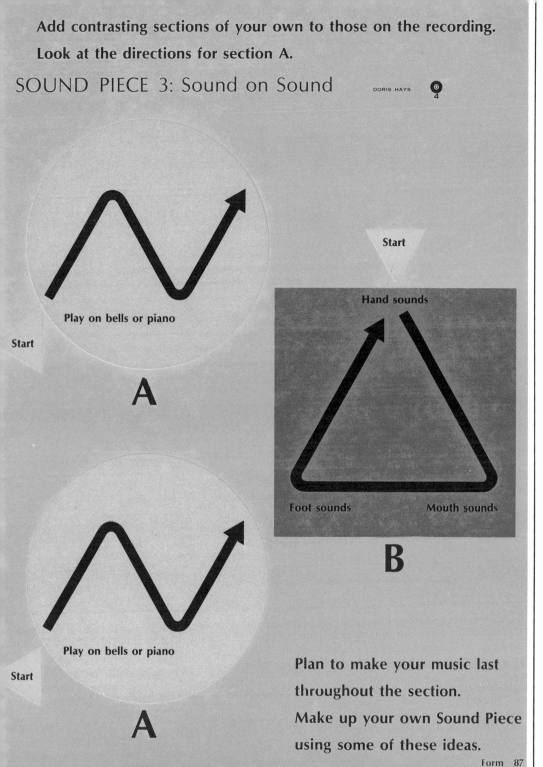

A

Play on bells or piano

Start

B

Start

Hand sounds

Foot sounds   Mouth sounds

A

Play on bells or piano

Start

Plan to make your music last throughout the section.

Make up your own Sound Piece using some of these ideas.

Form 87

FORM • Lesson 4

MATERIALS
Record 4, Hays: *Sound Piece 3: Sound on Sound;* Pupil's Book, p. 87; bells or piano

VOCABULARY
section A, section B, contrast, AABA form

IDEAS FOR TEACHING
1. Children have experienced several ways to make contrast in music. Question: What is a contrast to high? (Low) Loud? (Soft) Fast? (Slow) Meter in 2? (Meter in 3) Long sounds? (Short sounds) Accents? (No accents)

2. Play the recording of *Sound Piece 3.* Question: What makes the contrast in this music? (The long, sustained sounds in section A contrasted with the short, quick sounds in section B) Note: Lead children to discover that section A is played three times, making the form AABA.

3. Before asking children to add their own sounds to those on the recording, help them follow the drawing for each section on p. 87. Section A is shown by a circle, section B by a square.

4. One child can accompany section A. The same child, or a group of children, can accompany section B. The group may start the three different sounds of section B—hand sounds, foot sounds, mouth sounds—one after the other in follow-the-leader fashion.

TRY THIS

Have children make their own arrangement of section B, using percussion instruments instead of natural sounds. Encourage them to notate the sounds they create in their own way.

TEACHER INFORMATION

Doris Hays (American, 1941–) *Sound Piece 3: Sound on Sound:* This composer performed *Sound Piece 3* on a synthesizer. A photograph of Doris Hays with a synthesizer appears on p. 58, lower right.

MATERIALS

Record 4, "Little David, Play on Your Harp"; Pupil's Book, pp. 88 and 89; recorder or bells

VOCABULARY

contrast, tone color, ABA form, staff, G-clef sign

IDEAS FOR TEACHING

1. Play the recording of "Little David, Play on Your Harp" and ask children to listen for the tone colors of the voices and instruments. (The music is performed three times—vocal, instrumental, vocal.) Question: What makes the contrast between sections A and B? (In the vocal performance, children sing section A; a man sings section B. In the instrumental performance, the melody of section A is played on recorder; a cello plays the melody in section B.)

2. Have children add the tone color of their voices to the children's voices in section A on the recording.

3. Direct attention to the graphics at the top of p. 88. Play the recording and ask children to listen for the form of the song. Question: Which drawing in your book shows the form of "Little David, Play on Your Harp"? (Circle, square, circle; ABA—the repetition of section A is indicated by *D.C. al Fine,* which means "repeat from the beginning and continue to the word *Fine.*") See Review/Reinforcement below. ⟶

Which set of shapes and letters shows the form of "Little David, Play on Your Harp"?

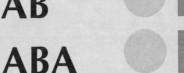

AB

ABA

Follow the notes for each section as you sing the song.

LITTLE DAVID, PLAY ON YOUR HARP   BLACK SPIRITUAL

Orff acc. p. 281

REFRAIN

Lit-tle Da-vid, play on your harp, Hal-le-lu, hal-le-lu,

Fine

Lit-tle Da-vid, play on your harp, Hal-le-lu.

VERSE

Lit-tle Da-vid was a shep-herd boy,____

D.C. al Fine

He killed Go-li-ath and shout-ed for joy.

88 Form

TRY THIS

For an additional focus on vocal tone color as a means for showing contrast, select children to sing the verse (section B) of "Little David, Play on Your Harp" as a solo; others can sing the refrain (section A).

REVIEW/REINFORCEMENT

For other songs with the indication *D.C. al Fine,* see the following songs.

- Oh, What a Beautiful City, p. 82
- Michie Banjo, p. 20
- Oh, Won't You Sit Down? p. 90
- Bella Bimba, p. 101
- German Instrument Song, p. 136
- This Land Is Your Land, p. 202

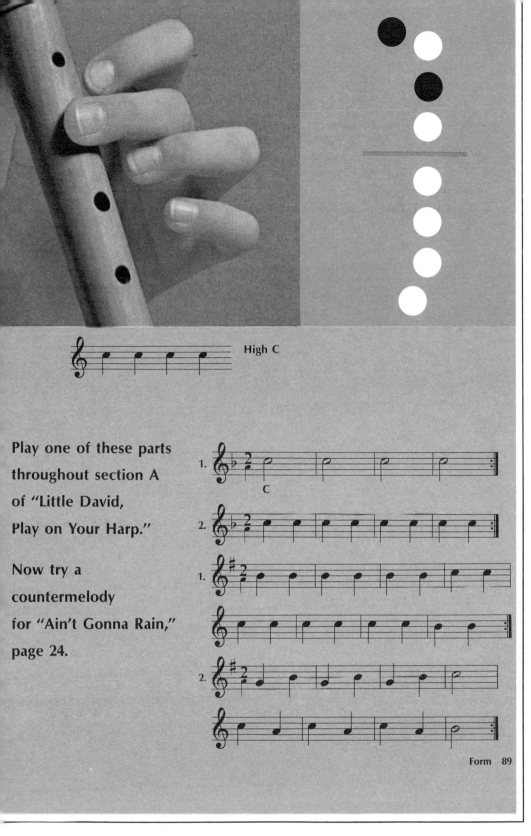

Play one of these parts throughout section A of "Little David, Play on Your Harp."

Now try a countermelody for "Ain't Gonna Rain," page 24.

High C

Form 89

4. Children who have been playing the recorder can learn the fingering for the new note (high C) by studying the photograph on p. 89 in their book. <u>Note</u>: You may need to point out that the group of five lines and the spaces between, on which notes are written, is called a *staff*. (The function of lines and spaces is introduced on p. 4 in Beginning Experiences.) Also, call attention to the G clef (𝄞), the sign that shows the line G, second from the bottom on the staff.

5. Give recorder players an opportunity to practice playing high C. When they are ready, have them play one of the recorder parts, notated in their book, throughout section A of "Little David, Play on Your Harp." <u>Note</u>: The recorder parts can also be played on the bells.

6. Children can practice playing one or both of the countermelodies for the song "Ain't Gonna Rain, p. 24, that are notated at the bottom of p. 89. <u>Point out</u>: A countermelody is a second melody sounding simultaneously with another melody.

7. When children are ready, have them play one of the countermelodies as others sing "Ain't Gonna Rain." To fill out the ensemble, let children take turns playing the Autoharp part for "Ain't Gonna Rain"—this part is found on p. 25 in the Pupil's Book.

TRY THIS

For further practice in playing high C, here are two additional parts that children can use with the song "A Ram Sam Sam" (p. 33). Write the parts on the chalkboard or on a chart so that children can practice on their own.

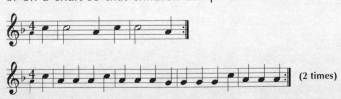

(2 times)

MATERIALS

Record 4, "Oh, Won't You Sit Down?"; *Call Chart 3: Form; Call Chart 4: Form;* Pupil's Book, pp. 90 and 91

VOCABULARY

contrast, form, AB, ABA, AABA, AABB

IDEAS FOR TEACHING

1. Play the recording of "Oh, Won't You Sit Down?" and have children follow the notation as they listen. Call attention to the letters and shapes that show the sections—Ⓐ Ⓑ. Question: Is the form of the song AB, or ABA? (ABA) Note: Most children will hear that section A repeats, making the form ABA. The repetition of section A is indicated by *D.C. al Fine,* which means "repeat from the beginning and continue to the word *Fine.*"

2. To reinforce the concept of ABA form, have children show a contrast between sections of the song by doing a stamp-clap pattern (stamp on one beat, clap on the next, etc.) during section B. During section A, and the repeat of A, they stand still and listen.

3. When they know the song, choose children to sing the verses (section B) as a solo; others can sing the refrain (section A). ⟶

OH, WON'T YOU SIT DOWN? BLACK SPIRITUAL

Piano acc. p. 244

TRY THIS

Children can play a bell part during section B of "Oh, Won't You Sit Down?" Before they play, you may want to review the relative duration of quarter notes and quarter rests. (A quarter rest is introduced in Beginning Experiences, p. 16.) Also, call attention to the words in the last measure. It helps to use the words of a song as a frame of reference when playing more difficult rhythms.

Mo-ses led.__

TEACHER INFORMATION

Mainstreaming: Suggestions for using "Oh, Won't You Sit Down?" appear in the song list in *Silver Burdett Music for Special Education.*

Must be the chil-dren of the Is-rael-ite. _____

D.C. al Fine

2. Who's that yonder dressed in blue?

   Must be the children that are comin' through.

   Who's that yonder dressed in black?

   Must be the hypocrites a-turnin' back. *Refrain*

4. Note: The Call Charts in the Pupil's Book will help them hear and feel different sections. When the music starts and the voice on the recording says "one," the chart shows the letter A. At each number that follows, the chart will tell them whether they are hearing repetition or contrast.

5. Play *Call Chart 3* and *Call Chart 4*, then help children discover that the music in Chart 3 is in AABA form; that the music in Chart 4 is in AABB form.

Note: *Call Chart 4* is available in the form of a What Do You Hear? lesson. It appears as *What Do You Hear? 15* in *Silver Burdett Music What Do You Hear? Spirit Masters, 3.*

Can you hear and feel different sections in other music?

Look at the charts to help you.

CALL CHART 3: FORM 🎯 ## CALL CHART 4: FORM 🎯

1. *A*	**1.** *A*
2. *A (REPETITION)*	**2.** *A (REPETITION)*
3. *B (CONTRAST)*	**3.** *B (CONTRAST)*
4. *A (REPETITION)*	**4.** *B (CONTRAST)*

Tchaikovsky: "Trepak"

Purcell: *Trumpet Tune*

Form   91

TEACHER INFORMATION (for *Call Chart 3* and *Call Chart 4*)

Peter Ilyitch Tchaikovsky (Russian, 1840–1893) *Nutcracker Suite,* "Trepak": The ballet music of this composer (including *The Nutcracker, Swan Lake,* and *The Sleeping Beauty*) is among the most popular ever written. Captivating melodies, lively rhythms, and colorful use of instruments help account for this music's appeal. Ballet music is often played as a concert number. "Trepak" is one of a set of eight pieces in *Nutcracker Suite* and takes its name from a popular Russian folk dance.

Henry Purcell (English, c. 1659–1695) *Trumpet Tune:* This famous English composer lived at a time when music depended upon the support of the rich members of royal families. When he was only eighteen, Purcell became composer for the king's violins who played at court affairs, as well as for the entertainment of guests at mealtimes.

MATERIALS
Record 4, "Piñata Song"; Pupil's Book, p. 92; tambourine

VOCABULARY
repetition, contrast, section A, section B, AB form, meter in 2, meter in 3

IDEAS FOR TEACHING

1. By looking at the music, some children may notice that "Piñata Song" has two sections, A and B. Play the recording and have children follow the notation as they listen to find out how section B contrasts with section A. <u>Note</u>: If children have worked through the material on meter, pp. 60–69, some of them may hear that section A has meter in 3 and section B has meter in 2. Call attention to the meter signature in each section.

2. Have children make up a tambourine part for each section to accompany the singing of the song. For example:

<u>Note</u>: The tambourine parts that children create should also show contrast. This might be evident in such qualities as rhythm pattern, dynamics, and tone color (playing on the head, on the rim; hitting; shaking; etc.).

Make up a tambourine part for each section of this song.

Which section has meter in 3?

Which section has meter in 2?

Piano acc. p. 250

PINATA SONG
CHRISTMAS SONG FROM MEXICO   ENGLISH WORDS BY VERNE MUNOZ

In the hap - py days of Christ - mas,___

Sounds of glad - ness fill the air;___

When it's time for the pi - ña - ta,___

There's ex - cite - ment ev - 'ry - where.___

Take a stick and whack it, Be the one to crack it;

Win pi - ña - ta's trea - sure, Can - dies for your plea - sure.

92 Form

TRY THIS

Have children make up percussion parts for each section of "Piñata Song," using appropriate instruments such as guiro, claves, maracas, and tambourine. For example:

Section A

Tambourine

Guiro

Section B

Claves

Maracas

TEACHER INFORMATION

There are nine days of Christmas celebrations in Mexico. On the ninth day (Christmas Eve) there is a gay social evening with dancing and many special treats. As a climax of the evening's festivities comes the breaking of the *piñata* (an earthenware bowl or paper bag made to look like a bird or an animal), which is hung high above an open space. The piñata, full of fruits, candies, small gifts, and lucky charms, swings gently from side to side. Each child is blindfolded and has a turn to swing at the piñata with a heavy stick, hoping to break it. When the piñata is finally broken, all the children rush to pick up the treats.

WHAT DO YOU HEAR? 5: FORM

When the music starts and the voice on the recording says "one," you are hearing section A, as shown on the chart.

At each number that follows, decide whether the section is a *repetition* of A or a *contrast* of A.

1. A

2. REPETITION ~~CONTRAST~~

3. ~~REPETITION~~ CONTRAST

4. REPETITION ~~CONTRAST~~

5. ~~REPETITION~~ CONTRAST

Giuliani: *Grand Sonata in A Major for Flute and Guitar*, "Scherzo" (excerpt)

1. A

2. ~~REPETITION~~ CONTRAST

3. REPETITION ~~CONTRAST~~

4. ~~REPETITION~~ CONTRAST

Pinto: "Run Run"

Form 93

MATERIALS
Record 5, *What Do You Hear? 5: Form*; spirit master

VOCABULARY
section A, repetition, contrast

TEACHER INFORMATION

In *What Do You Hear? 5,* children are asked to identify repetition and contrast.

Because it may be necessary to play the pieces more than once, take time to have children listen to and talk about the repetitions and contrasts before they circle their answers on their paper.

For example, help children recognize section A in the first piece by discussing how it begins—repeated tones, followed by a leap upward.

Help children hear that section A in the second piece consists of crisp, short, fast sounds.

MODULE 8

OBJECTIVES, p. xii

THE ARTS: Repetition and Contrast

MATERIALS
Record 5, *But You Are Mine;* Pupil's
Book, pp. 94 and 95

VOCABULARY
repetition, contrast

IDEAS FOR TEACHING
1. Ask children to look around the
room to find things that *repeat*.
(Chairs, desks, windows, light
fixtures, etc. Also, explore repeats in
clothing patterns, buttons, shoes,
etc.)

2. Ask children to find things that
contrast. (Books of different colors
on a shelf, light and dark wall
surfaces, etc. Also, contrasts in
clothing patterns, clothing colors,
etc.)

3. Have children play a "Repeat and
Contrast" game. Prepare a set of
cards—one for each child. On half
the cards, write *R* (for repeat); on the
other cards write *C* (for contrast).
Shuffle the cards and ask each child
to take one. (For the game, see
below.)

4. Take time for children to study
the painting *The White American
Barn*. (Make sure they understand
that this is one painting, extending
over two pages.) <u>Questions</u>: Can you
find things that repeat in this
painting? (Two doorways, yellow
mats, lightning rods on roof, grill on
door, windowpanes, three white wall
sections) Can you ⟶

Look around your classroom.

What can you find that repeats?

What can you find that contrasts?

Can you find repetition and contrast in this painting?

Can you find repetition and contrast in this poem?

BUT YOU ARE MINE ⊙
5

Someone would like to have you for her child

but you are mine.

Someone would like to rear you on a costly mat

but you are mine.

Someone would like to place you on a camel blanket

but you are mine.

94   MODULE 8: The Arts—Repetition/Contrast

GAME

Children stand. The teacher, or a child-leader, claps a
rhythm pattern. For example:

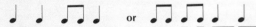

Depending upon the letter on the card, the first player
repeats the pattern (R), or claps a contrasting pattern (C).
The leader claps the original pattern again and a second
player responds, etc. A child who responds incorrectly is
out of the game.

TEACHER INFORMATION

Georgia O'Keeffe (American, 1887–) *The White
Canadian Barn:* The paintings of this American artist often
emphasize enlarged details of flowers or dried bones or
western barns, or churches—like closeup camera
photographs. The photolike, stark bareness of this painting
almost turns it into an abstract painting of repeated and
contrasted shapes.

© GEORGIA O'KEEFFE. THE WHITE CANADIAN BARN, NO. 2.
THE METROPOLITAN MUSEUM OF ART. THE ALFRED STIEGLITZ COLLECTION, 1949.

I have you to rear on a torn old mat.

Someone would like to have you as her child

but you are mine.

—From Africa

Now say the poem to find the ideas that contrast.

There is repetition and contrast in music and painting and poetry.

Each art uses repetition and contrast in its own way.

95

find things that contrast? (Colors contrast—blue, black, white, green, yellow; contrast in width of color bands—narrow blue at the top, wide black roof, very narrow blue-grey and white lines at top of walls, wide white walls, narrow green grass. Shapes contrast—different-sized rectangles.)

5. Point out that in the painting we see all the contrasts *together at the same time.* In music, as in the "Repeat and Contrast" game, one thing happens, then another thing happens—spread out through time.

6. Have children listen to the recording of *But You Are Mine.* Questions: What repeats in the poem? (*Someone would like to, but you are mine, child, mat*) What contrasts in the poem? (*to have you, to rear you, to place you; costly mat, torn old mat.* All lines begin with the word *but* except line 7, which begins wih the contrasting word *I.*)

7. Point out that a poem, like music, has one thing happening at a time. In music and poetry we must *remember* what has happened. In a painting, we don't need to remember—it is all there and doesn't go away.

When students complete this lesson, they are ready to take Test 1 for Book 3. Additional information about *Silver Burdett Music Competency Tests* is found in the introduction of this book.

REVIEW/REINFORCEMENT

Songs: "Hawaiian Rainbows" (two contrasting phrases—ABAB), p. 146; "Hill an' Gully" (repeated chorus parts), p. 180; "America, the Beautiful" (repeated rhythm pattern ♩ | ♩. ♪ ♩), p. 184

Visuals: Paintings of George Washington, p. 156; Kitten photographs, p. 192

Poems: *Rain Sizes,* p. 70, Paper I, p. 145

TRY THIS

1. Children can paint or draw pictures with obvious repetitions and contrasts, some representational (houses, scenes, people, etc.) and some nonrepresentational (shapes, colors, lines). Have children explain how repetitions were created and how contrasts were created.

2. Children can take a "Repetition and Contrast Walk" around the school building, inside and out, looking for obvious and hidden repetitions and contrasts in the architecture and its environment.

MODULE 9

OBJECTIVES, p. xii

REGISTER • Lesson 1

MATERIALS
Pupil's Book, pp. 96 and 97;
Autoharp, drums, bells, water glasses

VOCABULARY
high; low; vibration; fast vibration—
higher sounds; slow vibration—lower
sounds

IDEAS FOR TEACHING
1. Point out that sound is made by a
kind of motion called *vibration*—
movement back and forth. We can
make things vibrate by striking,
blowing, or plucking. Help children
feel vibration by having them touch
a string of the Autoharp after
plucking it or a drumhead after
striking it.

2. Fast vibrations make high sounds.
Slow vibrations make low sounds.
When there is no vibration, there is
no sound. Illustrate how the sound
stops when you *damp* (stop the
vibration with the hand) the
Autoharp strings after plucking or
strumming them. Let children
try this.

3. Have children experiment with
vibration. They will need hands-on
experience in order to answer the
questions in their book. It is
doubtful that children will be able to
see the faster or slower vibration in
their experiments. However, they will
be able to conclude that a short bell
sounds higher than a long one. A
thick string sounds lower than a thin
one. A glass ⟶

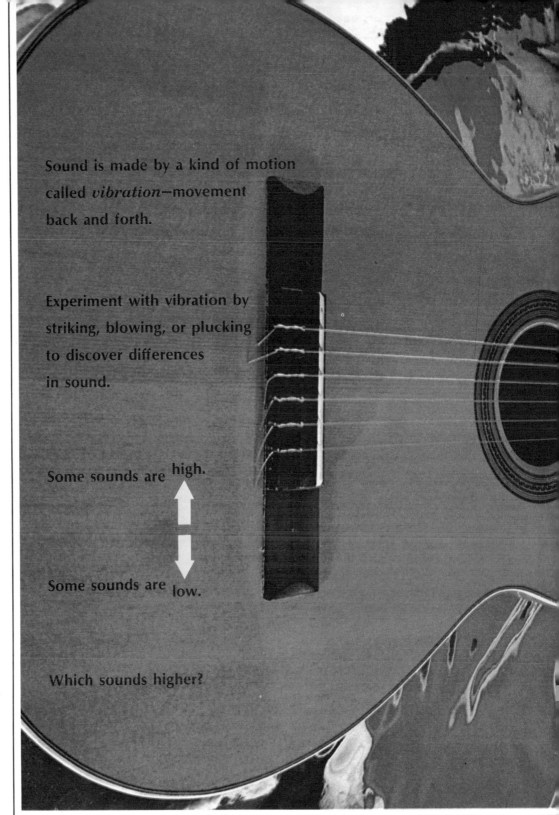

Sound is made by a kind of motion
called *vibration*—movement
back and forth.

Experiment with vibration by
striking, blowing, or plucking
to discover differences
in sound.

Some sounds are high.

Some sounds are low.

Which sounds higher?

TEACHER INFORMATION

Mainstreaming: It is important that hearing-impaired
children experience the *feel* of vibrations that result in
sound. Examples are the low strings of a piano or guitar,
the snares on a snare drum, a resonator bell.

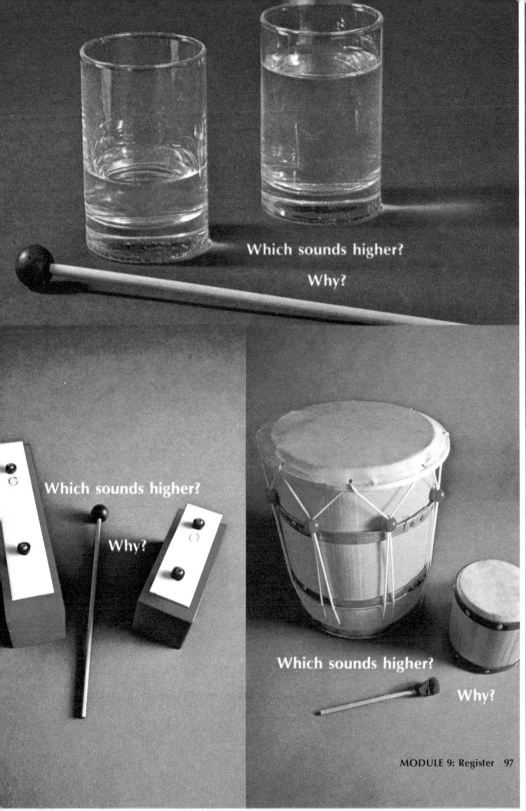

Which sounds higher?

Why?

Which sounds higher?

Why?

Which sounds higher?

Why?

MODULE 9: Register 97

filled with less water sounds higher, when struck, than a glass filled with more water. A drum with a larger head sounds lower than one with a smaller head.

4. For a pitch-discrimination game, choose a child to play two bells (from a set of bells), one high and one low, or one low and one high. Ask the class (with eyes closed) to determine how the bells were played—high-low, or low-high. Eventually, other bells can be added to produce high-high-low; low-high-low; etc.

MATERIALS

Record 5, "The Sow Took the Measles"; *Call Chart 5: Register;* Pupil's Book, pp. 98 and 99; drums, Autoharp, bells

VOCABULARY

high, low

IDEAS FOR TEACHING

1. Use songs children know to start this lesson. Have children find two drums with different pitches—one high and one low. Then let them take turns playing a high-low pattern on the drums to accompany "Oh, What a Beautiful City," p. 82. They can improvise their own patterns, or they can start with one of these.

Let children take turns playing a low-high strum on the Autoharp (they will press the F button) as others sing the A section (refrain) of "Little David, Play on Your Harp," p. 88.

2. Play the recording of "The Sow Took the Measles" and have children keep time to the steady beat by tapping knees, using alternate hands.

3. Direct attention to the three bell parts on p. 99 in the Pupil's Book. Help children discover the "low-high" pattern in each part: (1) low-high; (2) low-low-high-high; (3) low-low-low-high. ⟶

THE SOW TOOK THE MEASLES

AMERICAN FRONTIER SONG

Piano acc. p. 258

REFRAIN

How do you think I be-gan in the world?

I got me a sow and sev-'ral oth-er thing.

The sow took the mea-sles and she died in the spring.

VERSE

1. What do you think I made of her hide?

The ver-y best sad-dle that you ev-er did ride.

Sad-dle or bri-dle or an-y such thing,

D.C. after verse

The sow took the mea-sles and she died in the spring.

2. What do you think I made of her nose?

The very best thimble that ever sewed clothes.

Thimble or thread or any such thing,

The sow took the measles and she died in the spring.

98 Register

TRY THIS

1. "The Sow Took the Measles" has two sections—A (refrain) and B (verse). Call attention to the upward direction of the notes (*died in the spring*) at the end of each section. Children can play these notes (C, D, E, F) on the bells when they come in the song.

2. Some children might want to practice playing the last line of the verse on the bells. It starts on high C, repeats high C four times, leaps down to low C, repeats low C three times, then moves upward by step—D, E. F.

TEACHER INFORMATION

Mainstreaming: It is well to remember that sight-impaired children can readily play the Autoharp.

What do you think I made of her tail?

The very best whup that ever sought sail.

Whup or whupsocket or any such thing,

The sow took the measles and she died in the spring.

What do you think I made of her feet?

The very best pickles that you ever did eat.

Pickles or glue or any such thing,

The sow took the measles and she died in the spring. *Refrain*

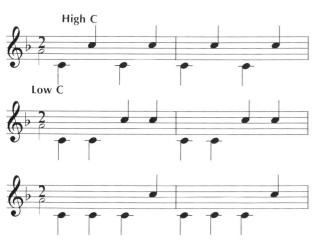

4. Have children take turns playing one of the bell parts throughout "The Sow Took the Measles." They will play the low-C bell with a mallet held in the left hand; the high-C bell with a mallet held in the right hand.

5. After they have worked through items 1–4 above, play the recording of *Call Chart 5* and have children follow the chart on p. 99 as they listen. This will help them hear how a composer organized sounds in different registers: sometimes mostly low, sometimes mostly high; other times, both high and low together.

The Call Chart will help you hear when the music is mostly low, mostly high, and both low and high.

CALL CHART 5: REGISTER

1. *MOSTLY LOW*

2. *MOSTLY HIGH*

3. *BOTH LOW AND HIGH*

4. *MOSTLY LOW*

Mussorgsky: *Pictures at an Exhibition*, "Samuel Goldenberg and Schmuyle"

Register 99

TRY THIS

Children can take turns accompanying "The Sow Took the Measles" on the Autoharp. Have them make up a strum pattern, using the low and high strings. The chord letters in the music will tell them when to play each chord. Two children can work at one Autoharp, one to press the chord buttons and one to strum the low and high strings.

TEACHER INFORMATION (for *Call Chart 5*)

Modest Mussorgsky (Russian, 1839–1881) *Pictures at an Exhibition*, "Samuel Goldenberg and Schmuyle": The music of this composer is often of a programmatic (storytelling) nature. *Pictures at an Exhibition* was written to honor the memory of his friend, the painter Victor Hartmann, some of whose paintings Mussorgsky describes in musical terms. This composition was written originally for piano, but the work has been made famous by the brilliant orchestration of the French composer Maurice Ravel.

MATERIALS
Record 5, "Bella Bimba"; Pupil's
Book, pp. 100 and 101; drums,
Autoharp

VOCABULARY
high, low, meter in 3, ABA form

IDEAS FOR TEACHING

1. Have children take turns playing a
low-high-high pattern on drums.
Suggestion: Children can use bongo
drums or two drums of different
sizes (one that sounds lower, the
other higher), playing the lower
sound with the left hand; the higher
sound with the right hand.

2. As someone plays the drum
pattern, have other children walk a
low-high-high pattern. They will
bend the knee and dip for "low"
and walk on tiptoe for "high-high."
It will help if they think "down-
up-up." Note: Because the "down"
step comes on alternate feet in a
pattern of threes, it will take time
for some children to feel this
waltz-walk.

3. Direct attention to the drum part
notated on p. 100. Questions: Does
the drum part use meter in 2, or
meter in 3? (Meter in 3) How is the
low-high-high pattern shown in the
notation? (Notes with stems pointing
down show low sounds; those with
stems pointing up show high
sounds.) Call attention to the repeat
sign.

4. Select one or two children to
practice a low-high-high pattern
(using the low and high strings) on
an Autoharp. Have them follow the
chord pattern notated on p. 100. →

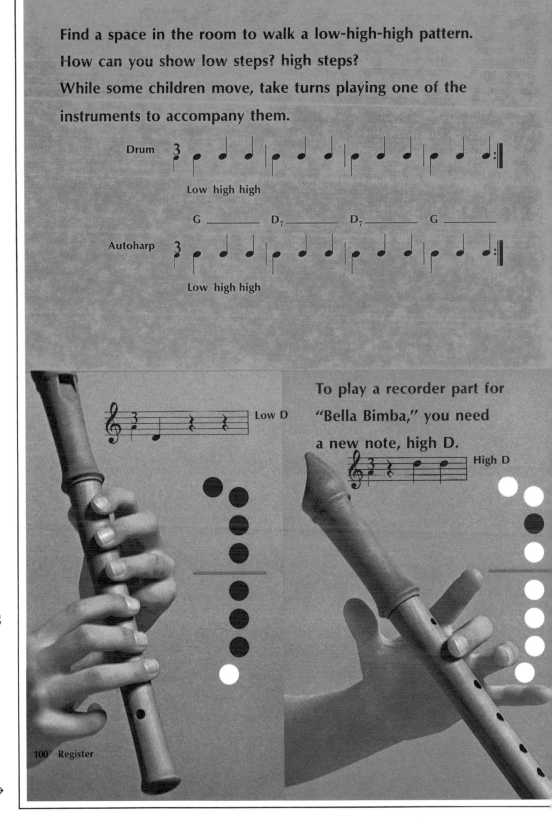

Find a space in the room to walk a low-high-high pattern.

How can you show low steps? high steps?

While some children move, take turns playing one of the

instruments to accompany them.

Drum

Low high high

G ——— D₇——— D₇——— G ———

Autoharp

Low high high

To play a recorder part for
"Bella Bimba," you need
a new note, high D.

Low D

High D

dd your accompaniment to section A of this song.

op and listen to section B.

Piano acc. p. 241

ELLA BIMBA
FOLK SONG FROM ITALY   ENGLISH WORDS BY RICHARD MORRIS

REFRAIN

How well you dance, my *bel - la bim - ba, bel - la*

bim - ba, bel - la bim - ba. How well you dance, my *bel - la*

bim - ba, bel - la bim - ba, how you dance!

VERSE

1. Bright as a sun - beam, Grace - ful and fair,

Light as a feath - er, Float - ing on air.

Whirling and twirling,

Round and around,

Feet always moving

When music sounds.

Register 101

5. Point out that the song "Bella Bimba" has two sections, A and B. Play the recording and ask children to follow the notation to discover the form of the music. Question: Is the form ABA, or AB? (Most children will hear that section A repeats, making the form ABA. The repetition of section A is indicated by *D.C. al Fine,* which means "repeat from the beginning and continue to the word *Fine*."

6. While some children sing "Bella Bimba," others can accompany section A by playing the low-high-high pattern on drums and on the Autoharp. Still others can walk the low-high-high pattern. Suggestion: Children can practice one part at a time with the recording. Encourage them to practice on their own. Then, when they are ready, they can put all the parts together to form an ensemble.

TEACHER INFORMATION

Mainstreaming: An adaptation of "Bella Bimba" appears in *Silver Burdett Music for Special Education.*

TRY THIS

1. To play a low-high-high pattern on recorder, recorder players will need a new note, high D. Children will find the fingering for high D on p. 100 in their book. (Low D is introduced on p. 72.) Children will play low D on the strong beat (first beat) and high D for beats 2 and 3.

2. For a "Bella Bimba" ensemble, combine singing, playing instruments (drums, Autoharp, recorder), and the waltz-walk for section A of the song. All will stop and sing the verses (section B). These contrasting activities will give children an opportunity to think about their part in relation to the whole.

As in all ensembles, children should be aware of working together to create a blend of sound. Each part has a particular function. Make children aware of how loud or soft they should play to create a blend they and you are satisfied with.

MATERIALS

Record 5, "Bella Bimba"; Pupil's Book, p. 102; bells

VOCABULARY

high sounds, low sounds, octave

IDEAS FOR TEACHING

1. Direct attention to the three bell parts on p. 102. These bell parts can be used with section A of "Bella Bimba," p. 101. Before children try playing the bell parts, call attention to the following:

Bell part 1: Measures 1 and 4 start on G followed by two high D's; measures 2 and 3 start on low D followed by two high D's.

Bell part 2: The two notes, low D and high D, are an octave apart (*octa-* means "eight"). Note: When counting from a lower note to a higher note, call the lower note "one" and count all the lines and spaces to the higher note.

Bell part 3: The low-D and the high-D bells are played simultaneously.

2. Point out that when playing bell parts 1, 2, and 3, the notes that are played with the left hand have stems going down. The ones that are played with the right hand have stems going up.

3. Have children take turns playing one of the bell parts to accompany the singing of "Bella Bimba" (section A).

You have played high and low sounds on a drum, on the strings of an Autoharp, or on a recorder.

Now play a bell part to accompany section A of "Bella Bimba."

Call the lower note "one" and count all the lines and spaces to the higher note. It will be "eight." The two notes are an *octave* apart.

Now play the notes, *octave* D, at the same time to discover that they sound alike.

Find other bells that sound the same when played together.

Your ears will tell you when you are playing octaves.

Play octaves to accompany "Bella Bimba."

Play octave D during section A.

Play octave B during section B.

Make up your own rhythm pattern.

TEACHER INFORMATION

If children have trouble making up a rhythm pattern for bell parts 2 and 3, here are some they can start with.

TRY THIS

Have children play an octave B to accompany section B of "Bella Bimba" as others sing.

WHAT DO YOU HEAR? 6: REGISTER ⦿

Each time a number is called, decide whether the music
is mostly high or mostly low.

If you think it is mostly high, circle the words MOSTLY HIGH.
If you think it is mostly low, circle the words MOSTLY LOW.
Listen. Then circle what you hear.

1	*MOSTLY HIGH*	*(MOSTLY LOW)*
2	*MOSTLY HIGH*	*(MOSTLY LOW)*
3	*(MOSTLY HIGH)*	*MOSTLY LOW*
4	*(MOSTLY HIGH)*	*MOSTLY LOW*
5	*(MOSTLY HIGH)*	*MOSTLY LOW*
6	*MOSTLY HIGH*	*(MOSTLY LOW)*

Haydn: *Symphony No. 103,* "Adagio"

1	*MOSTLY HIGH*	*(MOSTLY LOW)*
2	*MOSTLY HIGH*	*(MOSTLY LOW)*
3	*(MOSTLY HIGH)*	*MOSTLY LOW*

Grieg: "In the Hall of the Mountain King"
Beethoven: *Symphony No. 7,* Movement 4
Britten: *The Young Person's Guide to the Orchestra*

Register 103

REGISTER • Lesson 5

MATERIALS
Record 5, *What Do You Hear? 6:
Register;* spirit master

VOCABULARY
mostly high, mostly low

TEACHER INFORMATION

In *What Do You Hear? 6,* children
are asked to listen to music that is
mostly high or mostly low.

Because it may be necessary to play
the pieces in this lesson more than
once, take time to have children
listen to the recording first. Then
when they hear the music a second
time, they can circle their answers
on their paper.

MATERIALS

Record 5, "One Day My Mother Went to the Market"; *Cat!*; Pupil's Book, pp. 104 and 105

VOCABULARY

high sounds, low sounds

IDEAS FOR TEACHING

1. Remind children that they have explored high and low sounds on drums (pp. 96, 98, 100), Autoharp (pp. 96, 98, 100), and bells (pp. 96, 98, 102).

2. Point out that "One Day My Mother Went to the Market" has two sections, A and B. Then play the recording and ask children to listen for the parts that are spoken, not sung. Question: Do you hear spoken parts in section A, or section B? (Children will hear two places in section A where speaking voices are used.)

3. This time, have children join in on the spoken parts. Suggestion: Encourage children to explore the range of their speaking voices, making their voices very high and very low. An expressive use of the speaking voice tends to improve the singing voice.

4. When they are familiar with the song, have the class sing it. Let children take turns saying the speaking parts.

5. Play the recording of *Cat!* and ask children to listen for the different voice registers that are used. Then have the children experiment with different voice registers. Ask them to decide which words of the poem →

ONE DAY MY MOTHER WENT TO THE MARKET

FOLK SONG FROM ITALY   ENGLISH WORDS BY LEO ISRAEL   COLLECTED AND ADAPTED BY RUDOLPH GOEHR

FROM LITTLE FOLK SONGS. © COPYRIGHT 1958, 1964, SHAWNEE PRESS, INC., DELAWARE WATER GAP, PA 18327. INTERNATIONAL COPYRIGHT SECURED. ALL RIGHTS RESERVED. USED WITH PERMISSION.

Piano acc. p. 270

1. One day my moth-er went to the mar-ket
And she bought a hand-some roost-er.
A roost-er? A roost-er!
But when my moth-er start-ed to cook him,
He did ev'-ry-thing he use-ta.
He use-ta? He use-ta!
Oh, he said, "Cock-a-doo-dle-doo,
How I love you, how I love you."

104 Register

TRY THIS

1. Children can accompany "One Day My Mother Went to the Market" on the Autoharp. The song uses three chords, F, C$_7$, and B$^\flat$. (The chord letters in the music will tell them when to play each chord.) Children can strum on the high strings or on the low strings. They also can tap the side of the Autoharp to play the rhythm of the spoken words.

2. Select children to practice a bell part to play during section B. The part can be played in a high register or a low register on the keyboard or on bells.

C   D   B$^\flat$ A   G

Some children will hear the harmony made by the voice part and the bell part when they are performed together.

Oh, he said, "Cock - a doo - dle - doo,"

And a - way he flew, and a - way he flew.

2. . . . and she bought a little pig . . .

But when my mother started to cook him,

He got up and danced a jig . . .

Oh, he said, "Oink, oink, oink,

Though I'd like to stay, though I'd like to stay."

Oh, he said, "Oink, oink, oink,"

And he ran away, and he ran away.

3. . . . and she bought a pretty lamb . . .

But when my mother started to cook him,

He said, "Who do you think I am?" . . .

Oh, he said, "Baa, baa, baa,

I'm silly, it's true, I'm silly, it's true."

Oh, he said, "Baa, baa, baa,

Not as silly as you, not as silly as you."

4. . . . and she bought a lovely hen . . .

But when my mother started to cook her,

She began to cluck again . . .

Oh, she said, "Cluck, cluck, cluck, cluck, cluck."

But she forgot, but she forgot,

Oh, she said, "Cluck, cluck, cluck, cluck, cluck,"

And fell into the pot, and fell into the pot.

Register   105

they will say with a high-pitched
voice, a low-pitched voice. Will they
go from high to low or from low to
high?

CAT!

> *Cat!*
> *Scat!*
Atter her, atter her,
Sleeky flatterer,
Spitfire chatterer,
Scatter her, scatter her
> Off her mat!
> *Wuff!*
> *Wuff!*
> Treat her rough!
Git her, git her,
Whiskery spitter!
Catch her, catch her,
Green-eyed scratcher!
> Slathery
> Slithery
> Hisser,
> Don't miss her!
Run till you're dithery,
> Hithery
> Thithery!
> *Pfitts! pfitts!*
> How she spits!
> *Spitch! spatch!*
> Can't she scratch!
Scritching the bark
Of the sycamore-tree,
She's reached her ark
And's hissing at me
> *Pfitts! pfitts!*
> *Wuff! wuff!*
> Scat.
> Cat!
> That's
> *That!*

Eleanor Farjeon

TEACHER INFORMATION

Many poems can be used to reinforce music concepts
such as dynamics, tempo, steady beat, accents. Ask
children to bring in a favorite poem. Have them use it to
illustrate one of the concepts.

Other poems in the Pupil's Book can be used also.
• *Rain Sizes,* p. 70
• *But You Are Mine,* p. 94
• *Lewis Has a Trumpet,* p. 126

MODULE 10

OBJECTIVES, p. xii

STYLE: Renaissance, Romantic

MATERIALS
Record 5, Locke: *Courante*; Brahms: *Hungarian Dance No. 6*; Scriabin: *Prelude No. 18 in F Minor*; Bull: *In Nomine*; Pupil's Book, pp. 106 and 107

VOCABULARY
beat, register, small and large groups of instruments, accents, dynamics, style

IDEAS FOR TEACHING

1. Direct attention to the symbols on pp. 106 and 107. Through questioning and discussion, help children discover that the symbols represent certain qualities of music.

2. <u>Note</u>: In the left-hand column of each page, children will see (1) steady beat, (2) register very high and very low, (3) small group of instruments, (4) accents, (5) few dynamic changes. Children will see the opposite quality in each right-hand column.

3. Play the recording of Locke's *Courante* and ask children to listen for the five qualities of music they hear that are represented by the symbols in their book. (The symbols will help focus the children's listening.)

Help children hear that in *Courante* the beat is steady, there are few changes in dynamics, and there are no accents. A small group of brass instruments plays in a medium →

Tempo, dynamics, beat, direction, register, and tone color are some of the *qualities* of music.

They can be put together in different ways to make different *styles*. As you listen to two pieces in different styles, look at the symbols to find some of the qualities you hear.

Each piece has a different style, or general sound.

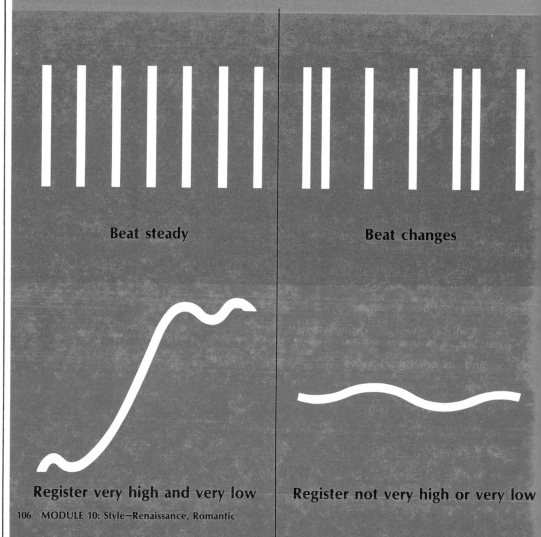

Locke: Courante   Brahms: Hungarian Dance No. 6

Beat steady   Beat changes

Register very high and very low   Register not very high or very low

106   MODULE 10: Style—Renaissance, Romantic

TEACHER INFORMATION

Matthew Locke (English, 1632–1677)   *Courante:* This composer was a favorite of the court of King Charles II. His *Courante* (a French dance that originated in the 16th century) is typical of the dances of such a court.

Johannes Brahms (German, 1833–1897)   *Hungarian Dance No. 6:* Brahms's Hungarian Dances and many other similar works clearly show his musical romanticism in their driving rhythms, flowing melodies, lush harmonies, and elaborate use of a large orchestra. Throughout different periods of music history, composers have used folk songs in their compositions. Brahms used a Hungarian folk tune as the main theme in *Hungarian Dance No. 6.*

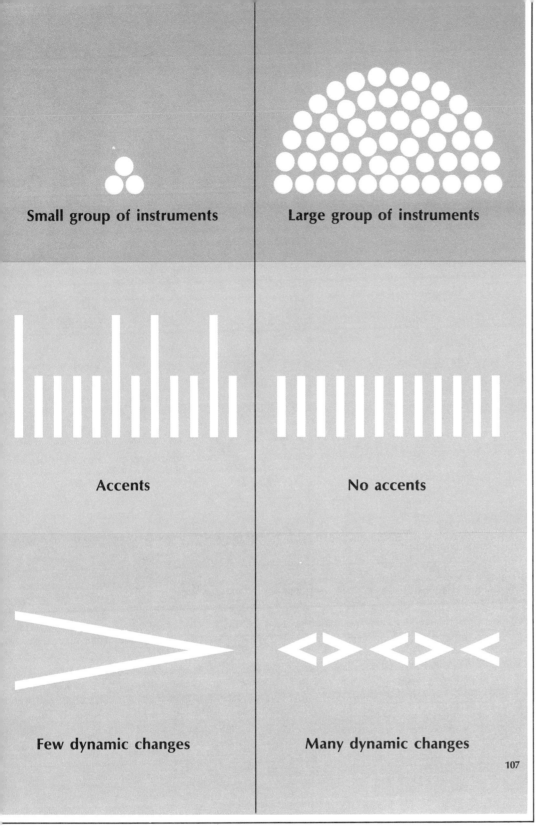

Small group of instruments

Large group of instruments

Accents

No accents

Few dynamic changes

Many dynamic changes

register, neither very high nor very low. Combined, these qualities result in a certain style. Note: Even though children may not hear everything at once, they will get a general impression of style.

4. Play the recording of the Brahms piece and ask children to look at the symbols as they listen.

Help children hear that in the Brahms piece there are many changes of beat, many accents, and many changes in dynamics. A large group of instruments (an orchestra) plays in a wide range, including very high and very low sounds. When these qualities are combined, another sound (a contrasting style) is created.

5. Have children play a "Style-Matching Game":
• Play the recording of Scriabin's *Prelude.* Question: Is this music like the Locke piece, or the Brahms piece?
• Play the recording of Bull's *In Nomine.* Question: Is this music like the Locke piece, or the Brahms piece?

Discussion: The Scriabin piece has the same qualities as the Brahms, except that it is played by a solo instrument (piano) rather than by a large group of instruments. The Bull piece is in the same style as Locke's *Courante,* except it is played by a group of recorders rather than by brass instruments.

107

TEACHER INFORMATION

Alexander Scriabin (Russian, 1872–1915) *Prelude No. 18 in F Minor:* Scriabin was Russia's first important composer of piano music. He is sometimes called the "Russian Chopin." He used harmonies of his own invention, approaching what later was to become atonal music (no single pitch provides a focus for the ear).

John Bull (English, 1562–1628) *In Nomine:* Bull was a famous organist of his time. He served many royal families and large churches as composer and performer. *In Nomine* means "in the name."

MODULE 11

OBJECTIVES, p. xii

DURATION • Lesson 1

MATERIALS
Record 5, *Blum; "*What Is Love?";
Pupil's Book, pp. 108 and 109

VOCABULARY
short sounds, long sounds, whole
notes

IDEAS FOR TEACHING

1. Direct attention to the photograph
on p. 108. Help children discover
how the photograph illustrates short
and long.

2. Have children think of ways to
show short and long with their
voices. For example, a short whistle,
a long whistle; a short "rah," a long
"raaaah."

3. Play the recording of *Blum* and
have children listen to the way the
reader says the words in the
poem—she says some words shorter
and some words longer. <u>Question</u>:
Which word lasted the longest?
(*Blum*) <u>Discussion</u>: The way the
poem is read gives it its own feeling
because of the many short sounds
and the few long sounds.

4. Let children take turns saying
several lines of the poem, making
some words long and some words
short.

5. Point out that music uses long
and short sounds. Then play the
recording of "What Is Love?" and
have children listen, with books
closed, for the longest sounds in the
song. These sounds are shown in the
notation as whole notes ($_o$). ⟶

Words can have short
sounds or long sounds.
Listen to this poem.
Which sound is the
longest on the recording?
◎
5

BLUM

Dog means dog,

And cat means cat;

And there are lots

Of words like that.

A cart's a cart

To pull or shove,

A plate's a plate,

To eat off of.

But there are other

Words I say

When I am left

Alone to play.

Blum is one.

Blum is a word

That very few

Have ever heard.

I like to say it.

"Blum, Blum, Blum"—

I do it loud

Or in a hum.

All by itself

It's nice to sing:

It does not mean

A single thing.

Dorothy Aldis

108   MODULE 11: Duration

TRY THIS

Have children bring in pictures that illustrate short and
long. A collage of pictures that children collect would
make an attractive bulletin-board display. In this way,
children can share what they have learned about duration
with others in the school.

Music can have long and short sounds, too.

Which sounds are short and which are long in this song?

Piano acc. p. 268

HAT IS LOVE? WORDS AND MUSIC BY CHRIS DEDRICK © 1972 ALMITRA MUSIC COMPANY, INC.

I know a ver-y hard ques-tion: What is love?

Ver-y wise peo-ple can't find the words to say what love is.

I fig-ured out that there can't be words for some-thing quite that good.

If you stop, If you stop to think a-bout your friends, your folks,

Your pup-py, your cat, the sun-shine, the trees and e-ven your-self—

You know all a-bout love; Al-most ev-'ry-one does.

Love, love, I know all a-bout love, but I can't tell.

Love, love, Words can't tell a-bout love, it's just as well.

Do you *see* what you *hear?*

Sing the song and point to the longest sounds.

109

6. Play the recording again and ask children to follow the notation as they listen. Have them pretend to stretch an elastic band to measure the length of each whole note. Note: In this song, the whole note is the same as four quarter notes tied together. It lasts four beats.

7. Play the recording again. This time, ask children to listen for the shorter sounds in the song. These are shown as quarter notes and eighth notes.

8. Call attention to the fourth and fifth lines of the song. When children sing these lines, they will be singing mostly short sounds. Point out the fermata sign (⌒) over the last note in the fifth line. Remind children that the fermata means "the beat stops and holds."

REVIEW/REINFORCEMENT

This would be a good time to review long and short sounds in *Kites Are Fun,* p. 39.

TRY THIS

1. Play a long sound on any ringing instrument (e.g., finger cymbals, triangle, gong). As long as the sound rings, children will move their head, arm, shoulder, leg in one direction (up, down, or sideways). On the next ring, they move in another direction. Each movement should continue as long as the sound lasts.

Have children contrast the long movement by making short movements with arm, leg, head, shoulders (up, down, forward, backward, etc.) when they hear short sounds played on woodblock, claves, or drum.

2. Help children organize the long and short sounds to make a long-short sound piece to which they can move. For example:

| Long | Short | Long and short | Long |

(Each box represents a phrase of 8 beats.)

Add flashlights to the movement. Keep the light moving during the long sounds; flick the light off and on during the short sounds. This is a good activity for non-ambulatory children.

MATERIALS

Record 5, "What Is Love?"; *Call Chart 6: Duration*; Pupil's Book, pp. 109–111; percussion instruments, bells, and recorder

VOCABULARY

quarter notes, half notes, whole notes, eighth notes

IDEAS FOR TEACHING

1. Direct attention to the first four lines of notes on p. 110. Then help children answer the questions below the lines of notes. (The answers are surprinted in the Teacher's Edition.)

2. As soon as children understand how duration is written (with quarter, half, eighth, and whole notes), and what the relationship is of one note to another, point out how notes can be combined to make rhythm patterns. Note: The rhythm patterns at the bottom of p. 110 are all found in "What Is Love?" (p. 109). Help children find each pattern where it occurs in the song.

3. Select four children, each to tap, clap, snap, or play on a percussion instrument one of the rhythm patterns when it comes in the song.

4. Ask children to find rhythm patterns that use the notes ♩, ♪, 𝅝, ♫ in other songs they know.
Suggestion: The songs on pp. 42, 50, 62, 63, 75, and 98 would be good ones to start with. ⟶

HOW TO WRITE LONG AND SHORT SOUNDS
Find these notes in the song "Love" on page 109.

Quarter notes	
Half notes	
Whole notes	
Eighth notes	

How many quarter notes can take the place of a half note? 2

How many eighth notes can take the place of a half note? 4

How many eighth notes can take the place of a quarter note? 2

How many quarter notes can take the place of a whole note? 4

Long and short sounds can make a rhythm pattern.

Find these patterns in the music on page 109.

1.   line 1, meas. 1 and 2

2.   line 5, meas. 1 and 2

3.   line 6, meas. 1 and 2

4.   line 1, meas. 3 and 4

110   Duration

TEACHER INFORMATION

A rhythm pattern can use silence as well as sound. Have children find these patterns in the song "What Is Love?":

♩♩♩♩ (line 2, measure 2; line 3, measure 2 or 3)
♩ 𝄽 𝄽 ♫ (line 3, measure 1)

A quarter rest (𝄽) can take the place of a quarter note.
A half rest (➖) can take the place of a half note.
Eighth rests (𝄾 𝄾) can take the place of eighth notes.

TRY THIS

1. Have a child play one of the patterns on p. 110 on a percussion instrument. Others try to identify the pattern.
2. Recorder players play one of the patterns on the tones they know (B, A, G, E, low D, high D, C). They may play the pattern on one tone, or they may use a combination of tones.
3. Using percussion instruments, have children create a sound piece by combining several rhythm patterns. Ask children to decide on the tempo, the dynamics, and the form.

F#

daah daah daah daah

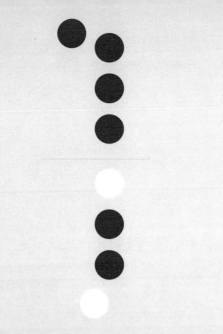

Play this pattern when it comes in the song "Love."

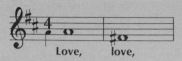

Love,   love,

Can you hear long and short sounds in a piano piece?

Listen to the recording and check the chart to help you.

CALL CHART 6: DURATION

Chopin: *Scherzo No. 3 in C# Minor*

1. LONG SOUNDS	**4.** SHORT SOUNDS
2. SHORT SOUNDS	**5.** LONG SOUNDS
3. LONG SOUNDS	**6.** SHORT SOUNDS
	7. LONG SOUNDS

Duration 111

5. <u>Note</u>: Children will find the recorder fingering for a new note (F#) in their book. Those who have been playing the recorder can practice playing the new note on their own.

6. When they are ready, children can play the pattern notated on p. 111 when it comes in "What Is love?" (The pattern occurs at the beginning of the last two lines of the song.) <u>Note</u>: Those who do not play the recorder can play the pattern on the bells. They will need the A and F# bells.

7. Children will hear long and short sounds played on the piano in *Call Chart 6.* Play the recording and have them follow the chart in their book as they listen. <u>Suggestion</u>: Because the events in this excerpt by Chopin move very quickly, play the recording several times.

TRY THIS

1. Children can play each whole note on recorder or bells when it comes in the song "What Is Love?" They will need:

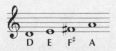

D   E   F#   A

2. When the class sings each whole note, some children can play short sounds on recorder or bells, using the appropriate pitch—D, E, F#, or A.

TEACHER INFORMATION

Frédéric Chopin (Polish, 1810-1849) *Scherzo No. 3 in C Sharp Minor*: While Chopin composed a great deal of music, practically all of it was written for a single instrument—the piano. These piano pieces are basic in the repertoire for the piano, being among the most challenging yet rewarding compositions any pianist can perform. Because they are so universally appealing, some of Chopin's melodies have become popular classics.

MATERIALS
Record 5, *Echo Rhythm Patterns;*
"Old Blue"; Record 6, Vivaldi, *The
Four Seasons* (Winter); Baldridge:
Let's Dance; Pupil's Book, pp. 112
and 113; percussion instruments

VOCABULARY
long sounds, short sounds, rhythm
patterns

IDEAS FOR TEACHING

1. Children have learned that long
and short sounds can be combined
in many different ways to make
rhythm patterns. Play the recording
of *Echo Rhythm Patterns* and let
children take turns echoing them by
clapping, tapping, or playing a
percussion instrument. <u>Note</u>: The
rhythm patterns children will hear
are notated below in Teacher
Information.

2. Play the recording of "Old Blue"
and ask children to listen for the
long sounds in the song. (In verse 1,
the long sounds occur on the words
dog, Blue, and *you.*)

3. While they sing each long sound
in the refrain of "Old Blue," let
children take turns filling in the span
of time by clapping their own
patterns of shorter sounds.
Encourage children to experiment
with many different rhythm patterns.

<u>Note</u>: Another time, divide the class
into two groups for the refrain. One
group begins to sing. When they
reach the first long sound in the
refrain, the other group begins. The
groups echo one another
throughout. ⟶

**Clap a pattern of shorter sounds each time you hear
a long sound in this song.**

OLD BLUE SOUTHERN MOUNTAIN SONG Piano acc. p. 256

1. I had an old dog,
And his name was Blue,
And I betcha five dollars he's a good dog, too.

REFRAIN
Come on, Blue, you good dog, you;
Come on, Blue, you good dog, you.

TEACHER INFORMATION

1. ("Ain't Gonna Rain," p. 24)

2. ("Old Joe Clark," p. 8)

3. ("The Ghost of John," p. 71)

4. ("Shepherd, Shepherd," p. 75)

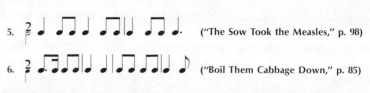

5. ("The Sow Took the Measles," p. 98)

6. ("Boil Them Cabbage Down," p. 85)

<u>Mainstreaming</u>: Suggestions for using "Old Blue" appear in
the song list in *Silver Burdett Music for Special Education.*

2. I grabbed my axe and I tooted my horn,

   Gonna git me a 'possum in the new-ground corn. *Refrain*

3. Chased that ol' 'possum up a 'simmon tree,

   Blue looked at the 'possum, 'possum looked at me. *Refrain*

4. Blue grinned at me, I grinned at him,

   I shook out the 'possum, Blue took him in. *Refrain*

5. Baked that 'possum all good and brown,

   And I laid them sweet potatoes 'round and 'round. *Refrain*

6. Well, old Blue died, and he died so hard,

   That he shook the ground in my back yard. *Refrain*

7. I dug his grave with a silver spade,

   I let him down with a golden chain. *Refrain*

8. When I get to heaven, first thing I'll do,

   Grab me a horn and blow for old Blue. *Refrain*

Can you hear two different rhythm patterns played at the same time in this music?

Vivaldi: *The Four Seasons* (Winter)

Baldridge: *Let's Dance*

Duration 113

4. When children clapped a rhythm pattern while singing the long sounds in "Old Blue," they did two things at one time. Play the recording of the Vivaldi piece (listed in Materials) and ask children to listen for violins playing both long and short sounds at the same time. (Some children may recognize that plucking the strings of a violin makes short sounds, while bowing makes longer sounds.)

Suggestion: If possible, arrange for a demonstration to show how a string instrument can be bowed or plucked. It is good practice to invite older children into the classroom to demonstrate orchestral instruments and play the melody of a song children know. There are many countermelodies and ostinato parts throughout the book that can be played on orchestral instruments.

5. Play the recording of the Baldridge piece and ask children to listen for long and short sounds in this dance music. (Sometimes they will hear both long and short sounds at the same time. At other times, they will hear mostly long or mostly short sounds.)

TEACHER INFORMATION

Antonio Vivaldi (Italian, 1678–1741) *The Four Seasons* (Winter): During Vivaldi's lifetime, new music was demanded for practically every occasion and a piece was not expected to be popular for very long. As a composer much in demand, Vivaldi turned out music at an astonishing rate—450 concertos, 49 operas, a great number of small instrumental pieces, etc. All his music is fresh in rhythmic energy and melodic inventiveness.

DURATION • Lesson 4

MATERIALS
Record 6, "The Pig"; Pupil's Book, p. 114; percussion instruments

VOCABULARY
rhythm pattern, quarter rest, phrase

IDEAS FOR TEACHING

1. Play the recording of "The Pig" and ask children to listen for the rhythm pattern in each two-measure phrase. Question: Did you discover anything about the rhythm pattern of each phrase? (Although the melody changes, some children may have heard that the rhythm pattern in each phrase is the same.)

2. To call attention to the silence at the end of each phrase (written as a quarter rest, ♩), have children take turns filling in the silence with a "surprise" sound, using any tone color—natural sound, percussion sound, voice sound, etc.

3. Play the recording again and ask children to tap the rhythm pattern in each phrase, followed by a "surprise" sound on the quarter rest.

4. For a "question and answer" activity, one child plays the first measure of the rhythm pattern on sticks or claves. Another child plays the second measure on a different percussion instrument—for example, guiro. Other children pretend to play a "surprise" sound at the end of each phrase to show the silence (♩).

THE PIG

FOLK TUNE FROM MEXICO   ENGLISH WORDS BY MARGARET MARKS

Piano acc. p. 265

Mis - sus Tor - res had a pi - hig,

Ver - y fat and ver - y bi - hig,

Dressed him in a fun - ny wi - hig,

Tried to make him dance a ji - hig.

But the pig, whose name was Sa - ham,

Said, "I'm ver - y sor - ry, Ma - ham,

Can't you leave me as I a - ham?

I don't want to be a ha - ham!"

114 Duration

TRY THIS

Recorders and bells play the second measure of the pattern each time it comes in "The Pig." The players will need the tones A, G, F♯, E, and low D.

Phrases 1, 4, 5

Phrases 2, 6

Phrases 3, 7

Phrase 8

REVIEW/REINFORCEMENT

As they listen to the recording, ask children to follow the notation of "The Pig" to find phrases that have the same melody. Phrases 1 and 5 are alike; phrases 2 and 6 are alike; phrases 3 and 7 are alike. Noticing repetition in a song makes it easier to learn.

AFRICAN RHYTHM COMPLEX

Chant the numbers in each line. Clap each time you say a large-size number.

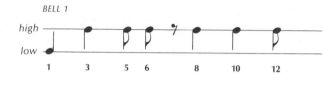

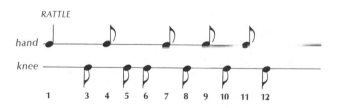

Look at the notation for the rhythms you clapped.

BELL 1

BELL 2

RATTLE

115

DURATION • Lesson 5

MATERIALS
Record 6, *African Rhythm Complex;* Pupil's Book, p. 115; African bells (or tin cans), rattle or maraca

VOCABULARY
rhythm patterns, polyrhythm

IDEAS FOR TEACHING

1. Establish a steady beat and have children chant the first line of numbers, clapping on each enlarged number. Have them repeat the line several times without pause. Then have them just *think* the numbers while clapping on each enlarged number. Performing the line over and over in this manner will help them feel the rhythm. Repeat the activity for the second and third lines.

2. When children are ready, divide the class into groups to perform two lines, then three lines, simultaneously. Note: When two or three lines are combined, children are experiencing *polyrhythm* (several different rhythms performed at the same time).

3. Call attention to the notation for the rhythms children clapped. (For an explanation of the instruments used, see Teacher Information, below.)

4. Have children follow the notation to play the rhythms, playing one part at a time at a moderate tempo before trying to combine parts. Silently counting from *one* to *twelve* will help them play accurately.

5. Have children follow the notation as they listen to the recording. They will be seeing and hearing polyrhythm.

TEACHER INFORMATION

In Africa, the first two rhythms might be played on an *gankogui* (gahn-koh'-gwee), a metal bell that is struck with a stick. The gankogui has a large section that produces a low pitch and a small section that produces a high pitch. The third rhythm might be played on an *axatse* (ahks-ah'-tsay), a gourd rattle covered with beads.

If African instruments are not available, children can use large and small tin cans for the bell rhythms and a maraca for the rattle rhythm. For the rattle rhythm, the instrument is hit against the hand or the knee as indicated in the notation.

Suggestion: If stereo equipment is available, use the Pick-a-Track technique to help children practice the parts. Bell parts 1 and 2 are recorded on one channel; rattle part on the other channel.

MATERIALS
Record 6, "Scratch, Scratch"; "Rabbit Hash"; Pupil's Book, p. 116; percussion instruments

VOCABULARY
sound and silence, quarter notes, quarter rests, half notes, half rests, eighth notes, eighth rests, triplet, whole rest

IDEAS FOR TEACHING

1. Play the recording and ask children to listen for the silences that occur after the word *back* in the second section (refrain) of the song.

2. Have children choose a percussion instrument that makes a scratching sound (notched stick, guiro, finger-nails across drumhead) and use it to fill in the silences that follow the word *back* in the second section.

3. As others sing the song along with the recording, children can take turns filling in the span of time after the word *back* with *sound,* or *silence.*

4. Ask children to look at the notation of "Scratch, Scratch" to find the signs that show all the silences. The children should find quarter rests, a half rest, and eighth rests.

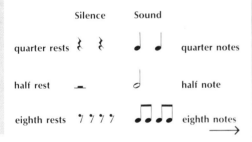

Sound and silence can work together in a rhythm pattern.

SCRATCH, SCRATCH
WORDS AND MUSIC BY HARRY BELAFONTE AND LORD BURGESS

"SCRATCH, SCRATCH ME BACK" BY HARRY BELAFONTE AND LORD BURGESS © COPYRIGHT 1957 BY CLARA MUSIC PUBLISHING CORPORATION. ALL RIGHTS RESERVED. USED BY PERMISSION.

116 Duration

REVIEW/REINFORCEMENT

Review the relationship of note values.
• How many quarter notes can take the place of a half note? (2)
• How many eighth notes can take the place of a half note? (4)
• How many eighth notes can take the place of a quarter note? (2)
• How many quarter notes can take the place of a whole note? (4)

<u>Note</u>: The relationship of note values is introduced on p. 3 and developed further on pp. 4, 5, 13, 14, 16, 17, 19, 24, 35, 45, 61, 72, 89, 91, 92, 98, 102, 109, and 112 in the Teacher's Edition.

Well, I was quite embarrassed,

Till my two friends I did see,

Well, they were madly itching,

And they were screaming louder than me.

Refrain

3. Now, this scratching was contagious,

And it didn't take very long,

Ev'rybody there was itching,

As they joined me in this song.

Refrain

5. Play the recording of "Rabbit Hash" and have children keep time to the steady beat by patting knees. (Children will hear the steady beat being clapped on the recording.)

6. To focus attention on the silence (𝄽) that occurs on the second beat of the measure in lines 1, 3, and 5, have children use this hand pattern to keep time to the steady beat—they will use both hands.

7. Have some children chant while others perform the hand pattern. Take time to switch groups so that at a later time, all can chant while doing the hand pattern.

8. Point out the places where triplets are used. The notation for a triplet indicates that there are three sounds to one beat. <u>Note</u>: Children have now observed and performed notation that represents one sound to a beat (♩), two sounds to a beat (♫), and three sounds to a beat.

9. Call attention to the notation for silences. Point out the whole rest (▬) at the end of line 2. A whole rest indicates that a silence lasts for the whole measure—in this case, two beats.

Children should notice that a quarter rest occurs on the first beat of the measure at the beginning of lines 2 and 6. Also, help them discover that the eighth rest that follows it takes the place of an eighth note.

eep time to the steady beat as you say this patting chant.

otice how sound and silence work together.

ABBIT HASH PATTING CHANT

CTED, ADAPTED AND ARRANGED BY JOHN A. LOMAX & ALAN LOMAX   TRO—© COPYRIGHT 1934 AND RENEWED 1962 LUDLOW MUSIC, INC., NEW YORK, N.Y. USED BY PERMISSION

Duration 117

TRY THIS

When children know the chant, they can devise their own routine, or hand jive, using combinations of patting, clapping, snapping, stamping, etc., to keep the steady beat. Encourage them to experiment with changes of tempo and changes of dynamics.

After they feel secure, have children try the routine as a round. Group 2 begins when group 1 reaches the end of the second measure.

DURATION • Lesson 7

MATERIALS
Record 6, "The Barnyard"; Bartók: *Roumanian Dance No. 6;* Pupil's Book, pp. 118 and 119; percussion instruments

VOCABULARY
rhythm patterns, accents

IDEAS FOR TEACHING

1. Play the recording of "The Barnyard" and ask children to join in when they can. The many repetitions in melody and rhythm encourage immediate participation.

2. After children have sung "The Barnyard," point out that the song is made up of three different rhythm patterns. You may want to write the patterns on the chalkboard. Note: The ✗'s in pattern 3 indicate that an animal sound is performed at an indeterminate pitch.

3. Have children tap out the rhythm of the melody to hear each pattern and the repetitions of each pattern. Instead of tapping, have them make an animal sound for each ✗.

4. Have children use a percussion instrument to play an accent on the quarter rest (𝄽) before each animal sound (*Moo, Quack, Honk, Cluck*) in the song. Note: Children have ⟶

Tap out the rhythm pattern of the melody to hear the rhythm patterns that repeat.

THE BARNYARD
WORDS AND MUSIC BY CARMINO RAVOSA

©1972 Carmino Ravosa

Piano acc. p. 222

1. Barn - yard, barn - yard, all a-round the barn - yard,
Hear the cow go, "Moo, moo."
Barn - yard, barn - yard, all a-round the barn - yard,
Hear the duck go, "Quack, quack."
All a-round the barn-yard, An - i - mals are talk - ing;
Though it sounds to you like Just a lot of squawk-ing.
Barn - yard, barn - yard, all a-round the barn - yard,

118 Duration

TRY THIS

1. The melody for the animal sounds can be played on recorder or bells.

F♯ G

2. Children can play the first measure of lines 1-4 and lines 7-10 on bells or recorder.

B G B G

TEACHER INFORMATION

For biographical information on Carmino Ravosa, composer of "The Barnyard," see p. 68.

Mainstreaming: Suggestions for using "The Barnyard" appear in the song list in *Silver Burdett Music for Special Education.*

Hear the goose go, "Honk, honk."

Barn-yard, barn-yard, all a-round the barn-yard,

Hear the chick-en, "Cluck, cluck, Cluck, cluck."

Barnyard, barnyard, all around the barnyard,

Hear the pig go, "Oink, oink."

Barnyard, barnyard, all around the barnyard,

Hear the sheep go, "Baa, baa."

All around the barnyard,

Animals are talking;

Though it sounds to you like

Just a lot of squawking.

Barnyard, barnyard, all around the barnyard,

Hear the horse go, "Neigh, neigh."

Barnyard, barnyard, all around the barnyard,

Hear the donkey, "Hee-haw, Hee-haw."

Bartók: *Roumanian Dance No. 6*

119

learned that in music, a sudden loud sound is called an *accent*. (Accents are introduced in the song "A Ram Sam Sam" on p. 33. Children have had further experience with accents in the music on pp. 43, 67, 78, 85, and 106.)

5. After children have experienced qualities of music such as accents and shorter and longer sounds, they should listen to discover how a composer uses these qualities in a piece of music.

Play the Bartók piece (listed in Materials) and ask children to listen for accents and for shorter and longer sounds. Questions: Did you hear many accents, or few accents? (Many accents) Did you hear mostly short, or mostly long, sounds? (Mostly short)

Note: Some children will hear that the last sound is the only long sound in the melody (played by upper strings) and that throughout the piece, longer sounds are played by the lower strings.

Since this excerpt is very short, you may want to play it several times so that all children can answer the questions successfully.

TEACHER INFORMATION

Béla Bartók (Hungarian, 1881–1945) *Roumanian Dance No. 6:* Bartók was a virtuoso pianist as well as an important composer. From the beginning he was attracted by the folk music of eastern Europe, especially the folk music of Hungary and Romania. His music blended folk idioms into serious, complex works, many of them considered to be among the greatest of this century. The set of dances of which *Roumanian Dance No. 6* is a part is particularly popular.

DURATION • Lesson 8

MATERIALS

Record 6, "Shepherds Came to Bethlehem"; Pupil's Book, pp. 120 and 121; percussion instruments (drum, finger cymbals, tambourine), bells or recorder

VOCABULARY

accents, phrases, contrasting sections

IDEAS FOR TEACHING

1. Play the recording of "Shepherds Came to Bethlehem." Have children follow the notation in their book as they listen for all the accents in the song. <u>Note</u>: Have children find the sign that shows the accents (>).

2. Play the recording again and have children clap on all the accents.

3. Children can play the accents on a percussion instrument along with the recording. Ask them to listen especially for accents played on the drum.

4. Now have children show accents through movement:

Section A
• Clap accents at the end of phrase 1 (*Christ-mas Day*).
• Pat knees on accents at the end of phrase 2 (*pipes did play*).

Section B
• Stamp feet and clap hands on accents (*peace on earth*).

5. Before teaching the dance (directions below), tell children that the song has two contrasting sections, A and B. Call attention to →

In music, a sudden loud sound is called an ***accent.***

Find the sign (>) that shows accent in this song.

Orff acc. p. 282

SHEPHERDS CAME TO BETHLEHEM POLISH CAROL

ENGLISH WORDS BY ROSEMARY JACQUES

1. Shep-herds came to Beth-le-hem on Christ-mas Day.

How the Ba-by smiled as they their pipes did play.

Glo-ry, sing glo-ry to God in the high-est,

And peace on earth, Peace on earth.

2. Then a shepherd beat upon a little drum.

How it pleased the Baby with its rum-tum-tum.

Glory, . . .

3. As the shepherds bowed before the blessed Boy,

All the heavens rang with sounds of wondrous joy.

Glory, . . .

Play the accents on a small drum or on finger cymbals.

120 Duration

DANCE DIRECTIONS

Form a double circle of dancers, one circle facing the other. Children standing opposite each other are partners.

Secion A
• Phrase 1: Take four steps backward, away from partner (meas. 1 and 2). Stop and clap hands three times, once on each accent (meas. 3 and 4).
• Phrase 2: Take four steps toward partner (meas. 5 and 6). Stop and pat knees three times, once on each accent (meas. 7 and 8).

Section B
• Each dancer swings his or her partner once around, stopping to simultaneously stamp feet and clap hands on the accented beats (meas. 13 and 14). Everyone stands still and sings the last two measures.
• Repeat the movements for section B. (After swinging partners, it is important for children to be back in their places in the circle before changing partners.) As everyone sings the last two measures, they take two sliding steps to the right, stopping in front of a new partner. The dance begins again.

To accompany "Shepherds Came to Bethlehem," play one of the parts on the bells or recorder.

Here is a part to play on a tambourine.

121

TRY THIS

1. Before children try playing one of the instrumental parts on p. 121 to accompany "Shepherds Came to Bethlehem," you may need to review the relative duration of half notes, quarter notes, and eighth notes.

Also, call attention to the whole rest (━) in the first instrumental part. Remind children that a whole rest indicates a silence that lasts for a whole measure—in this case, two beats. (A whole rest is introduced in "Rabbit Hash," p. 117.) Children should also be aware of the quarter rests (𝄽) that occur on the last beat in lines 1, 2, and 4 of the tambourine part. Each quarter rest lasts for one beat.

2. Those children who elect to play one of the instrumental parts can practice on their own. When they are ready, have the instrumental players accompany the singing of "Shepherds Came to Bethlehem."

MATERIALS
Record 6, *What Do You Hear? 7: Duration*; spirit master

VOCABULARY
long sounds, short sounds, long and short sounds

TEACHER INFORMATION

In *What Do You Hear? 7*, children are asked to listen for mostly short sounds, mostly long sounds, or short and long sounds played together.

The music includes excerpts from a review song, "Mama Paquita," p. 18; a Sound Piece from p. 87; a composition that is used as an integrated listening selection, p. 113; and a new selection—Ebreo: *Falla con misuras.*

The What Do You Hear? evaluation can be done with a large group in a classroom situation or with a small group using earphones. Spirit masters are available so that each child can respond individually.

Mainstreaming: In *What Do You Hear? 7*, the evaluation can also be done through movement. A child makes short movements, long movements, or short and long movements alternately as he or she responds to the music on the recording.

WHAT DO YOU HEAR? 7: DURATION ◉
6

What do you hear? Each time a number is called, decide whether you hear mostly short sounds, mostly long sounds, or short and long sounds played together.

Listen. Then circle what you hear.

---

1. *SHORT SOUNDS*
(LONG SOUNDS)
SHORT AND LONG SOUNDS PLAYED TOGETHER

---

2 *SHORT SOUNDS*
LONG SOUNDS
(SHORT AND LONG SOUNDS PLAYED TOGETHER)

---

3 *SHORT SOUNDS*
LONG SOUNDS
(SHORT AND LONG SOUNDS PLAYED TOGETHER)

---

4 *(SHORT SOUNDS)*
LONG SOUNDS
SHORT AND LONG SOUNDS PLAYED TOGETHER

Hays: *Sound Piece 3*
Vivaldi: *The Four Seasons* (Winter)
Ebreo: *Falla con misuras*
Mama Paquita

122 Duration

WHAT DO YOU HEAR? 8: RHYTHM PATTERNS 🔴

What do you hear? As each number is called, look at the notation and circle the rhythm pattern you hear.

The Lilly Bud
Mozart: *Symphony No. 40*
The Pig
Bach: *Passacaglia in C Minor*

123

DURATION • Lesson 9

MATERIALS
Record 6, *What Do You Hear? 8: Rhythm Patterns;* spirit master; percussion instruments

VOCABULARY
rhythm patterns

TEACHER INFORMATION

If necessary, use this page to review the relative duration of note values.

Before they listen to the recording, have children tap, clap, or play the patterns on a percussion instrument, or on recorder or bells, using a single pitch.

Before children respond on their answer sheet, make sure they understand that each rhythm pattern they hear on the recording will be played several times.

MODULE 12

OBJECTIVES, p. xiii
THE ARTS: Pattern

MATERIALS
Record 6, Anonymous: *Coranto;*
Pupil's Book, pp. 124 and 125

VOCABULARY
patterns

IDEAS FOR TEACHING
1. Ask children to look around the room to find patterns (things that are repeated over and over). Help them discover patterns in clothing (flowers, stripes, colors, etc.); in things in the classroom (light fixtures, grills, windowpanes, etc.). Point out: Patterns are all around us. Many artists use patterns in their works to help organize what we see.

2. Direct attention to Mary Slatter's *Sampler* on pp. 124 and 125. (Make sure children understand that this is one piece of art, extending over two pages.) Question: Can you find patterns in this sampler? (Practically everything in the sampler functions as a pattern: zigzag lines around the edge, flowers, leaves, fruits, birds, trees. Nothing is "one of a kind." Everything repeats, at least once, but usually several times. Even the people are enough alike to seem like patterns.)

3. Point out: In this work of art the patterns are seen all together—all at the same time, each one having an effect on all the others. Your eyes can focus on one pattern at a time, →

TEACHER INFORMATION

Mary Slatter (British) *Sampler:* Mary Slatter was a British artist, active around the time of the American Revolution (this sampler is dated 1792). Samplers were a popular folk art form, but as in this example, they were sometimes very complicated and sophisticated. We are presented with what is almost an "eye-puzzle," being challenged to see all the clever repetitions the artist's skill created.

but you can see all of them together, too.

4. Music uses patterns also—repeated rhythms or melodies. Play the recording of *Coranto.* (Since this piece is short, you may want to play it several times before asking the question.) <u>Question</u>: What pattern did you hear repeated in the music? (The tambourine rhythm is used over and over.)

5. <u>Point out</u>: In music the patterns happen one after another and your ears and your mind *remember* what you have heard and that you are hearing it again.

REVIEW/REINFORCEMENT

1. Point out repeated rhythm patterns in familiar songs. For example:

"Hey Ho, Hey Lo," p. 42

"The Pig," p. 114

2. Have children play a repeated melody pattern (ostinato) on bells throughout a song they know. For example:

"Lady, Come," p. 22

"Pray God Bless," p. 78

TRY THIS

1. Children can make "pattern pictures" in a variety of ways. For example, they can cut out a shape, using construction paper, then trace the shape over and over in interesting arrangements on a white or colored background.

2. Children can collect wallpaper and fabric samples that use patterns. Have them choose several and make a pattern collage by cutting shapes and pasting the cutouts on a background.

MODULE 13

OBJECTIVES, p. xiii

TONE COLOR • Lesson 1

MATERIALS
Record 6, *Lewis Has a Trumpet;*
Hammer Ring; Vocal Tone Colors;
Pupil's Book, p. 126

VOCABULARY
tone color

IDEAS FOR TEACHING

1. Have children experiment with a variety of voice sounds. They can imitate someone who performs on television, a space rocket, an automobile horn, an animal, a bird. Point out: Your voice can imitate many different tone colors, too. Words imitate tone color, also—a cat *purrs,* or a bee *buzzes.* Ask children to think of other words that imitate sounds. Suggestions: *thud, jingle, squish, shush, chop, crunch, crackle.*

2. Let children take turns reading *Lewis Has a Trumpet,* emphasizing the tone colors of the words printed at the right of the poem. Then have them listen to the recorded version of the poem.

3. Now play the recording of *Hammer Ring.* (A man sings the solo parts; children sing the chorus parts.) Have children fill in the chorus parts with shouting, humming, or whispering.

4. Play the recording of *Vocal Tone Colors* and ask children to decide whether a man, a woman, or children are singing. (See Teacher Information below.)

You can use your voice to make different tone colors.

Find words that imitate sounds in this poem.

When you say the poem, make your voice imitate the sounds.

LEWIS HAS A TRUMPET

A trumpet

A trumpet

Lewis has a trumpet

A bright one that's yellow

A loud proud horn.

He blows it in the evening

When the moon is newly rising

He blows it when it's raining

In the cold and misty morn

It honks and it whistles

It roars like a lion

It rumbles like a lion

With a wheezy huffing hum

His parents say it's awful

Oh really simply awful

But

Lewis says he loves it

It's such a handsome trumpet

And when he's through with trumpets

He's going to buy a drum.

Karla Kuskin

TEACHER INFORMATION

On the recording of *Vocal Tone Colors,* children will hear excerpts from the songs "Two-Feather Crow" (man), "All the Pretty Little Horses" (woman), "All Hid" (man and children), and "Scratch, Scratch" (children).

TRY THIS

Let children experiment with vocal tone colors, using this poem or others that are available.

WIND

The wind has lots of noises:
it sniffs,
it puffs,
it whines;
it rumbles like an ocean
through junipers and pines;
it whispers in the windows,

it howls,
it sings,
it hums;
it tells you VERY PLAINLY
every time it comes.

Aileen Fischer

The recorder has its own tone color. When you play a recorder, you make the sound by blowing. All instruments that are played by blowing are called *wind instruments*. How many do you know?

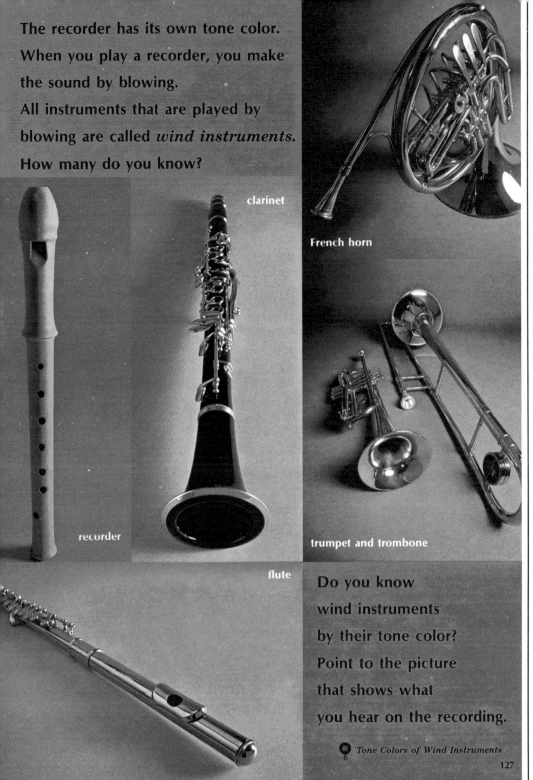

clarinet

French horn

recorder

trumpet and trombone

flute

Do you know wind instruments by their tone color? Point to the picture that shows what you hear on the recording.

Tone Colors of Wind Instruments

127

MATERIALS
Record 6, *Tone Colors of Wind Instruments*; Pupil's Book, p. 127; recorder

VOCABULARY
tone color

IDEAS FOR TEACHING
1. Play the recording of *Tone Colors of Wind Instruments* and ask children to find the picture of the instrument or instruments they hear. The instruments are played in this order on the recording:
• Debussy: *Syrinx* (flute)
• Gabrieli: *Canzona per sonare* (trombones and trumpets)
• Roussel: *Pipe in D Major* (recorder)
• Mozart: *Horn Concerto in E Flat Major* (French horn)
• Messiaen: *Quartet for the End of Time*, "Abyss of the Birds" (clarinet)
Point out: All the instruments that are played by blowing are called *wind instruments*. Suggestion: This would be a good time to invite older children who play wind instruments to perform for the class.

2. Let children who have been practicing recorder play one of the parts they know for the class. Have them choose a part from the following list of ostinatos and countermelodies.

• Ain't Gonna Rain, p. 29
• Brother Noah, p. 30
• Skin and Bones, p. 53
• New Year's Song, p. 61
• Love, p. 68
• The Ghost of John, p. 73
• Pray God Bless, p. 78
• Shepherds Came to Bethlehem, p. 121

MATERIALS

Record 6, "Hana ichi momme"; "Imagination of Grand Sea"; "Ay, di, di, di"; Pupil's Book, pp. 128 and 129; Autoharp, recorder, bells, percussion instruments (finger cymbals, woodblock, triangle)

VOCABULARY

tone color

IDEAS FOR TEACHING

1. Have recorder players choose one of the songs on pp. 128 and 129 to practice. If necessary, have them review the fingerings for low D (p. 72), E (p. 53), F♯ (p. 111), G, A, B (pp. 28 and 29), C (p. 89), and high D (p. 100).

2. For "Hana ichi momme," recorder players will need these tones:

D E G A B

For a "Hana ichi momme" ensemble, recorders play the melody. Other recorder players can play the countermelody notated at the bottom of the Pupil's Book. Other children can play the woodblock part (indicated in the music by ✗), or the bell parts (notated in the Pupil's Book), or they can participate in the game (directions given below). ⟶

Here are some songs to play on the recorder.

HANA ICHI MOMME

FOLK SONG FROM JAPAN

Piano acc. p. 271

Ka - te u - re - shii___ ha - na i - chi mom - me.

Mu - ka - i no da - re ka san chot - to o - i - de.

Literal translation:
How happy I am to see the flowers.
Mother, come quickly and buy one for me.

Add the tone color of the woodblock when it comes in the song.

Add one of these parts to the melody.

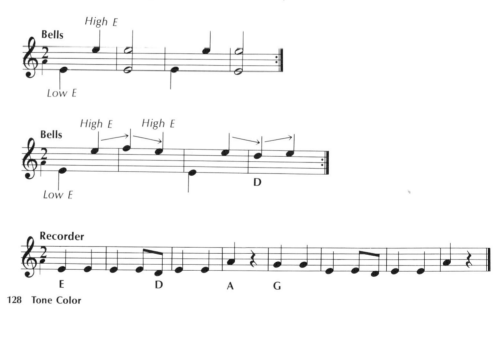

GAME DIRECTIONS

Children form two lines, facing each other. The children facing each other at one end of the lines are the leaders.
First time, Phrase 1: With hands joined, children in each line walk forward, taking small steps. They stop and place heel of right foot in front when woodblock sounds at end of phrase.
First time, Phrase 2: Children in each line walk backward, taking small steps. They stop and place heel of right foot in front when woodblock sounds.

Second time, Phrase 1:

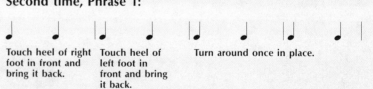

Touch heel of right foot in front and bring it back.   Touch heel of left foot in front and bring it back.   Turn around once in place.

Second time, Phrase 2: Same sequence as phrase 1, but use heel of left foot first.
Instrumental interlude: Leaders grasp hands and pull. Whoever pulls the other to his or her line wins. Both leaders then go to the other end of the leader's line and the game begins again.

IMAGINATION OF GRAND SEA

Piano acc. p. 223

FOLK SONG FROM JAPAN

ENGLISH WORDS BY RICHARD MORRIS

U - mi wa hi - ro - i na oh - ki - i na,

Tsu - ki ga no - bo - ru shi hi ga shi - zu - mu.

1. *Grand is the evening sea, majestic and deep;*
   There, as the moon awakes, the sun will go to sleep.

2. *Calm are the mighty waves; the water, so blue;*
   I wonder where the sea and all the waves go to.

3. *Many the tiny ships that float on the sea;*
   Some day to foreign lands those ships will carry me.

AY, DI, DI, DI

Piano acc. p. 257

HASIDIC MELODY

Ay, di, di, di, ay, di, di, di, di;

Ay, di, di, di, di, ay, di, di, di, di.

Tone Color 129

---

3. For "Imagination of Grand Sea," recorder players will need these tones:

D E G A B D

Children who do not play recorders can perform the percussion parts shown below when the class sings "Imagination of Grand Sea." Note: Call attention to the whole rests (𝄻) in the triangle part. A whole rest indicates a silence that lasts for a whole measure—in this case, three beats.

Finger cymbals

Woodblock

Triangle

To add the tone color of strings, have children alternately pluck the low-G string on the Autoharp and the D above it throughout "Imagination of Grand Sea." They should let each sound ring for three beats (♩.).

4. For "Ay, di, di, di," recorder players will need these tones:

D F♯ G A C D

Here is a bell part that can be played throughout "Ay, di, di, di." Children will need the G, and high-D bells.

TEACHER INFORMATION

Although many of the lessons in SILVER BURDETT MUSIC are presented through a group experience, it is most beneficial to a child's musical growth to have the opportunity for individual experiences as well. Most lessons lend themselves readily to individual instruction modes that are used in other subjects. The teacher should feel free to adapt these materials to a variety of individualized instruction opportunities.

The activities suggested on pp. 128 and 129 will extend over a period of time. Provide opportunities for children to practice individually or in small groups.

TONE COLOR • Lesson 4

MATERIALS
Record 7, "Yankee Doodle"; "Battle Hymn of the Republic"; "Jingle Bells"; Pupil's Book, pp. 130 and 131; percussion instruments (drum, cymbals, woodblock, jingle bells)

VOCABULARY
tone color, quarter note, half note, eighth notes, quarter rest, half rest

IDEAS FOR TEACHING
1. Children can have firsthand experience with the tone color of percussion instruments by playing an accompaniment for three familiar songs. They will use drum and cymbals with "Yankee Doodle" and "Battle Hymn of the Republic"; woodblock and jingle bells with "Jingle Bells."

2. Point out that whereas the sound of wind instruments is produced by blowing, the sound of percussion instruments is produced by striking or shaking.

3. Play the recording of "Yankee Doodle." Ask children to follow the drum and cymbals parts (one at a time) in their book and try to figure out how to play them. Call attention to the repeat sign at the end of each part.

4. Use the procedure in item 3 above and play the recording of "Battle Hymn of the Republic." →

YANKEE DOODLE
TRADITIONAL   WORDS BY DR. RICHARD SHUCKBURGH

Piano acc. p. 218

1. Fath'r and I went down to camp,
2. And there we saw a thou-sand men,

A-long with Cap-tain Good-in',
As rich as Squire_____ Da-vid;

And there we saw the men and boys
And what they wast-ed ev-'ry day,

As thick as hast-y pud-din'.
I wish it could be sav-ed.

REFRAIN
Yan-kee Doo-dle, keep it up, Yan-kee Doo-dle dan-dy,

Mind the mu-sic and the step And with the girls be hand-y.

3. And there was Captain Washington
Upon a slapping stallion,
A-giving orders to his men;
I guess there was a million.

130 Tone Color

TEACHER INFORMATION

Many legends are attached to our national songs. Numerous conflicting stories are told about "Yankee Doodle." There is one fact, however, that is known to be true. The song was used by the British to make fun of the Yankees, and later, during the Revolutionary War, the Yankees adopted it as their own song.

No one knows exactly where or when the tune of "Yankee Doodle" was first sung. We do know that many sets of verses have been written for the tune. Today the best known verse is: "Yankee Doodle came to town/ Riding on a pony,/ Stuck a feather in his cap/ And called it macaroni."

During the Revolutionary War, *macaroni* was a slang word meaning "stylish" and referred to a man who was overly concerned about his clothes and appearance.

BATTLE HYMN OF THE REPUBLIC

WORDS BY JULIA WARD HOWE

MUSIC BY WILLIAM STEFFE

Piano acc. p. 254

JINGLE BELLS

WORDS AND MUSIC BY JAMES PIERPONT

Piano acc. p. 264

131

5. Write these instrumental parts on the chalkboard, then use the procedure in item 3 (p. 130) and play the recording of "Jingle Bells."

Woodblock

Jingle bells

REVIEW/REINFORCEMENT

This would be a good time to reinforce the concept of duration introduced in Module 11, pp. 108–123:

- One quarter note ($\quarternote$) has the same number of beats as two eighth notes ($\eighthnote\eighthnote$).
- One half note ($\halfnote$) has the same number of beats as two quarter notes ($\quarternote\quarternote$).
- A quarter rest ($\quarterrest$) can take the place of a quarter note ($\quarternote$).
- A half rest ($\halfrest$) can take the place of a half note ($\halfnote$).

TRY THIS

1. When children have played one of the instrumental parts for "Yankee Doodle" or for "Battle Hymn of the Republic," have them play as they march. In this way they will experience two things at once—the steady beat with their feet and a rhythm pattern with their hands.

2. Some children may be able to play a bell part (notated below) to accompany "Jingle Bells." Write the part on the chalkboard or on a chart so that children can practice on their own.

BELL PART for "Jingle Bells"

MATERIALS

Record 7, "For Health and Strength";
"Frère Jacques"; "Oh, Susanna";
Record 1, Eddleman: *Autoharp Sound
Piece;* Pupil's Book, pp. 132 and 133;
Autoharp

VOCABULARY

tone color, chords

IDEAS FOR TEACHING

1. One way children can experience
the tone color of a string instrument
is to play the Autoharp. The
Autoharp sound can be produced in
many ways. Play the recording of
Autoharp Sound Piece (see p. 23).
This piece can serve as a model for
student experimentation.

2. All children should be given an
opportunity to strum the strings of
the Autoharp to accompany a song.
Let them experiment with a one-
chord song like "For Health and
Strength" to discover that strumming
chords provides a stronger
accompaniment than plucking
individual strings.

Children will strum the F chord
throughout "For Health and
Strength." They will start strumming
on the first strong beat (on the word
health).

3. "Frère Jacques" can be played,
using two chords—F and C₇.
Children should use the left index
finger to press the F button; the left →

You can add the tone color of the Autoharp when
you sing these songs.

132

TEACHER INFORMATION

Pronunciation guide

Frè-re   Jac-ques, Frè-re   Jac-ques, Dor-mez-vous, Dor-me -vous?
freh-ruh zhah-kuh freh-ruh zhah-kuh dor-meh-voo   dor-mel -voo

Son-nez les ma-ti-nes,   Son-nez les ma-ti-nes,
sun-neh leh mah-tee-nuh sun-neh leh mah-tee-nuh

Din din don,   Din din don.
deen deen doh(N) deen deen dohn(N)

OH, SUSANNA

WORDS AND MUSIC BY STEPHEN FOSTER 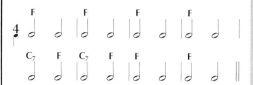 Piano acc. p. 231

I came from Al - a - ba - ma With my ban - jo on my knee,

I'm going to Loui - si - an - a, My true love for to see;

It rained all night the day I left, The weath-er it was dry;

The sun so hot I froze to death; Su-san - na, don't you cry.

REFRAIN

Oh, Su - san - na, Oh, don't you cry for me,

I've come from Al - a - ba - ma With my ban - jo on my knee.

I had a dream the other night,

When ev'rything was still.

I thought I saw Susanna

A-coming down the hill.

The buckwheat cake was in her mouth,

The tear was in her eye.

Says I, "I'm coming from the South,

Susanna, don't you cry." *Refrain*

Tone Color   133

---

middle finger to press the C₇ button.

Note: The Autoharp accompaniment for "Frère Jacques" is intended for singing in unison only, not as a round.

4. "Oh, Susanna" uses three chords—F, C₇, and B♭. Children should use the fingers of the left hand to press the chord buttons—index finger for F, middle finger for C₇, and ring finger for B♭. The chord letters in the music will tell them when to change from one chord to another.

Suggestion: Other songs that children can accompany on the Autoharp are:
• Swing Low, Sweet Chariot (F chord throughout)
• Skip to My Lou (F, C₇)
• Sandy Land (F, C₇)
• Row, Row, Row Your Boat (C chord throughout)
• He's Got the Whole World in His Hands (C, G₇)
• Michael, Row the Boat Ashore (C, G₇, F)
• Clementine (G, D₇)
• She'll Be Coming Round the Mountain (G, D₇, C)

Encourage children to experiment with different kinds of strums on the Autoharp—long strums, short strums, strums on the high strings, strums on the low strings, etc.

English version for "Frère Jacques"
Are you sleeping, Are you sleeping,
Brother James, Brother James?
Morning bells are ringing, Morning bells are ringing,
Ding ding dong, Ding ding dong.

MATERIALS
Record 7, "Nobody's Business";
Record 6, Vivaldi: *The Four Seasons*
(Winter); Pupil's Book, pp. 134 and
135; Autoharp

VOCABULARY
tone color, chords

IDEAS FOR TEACHING

1. Play "Nobody's Business" and ask
children to listen for the tone colors
of the instruments used in the
recording. Some children may be
able to identify fiddle, guitar, string
bass, piano, and percussion.

2. Play the recording again and have
children follow the chord letter
names—D, A₇, G—in the music.

3. Select some children to practice
the Autoharp part so they can
accompany the singing. <u>Note</u>:
Because of the many chord changes,
children may need help in following
the letters. Write the chord names D,
A₇, G on the chalkboard and point
to them to lead children in playing
the chords as others sing.

4. If a violin or a guitar is available,
children can add the tone color of
the plucked strings—D, A, and G.

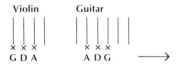

NOBODY'S BUSINESS

AMERICAN FOLK SONG

Piano acc. p. 256

FROM PLAY-PARTY GAMES OF PIONEER TIMES. PUBLISHED BY COOPERATIVE RECREATION SERVICE, INC. USED BY PERMISSION.

1. I went to town in a lit-tle red wag-on,

Come back home with the hub a-drag-gin',

It's no-bod-y's busi-ness what I do.

It's no-bod-y's busi-ness, busi-ness,

No-bod-y's busi-ness, busi-ness,

No-bod-y's busi-ness what I do.

2. I've got a wife and she's a daisy,
   She won't work and I'm too lazy,
   It's nobody's business what I do. *Refrain*

Add the tone color of one of the parts on page 135

as others sing this song.

134 Tone Color

SINGING GAME for "Nobody's Business"

Verse: All join hands in a circle. Three children, the
leaders, stand in the center. During the verse the circle
moves counterclockwise as children walk the steady beat.
As the verse comes to an end (the cadence), each leader
"captures" two children from the circle (nine children are
now inside the circle).

Refrain: Each leader swings one of his or her "captives,"
snubbing the other one. Everyone else keeps time by
clapping hands. As the refrain comes to an end (the
cadence), the "swinging" children join the circle, leaving
the three "snubbed" children in the center. These children
are the new leaders as the game continues.

Which part will you play?

This part uses B A G only.

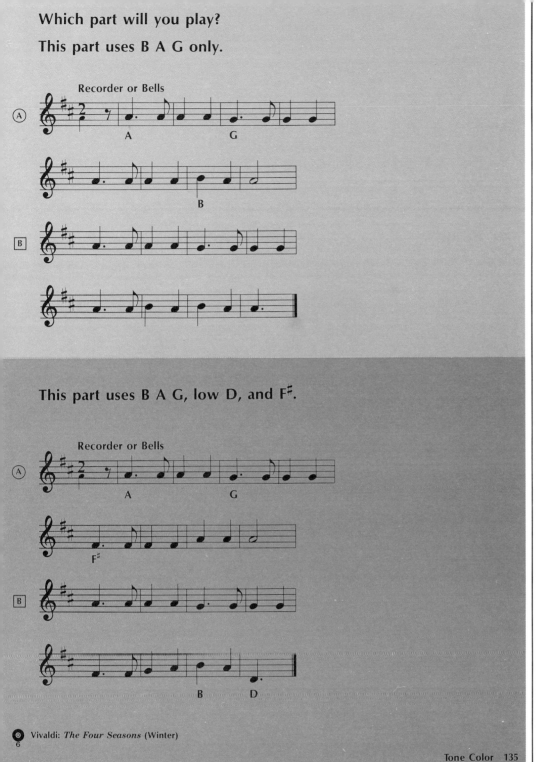

Recorder or Bells

This part uses B A G, low D, and F♯.

Recorder or Bells

Vivaldi: *The Four Seasons* (Winter)

5. Play the recording of the Vivaldi piece (listed in Materials) and have children listen to hear how the string instruments are played. (They are played both by bowing and plucking.)

Suggestion: If schedules permit, you may want to invite string players in the community (private teachers, community orchestra members) to demonstrate how the violin works by showing various kinds of bowing as well as plucking. Ask visitors to play one of the children's favorite songs, as well as a characteristic piece for the instrument.

TRY THIS

The two instrumental parts notated on p. 135 will allow bell and recorder players to add other tone colors to an ensemble for "Nobody's Business." The first part uses three tones—G, A, and B; the second uses five tones—D, F♯, G, A, and B.

Encourage children to practice one of the parts on their own. When they are ready, have them add their part to the ensemble.

Suggestions for ensembles:
• Voices, Autoharp, bells
• Voices, recorder, Autoharp
• Voices, Autoharp, bells, recorder

TEACHER INFORMATION

For biographical information on Vivaldi, composer of *The Four Seasons*, see p. 113.

Mainstreaming: An adaptation of "Nobody's Business" appears in *Silver Burdett Music for Special Education.*

MATERIALS
Record 7, "German Instrument Song"; Pupil's Book, pp. 136 and 137; bells, violin, recorder, Autoharp, drum

VOCABULARY
tone color, harmony

IDEAS FOR TEACHING

1. Ask children to look at the pictures of instruments on p. 137. From left to right they show violin, recorder, drum, and Autoharp. (For a picture of bells, direct attention to p. 86.) Write the list of instruments on the chalkboard.

2. As children listen to the recording of "German Instrument Song," choose a child to number the list in the order in which the instruments are heard—bells, fiddle (violin), pipe (recorder), Autoharp, drum.

3. Play the recording of verse 1 only and have children follow the notation of the bell part to see how the tones move. Call attention to the repeated notes on the staff and to those that move in a downward direction.

4. Choose someone to line up the bells in the order F♯, G, A, and B. As others sing the song, let children try playing the bell part from the notation. The bell part starts on B.

5. Have several children each choose one of the other instrumental parts (notated on p. 137) to play during section B. Provide time for them to practice before trying to play the part within the song. <u>Note</u>: If a violin is not available, have children ⟶

Listen for the bell part in this song.

Do you see it in section A, or in section B? Section B

GERMAN INSTRUMENT SONG FOLK SONG FROM GERMANY
ENGLISH WORDS BY TULLA STATLER
Piano acc. p. 234

1. If I had a bell to play a tune on,
   If I had a bell, oh, how I'd *ring.*

2. If I had a fiddle, fiddle, fiddle,
   If I had a fiddle, how I'd *bow.*

3. If I had a pipe to play a tune on,
   If I had a pipe, oh, how I'd *blow.*

4. If I had an Autoharp to play on,
   If I had an Autoharp, I'd *strum.*

5. If I had a drum that I could play on,
   If I had a drum, oh, how I'd *beat.*

6. Now we have a tune to play together,
   Now we have a tune, oh, how we'll *play.*

136 Tone Color

Add the tone color of other instruments to the bell part in "German Instrument Song."

When the instruments play together, you hear *harmony*.

pretend to bow the rhythm of the part.

Suggestion: It is good practice to invite older children into the classroom to demonstrate orchestral instruments. Ask a violin player from an upper grade to play the violin part.

6. The final verse of the song suggests that the various instruments play together. Call attention to the harmony that results when the violin, recorder, or Autoharp part is added to the bell part, and when all the instruments play in verse 6.

TEACHER INFORMATION

Playing in an ensemble for "German Instrument Song" will be a new experience for many children. As in all ensembles, children should be aware of working together to create a blend of sound. Each part has a particular function. For instance, the Autoharp chords must be heard even though there are several other parts being played.

Make children aware of the dynamics—how loud or soft they should play to create a blend they and you are satisfied with.

MATERIALS
Record 7, *Call Chart 7: Tone Color;*
Pupil's Book, pp. 138 and 139

VOCABULARY
tone color

TEACHER INFORMATION

Call Chart 7, like other Call Charts in the book, is a teaching device to focus children's attention on a specific quality in music. On this Call Chart recording, children are led to hear a variety of tone colors. As they listen, have children match the sounds with the pictures on p. 139.

The music excerpts are heard in the following order:
1. *Old Bald Eagle* (dulcimer)
2. Ibert: *Divertissement,* "Parade" (bass drum)
3. Mozart: *Adagio and Fugue in C Minor,* K 546 (organ)
4. Ussachevsky: *Four Miniatures,* No. 1 (electronic instrument)
5. Satie: *Sports et Divertissements,* "Le Water-Chute" (piano)
6. Nielson: *Quintet Op. 43* (bassoon)
7. Rooker: *Horn in the West,* "Drum Theme" (timpani)
8. McHugh: *Vegetables II* (guitar)

CALL CHART 7: TONE COLOR

Some musical sounds are made by voices.

Others are made by instruments.

When a number is called, look at the pictures

to discover how the sound is made.

Match the sounds with the pictures.

1. The *dulcimer* is strummed, plucked, or struck with mallets.

2. The *bass drum* is struck.

3. To play the *organ,* the player strikes the keys;
   a machine blows air across and through the pipes.

4. In an electronic laboratory, electric machines make sounds.

5. The player strikes the keys of the *piano.*
   Hammers then strike the strings. Sometimes the player may strike, pluck, or strum the strings without using the keys.

6. The *bassoon* is played by blowing.

7. The *timpani* are struck with mallets.

8. A *guitar* can be strummed or plucked.
   Sometimes the player strikes the body of the guitar.

Old Bald Eagle
Ibert: "Parade"
Mozart: *Adagio and Fugue in C Minor*
Ussachevsky: *Four Miniatures No. 1*

Ibert: "Le Water-Chute"
Nielson: *Quintet Op. 43*
Rooker: *Horn in the West,* "Drum Theme"
McHugh: *Vegetables II*

138   Tone Color

Whenever possible, use community resources. It would be enriching for children to visit an electronic studio; go to a high school orchestra or band concert; visit a local church to see how an organ is played, etc.

A sound/color filmstrip titled "A Youth Orchestra" is included in *Silver Burdett Music: Sound/Color Filmstrips,* which focuses on the tone colors of the orchestra.

Picture 1 on p. 139 shows Jean Richie playing a mountain dulcimer. She recorded the first excerpt in *Call Chart 7.*

The American mountain dulcimer is a homemade instrument that looks like an elongated violin. It is held across the knees, with the neck at the player's left. The tone is produced by brushing a sharpened turkey quill or a wooden pick back and forth across the strings (unlike the European dulcimer, which is played with mallets).

Jean Richie is also a collector of folk songs. See "Skin and Bones," p. 52.

MATERIALS

Record 7, "Forty-Nine Angels";
Pupil's Book, p. 140; Autoharp, bells,
triangle

VOCABULARY

tone color

IDEAS FOR TEACHING

1. Play the recording of "Forty-Nine
Angels" and have children follow the
chord letter names—F, C₇, Bᵇ—in the
music.

2. After they know the song, let
children try accompanying it on the
Autoharp. For each letter, they will
continue to strum the chord until
they come to a different letter in the
music. Some children may need help
in following the letters. Write the
chord names on the chalkboard and
point to them to lead children in
playing the right chord at the right
time.

3. When children are able to change
from one chord to another, have
them create a two-measure
strumming pattern of their own. For
example:

FORTY-NINE ANGELS

WORDS AND MUSIC BY ROBERT SCHMERTZ

FROM A PICTURE BOOK OF SONGS AND BALLADS BY ROBERT SCHMERTZ USED BY PERMISSION

Orff acc. p. 287

For-ty-nine an-gels look-ing down, Sev-en all a-round a gold-en crown,
For-ty-nine an-gels look-ing down, Sev-en weav-ing lin-en for a gown,

Sev-en with a harp and sev-en with a horn Play for the Ba-by
Sev-en to em-broid-er, sev-en to a-dorn A dress for the Ba-by

new-ly born, Play for the Ba-by new-ly born.
new-ly born, A dress for the Ba-by new-ly born.

And where are the rest of the for-ty-nine? One takes a star, makes it

bright-ly shine; Two tell the news o-ver Gal-i-lee;

Three show the way to the Wise Men three; And lit-tle For-ty-Nine this

bless-ed morn Sings for the Ba-by new-ly born,

Sings for the Ba-by new-ly born.

140

TRY THIS

Some children can add the tone colors of bells and
triangle to the voice and Autoharp parts. (Bell and triangle
parts are notated at the right.)

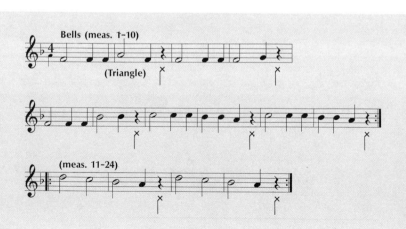

When each number is called, decide what tone color you hear.

Listen. Then circle your answer.

1	*TRUMPET AND TROMBONE*	(*FLUTE*)	*CLARINET*	*AUTOHARP*
2	*TRUMPET AND TROMBONE*	*FLUTE*	(*CLARINET*)	*AUTOHARP*
3	*TRUMPET AND TROMBONE*	*FLUTE*	*CLARINET*	(*AUTOHARP*)
4	(*TRUMPET AND TROMBONE*)	*FLUTE*	*CLARINET*	*AUTOHARP*
5	*TRUMPET AND TROMBONE*	*FLUTE*	(*CLARINET*)	*AUTOHARP*

Debussy: *Syrinx*
Mozart: *Concerto for Clarinet and Orchestra*, K. 622, "Adagio"
Eddleman: *Autoharp Sound Piece*
Gabrieli: *Canzona Noni Toni*
Messiaen: *Abyss of the Birds*

Tone Color   141

TONE COLOR • Lesson 10

MATERIALS
Record 7, *What Do You Hear? 9: Tone Color;* spirit master

VOCABULARY
tone color

TEACHER INFORMATION

In *What Do You Hear? 9,* children are asked to identify different instrumental tone colors. Before they listen to the recording, play the recording of *Tone Colors of Wind Instruments* (p. 127) and call attention to the photographs of trombone, trumpet, flute, and clarinet on p. 127.

TRY THIS

Some children may be interested in creating their own What Do You Hear? charts, using other instrumental compositions in their book. For example, they could choose four or five selections from the following list:

- Anonymous: *Dadme Albricias, Hijos d'Eva* (recorders), p. 26
- Bull: *In Nomine* (recorders), p. 106
- Locke: *Courante* (recorders), p. 106
- Smith: *Three Brevities for Solo Flute* (flute), p. 33
- Ibert: *Entre'acte* (flute and guitar), p. 43
- Sor: *Variations on a Theme by Mozart* (guitar), p. 33
- Locke: *Saraband* (brass), p. 73
- Purcell: *Trumpet Tune* (brass), p. 91
- Pinto: *Run Run* (piano), p. 93
- Chopin: *Scherzo No. 3 in C Sharp Minor* (piano), p. 111
- Handel: *Water Music,* "Air," Version 1 (strings), p. 41
- Vivaldi: *The Four Seasons* (Winter) (strings), p. 113
- Reimer: *Speed of the Beat* (synthesizer), p. 42
- Kingsley: *Piece in Two Meters* (synthesizer), p. 64

MODULE 14

OBJECTIVES, p. xiii

STYLE: Classic/Rock

MATERIALS
Record 7, Mozart: *Horn Concerto in E♭ Major,* Movement 3; Phillips: *California Dreamin';* Pupil's Book, pp. 142 and 143

VOCABULARY
style

IDEAS FOR TEACHING

1. Direct attention to the photographs on p. 142. Questions: Which are the old cars? Which are the new cars? (Encourage discussion: The old cars look old-fashioned; the new cars have a modern, sleek look.) Do the older cars have fenders? (Yes) Do the modern cars have fenders? (Yes) Do both styles of cars have headlights? (Yes) Point out: Both styles of cars use many of the same things, but each style looks different.

2. Point out that music can be in different styles even though some of the same things are used. Play the Mozart piece (see Materials) and have children follow the Mozart chart on p. 143 as they listen. If necessary, help children to read the words in each item of the chart so they will understand the musical qualities they will be listening for (steady beat, beats moving in twos, etc.).

3. Play the Phillips piece and have children follow the Phillips chart on p. 143. Point out: Aside from different instruments and the use of
→

TEACHER INFORMATION

Wolfgang Amadeus Mozart (Austrian, 1756–1791) *Horn Concerto in E♭ Major,* Movement 3: This child genius (he began composing when he was four years old) fulfilled all his youthful potential. In his short life he composed enduring music that is the essence of classic style. His works range from light and entertaining to the most profound.

usic has styles, too.

ow many of these things
n you hear
 a piece in *classic style?*

Mozart: *Horn Concerto in E♭*

STEADY BEAT

BEATS MOVING
IN TWOS

LONG AND SHORT
PHRASES

TONAL
(FOCUSES ON THE
IMPORTANT TONE)

MELODY
WITH HARMONY

TONE COLOR:
FRENCH HORN AND
ORCHESTRA

Listen to another piece.

**Do you think it is
in the same style,
or does it sound different?**

Phillips: *California Dreamin'*

1 STEADY BEAT

2 BEATS MOVING
  IN TWOS

3 LONG AND SHORT
  PHRASES

  TONAL
4 (FOCUSES ON ONE
  IMPORTANT TONE)

5 MELODY
  WITH HARMONY

  TONE COLOR:
6 BASS GUITAR, DRUMS,
  TRUMPETS, ORGAN, VOICES

voices, the Phillips piece uses many of the same qualities as the older piece. Yet it has its own special sound, or style, called *folk rock.* The Mozart piece is in a style called *classic.*

▪st as cars in different styles can have some of the same parts,

▪ieces of music in different styles can have some of the same parts.

▪he same parts can create a different look or sound, called *style.*

MODULE 14: Style—Classic/Rock 143

TEACHER INFORMATION

The period in music's history from around 1750 to 1800 was called the Classic period. Mozart and Haydn were the two major composers of that time. Their music has clear forms, regular phrases, simple yet very sophisticated melodies, and regular meters.

There are many styles of popular rock music, ranging from the hard-driving, dissonant *acid rock* to the perky, easy-to-bounce-to *bubble-gum rock.* Folk rock retains its connection to the simplicity and directness of folk songs, while adding the typical rock rhythmic drive and more elaborate accompaniment.

MODULE 15

OBJECTIVES, p. xiii

PHRASES • Lesson 1

MATERIALS
Record 7, "How D'ye Do and Shake Hands"; Hovhaness: *Fantasy on Japanese Woodprints; Paper I; April Fool's Day;* Pupil's Book, pp. 144 and 145

VOCABULARY
long and short phrases, steady beat

IDEAS FOR TEACHING
1. Play the recording of "How D'ye Do and Shake Hands" and ask children to follow along in their book to discover the long and short phrases in the song. The phrase marks (⁀) will tell them that phrases 1–4 are long, and that phrases 5–8 are short. Note: On the recording, phrases 5–8 are sung four times. The first two times, the lower notes are sung at the end; the last two times, the upper notes are sung. Also, dialogue occurs before the first and second repetitions.

2. As preparation for the dance for "How D'ye Do and Shake Hands" (directions below), have partners face and shake hands throughout each short phrase (phrases 5–8). If children keep time to the steady beat, there will be four handshakes for each short phrase. Note: In the dance, children will move to both long and short phrases of the song.

3. After children have moved to "How D'ye Do and Shake Hands," play the recording of the Hovhaness piece (see ⟶

Music has long and short phrases. Follow the long and short phrase lines as you listen to this song.

HOW D'YE DO AND SHAKE HANDS

MUSIC BY OLIVER WALLACE

WORDS BY CY COBEN
© 1951 WALT DISNEY MUSIC COMPANY. REPRINTED BY PERMISSION.

Piano acc. p. 254

You go through life and nev-er know the day when fate may bring

A sit-u-a-tion that will prove to be em-bar-rass-ing.

Your face gets red, you hide your head, and wish that you could die,____

But that's old-fash-ioned, here's a new thing you should real-ly try.

Say "How d' ye do" and shake hands, Shake hands, shake hands,

Say "How d' ye do" and shake hands, State your name and bus'-ness.

*Sing from here to the end four times.

144 MODULE 15: Phrases

DANCE DIRECTIONS

Partners stand side by side in a circle, facing the center, leaders to left of their partners.

Phrase 1: All leaders walk to center of circle (4 beats), turn around and walk back to place (4 beats).

Phrase 2: Their partners do the same.

Phrase 3. Partners face each other. With right hands joined, circle once around. Be sure to get back to original place, facing partner, by end of phrase (8 beats).

Phrase 4: With left hands joined, circle once around. Be sure to get back to original place, facing partner, by end of phrase (8 beats).

Phrase 5: Shake right hands throughout phrase.

Phrase 6: Shake left hands throughout phrase.

Phrase 7: Shake right hands throughout phrase.

Phrase 8: Shake left hands throughout phrase.

Music has phrases. Poems have phrases, too.

PAPER I 🔊

Paper is two kinds, to write on, to wrap with.

If you like to write, you write.

If you like to wrap, you wrap.

Some papers like writers, some like wrappers.

Are you a writer or a wrapper?

Carl Sandburg

APRIL FOOL'S DAY 🔊

Look out! Look out! You've spilt the ink.
You're sitting in a purple puddle.
Your pants are ripped and I should think
You'd hate to have a nose so pink
And hair in such a dreadful muddle.

Look out! Behind you there's a rat.
He's hiding now behind the stool.
He's going to jump upon your hat.
Look out! Watch out! Oh dear, what's THAT?
It's only you, you April fool!

Marnie Pomeroy

Phrases   145

Materials) and ask children to decide whether the phrases are all the same length or different lengths. (The phrase lengths are different—some longer, some shorter.)

4. Phrases help music to be organized. Poems have phrases, too. Some phrases have strong endings, giving a strong feeling of coming to a resting place. Some have weak endings. Play the recording of the two poems listed in Materials and have children listen for the strong and weak endings. (If necessary, relate the notion of strong and weak to the rise and fall of the voice—it remains higher at a weak ending and falls at a strong ending.)

TEACHER INFORMATION

Alan Hovhaness (American, 1911–) *Fantasy on Japanese Woodprints:* This composer is influenced by his Armenian heritage. He has also used elements of music from India and the Orient, as in his *Fantasy on Japanese Woodprints.*

MATERIALS

Record 8, "Hawaiian Rainbows";
Pupil's Book, p. 146

VOCABULARY

phrase, cadence

IDEAS FOR TEACHING

1. Play the recording of "Hawaiian Rainbows" and ask children to follow the phrase marks (⌒) in their book as they listen. The phrase marks will help them *see* as well as hear that the phrases are all the same length.

2. To help them feel the phrase lengths, have children make the motions that go with the song. (See directions in the music.)

3. While some do the motions, have other children sing and listen especially for the end of each phrase. This is called a *cadence.*
Note: Help children hear that phrases 1 and 3 end on a weak cadence. A weak cadence gives the same feeling as a comma in language (a pause). Phrases 2 and 4 end on a strong cadence. A strong cadence gives the same feeling as a period (a full stop).

REVIEW/REINFORCEMENT

Call attention to the rhythm pattern of each phrase—the pattern is the same throughout.

HAWAIIAN RAINBOWS

HAWAIIAN FOLK SONG   Piano acc. p. 232

Dance Directions
Children kneel and sit low on their heels. They stretch both arms out to the left with fingers pointing up and palm facing out.

Ha - wai - ian rain - bows,   white clouds roll by;

Slowly swing arms over the head from left to right to show the shape of a rainbow.   Swing arms back from right to left. At the same time, roll one hand over the other to show clouds.

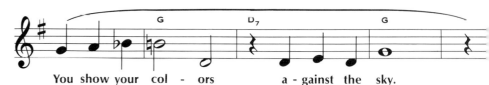

You show your col - ors   a - gainst the sky.

Swing arms from left to right. At the same time, make a rippling motion with the fingers as if pointing to all the colors of the rainbow.   Raise both hands high to the right (palms up). Move the left hand "across the sky" to the left side.

Ha - wai - ian rain - bows,   it seems to me,

Slowly swing arms over the head from left to right to show the shape of a rainbow.   Place the right hand under the left elbow and point the index finger of the left hand toward the chest ("It seems to me").

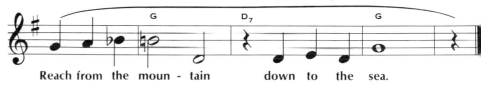

Reach from the moun - tain   down to the sea.

Raise both hands high to the left.   Slowly lower hands toward the right knee and continue moving them out to the right ("Down to the sea").

YOU CAN'T MAKE A TURTLE COME OUT

WORDS AND MUSIC BY MALVINA REYNOLDS   © COPYRIGHT 1962 BY SCHRODER MUSIC CO. (ASCAP) USED BY PERMISSION.   Piano acc. p. 261

1. You can't make a tur - tle come out,

146 Phrases

TRY THIS

Some children can accompany "Hawaiian Rainbows" on the Autoharp. They can follow the chord letter names—G, D₇, C—in the music. They will start on the first syllable of *rainbows,* and continue to strum the chord until they come to a different letter.

Have them try strumming one chord per measure; two chords per measure. Help them experiment to discover ways to make an interesting accompaniment. For example, when playing two chords per measure, have children strum

only the low strings for the first chord, only the high strings for the second.

Also, have a variety of picks—metal, plastic, rubber (a wedge-shaped rubber doorstop can be used), felt, etc.—available so that children can experiment to find the tone color most suitable for their accompaniment. Picks made of hard materials, like plastic, give a crisp sound; those made of soft materials, like felt, give a mellow sound.

You can't make a tur-tle come out,

You can call him or coax him or shake him or shout,

But you can't make a tur-tle come out, come out,

You can't make a tur-tle come out.

If he wants to stay in his shell, (*2 times*)

You can knock on the door but you can't ring the bell,

And you can't make a turtle come out, come out,

You can't make a turtle come out.

Be kind to your four-footed friends, (*2 times*)

A poke makes a turtle retreat at both ends,

And you can't make a turtle come out, come out,

You can't make a turtle come out.

So you'll have to patiently wait, (*2 times*)

And when he gets ready he'll open the gate,

But you can't make a turtle come out, come out,

You can't make a turtle come out.

And when you forget that he's there, (*2 times*)

He'll be walking around with his head in the air,

But you can't make a turtle come out, come out,

You can't make a turtle come out.

Phrases 147

MATERIALS
Record 8, "You Can't Make a Turtle Come Out"; Pupil's Book, pp. 146 and 147; woodblock

VOCABULARY
short and long phrases

IDEAS FOR TEACHING

1. Play the recording of "You Can't Make a Turtle Come Out" and have children follow the phrase marks in their book as they listen. <u>Point out</u>: Phrases 1, 2, and 4 are short; phrase 3 is long.

2. Play the recording again and have children trace the phrases in the air (from left to right for each phrase). This will help them feel the phrase lengths.

3. To reinforce the concept of short and long phrases, children can play a woodblock on the last word of each phrase.

4. Show long and short phrases for other songs children know by using long and short phrase marks. For example:

"Battle Hymn of the Republic," p. 131

<u>Note</u>: Long and short phrases are clearly indicated in this module for the purpose of teaching the concept. There may be some differences of opinion, however, because phrasing in performance is a matter of personal preference.

TRY THIS

Have children take turns playing the melody of the last phrase on bells. Help them analyze the way the tones move. (Except for the small leap from G down to E, the tones move upward, then downward by step.)

Play the last phrase, ending in an upward direction. (The melody moves upward, then downward, then upward

again by step. There are no leaps.)

When the last phrase is played or sung both ways (in contrasting directions) at the same time, children will hear harmony.

MATERIALS
Pupil's Book, pp. 148 and 149;
Autoharp, bells, gong or cymbal

VOCABULARY
long and short phrases, loud and
soft, sound and silence

IDEAS FOR TEACHING
1. Before making up their own
sound piece using the suggestions
on p. 148, children should have had
the experience of measuring the
length of phrases in songs such as
"Che che koolay," p. 34, or
"Hawaiian Rainbows," p. 146.

2. Have children make up their own
phrase, using sounds suggested in
their book—Autoharp, bells, gong or
cymbal.

3. Encourage children to make up a
phrase of sound using other
instruments. A piano with damper
pedal depressed may be substituted
for the Autoharp; piano keyboard
may be substituted for bells; bongos
may be substituted for gong or
cymbal.

4. After children have had the
experience of playing a phrase of
sound, have them create a phrase of
silence by pretending to play the
instrument. Then have them
combine phrases of sound and
silence to create a sound piece of
their own. For example:

1. Sound   Sound   Silence
2. Sound   Silence   Sound

Make up your own phrase of sound by following one of the parts below.

Make the phrase as long or as short as you wish.

On Autoharp

Strum from left to right.   *Pluck* a high string and let it ring.   *Pluck* a low string and let it ring.   *Stop sound* with your hand or arm.

On bells

Strike two high bells loud.   *Strike* two low bells soft.   *Strike* two high bells loud.   *Strike* highest and lowest bells soft.

On gong or cymbal

Strike loud.   *Strike* soft.   *Keep hitting* with mallet to make sound last.   *Snap* fingers against gong.

148   Phrases

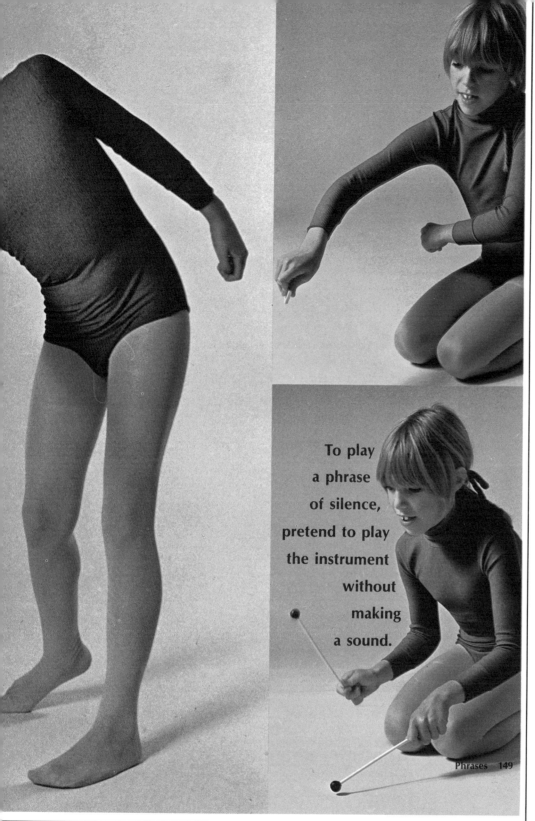

To play
a phrase
of silence,
pretend to play
the instrument
without
making
a sound.

Phrases 149

REVIEW/REINFORCEMENT

Children have shown long and short phrases through movement. You may want to review phrases in one or two of the following songs.
• Che che koolay, p. 34
• Boil Them Cabbage Down, p. 85
• Shepherds Came to Bethlehem, p. 120
• Hana ichi momme, p. 128
• How D'ye Do and Shake Hands, p. 144
• Hawaiian Rainbows, p. 146

MATERIALS

Pupil's Book, p. 150; Autoharp, bells, gong or cymbal

VOCABULARY

phrases, ABA form, sound and silence

TEACHER INFORMATION

Children can combine phrases of sound and silence to create a piece in ABA form.

Give children an opportunity to work out a *Sound and Silent Motion* sound piece of their own, using the suggestions on p. 150 in their book. They may want to substitute other instruments for Autoharp, bells, gong, or cymbal. Also, the player can alter the ABA plan shown in the Pupil's Book by switching the parts, using a silent phrase for the A sections and a phrase of sound for the B section.

When they are ready, let children perform for the class.

You have played a phrase of *sound* on the Autoharp, bells, gong, or cymbal.

Show a phrase of silence by pretending to play.

Now put the phrases together in ABA form.

SOUND PIECE 4: Sound and Silent Motion ELIZABETH CROOK

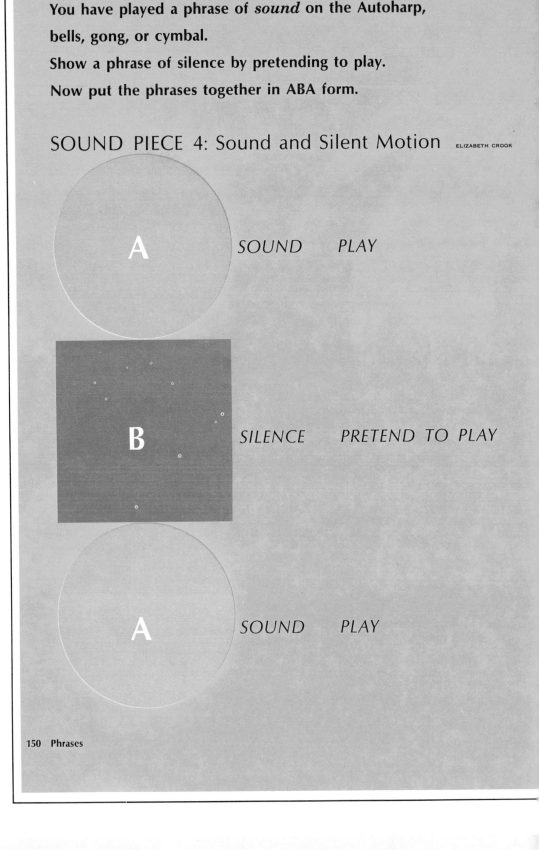

A   SOUND   PLAY

B   SILENCE   PRETEND TO PLAY

A   SOUND   PLAY

150   Phrases

Can you feel the length of the phrases in songs you know?

Listen for the number of phrases in each song.

Then look at the chart to see if you are right.

CALL CHART 8: PHRASES

1. *Oh, What a Beautiful City*	**FOUR**
2. *Join into the Game*	**FOUR**
3. *Oh, Susanna*	**SIX**
4. *Hana ichi momme*	**TWO**
5. *The Mad Man*	**ONE**

Phrases 151

PHRASES • Lesson 6

MATERIALS
Record 8, *Call Chart 8: Phrases;*
Pupil's Book, p. 151

VOCABULARY
phrases

TEACHER INFORMATION

Before children open their book, play the recording of *Call Chart 8* and have them decide how many phrases they hear in each of the five songs. Then play the recording again and have children follow the Call Chart to check their answers.

TRY THIS

Have children make up their own call chart, using songs they know. For example:

1. All the Pretty Little Horses (p. 49) FOUR

2. Valentine Round (p. 78) TWO

3. Battle Hymn of the Republic (p. 131) THREE

4. The Ghost of John (p. 71) FOUR

5. The Pig (p. 114) EIGHT

MATERIALS

Record 8, "Joyous Chanukah"; Pupil's Book, pp. 152 and 153; tambourine

VOCABULARY

phrase, strong cadence

IDEAS FOR TEACHING

1. Have children play the "Spin the Dreydl" game (directions below). Point out: When you play the game, you *see* the dreydl spin a certain length of time—sometimes short and sometimes long.

2. Point out that in music, you *hear* a phrase last a certain length of time. Play the recording of "Joyous Chanukah" and have children listen for the phrases. Question: Are the phrases all the same length, or different lengths? (Same length—four measures each)

3. To accompany the singing, have children take turns playing the tambourine part on p. 152 in their book. Point out: Each phrase in the tambourine part ends with a "shake" (♪).

4. Play the recording again and ask children to listen for the phrase that ends with a strong cadence—a strong feeling of coming to rest. (The fourth, or last, phrase ends with a strong cadence.)

Note: You may want to review strong and weak cadences in "Join into the Game," p. 11, and "Hawaiian Rainbows," p. 146.

Follow the notes to help you see and hear which phrase ends with a strong cadence.

JOYOUS CHANUKAH

HEBREW FOLK SONG   ENGLISH WORDS BY PHYLLIS RESNICK

To accompany "Joyous Chanukah," add a tambourine or recorder part.

Tambourine

Play 4 times

Shake

Play steady beats.

Recorder or Bells

GAME

Children sit in a circle and take turns spinning the dreydl, a four-sided top with a Hebrew letter on each side. When the dreydl stops spinning and falls on one side, the Hebrew letter on the side facing up indicates whether the child wins or loses the pot. The game is usually played with toothpicks or candy as the stake. (*Nun*—lose all; *Gimmel*—take all; *Hay*—take half; *Shin*—add to the pot.) The Hebrew letters stand for *ness gadol haya sham*, which means "a great miracle happened then."

REVIEW/REINFORCEMENT

Children can review quarter, eighth, and half notes by playing the two recorder/bell parts notated in the Pupil's Book. The first part (p. 152) uses quarter notes only. The other part (p. 153) follows the rhythm of the words of the song, using quarter notes, half notes, and eighth notes.

quarter notes

half notes

eighth notes

...ay the rhythm of the words.

EBKA HORA   FOLK SONG FROM ISRAEL

BY PERMISSION OF © LAWSON-GOULD MUSIC PUBLISHERS, INC.

La la la la la la la la, *(clap)*

La la la la la la la la. *(clap)*

La la la la la la la · la la la,

La la la la la la la la. *(clap)*

Phrases 153

PHRASES • Lesson 8

MATERIALS
Record 8, "Debka hora"; Pupil's Book, p. 153; tambourine

VOCABULARY
phrases, strong and weak cadence

IDEAS FOR TEACHING
1. Play the recording of "Debka hora" and ask children to listen for the phrases. <u>Point out</u>: "Debka hora" has three phrases. The first two are each two measures long; the last one is four measures long.

2. Play the recording again and ask children to listen for the weak and strong cadences. (Phrase 1 is weak; phrases 2 and 3 are strong.)

3. When children sing the song, have them clap (as indicated in the music) at the end of phrases. <u>Suggestion</u>: Children can play the "claps" on an instrument such as a tambourine.

4. Here is a bell or Orff-instrument part to play throughout the song. (If Orff instruments are available, children can use the alto or bass xylophones.)

5. When children know the song well, have them try it as a two-part round. The parts sung together make *harmony.*

DANCE DIRECTIONS

To dance a simple hora, have children practice this pattern throughout the song:

Step, hop, step, hop

When they can step-hop in time with the steady beat, have them try dancing in a line of eight or nine children. Each child places his or her *right* hand on the *left* shoulder of the person directly in front. The child at the head of the line leads the line wherever there is adequate room.

TEACHER INFORMATION

<u>Mainstreaming</u>: Non-ambulatory children and those with motor difficulty may accompany the dance on classroom instruments or by clapping, emphasizing the ends of phrases.

MATERIALS

Record 8, "Shepherds, Bring Candy and Milk"; Pupil's Book, p. 154; triangle or finger cymbals, bells

VOCABULARY

phrases, strong and weak cadence, steady beat

IDEAS FOR TEACHING

1. Play the recording and have children decide how many phrases there are in the music. (There are four phrases.)

2. To help children feel the four phrases, let them take turns playing finger cymbals or triangle on the last word (beat) of each phrase as others sing along with the recording.

3. This time, have children listen for strong and weak cadences. (Phrases 1 and 4 have strong cadences; phrases 2 and 3 have weak cadences.)

4. Before children try playing the bell part notated at the bottom of this page, play the recording of the song and have children feel the steady beat by swaying from side to side or rocking back and forth. They will feel two beats in a measure throughout.

Point out. In the bell part, the bells are played on the steady beats.

SHEPHERDS BRING CANDY AND MILK

17TH-CENTURY CHRISTMAS SONG FROM BELGIUM   ENGLISH WORDS BY SALLI TERRI
FROM BELGIAN CHRISTMAS SONGS. SET I © 1971 BY LAWSON-GOULD MUSIC PUBLISHERS, INC. USED BY PERMISSION

Piano acc. p. 255

Shep-herds, bring can-dy and milk to the Child.

See lit-tle Je-sus cry - ing there.

Hang up your coats to keep out the wind.

Jo-seph is rock-ing the Ba-by so mild.

2. Mary and angels are singing a song,

There in the stable shabby and bare.

Joseph so weary comes from the stream.

He washed the swaddling clothes all the day long.

3. Mary and Jesus are lying there.

Joseph is gath'ring wood for the fire.

See how he tends to all of the chores.

He loves the Baby and Mary fair.

154 Phrases

BELL PART

If Orff instruments are available, this bell part can be played on the glockenspiel.

WHAT DO YOU HEAR? 10: PHRASES (CADENCE) 🎧

Can you hear strong and weak cadences in music?

Decide whether the phrase ends with a strong cadence or

a weak cadence. Listen, then circle your answer.

1 (STRONG)   WEAK

2 (STRONG)   WEAK

3 STRONG   (WEAK)

4 (STRONG)   WEAK

Join into the Game

1 STRONG   (WEAK)

2 (STRONG)   WEAK

3 STRONG   (WEAK)

4 (STRONG)   WEAK

5 STRONG   (WEAK)

6 (STRONG)   WEAK

Oh, Susanna

Phrases 155

PHRASES • Lesson 10

MATERIALS
Record 8, *What Do You Hear? 10: Phrases (Cadence)*; spirit master

VOCABULARY
phrase, strong cadence, weak cadence

TEACHER INFORMATION

In *What Do You Hear? 10*, children are asked to identify strong and weak cadences. Before they listen to the recording, make sure they understand the difference between strong and weak cadences. A strong cadence gives a strong feeling of coming to a resting place. A weak cadence gives an "unfinished" feeling as though there is more music to come.

If necessary, review the poems on p. 145 (a strong cadence gives the same feeling as a period in language—a full stop; a weak cadence gives the same feeling as a comma—a pause). You may also want to review the song, "Hawaiian Rainbows," and the activities suggested on p. 146.

When students complete this lesson, they are ready to take Test 2 for Book 3. Additional information about Silver Burdett Music Competency Tests is found in the introduction of this book.

MODULE 16

OBJECTIVES, p. xiii

THE ARTS: Varying a Subject

MATERIALS
Record 8, Stamitz: *Sonate for Viola d'amore and Viola* (theme); *Call Chart 9: Theme and Variations;* Pupil's Book, pp. 156 and 157

VOCABULARY
variation, varying a subject

IDEAS FOR TEACHING
1. Ask children to look at the four paintings in their book. Questions: All of the paintings are of the same man. Do you know who he is? (George Washington) Each is a picture of the same man, but what makes the paintings different? (Three show the face and the upper part of the body and one is a full figure; each has a different combination of colors; two face right and two face left; the painting at the lower right is not finished. Point out: The subject of these paintings is George Washington. Each painting is a *variation* of the same subject—a different way of presenting the same thing.

2. Have children listen to a subject in music—a melody idea called a *theme.* (Usually *subject* and *theme* are used interchangeably.) Play the theme of Stamitz's *Sonate.* Question: Do you recognize it? (The theme is a melody from France. We sing it in this country, with slight changes, with the words *For he's a jolly good fellow* or *The bear went over the mountain.*

3. Play *Call Chart 9,* helping children →

TEACHER INFORMATION

Edward Savage (American, 1761-1817)   *George Washington,* upper left;
Gilbert Stuart (American, 1775-1828)   *George Washington,* upper and lower right;
John Trumbull (American, 1756-1843)   *General George Washington at the Battle of Trenton,* lower left.

Each of these American artists captured a somewhat different glimpse of their famous leader: Savage's aristocratic aspect, Trumbull's man of action, Stuart's more human aspect. Each painting uses a different background and colors, and each presents a different dimension of the complex human being Washington was.

Look at the paintings of George Washington.

What makes the paintings different?

Listen to a subject in music, called a *theme*.

Stamitz: *Sonate for Viola d'amore and Viola* (theme)

Now listen to the same theme played in several different ways.

As each number is called, look at the chart.

It will help you hear many variations of this same subject.

CALL CHART 9: THEME AND VARIATIONS

1. *SUBJECT*	*LOUD, FAST*	
2. *FIRST VARIATION*	*CHANGE OF RHYTHM PATTERNS*	
3. *SECOND VARIATION*	*SOFT, SLOW*	
4. *THIRD VARIATION*	*VERY FAST, MANY SHORT NOTES*	

Stamitz: *Sonate for Viola d'amore and Viola*

MODULE 16: The Arts—Varying a Subject   157

---

follow as the subject and three variations of it are heard.

4. Point out: In painting, a subject can be varied by using differences in shape, line, and color. In music, a subject (theme) can be varied by changing tempo (fast-slow), dynamics (loud-soft), register (high-low), etc.

TRY THIS

1. Children can try varying a story subject. Present an idea: "Tom's mother gave him some money and asked him to go to the store to get some milk. On the way he lost the money. He didn't know what to do. So he . . ." Children can take turns starting the story in their own words and finishing it with their own ending.

2. Choose a familiar song. After they have sung the song, ask children how it might be varied. Suggestions: Try singing it louder, softer, faster, slower, more smoothly (legato), more detached (staccato). Try using different accompaniments—clapping, foot tapping, playing percussion instruments, etc. Each new way will be a variation of the song.

3. To reinforce the idea of variation, call attention to the other visuals: The composer photographs on p. 58 have the same subject—a composer at work. Each photograph is a variation of that subject. The automobile photographs on p. 142 are also variations of the same subject.

TEACHER INFORMATION

Karl Stamitz (German, 1745–1801)   *Sonate for Viola d'amore and Viola,* "Andante con Variozione": Stamitz was the son of a famous composer (Johann Stamitz, 1717–1757) who helped establish the Classic style. Karl was a virtuoso string player—viola and violin. (The name *viola d'amore* may refer to the instrument's scroll, which usually was carved like a blindfolded face resembling that of the god Amor.) Karl Stamitz composed much instrumental music, including more than seventy symphonies.

MODULE 17

OBJECTIVES, p. XIV

THE ARTS: Focus, No Focus

MATERIALS
Pupil's Book, pp. 158 and 159

TEACHER INFORMATION

The photographs on pp. 158 and 159 in the Pupil's Book can be used to introduce the lesson, *The Arts: Focus, No Focus,* that begins on p. 160.

In the picture on p. 158, your eyes are drawn to one place—the center—where the head's of the dolls converge. In this picture, the dolls' heads focus on one specific place.

In the picture on p. 159, your eyes tend to wander around with no one focus to go to.

<u>Note:</u> The Guatemalan miniature dolls that are used in the photographs are approximately one inch high. They are made of bits of wire and fabric with colorful threads wrapped around the wire to form the arms and legs. The costumes are indicative of the costumes of the men and women in the Indian tribes who make them.

The dolls come from Chickecastenango, the central market of Guatemala where Indians gather twice a week for market day. Some of the people who sell their wares there travel on foot for two days to reach the market, carrying their wares in giant bundles on their backs, or heads.

Look at the paintings on the
next two pages. Can you *see* which painting
has a center of interest? Some music has focus.
Some does not. Can you hear which piece of music has focus?

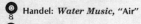 Handel: *Water Music,* "Air"
Ives: *The Cage*

In painting, *focus* refers to a
center of interest for your
eyes to see. In music, *focus* refers to a
sound for your ears to hear.

THE ARTS: Focus, No Focus

MATERIALS
Record 8, Handel: *Water Music*,
"Air"; Ives: *The Cage*; Pupil's Book,
pp. 160 and 161

VOCABULARY
focus, no focus, center of interest,
tonal center

IDEAS FOR TEACHING
1. Ask children to look at the two
paintings on pp. 160 and 161. (The
painting on p. 160 extends a little
into p. 161.) Point out: In one of the
paintings (p. 161), your eyes are
drawn to one place—a center of
interest, or focus. In the other, your
eyes wander around with no one
focus to go to. Questions: Which
painting has a focus? Which does
not? (Balla's *Street Light*, p. 161, has
a focus on the yellow oval shape.
Pollock's *Number 27*, p. 160, is
without one central focal point.)

2. Point out: Just as your eyes can
see a focus, your ears can *hear* a
focus. If the tones of a melody lead
your ears to hear one of them as the
most important, that one tone
becomes the focus tone of the
music. (Some music does not use a
focus tone—all the tones are equally
important. That kind of music
sounds very different.)

3. Play the recording of the Handel
piece, then the Ives piece, and ask
children to listen to hear which of
these two pieces has a focus and
which does not. (The Handel piece
has a strong tonal center. Almost
every phrase ends on the keynote,
giving a feeling of "arrival"—of a
"resting place." The Ives piece has
no such ⟶

The Arts: Focus/No Focus

TEACHER INFORMATION

Jackson Pollock (American, 1912–1956)   *Number 27*: The
name "abstract expressionist" well describes this artist and
the artistic movement of which he was a part—"abstract"
because there was nothing pictured, "expressionist"
because there was an attempt to allow for spontaneous
expression by quick, intuitive, somewhat random acts.
Pollock's technique was to dribble paint onto a canvas
stretched on the floor. However improvisational this may
be, the unfolding painting is controlled and guided by a
masterfully sensitive artist's eye. The result is a "structured
explosion."

Giacomo Balla (Italian, 1871–1958)   *Street Light*: This artist
was a futurist painter (the Futurists attempted to capture a
sense of action as a dynamic, moving thing—not "frozen" as
in paintings of the past). Balla tried to make the flat
surface radiate with compelling movement. Even a still
scene such as a streetlight at night can give an experience
of pulsating energy.

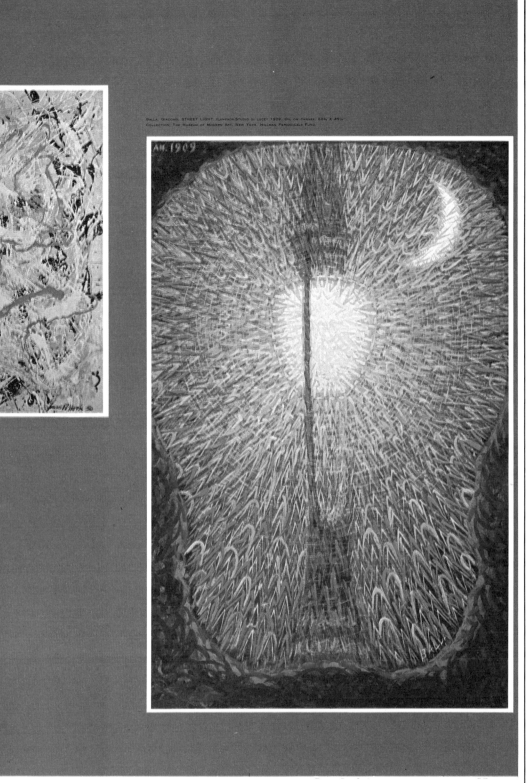

BALLA, GIACOMO. STREET LIGHT (LAMPADA STUDIO DI LUCE) 1909. OIL ON CANVAS. 68¾" X 45¼".
COLLECTION: THE MUSEUM OF MODERN ART, NEW YORK. HILLMAN PERIODICALS FUND.

strong keynote. The music wanders, with no single resting place for the ears.)

TRY THIS

1. Ask children to look for pictures and photographs that have a strong center of interest, or no strong center of interest. Discuss how the eyes are helped to see the difference.

2. Children can create their own visuals to show a strong focus and no focus by painting different shapes of different colors and arranging them on a neutral background.

REVIEW/REINFORCEMENT

Have children sing two or three of the following songs, holding back the final tone a few seconds and then "landing" on it to emphasize its function as a resting place or keytone for the song.
• On the First Thanksgiving Day, p. 56
• Marching to Pretoria, p. 4
• Ain't Gonna Rain, p. 24
• Battle Hymn of the Republic, p. 131
• Find the Ring, p. 62

TEACHER INFORMATION

For biographical material on George Frideric Handel, see p. 40.

Charles Ives (American, 1874–1954) *The Cage:* This New Englander (who spent his life in the insurance business) was an astonishingly original composer. He used very modern techniques years before most other composers even thought about them. His music often has a dissonant, angular, jagged quality, although this song uses only small steps.

Mainstreaming: Because of color blindness, students with visual and neurological impairments should be given paper with sharp contrasts of color. As diagonal lines and combinations of curved and straight lines are difficult for them to perceive, you may want to have them create a pattern based on triangles, circles, and squares already cut out for them.

MODULE 18

OBJECTIVES, p. xiv

TONALITY • Lesson 1

MATERIALS
Record 8, "The Mad Man"; Pupil's Book, pp. 162 and 163; bells

VOCABULARY
tonal center, phrase

IDEAS FOR TEACHING

1. Have children sing one of the following songs:

• Mama Paquita, p. 18
• Brother Noah, p. 6
• You Can't Make a Turtle Come Out, p. 146

2. Now have them sing just the last phrase (last line) of the song.
Point out: The melody has a focus on one particular tone. All the tones lead to the final tone, which makes the melody sound finished.

3. Choose a child to play the last phrase on the bells, leaving out the last tone—other children will sing the last tone to end the phrase.

4. Play the recording of "The Mad Man" and have children play the tone G on the bells on the last word of every verse. Point out: The whole melody seems to focus on the last tone, G. Music that focuses on one important tone, a center, is called *tonal music.* Music that does not focus on a tonal center is called *atonal music.* Each has its own special way of feeling. ——→

Play the important tone on the G bell at the end of every verse of this song.

Piano acc. p. 233

THE MAD MAN
AMERICAN FOLK TUNE   WORDS BY JEANNE WILHELMS

1. In old - en days there was a man
And he fell in a fry - ing pan.

2. The frying pan it was so nice
And he fell in a bag of ice.

3. The bag of ice it turned to slush
And he fell in a pan of mush.

4. The pan of mush it was so cold
And he fell in a pot of gold.

5. The pot of gold it was so rich
And he fell in a muddy ditch.

6. The muddy ditch it was so deep
And he fell in a flock of sheep.

7. The flock of sheep did moan and groan
And he fell in an ice-cream cone.

8. The ice-cream cone it was so sweet
And he fell on his own two feet.

162   Tonality

5. To reinforce the idea of a tonal center, have children play one of the bell parts on p. 163 in their book while others sing the song. For parts 1 and 2 they will need the low-G bell or the high-G bell. For parts 3 and 4 they will need both G bells.

TRY THIS

Have children make up original verses for "The Mad Man." Each time the rhyming word will be sung on the tone that is the tonal center. For example:

His own two feet were slippery
And he fell in the apple tree.

The apple tree did bend and shake
And he fell in a choc'late cake.

The choc'late cake he ate, they say,
And he fell into yesterday.

Play a bell part

throughout the song.

Try a different part

for each verse.

Notice the *focus* on the tone G,

both low G and high G.

163

MATERIALS

Record 8, "Ol' Clo'"; Hays: "Ol' Clo'"; Schoenberg: *Trio for Violin, Viola, and Cello;* Haydn: *Symphony No. 94,* Movement 2; Pupil's Book, pp. 164 and 165; bells, recorder

VOCABULARY

octave, scale, tone row, tonal music, atonal music

IDEAS FOR TEACHING

1. Have someone line up the bells from low G to high G as shown in the first bell diagram on p. 164—low G, A, B, C, D, E, F♯, high G.

2. Have children play all eight bells in order, from low G to high G, to hear and feel tones that pull to the final G. (The pull is intensified if there is a slight pause before the final tone.)

3. Have children play the bells in a downward direction, starting on high G. Point out: Children have played a *scale,* upward and downward. It is *tonal* because it focuses on one important tone—G.

4. Ask children to listen for the important tone—G—in the first version of "Ol' Clo'."

5. Now, have them sing and feel the important tone throughout the song. Suggestion: A bell part can be played to help focus on the tone G. Write the pattern on the chalkboard. (Some children may be able to play the pattern on the recorder.)

(4 times)
→

You have played low G and high G, an *octave,* to accompany "The Mad Man."

Now line up the bells from low G to high G. Feel the pull toward the final tone. You have played a scale.

Now line up these twelve bells as shown. You will need all the bells except high G.

Feel that there is *no* pull toward a final tone. You have played a *tone row.*

Play upward.
Play downward.

It is *tonal* because there is a *focus* on one important tone, G.

Play upward.
Play downward.

It is *atonal* because there is *no* focus on one important tone.

This song is *tonal.* Can you tell why?

OL' CLO' TRADITIONAL ROUND

FROM GIRL SCOUT SONG BOOK P. 91 AS PUBLISHED IN 1925 BY GIRL SCOUTS INC.

My un - cle he sells ol' clo',

He's a deal - er in chi - na, you know;

164 Tonality

TRY THIS

After the children know the traditional version of "Ol' Clo'" (p. 164), have them sing it as a two-part round. Each part focuses on the tone G.

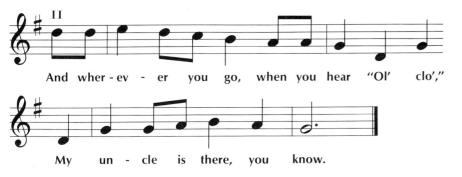

And wher-ev - er you go, when you hear "Ol' clo',"

My un - cle is there, you know.

Now listen to the recording. Do you *hear* what you *see?*

To hear how the melody focuses on the tone G, take turns playing the G bell throughout the song.

Make up your own rhythm pattern.

This song is *atonal.* Can you tell why?

L' CLO'

MUSIC BY DORIS HAYS   Piano acc. p. 246

mf My____ un - cle he sells ol' clo',

He's a deal - er in____ chi - na, you know;

And wher - ev - er you go, when you hear *rit.* "Ol'____ clo',"

a tempo My un - cle's there, *dim.* *mp* you know!

Now listen to the recording. Do you *hear* what you *see?*

6. Have someone line up twelve bells as shown in the second diagram—C♯, F♯, C, A, G, G♯, E, D♯, F, B, A♯, D.

7. Have children play the second bell arrangement upward and downward to hear sounds that do not focus on one tone. Point out: Children have played a *tone row.* It is *atonal* because there is no focus on one important tone.

8. Play the recording of the Hays version of "Ol' Clo'." Questions: Is the music tonal, or atonal? How do you know? (Atonal—the melody does not focus on one tone.)

9. Play the recording of the Schoenberg piece and the Haydn piece (listed in Materials) and ask children to tell which is tonal and which is atonal. (The Schoenberg is atonal; the Haydn is tonal.)

TEACHER INFORMATION

Arnold Schoenberg (Austrian, 1874-1951) *Trio for Violin, Viola, and Cello,* Op. 45: This composer invented a system of composing in which the traditional use of the scale was abandoned, each of the twelve scale tones now being of equal importance. Such music, called *atonal,* became one of the major styles in the 20th century, assuring Schoenberg of a place among the most influential of all composers.

Franz Joseph Haydn (Austrian, 1732-1809) *Symphony No. 94,* Movement 2: Along with Mozart, Haydn is the best known and most important composer of the Classic period (1750-1820). His symphonies (104 of them!) are models of classic form yet have a "special personality" that makes them very much his own.

MATERIALS
Record 8, "Twinkle, Twinkle, Little Star"; Eddleman: "Twinkle, Twinkle, Little Star"; Pupil's Book, p. 166; bells

VOCABULARY
tonal music, atonal music, ABA form

IDEAS FOR TEACHING
1. Before playing the recording of the traditional version of "Twinkle, Twinkle, Little Star," tell children that the form of the song is ABA. (The repetition of section A is indicated by *D.C. al Fine* [*Da Capo al Fine*—Dah Kah*poh ahl Fee*nay], which means "repeat from the beginning and continue to the word *Fine*.") Play the recording and ask children to follow the notation in their book as they listen.

2. Now have them sing along with the recording to feel the important tone, F, at the end of the A sections.

3. Have children take turns playing the last two measures of section A (*How I wonder what you are*) on the bells. This will help to focus on the important tone, F. Point out: The music is tonal because it focuses on one important tone.

4. Play the recording of Eddleman's version of "Twinkle, Twinkle, Little Star." Question: Is this music tonal—does it focus on one important tone? (No. The music is atonal—the melody does not focus on one tone.)

Listen to this old familiar song. It is *tonal*.

Can you tell why?

TWINKLE, TWINKLE, LITTLE STAR

Now listen to this "Twinkle, Twinkle, Little Star" song.

It is *atonal*. Can you tell why?

TWINKLE, TWINKLE, LITTLE STAR

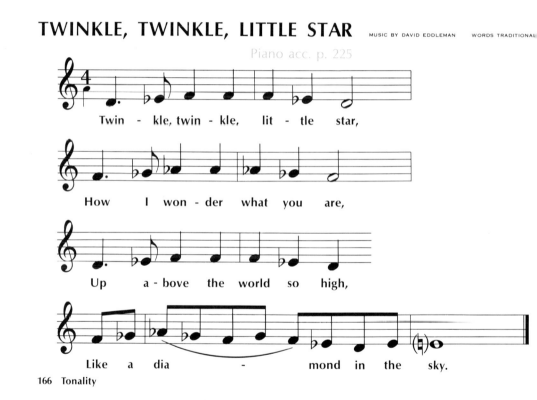

166 Tonality

TEACHER INFORMATION

For biographical material on David Eddleman, see p. 23.

WHAT DO YOU HEAR? 11: TONALITY

Some of the following pieces are *tonal* music.

Other pieces are *atonal* music.

As each number is called, decide whether the music is tonal, or atonal
Listen. Then circle what you hear.

1	(TONAL)	ATONAL	**Handel:** *Water Music,* "Air"
2	TONAL	(ATONAL)	**Schoenberg:** *Trio for Violin, Viola, Cello*
3	(TONAL)	ATONAL	**Ravosa:** *Love*
4	TONAL	(ATONAL)	**Hays:** *Ol' Clo'*
5	(TONAL)	ATONAL	**Mozart:** *Three German Dances,* No. 3
6	TONAL	(ATONAL)	**Subotnick:** *Touch*

Tonality   167

TONALITY • Lesson 4

MATERIALS
Record 8, *What Do You Hear? 11: Tonality;* spirit master

VOCABULARY
tonal music, atonal music

TEACHER INFORMATION

In *What Do You Hear? 11,* children are asked to identify music that is tonal and music that is atonal. Before they listen to the recording, make sure they know which symbol stands for tonal and which stands for atonal. In one drawing, the arrows pointing to one place direct the eyes to a focal point (tonal). In the other drawing, the arrows point in many directions—the eyes don't focus on any one place—atonal.

You may want to play the recording more than once so that children can feel confident when they make their responses on paper.

MODULE 19

OBJECTIVES, p. xiv

RHYTHM PATTERNS • Lesson 1

MATERIALS
Record 8, "Yesterday Morning";
Pupil's Book, pp. 168 and 169; drum,
maracas

VOCABULARY
steady beat, meter in 2, one sound
for each beat, two sounds for each
beat, quarter notes, eighth notes

IDEAS FOR TEACHING
1. Play the recording of "Yesterday
Morning." Have children feel the
steady beat by taking turns playing
the drum part on p. 169 in their
book. Point out that each quarter
note in the drum part lasts for one
beat. (They will play the notes with
stems down with the left hand, the
notes with stems up with the right
hand.) Questions: How many beats
are in each measure in the drum
part? (Two) Can you find lines that
separate the beats into sets of two?
(There is a bar line after every two
beats.)

2. Call attention to the meter
signature ($\frac{2}{4}$), which appears before
the first note of the drum part. The *2*
means there are two beats in each
measure. The *quarter note* means
that a quarter note lasts for one beat.

3. Ask children to sing the song (or
listen to the recording), feel the beat,
and play two sounds for each beat
on the maracas.

4. Ask children to look at the part
for maracas on p. 169. The maracas →

YESTERDAY MORNING
FOLK SONG FROM COLOMBIA

Piano acc. p. 259

ENGLISH WORDS BY JOAN GILBERT VAN POZNAK
FROM UNICEF BOOK OF CHILDREN'S SONGS, COMPILED AND WITH PHOTOGRAPHS BY WILLIAM I. KAUFMAN, COPYRIGHT 1970 BY WILLIAM I. KAUFMAN, PUBLISHED BY STACKPOLE BOOKS.

1. Oh, yes-ter-day at morn-ing, And then to-day at dawn,

Oh, yes-ter-day at morn-ing, And then to-day at dawn,

The tur-tle-doves were sing-ing, The roost-ers sang a-long,

REFRAIN
Ki-ki-ri, ki-ki-ri, I'm hap-py as can be;

Ki-ki-ri, ki-ki-ri, But who a-wak-en'd me?

2. The dogs for miles and miles
Were barking at the moon, } (2 times)
A silly goose was cackling,
And thought she sang a tune, *Refrain*

3. A heavy rain was falling,
And when it rains it pours, } (2 times)
With thunder, wind and lightning,
I wish I had some oars, *Refrain*

168 MODULE 19: Rhythm Patterns

TEACHER INFORMATION

Mainstreaming: To allow children with non-functioning
limbs and extremities to participate, have them do the
singing. Those with motor difficulties may feel the beat
silently and accompany the singing by clapping or tapping
two sounds per beat instead of playing the maracas.

How many sounds do the maracas play for each of the drum beats?

Which instrument will you play

to accompany the song "Yesterday Morning"?

Drum

Maracas

Listen to the instruments that accompany the song "Lemons"

on page 170. How many can you hear?

Guiro

Autoharp

Woodblock

Which instruments play the beat?

Which instrument plays the beat divided in three?

Take turns playing one of the parts with the recording as others sing.

Find the sign that shows that each measure has two beats.

Rhythm Patterns 169

---

part shows the sounds children have just played—two sounds for each beat. Help children practice playing two sounds for each beat as they sing the song.

5. Ask children to tell how the drum part and the part for maracas are different. (The drum part shows one sound for each beat—written as a quarter note. The maracas part shows two sounds for each beat—written as eighth notes.)

6. While some children play the drum part, others can play the maracas part. This can be done while children sing the song, or while the recording is played.

Suggestion: Although this module focuses on rhythm patterns, take time to reinforce other concepts. Ask children to listen for and look at the phrasing in "Yesterday Morning." Questions: How many phrases are there? (Five) Which ones are alike? (Phrase 2 is like phrase 1. Phrase 5 is like phrase 4.)

TRY THIS

1. Using a guiro or another percussion instrument, children can play a pattern of quarter notes and eighth notes throughout "Yesterday Morning." For example:

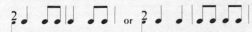

2. Select children to practice an Autoharp accompaniment. They will use the D, A₇, and G chords. Suggest that they strum quarter notes—one sound for each beat.

3. Here is a bell or recorder part that children can play to accompany the refrain of "Yesterday Morning":

A   D   D   G

MATERIALS
Record 8, "Lemons"; Pupil's Book, pp. 169–171; guiro, Autoharp, woodblock

VOCABULARY
steady beat, meter signature $\frac{2}{\cdot}$ two beats in a measure, three sounds for each beat

IDEAS FOR TEACHING

1. Ask children to feel beats in sets of two as they listen to the recording of "Lemons." <u>Point out</u>: The first strong beat comes on the first syllable of the word *silly*.

2. Direct children's attention to the notation of the instrumental parts (guiro, Autoharp, woodblock) at the bottom of p. 169 in their book and to the two questions below the notation.

3. Use verse 1 on the recording to help children hear that the guiro and Autoharp play the beat. <u>Point out</u>: In this song the beat is shown by a dotted quarter note (♩.). Also, call attention to the meter signature ($\frac{2}{\cdot}$) at the beginning of each instrumental part, which shows there are two beats in each measure.

4. Have them follow the woodblock part. It plays three sounds for each beat.

5. Provide time for children to practice the instrumental parts so they can accompany the singing.

6. Compare the instrumental parts for "Lemons" with the drum and maracas parts for "Yesterday Morning" at the top of p. 169. Call

→

Find the beats divided in three in this song.

Piano acc. p. 229

LEMONS
FOLK SONG FROM PUERTO RICO   ENGLISH WORDS BY ELIZABETH S. BACHMAN

1. A sil - ly old bird in a lem - on tree
Just sat the whole day through;
A sil - ly old bird in a lem - on tree
Just sat the whole day through.
Ah, 'tis true! Ah, 'tis true!
A sil - ly old bird in a lem - on tree

170 **Rhythm Patterns**

TRY THIS

1. For the song "Lemons," add the tone color of the bells when the melody moves in a downward direction—phrases 2 and 4. Call attention to the tones that repeat.

2. Play the rhythm of *Ah, 'tis true!* on a percussion instrument each time it comes in the song (three times).

Ah, 'tis true!

Just   sat,   and   all   that   he   could   see

Were   yel - low   lem - ons   hang - ing   on   the   tree.

Ah,   'tis   true!

7. Have a child play the steady beat on a woodblock as everyone sings the first verse of "Lemons." The class can tap the ♫♪ rhythm each time they sing three sounds to a beat.

He grabbed a lemon and took a bite,⎫
Then made an awful face.   ⎬ (*2 times*)

Ah, 'tis true! Ah, 'tis true!

He bit the lemon and made a face,

I guess he didn't like the taste

Of the yellow lemons hanging on the tree.

Ah, 'tis true!

That silly old bird was very mad,⎫
He shook the lemon tree.   ⎬ (*2 times*)

Ah, 'tis true! Ah, 'tis true!

That silly old bird was mad, you see,

With all his might he shook the tree,

And sent the lemons crashing down on me.

Ah, 'tis true!

Rhythm Patterns   171

TRY THIS

In some songs, when a beat has three sounds, children sing a word that has three sounds (syllables)—for example, the word *mer-ri-ly* in the round "Row, Row, Row Your Boat." Have children sing or chant this round in unison to feel three sounds to each beat when the words say *merrily, merrily, merrily, merrily*. Ask someone to play the steady beat on a percussion instrument while others chant or sing.

Have children substitute other three-syllable words for the word *merrily* in the song. Other adverbs ending in *-ly* can

be used: *happily, rapidly, playfully, carefully, cheerfully,* etc.

For other songs that have three sounds for a beat, see:
• Sing Together, p. 32
• How D'ye Do and Shake Hands, p. 144
• Shepherds, Bring Candy and Milk, p. 154

RHYTHM PATTERNS • Lesson 3

MATERIALS
Record 1, Anonymous: *Dadme Albricias, Hijos d'Eva;* Pupil's Book, pp. 172 and 173; percussion instruments

VOCABULARY
steady beat, three sounds to a beat, long-short pattern

IDEAS FOR TEACHING
1. Direct attention to the photographs on pp. 172 and 173 in the Pupil's Book. Children will see various fundamental movements represented through the pictures—walking, marching, running, jumping, leaping, galloping, skipping.

2. Have children try the movements to answer these questions:
• Which of the fundamental movements could show a steady beat (♩ ♩)? (Walking, marching, leaping, jumping)
• Which movement could show three sounds to a beat (♫♫ ♫♫)? (Running)
• Which movements have a long-short pattern (♩♪ ♩♪)? (Skipping, galloping)

3. Select one or two children to gallop while someone plays the "galloping" pattern on a percussion instrument.

4. Select children to combine their movements to make up a dance that shows all three patterns notated in their book. The dance will be in ⁶⁄₈(²) meter. They can make their dance fit the song "Lemons," p. 170. Or they can dance to a percussion accompaniment.
$\longrightarrow$

TRY THIS

1. Children can make up a percussion piece, using the three patterns on p. 173 in the Pupil's Book. Suggestions: Write each pattern on a separate index card (make five sets). Shuffle all the cards, then have children create a four-measure rhythm phrase by picking four cards at random and playing each pattern in turn without missing a beat.

2. Play the patterns on p. 173 on a percussion instrument, playing one pattern several times, then switching to another one. Children move as the patterns are played, changing their movement each time the percussion pattern changes. The movement should always fit the percussion sounds.

Find space
in the room
to gallop. Play the
pattern
made by
the sound of
galloping feet.

Find the pattern below.

1.

2.

3.

Now hear all three
patterns in
this music.

Anonymous:
Dadme Albricias, Hijos d'Eva

Rhythm Patterns 173

5. When children have experienced the rhythm patterns through the activities suggested above, play the recording of *Dadme Albricias, Hijos d'Eva* (listed in Materials). Encourage them to listen without moving or playing instruments and to try to feel the same patterns in this music. This piece, played by a recorder consort, is introduced on p. 26.

RHYTHM PATTERNS • Lesson 4

MATERIALS
Pupil's Book, pp. 174 and 175;
percussion instruments

VOCABULARY
steady beat, two sounds for a beat,
three sounds for a beat

IDEAS FOR TEACHING
1. Help children practice playing a
steady beat, then two sounds for
each beat, and three sounds for each
beat. Suggestion: To help children
recall and practice these patterns of
sounds, use the instrumental parts
for "Yesterday Morning" and
"Lemons" (p. 169).

Yesterday Morning

Lemons

2. Have children play the games
described on p. 174 as an additional
experience for feeling (1) the steady
beat, (2) two sounds to the beat, and
(3) three sounds to the beat. The
games can be played by any number
of partners, and children can play
them during free moments at school,
or at home.

METER GAMES

Choose one of the games to play.

To play either game, choose a partner.
You play the boxes in one direction and your partner plays
in the other direction at the same time.

The numbers in the boxes
tell you how many sounds to play for each beat.

Follow the arrows and play the boxes,
going first in one direction, then in the other.

When there are two boxes side by side, play either one or the other.

You will need to set a steady beat before you begin!

If both of you make the same choice when you reach the boxes
at the end, *you* win a point.
If you choose different boxes, your partner wins a point.
After five games, count up your points.

Another time, try the other game.

174

TRY THIS

1. In addition to clapping sounds, have children
experiment with a variety of tone colors, using percussion
sounds, natural sounds, or environmental sounds. Partners
might find it easier to tell whether or not they are ending
together if they use contrasting tone colors—for example,
woodblock and tambourine, triangle and sticks, two
different pitches on bells.

2. When children experiment outside of music class,
encourage them to tape their efforts for others to hear.

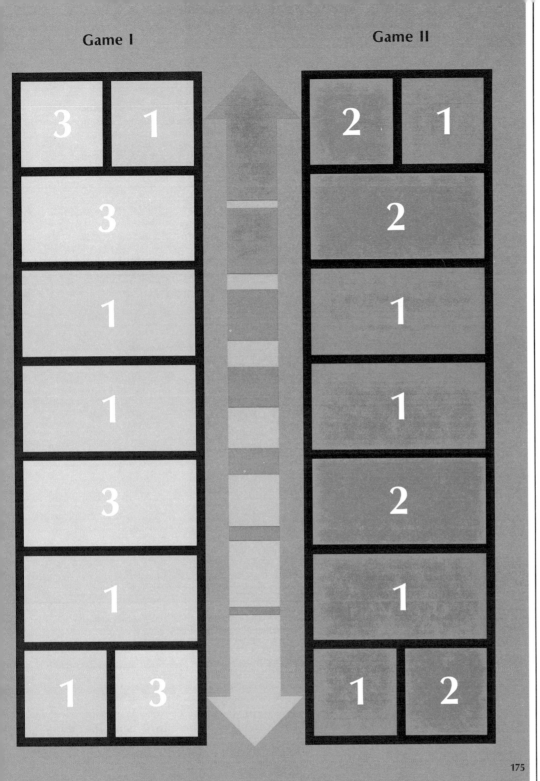

Game I

3	1

3
1
1
3
1

1	3

Game II

2	1

2
1
1
2
1

1	2

REVIEWING METER

Children have experienced meter through listening, singing, moving to music, and playing instruments. In all these experiences they can feel the steady beat and can recognize meter in 2 and meter in 3. To help children retain and build on what they know, try the following.

• Play excerpts from the recordings of "'Taters" (p. 66), "Ging Gong Gooli" (p. 67), and "Love" (p. 68) so that children can determine, by listening and feeling the beat, whether each excerpt has meter in 2 or meter in 3. ("'Taters" and "Ging Gong Gooli" have meter in 2; "Love" has meter in 3.)

• Using "Old Joe Clark" (p. 8) and "Buying Fish" (p. 65), children can experiment with singing, moving, and playing percussion instruments to show meter in each song. To involve all the children, a combination of these activities can be used with each of the songs.

• Play the recording of *Ton Moulin,* (see *What Do You Hear? 3,* p. 69). Ask children to listen and decide whether the meter stays the same or whether it changes. (The meter changes.)

175

MATERIALS

Record 8, "The Wee Falorie Man";
Pupil's Book, p. 176; percussion
instruments

VOCABULARY

steady beat, three sounds for a beat,
meter in 2, long-short pattern

IDEAS FOR TEACHING

1. Play the recording and ask
children to follow the notation on
p. 176. As they listen, ask them to
decide whether the music has meter
in 2 or meter in 3. (Meter in 2. Call
attention to the meter signature
that shows there are two beats in
each measure.)

2. Point out that the song uses two
familiar rhythm patterns—three
sounds for a beat (♫♫), and the
skipping or galloping pattern (♩♪♩♪)
that is introduced on p. 172.

3. Play the recording again and have
children play the steady beat on a
percussion instrument. They will play
this pattern throughout:

4. This time, have children play the
galloping pattern throughout the
song:

5. Write the patterns on the
chalkboard so that children can see
the notation for what they play.
Then have children choose one of
the patterns to play while others sing
the song.

THE WEE FALORIE MAN

FOLK SONG FROM IRELAND   COLLECTED BY DAVID HAMMOND

Piano acc. p. 244

1. I am the wee Fa - lo - rie man,
2. I am a good old work - in' man,

A rat - tlin', rov - in' I - rish - man,
Each day I carry my wee tin can,

⅞ I can do all that ev - er you can,
A large pen - ny bap and a clipe_____ of ham,

For I am the wee Fa - lo - rie man.
⅞ I am a good old work - in' man.

3. I am the wee Falorie man,

A rattlin', rovin' Irishman,

I can do all that ever you can,

For I am the wee Falorie man.

In the second verse, "clipe" means
a large thick hunk.
"Wee tin can" refers to the black can
in which a worker boils the tea.
"Bap" is a small loaf of bread.

THE OLD MAN   FOLK SONG FROM CANADA   Piano acc. p. 242

FROM TRADITIONAL SONGS FROM NOVA SCOTIA BY HELEN CREIGHTON. REPRINTED BY PERMISSION OF MCGRAW HILL RYERSON LIMITED.

1. There was an old man came o - ver the lea,
2. My moth - er she bade me o - pen the door,

TRY THIS

1. Play a steady-beat accompaniment on the Autoharp.
Write the pattern on the chalkboard or on a chart so that
children can practice on their own:

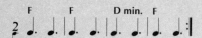

2. Play this rhythm pattern on the bells, alternately playing
the low- and high-F bells and the low- and high-D bells.

3. Play a recorder or bell part throughout the song. High C
on the recorder is introduced on p. 89; high D on p. 100.

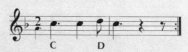

3. My mother she bade me set him a chair,

   Ho, ho, ho, but I won't have him!

   I set him a chair, but I didn't care

   For his long beard so newly shaven.

4. My mother, she bade me give him some meat,

   Ho, ho, ho, but I won't have him!

   I gave him some meat, but he wouldn't eat

   With his long beard so newly shaven.

5. My mother she bade me sit on his knee,

   Ho, ho, ho, but I won't have him!

   For I sat on his knee and he tried to kiss me

   With his long beard so newly shaven.

Rhythm Patterns   177

RHYTHM PATTERNS • Lesson 6

MATERIALS
Record 9, "The Old Man"; Pupil's Book, p. 177

VOCABULARY
fermata, steady beat, three sounds to a beat, long-short pattern

IDEAS FOR TEACHING

1. Play the recording and ask children to listen for the words that repeat. (The words in phrases 2 and 4 repeat in each verse with one exception—the last phrase in verse 3 begins *For his long;* in all other verses it begins *With his long.*) Note: Call attention to where the beat stops and holds—the fermata (⌢) over the last note on phrase 2 indicates this.

2. When they are familiar with the song, choose some children to sing each of the verses; the class will join in on phrases 2 and 4.

3. Introduce the chant notated below (you may want to write it on the chalkboard) to point up three different rhythm patterns in $^6_8$ ($^2_4$). Point out: The words in part 2 will change for each verse: verse 2—*open* the *door;* verse 3—*set* him a *chair;* etc.

Questions: Which part shows the steady beat? (Part 1) Which part uses words that show three sounds to a beat? (Part 2) Which part uses a pattern of long and short sounds? (Part 3)

4. Choose a child to read the words of the song. (Disregard the fermata for this activity.) Let the other children choose a line of the chant to perform throughout the reading. See suggestions below.

CHANT

Group 1: Low register, soft

Old man, Old man.

Group 2: Middle register, soft

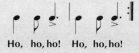

O - ver the lea, O - ver the lea.

Group 3: High and low registers, loud with accents

Ho, ho, ho! Ho, ho, ho!

Suggestions:
• Establish the tempo.
• Use the steady-beat pattern (group 1) throughout, as well as for an introduction and a coda (ending).
• Groups 2 and 3 start when the reader begins verse 1 and continue to chant throughout.
• It is important that children follow the dynamics indicated for each part. Also, using different voice registers will add interest to the performance.

MODULE 20

OBJECTIVES, p. xiv

STYLE: Modern

MATERIALS
Record 9, *Modern Sounds;* Pupil's Book, pp. 178 and 179

VOCABULARY
modern styles, folk-pop sound, electronic sounds

IDEAS FOR TEACHING

1. Play a few moments of each of the four excerpts on the recording, *Modern Sounds.* Questions: Do you think the sounds of these pieces are very old, or do you think they are from very new compositions? How can you tell? (They are very new—modern—pieces. Encourage discussion of the use of pop sounds and electronic equipment in the first excerpt and the strangeness of the sounds in the last three excerpts.)

2. Question: What are some things in our everyday lives that are new—that your grandfathers or grandmothers probably did not know about? (While children can be a little hazy about how old or how new some things can be, they can also identify that many modern inventions are indeed new. Encourage discussion of some of these new things, such as jet airplanes, space exploration, frozen foods, computers, etc. Point out that all these things are modern—new—and are part of our lives right now.)

3. Play the recording of *Modern Sounds* and discuss each excerpt in turn. Have children look at the photo- ⟶

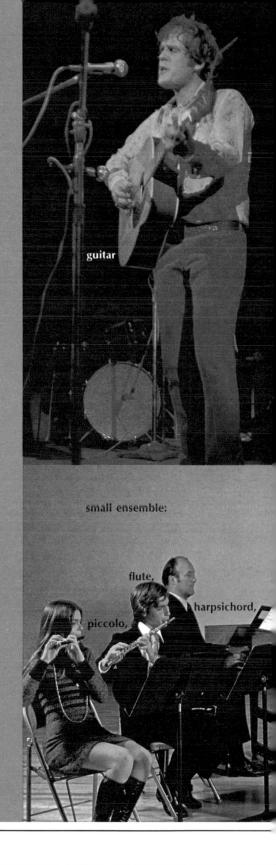

guitar

small ensemble:

flute,

harpsichord,

piccolo,

New things create a *modern style* of living.
New sounds create *modern styles* of music.
Follow the pictures as you listen to examples in modern styles.

🔴 9 *Modern Sounds*

Hardin (arr.): *Lonesome Valley*

Arel: *Stereo Electronic Music No. 1*

Erb: *Phantasama*

Oliveros: *Sound Patterns*

Modern music has many different styles for you to enjoy.

178　MODULE 20: Style—Modern

TEACHER INFORMATION

Bülent Arel (Turkish, 1918–　) *Stereo Electronic Music,* No. 1: Arel has studied and taught in the United States. Much of his music is electronic, but he has composed symphonies and theater music also.

Donald Erb (American, 1927–　) *Phantasma,* Op. 1, No. 1: The music of this composer-teacher has been performed by major orchestras around the world and by innumerable smaller groups. Erb often uses nontraditional sound makers (pop bottles, slide whistles, sleigh bells, etc.) in ways that make them very musical and emotionally powerful.

Pauline Oliveros (American, 1932–　) *Sound Patterns:* Oliveros is among those composers interested in expanding our ideas of "proper" sounds to use in music. She experiments with many nontraditional ways to use traditional instruments and the voice.

string bass

English horn, oboe

electronic studio

graphs on pp. 178 and 179 as they listen. <u>Note</u>: Children's attention spans vary. It is not necessary to play and discuss all the excerpts in one lesson.

Harden (arr.): *Lonesome Valley*—This pop-rock piece takes advantage of modern ways to record music, using elaborate studio equipment.

Arel: *Stereo Electronic Music*, No. 1—New electronic-sound-generating equipment has added a whole new world of possibilities for composers to explore. It is a very exciting thing for them, and a very challenging thing for the listener.

Erb: *Phantasma*, Op. 1, No. 1—Some modern composers prefer to use traditional instruments, but to do all sorts of unusual things with them, giving the old sounds a very new twist.

Oliveros: *Sound Patterns*—The oldest instrument of all—the voice—has also been used in very new, strange ways by modern composers who are searching for new challenges for their creativity.

REVIEW/REINFORCEMENT

When attention permits, play the recordings of a few other modern pieces, comparing the sounds with the ones in this lesson. Point out that there are many different styles in modern music. They are all modern, but each has a special sound.
- Smith: *Three Brevities for Solo Flute, p. 33*
- Kingsley: *Call Chart 1,* p. 64
- Stravinsky: *A Soldier's Tale Suite,* p. 36
- Schoenberg: *Trio for Violin, Viola, and Cello,* p. 164
- Hays: "Ol' Clo'," p. 165

TRY THIS

1. Explore unusual voice and mouth sounds with the children—hissing, tongue clicking, lip buzzing, swooping, etc. Try creating a modern, voice-sound piece with three sections, such as:
A—All voice sounds, soft, slow
B—All mouth sounds
C—A combination of A and B

2. A similar activity can be done using classroom instruments in unusual ways—strike a tambourine with a stick, play bells with a variety of different strikers, etc.

MODULE 21

OBJECTIVES, p. xiv

INTERVALS • Lesson 1

MATERIALS
Record 9, "Hill an' Gully"; Pupil's Book, p. 180; F bell, percussion instruments

VOCABULARY
repeated tones

IDEAS FOR TEACHING

1. Play the recording of "Hill an' Gully" and have children follow the notation to find out how the tones move in the chorus parts. (The tones repeat in each chorus part.)

2. This time have children sing all the chorus parts along with the children on the recording.

3. To reinforce the concept, have children take turns playing the repeated tones in each chorus part on an F bell. Call attention to the rhythm pattern, which is nearly identical each time (♫♫ ♩ and ♫♫ ♩).

4. During the singing of the chorus parts, one or two children can play the melody (repeated F) on any mallet instrument, while others play the rhythm on a percussion instrument.

Sing the chorus parts of "Hill an' Gully" to discover how the tones move.

Piano acc. p. 230

HILL AN' GULLY
CALYPSO FROM JAMAICA   ENGLISH WORDS BY MARGARET MARKS

1. Took my horse an' come down, Hill an'___ gul - ly.
But my horse done stum-ble down, Hill an'___ gul - ly.
An' the night-time come an' tum-ble down, Hill an'___ gul - ly.

2. Oh, the moon shine bright down,
   Hill an' gully.
   Ain't no place to hide in down,
   Hill an' gully.
   An' a zombie come a-ridin' down,
   Hill an' gully.

3. Oh, my knees they shake down,
   Hill an' gully.
   An' my heart starts quakin' down,

   Hill an' gully.
   Ain't nobody goin' to get me down,
   Hill an' gully.

4. That's the last I set down,
   Hill an' gully.
   Pray the Lord don' let me down,
   Hill an' gully.
   An' I run till daylight breakin' down,
   Hill an' gully.

180 Intervals

TRY THIS

Select four children, one for each verse, to sing the solo parts. Call attention to the first full measure of each line in the verse section of the song—the tones move downward mostly by leap. Point out the repeated tones in the last two lines.

LINE DANCE for "Hill an' Gully"

Phrase 1: Take four steps forward (4 beats); pat rhythm of *Hill an' gully* on knees (4 beats).
Phrase 2: Take four steps backward (4 beats); pat rhythm of "Hill an' gully on knees (4 beats).
Phrase 3: Starting with right foot, take three steps to the right, then clap once (4 beats); starting with left foot, take three steps to the left, then clap once (4 beats).
Phrase 4: Repeat phrase 3.
Phrase 5: Take four steps around in a circle in place (4 beats); clap the rhythm of *Hill an' gully* (4 beats).

Sing the chorus parts. Which ones use only repeated tones?

Which ones use a leap?

OLD HOUSE

AMERICAN FOLK GAME SONG   COLLECTED BY JOHN W. WORK

Piano acc. p. 237

SOLO · CHORUS

1. Old house. Tear it down!

Who's going to help me? Tear it down!

Bring me a ham-mer. Tear it down!

Bring me a saw. Tear it down!

Next thing you bring me, Tear it down!

Is a wreck-ing ma-chine. Tear it down!

2. New house. Build it up!

Who's going to help me? Build it up!

Bring me a hammer. Build it up!

Bring me a saw. Build it up!

Next thing you bring me, Build it up!

Is a carpenter man. Build it up!

Intervals 181

INTERVALS · Lesson 2

MATERIALS
Record 9, "Old House"; Pupil's Book, p. 181; G and B bells

VOCABULARY
repeated tones, leaps

IDEAS FOR TEACHING

1. Play the recording of "Old House" and ask children to listen for the words *Tear it down!* each time they come in the song. Have them follow the notation as they listen.

2. This time have children sing the chorus parts when they come in the song to discover how the melody works.

Sometimes the melody leaps to a higher tone.

Other times, the tones are all the same (repeated tones).

3. Direct attention to the two questions at the top of p. 181 in the Pupil's Book. Help children discover that chorus parts 2, 4, and 6 use only repeated tones and that chorus parts 1, 3, and 5 use a leap. Point out: Except for the fifth phrase, which ends with an eighth note, the rhythm is identical for each chorus part.

4. Let children take turns playing the chorus parts (on the bells) when they come in the song. See the notation in item 2 above.

TRY THIS

1. Have some children sing the solo parts; have others sing the chorus parts.
2. Add bells to the singing of the chorus parts.
3. Have one or two children play the rhythm of the chorus parts on a percussion instrument.
4. Select children to show the steady beat by dramatizing the work of a carpenter throughout the song. For instance, one child can pretend to pound a nail, while another sands the wood; one child uses a saw, while another planes the wood.

5. Have children dramatize the carpenter's movements in a way that shows duration. The children who are pounding the nail and sanding the wood perform their motions in this rhythm:

Those who are sawing and planing the wood use this rhythm:

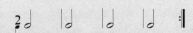

MATERIALS
Pupil's Book, p. 182; bells, recorder

VOCABULARY
steps, leaps, repeated tones

IDEAS FOR TEACHING
1. The parts of songs notated on p. 182 in the Pupil's Book may be played on the bells or on a recorder. Before they play, help children analyze how the tones move by asking the following questions:

Where do the tones move upward by step? (Nos. 1, 3, and 5)

Can you find tones that repeat? (No. 4. Some children may notice repeated tones at the beginning of No. 1, at the end of No. 5, and in the middle of No. 2.)

Can you find tones that leap from low to high? (Nos. 1 and 4)

Can you find tones that leap from high to low? (No. 3)

How does the melody work?

Do the tones repeat, move by step, or leap?

Play these melodies on bells or recorder.

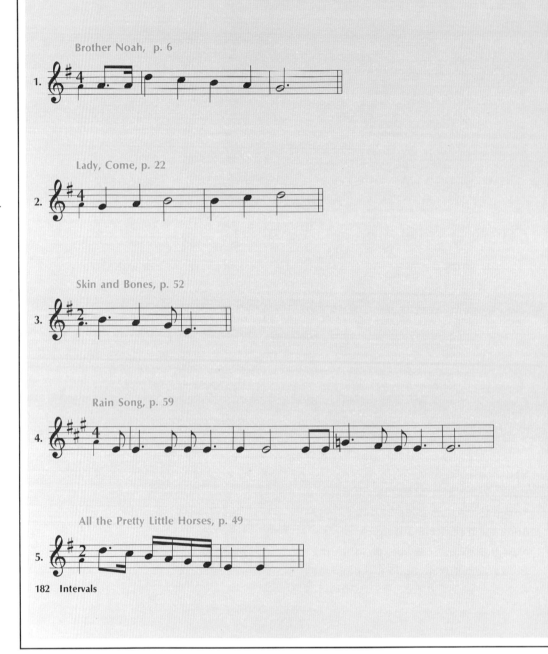

REVIEW/REINFORCEMENT

The following songs have accompanying bell or recorder parts. Review several and help children analyze how the tones move.

Pity the Poor Patat, p. 9; The Tree in the Wood, p. 10; Clover, p. 50; Skin and Bones, p. 52; Chicka Hanka, p. 54; New Year's Song, p. 60; Love, p. 68; The Ghost of John, p. 71; Pray God Bless, p. 78; Little David, Play on Your Harp, p. 88; Shepherds Came to Bethlehem, p. 120; Hana ichi momme, p. 128; Nobody's Business, p. 134; German Instrument Song, p. 136; Joyous Chanukah, p. 152.

Follow the notes as you sing a song you know.

Does the melody move mostly by *steps,* or by *leaps?*

Piano acc. p. 218

AMERICA   TRADITIONAL   WORDS BY SAMUEL FRANCIS SMITH

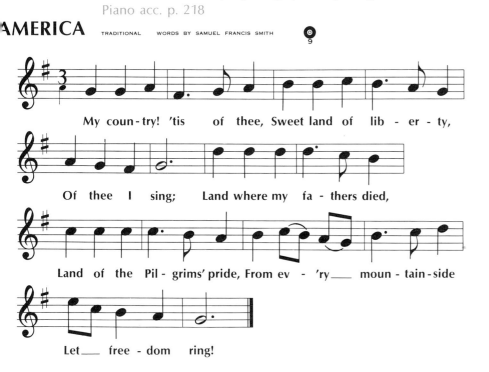

My coun-try! 'tis of thee, Sweet land of lib-er-ty,

Of thee I sing; Land where my fa-thers died,

Land of the Pil-grims' pride, From ev-'ry___ moun-tain-side

Let___ free-dom ring!

My native country, thee, Land of the noble free,

Thy name I love; I love thy rocks and rills,

Thy woods and templed hills, My heart with rapture thrills

Like that above.

Our fathers' God, to Thee, Author of liberty,

To Thee we sing; Long may our land be bright

With freedom's holy light; Protect us by Thy might,

Great God, our King!

Does the instrumental part move mostly by *steps,* or by *leaps?*

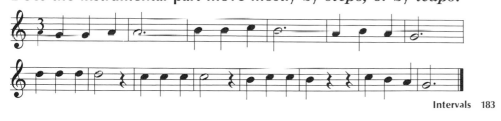

Intervals 183

INTERVALS • Lesson 4

MATERIALS
Record 9, "America"; Pupil's Book, p. 183; bells, recorder

VOCABULARY
steps, leaps, repeated tones

IDEAS FOR TEACHING

1. Play the recording of "America" and ask children to follow the notation to discover the tones that move by steps and those that leap. (Most children will find the leap between measure 6 and measure 7. Some children may begin to discover the small leaps at other places: between measures 1 and 2, measures 11 and 12, and in measure 13. Most of the tones move by step.)

2. Children who play G, A, B, C, and D on the recorder can play the instrumental part at the bottom of p. 183 in their book. This part may also be played on the bells. Help children to analyze the instrumental part so they will become more perceptive about how melodies work. In addition to the repeated tones, this part uses mostly tones that move by step.

Note: The patriotic songs, as well as other songs for special occasions, are used throughout this book to increase children's understanding and perception of musical qualities. However, this does not preclude the use of the songs for other reasons

TEACHER INFORMATION

When the founders of the United States had to decide which kind of government we would have, certain factions thought it right that George Washington, who had led the colonial army to victory, be crowned King of America. They supported this contention with a paraphrase of the British national anthem (wherein the words *God save our noble King,* etc., are sung to the tune we know as "America"), which began *God save George Washington.* The words we now sing to this melody were written for Washington's Birthday in 1832 by Samuel F. Smith, and first sung on July 4 of that year by a group of Boston Sunday-school children. This version was regarded, unofficially, as our national anthem until Congress passed a bill, in the early part of the 20th century, designating "The Star-Spangled Banner" as such.

MATERIALS

Record 9, "America, the Beautiful"; Pupil's Book, pp. 184 and 185; bells, recorder

VOCABULARY

steps, leaps, repeated tones, phrases, interval, contour

IDEAS FOR TEACHING

1. Direct attention to the photographs on pp. 184 and 185 that show high leaps. Point out that this lesson focuses on a leap from low to high (a wide interval) in "America, the Beautiful."

2. Play the recording and have children follow the notation to discover where the leap from low to high occurs. (The interval comes at the beginning of the third phrase on the first word *America.*) <u>Point out</u>: The steps, leaps, and repeated tones in "America, the Beautiful" help give the melody its shape, or contour.

3. Have children follow the contour of the melody as they sing along with the recording.

4. Help children discover that the four phrases in "America, the Beautiful" are all the same length (four measures) and have the same rhythm.

5. Help children analyze how the tones move in the instrumental part for "America, the Beautiful," p. 185, by asking the following questions:

How many phrases does the part have? (Four) $\longrightarrow$

This patriotic song has steps, leaps, and repeats.

Listen for the two words "America, America" as you sing. On which one does the melody leap from low to high?

AMERICA, THE BEAUTIFUL   MUSIC BY SAMUEL A. WARD   WORDS BY KATHARINE LEE BATES

Piano acc. p. 272

O beau - ti - ful   for spa - cious skies, For am - ber waves of grain,

For pur - ple moun - tain maj - es - ties A - bove the fruit - ed plain!

A - mer - i - ca!   A - mer - i - ca! God shed His grace on thee

And crown thy good with broth - er - hood From sea to shin - ing sea!

184 Intervals

REVIEW/REINFORCEMENT

Review other songs that have phrases of the same length and the same rhythm.
• Hawaiian Rainbows, p. 146

• The Pig, p. 114

TRY THIS

Tap out the rhythm of familiar songs and have children guess which ones they are. For example:
• Marching to Pretoria (refrain), p. 4
• Mama Paquita, p. 18
• Hey Ho, Hey Lo, p. 42
• Chicka Hanka, p. 54
• Ging Gong Gooli, p. 67

Recorder or bells

(A - mer - i - ca! A - mer - i - ca!)

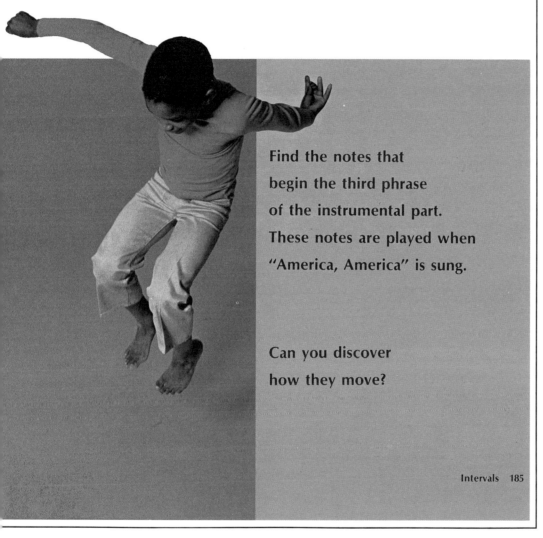

Find the notes that
begin the third phrase
of the instrumental part.
These notes are played when
"America, America" is sung.

Can you discover
how they move?

Intervals 185

Are the phrases the same length, or different lengths? (The same length)

Is there a wide interval when the first word *America* is sung? (No)

How do the tones move when the words *America, America* come in the instrumental part? (The tones repeat.)

Which phrase has a beginning identical to the *America, America* part of phrase 3? (Phrase 1)

Which phrase has a beginning identical to the *America, America* part of phrase 3, except for one note? (Phrase 2)

6. The instrumental part may be played on bells, keyboard, or recorder. Some children may be able to play all four phrases. However, encourage them to play one or two of the phrases before trying the entire part. Select a different child to play each phrase while others sing the melody on p. 184. <u>Note</u>: Children who are just beginning to play the recorder can play the first half of each phrase (tones G and A), leaving the second half of the phrase for more advanced players.

TEACHER INFORMATION

The story of how "America, the Beautiful" came to be written can be told over and over again. Briefly, it was inspired by the view that a schoolteacher got from a vantage point on top of Pike's Peak in Colorado. As Katharine Lee Bates looked out over the verdant panorama and saw a vast land of liberty and abundance, she felt the thrill of being an American. From this experience came the poem, which another American, Samuel Ward, set to music.

Only the first and fourth stanzas of the poem are included in the Pupil's Book, but children can hear the entire poem performed by The Mormon Tabernacle Choir and The Philadelphia Orchestra on Record 10.

Intervals · Lesson 5 · 185

MATERIALS

Record 9, "Wonders Never Cease";
Pupil's Book, pp. 186 and 187

VOCABULARY

steps, leaps, repeated tones, cadence

IDEAS FOR TEACHING

1. Play the recording of "Wonders
Never Cease" and have children follow the notation as they listen.
Point out: The form of the song will
help children learn the melody.
"Wonders Never Cease" is a cumulative song. In each verse, a phrase of
the melody is repeated one more
time than in the preceding verse—
the words are different for each repetition.

Note: For other cumulative songs in
this book, see Teacher Information at
the bottom of the page.

2. Direct attention to the notation
on p. 187 in the Pupil's Book. Children will see four endings, called cadences, which they can sing for the
last two measures of "Wonders
Never Cease." Help children analyze
how the tones move in each ending.

R—repeat; S—step; L—leap. The first
one is the ending of the song as
written.

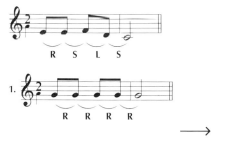

Follow the notes as you listen to this song.

Can you tell where the notes repeat, move by step,

and where they leap?

WONDERS NEVER CEASE

YIDDISH FOLK SONG   Piano acc. p. 232

ENGLISH WORDS BY ELIZABETH S. BACHMAN

"HOB ICH A POR OKSN" FROM A TREASURY OF JEWISH FOLKSONG EDITED BY RUTH RUBIN. COPYRIGHT ©1950 BY SCHOCKEN BOOKS INC. REPRINTED BY PERMISSION OF SCHOCKEN BOOKS INC

1. I've a pair of ox-en, ox-en,

Ox-en who cut noo-dles, noo-dles.

Do you mean you've nev-er seen An ox cut noo-dles by the oo-dles?

Won-ders nev-er cease, Oh, won-ders nev-er cease.

Repeat these two measures for additional lines in verses 2–6.

2. I've a pair of bears, bears,

   Bears who sweep the rooms, rooms.

   Do you mean you've never seen

   A bear sweep rooms without a broom?

   An ox cut noodles by the oodles?

   Wonders never cease,

   Oh, wonders never cease.

3. I've a pair of goats, goats,

   Goats who wheel the children, childre

   Do you mean you've never seen

   A goat so glad to wheel a lad?

   A bear sweep rooms without a broom

   An ox cut noodles by the oodles?

   Wonders . . .

186 Intervals

TEACHER INFORMATION

Other cumulative songs in this book are:

- The Tree in the Wood, p. 10
- My Twenty Pennies, p. 194
- When I First Came to This Land, p. 200

REVIEW/REINFORCEMENT

You might want to review cadences in one of two previous
lessons. See Ideas for Teaching, item 5, p. 11 in the Teacher's Edition and Ideas for Teaching, item 3, p. 146 in the
Teacher's Edition.

4. I've a pair of dogs, dogs,

 Dogs who write with ink, ink.

 Do you mean you've never seen

 A dog who'd think to write with ink?

 A goat so glad to wheel a lad?

 A bear sweep rooms without a broom?

 An ox cut noodles by the oodles?

 Wonders . . .

5. I've a pair of hens, hens,

 Hens who gather wood, wood.

 Do you mean you've never seen

 A hen so good at gath'ring wood?

 A dog who'd think to write with ink?

 A goat so glad to wheel a lad?

 A bear sweep rooms without a broom?

 An ox cut noodles by the oodles?

 Wonders . . .

6. I've a pair of birds, birds,

 Birds who like to bake, bake.

 Do you mean you've never seen

 A bird who baked a layer cake?

 A hen so good at gath'ring wood?

 A dog who'd think to write with ink?

 A goat so glad to wheel a lad?

 A bear sweep rooms without a broom?

 An ox cut noodles by the oodles?

 Wonders . . .

3. When children know the melody of "Wonders Never Cease," have them choose a cadence from the ones on p. 187 to sing for the final *wonders never cease* in each verse.

4. Have a small group of children choose one of the cadences to sing while the class sings the final *wonders never cease* as notated in the song. Call attention to the harmony that results when the two cadences are sung at the same time.

These endings are called *cadences*. How does each one move?

Which cadence will you sing to end each verse?

TRY THIS

1. Children can play the cadences on the bells.

(1) E E F D C

(2) G G G G G

(3) G G G G C

(4) G G A B C

MATERIALS
Record 9, Ives: "The Cage"; "Kookaburra"; *Call Chart 10;* Pupil's Book,
pp. 188 and 189; bells, recorder

VOCABULARY
repeated tones, steps, leaps, interval,
contour

IDEAS FOR TEACHING
1. "The Cage" is to be used primarily
as a listening experience. Play the recording and have children follow the
notation to discover how the tones
move. Note: Since the song is short,
you may want to play the recording
several times before helping children
analyze how the tones move. (With
the exception of a small leap—fourth
staff, measure 2, between the last
syllable of *won-der* and *Is*—the
tones move upward and downward
by step.)

2. The recording routine for the song
"Kookaburra," p. 189, is instrumental,
unison vocal, four-part round (4
times). Play the recording of the instrumental and unison vocal parts
only and ask children to follow the
notation to discover where the tones
of the melody move by step (measures 1, 1-2, 3, 3-4, 5, 5-6, 6, 6-7), by
leap (measures 2, 4, 4-5, 5, 6, 7), and
where they repeat (measures 1, 2-3,
3, 7, 7-8).

3. Question. Where is the widest interval? (An octave leap from low C
to high C occurs between the last
note in measure 4—*he*—and the first
note in measure 5—*Laugh*).

4. Children can accompany "Kookaburra" by playing on bells or on recorder one of the instrumental parts

$\longrightarrow$

Follow the notation as you listen to this song to discover that the melody moves upward and downward by steps.

This gives the melody its shape, or *contour.*

THE CAGE   CHARLES IVES
COPYRIGHT 1955 BY PEER INTERNATIONAL CORPORATION. USED BY PERMISSION.

A   leop - ard   went   a - round   his   cage   from   one   side

back to   the oth - er side; he stopped   on - ly when the keep-er

came   a - round with meat;   A   boy who had been there three

hours   he - gan   to   won - der,____   "Is____   life   an - y - thing

like   that?"

TEACHER INFORMATION

The kookaburra is a bird found in Australia. Like the king-
fisher, it has a large crested head and a short tail. Its call
sounds like loud laughter.

Charles Ives (American, 1874-1954)   "The Cage": This New
Englander (who spent his life in the insurance business)
was an astonishingly original composer. He used very
modern techniques years before most other composers
ever thought about them. His music has a dissonant, angular quality, although this song uses only steps and one
small leap.

KOOKABURRA

WORDS AND MUSIC BY MARION SINCLAIR

FROM THE DITTY BAG BY JANET E. TOBITT. COPYRIGHT © 1946 BY JANET E. TOBITT. USED BY PERMISSION.

I

Koo - ka - bur - ra sits on the old gum tree,_____

II

Mer - ry, mer - ry king of the bush is he;_____

III

Laugh, Koo - ka - bur - ra, laugh, Koo - ka - bur - ra, **IV** Gay your life must be.

Bells or Recorder

1.

2.

Bells

3.

CALL CHART 10: CONTOUR

1. *STEPWISE*

2. *LEAPWISE*

3. *STEPWISE*

4. *LEAPWISE*

Tchaikovsky: *Symphony No. 6*, Movement 1
Webern: *Five Pieces for Orchestra*
The Wongga
Debussy: "Golliwog's Cakewalk"

Intervals 189

notated on p. 189 in their book. Most children will notice that the tones in parts 1 and 3 move upward and then downward by step and that part 2 uses repeated tones.

5. Before playing the recording of *Call Chart 10*, point out that steps, leaps, and repeated tones give a melody its contour, or shape. When a melody uses mostly steps, its contour is stepwise. When it uses mostly leaps, its contour is leapwise.

6. Play the recording and have children listen for the contour of each of the melodies to hear which are stepwise and which are leapwise. Following the chart will help children hear the contour of each melody.

Note: Children will hear excerpts from the following selections:
(1) Tchaikovsky: *Symphony No. 6*, Movement 1 (stepwise)
(2) Webern: *Five Pieces for Orchestra*, Op. 10, No. 5 (leapwise)
(3) Australian aboriginal song: *The Wonnga* (stepwise)
(4) Debussy: *Children's Corner Suite*, "Golliwog's Cakewalk" (leapwise)

TRY THIS

1. When children know the melody of "Kookaburra," have them sing it as a two-part round. Some classes may be able to sing it as a three- or four-part round.

2. Have children try performing "Kookaburra" as a rhythm round. Assign four different percussion instruments, one to each part (for example, sandblocks, part 1; tambourine, part 2; woodblock, part 3; triangle, part 4) to play the rhythm of "Kookaburra," each part beginning at the appro-

priate time. Some children may notice both from the notation and from the percussion sounds that phrases 1 and 2 of the round have the same rhythm.

INTERVALS • Lesson 8

MATERIALS
Pupil's Book, p. 190; bells

VOCABULARY
steps, leaps, repeated tones, interval

IDEAS FOR TEACHING
1. The parts of familiar songs notated on p. 190 in the Pupil's Book can be played on the bells. Before they play, help children analyze how the tones move by asking the following questions:

Where do the tones move upward by step? (Nos. 3, 4, and 5)

Where do the tones move downward by step? (Nos. 3 and 6)

Can you find tones that repeat? (Nos. 1, 2, 3, 4, and 6)

Can you find tones that leap from low to high? (Nos. 1, 2, and 5)

Can you find tones that leap from high to low? (Nos. 1, 2, and 5)

Where do you find the widest interval? (No. 2—there is a leap of an octave, from high E to low E, between the first two notes in the last measure.)

Play these parts on the bells.

1. Sandy McNab, p. 63
   And had to be car - ried home in a cab.

2. 'Taters, p. 66
   Sab-bath, for a spe - cial treat, there's a 'ta - ter pud - ding!

3. The Ghost of John, p. 71
   Would - n't it be chill - y with no skin on!

4. Boil Them Cabbage Down, p. 85
   Boil them cab - bage down, down.

5. Lemons, p. 170
   Ah, 'tis true! Ah, 'tis true!

6. All the Pretty Little Horses, p. 48
   All the pret - ty lit - tle hors - es.

Intervals 190

REVIEW/REINFORCEMENT

The following songs have accompanying bell or recorder parts. Review several and help children analyze how the tones move.

Pity the Poor Patat, p. 9; The Tree in the Wood, p. 10; Clover, p. 50; Skin and Bones, p. 52; Chicka Hanka, p. 54; New Year's Song, p. 60; Love, p. 68; The Ghost of John, p. 71; Pray God Bless, p. 78; Shepherds Came to Bethlehem, p. 120; Hana ichi momme, p. 128; Nobody's Business, p. 134; German Instrument Song, p. 136; Joyous Chanukah, p. 152.

Listen to these melodies as you follow the notes.

Do the tones move mostly by step, mostly by leap,

or mostly by repeated tones?

As you hear each number called, look at the chart to help you.

CALL CHART 11: INTERVALS

1. LEAPS

Saint-Saëns: "Kangaroos"

2. LEAPS

Bugle Call: *Taps*

3. REPEATED TONES

McHugh: *Rain Song*

4. STEPS

Handel: *Messiah*, "Pastoral Symphony"

5. STEPS

Tchaikovsky: *Symphony No. 6*, Movement 1

Intervals 191

INTERVALS • Lesson 9

MATERIALS
Record 9 *Call Chart 11*; Pupil's Book, p. 191

VOCABULARY
steps, leaps, repeated tones, contour

TEACHER INFORMATION

Before playing the recording of *Call Chart 11*, direct attention to the melodies notated on p. 191 in the Pupil's Book. Encourage children to analyze the contour, or shape, of each melody. Question: Do the notes in each example move mostly by steps, by leaps, or mostly by repeated tones?

Play the recording and have children look at the chart in their book as each number is called. This will help them to *see* as well to *hear* a melody moving mostly by steps, mostly by leaps, or mostly by repeated tones.

Children will hear excerpts from the following selections:
1. Saint-Saëns: *Carnival of Animals*, "Kangaroos" (leaps)
2. Bugle call: *Taps* (leaps)
3. McHugh: *Rain Song* (repeated tones)
4. Handel: *Messiah*, "Pastoral Symphony" (steps)
5. Tchaikovsky: *Symphony No.6*, Movement 1 (steps)

Note: This experience will prepare children for *What Do You Hear? 12* (p. 195), in which they are asked to identify melody contour without looking at notation.

MATERIALS
Pupil's Book, pp. 192 and 193; bells
or piano

VOCABULARY
steps, leaps, repeated tones, melody
contour, tempo, meter, dynamics,
beat, rhythm patterns

IDEAS FOR TEACHING
1. Point out that one way to get an
idea for the contour of a melody is
to look at the contour of pictures.
Direct attention to the top row of
pictures on p. 192 in the Pupil's
Book.

2. Through questioning and discussion, help children discover that the
first picture is that of a kitten. The
second picture shows the same kitten, but dots have been added at
certain places on the kitten's head.
In the third picture, lines have been
added to connect the dots.

3. Using the same procedure, discuss
the second and third rows of pictures. Then call attention to the contour lines in the pictures in column
3. Some seem to leap upward, some
downward. Some stay on the same
level. Some seem to move upward
and downward by step.

4. Let children try to change each
contour line into a melody by playing it on the bells or on the piano.
They may start anywhere and stretch
the melody over a large or a small
area of the keyboard. Help them follow the general contour of steps,
leaps, and repeated tones.

<u>Note:</u> Give children an opportunity
to experiment in class—in small
groups ⟶

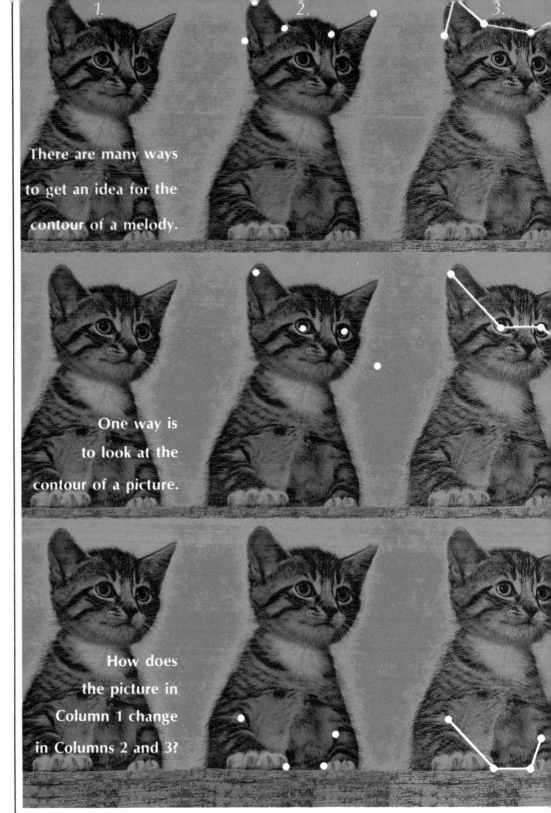

There are many ways
to get an idea for the
contour of a melody.

One way is
to look at the
contour of a picture.

How does
the picture in
Column 1 change
in Columns 2 and 3?

SOUND PIECE 5: Picture Piece

DAVID S. WALKER

Here are some contour lines taken from the ideas

in Columns 1, 2, and 3.

Play the tones they suggest to you, on bells

or on a piano.

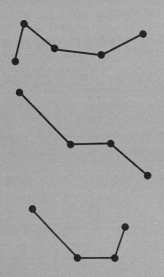

Will you use a steady beat, or no beat?

Will your piece be fast, or slow?

Will you use short sounds, long sounds, or both?

Will your piece move in twos, or threes?

Will it be loud, soft, or will the dynamics change?

Make up your own Sound Piece, using some of these ideas.

Intervals   193

or alone. Make the materials available for them to work outside of class, or at home, as well as in the classroom. This experience will last over a period of time.

5. Children will find a Sound Piece (based on the pictures of the kitten) on p. 193 in their book. Let them experiment and try to create a musical composition based on the Sound Piece. Encourage them to apply concepts they have learned throughout the year: tempo (fast-slow), meter (twos-threes), dynamics (loud-soft), contrast and repetition, rhythm pattern, and tone color. Also, encourage them to notate their compositions for others to play.

TEACHER INFORMATION

Sound Piece 5, as well as other Sound Pieces throughout the book, provides opportunities for creating music, using what the children know. At the same time, children are introduced to different ways of notating sound.

The Sound Pieces serve as examples that may encourage some children to make up their own music and to invent ways to notate what they create.

MATERIALS

Record 9, "My Twenty Pennies"; Pupil's Book, p. 194

VOCABULARY

steps, leaps, repeated tones

IDEAS FOR TEACHING

1. Play the recording and have children follow the notation on p. 194 in their book as they listen.

2. Direct attention to the melody of the cumulative part of the song (fourth line) and help children analyze how the tones move. (The melodic movement is stepwise except for the leaps from the fourth to fifth note and from the fifth to sixth note and the repeated tones at the end.)

TRY THIS

1. Encourage individual singing by assigning each cumulative line to a different solo singer.
2. Add a different percussion sound for each animal. Children choose six different instruments. Each instrument will be played two ways—one to indicate the grown animal, the other to indicate the baby animal. For example: a tambourine can be rapped for *pava*, shaken for *pavito*; a woodblock can be struck with the ball of the mallet for *gata*, struck with the stick end for *gatito*, etc.

How do the notes move in this song?

MY TWENTY PENNIES
FOLK SONG FROM VENEZUELA   TRANSLATION BY J. OLCUTT SANDERS

COPYRIGHT © 1948 BY COOPERATIVE RECREATION SERVICE. RENEWED 1976. USED BY PERMISSION.   Orff acc. p. 289

1. With twen-ty pen - nies, with twen-ty pen - nies,

With twen-ty pen - nies I bought a *pa - va*.

The *pa - va* had a *pa - vi - to,*

I have the *pa - va* and the *pa - vi - to;*

And so I still have my twen - ty pen - nies.

Repeat for additional lines in verses 2–6.

2. With twenty pennies, with twenty pennies,

   With twenty pennies I bought a *gata*.

   The *gata* had a *gatito*,

   I have the *gata* and the *gatito*;

   I have the *pava* and the *pavito*;

   And so I still have my twenty pennies.

194 Intervals

3. . . . *chiva . . . chivito . . .*

4. . . . *mona . . . monito . . .*

5. . . . *lora . . . lorito . . .*

6. . . . *vaca . . . vaquito . . .*

TEACHER INFORMATION

Each Spanish word names an animal. The words having the suffix *-ito* refer to the diminutive form of the animal: *pavito*—little turkey; *gatito*—kitten. The meanings of the Spanish words are as follows:

pava, pavito (pah-vah, pah-vee-toh)—turkey
gata, gatito (gah-tah, gah-tee-toh)—cat
chiva, chivito (chee-vah, chee-vee-toh)—goat
mona, monito (moh-nah, moh-nee-toh)—monkey
lora, lorito (loh-rah, lor-ree-toh)—parrot
vaca, vaquito (vah-kah, vah-kee-toh)—cow

REVIEW/REINFORCEMENT

In "My Twenty Pennies," meter in 3 seems strongly accented because of the persistent use of this rhythm pattern:

To help children feel the meter in 3, have them play the pattern on a tambourine to accompany the song. They will tap on the first beat and shake on the second and third beats.

WHAT DO YOU HEAR? 12: INTERVALS 🔘

Listen to the following pieces. Each time a number is called, decide whether the contour of the melody is mostly stepwise, or mostly leapwise.

Listen. Then circle your answer.

---

1 *MOSTLY STEPWISE* ⟨*MOSTLY LEAPWISE*⟩

Saint-Saëns: *Carnival of the Animals*, "Kangaroos"

---

2 ⟨*MOSTLY STEPWISE*⟩ *MOSTLY LEAPWISE*

Ives: *The Cage*

---

3 ⟨*MOSTLY STEPWISE*⟩ *MOSTLY LEAPWISE*

For Thy Gracious Blessing

---

4 *MOSTLY STEPWISE* ⟨*MOSTLY LEAPWISE*⟩

Webern: *Five Pieces for Orchestra*, Op. 10, No. 5

---

5 ⟨*MOSTLY STEPWISE*⟩ *MOSTLY LEAPWISE*

Bock-Harnick: *Sunrise, Sunset*

---

6 *MOSTLY STEPWISE* ⟨*MOSTLY LEAPWISE*⟩

Debussy: *Children's Corner Suite*, "Golliwog's Cakewalk"

Intervals   195

INTERVALS • Lesson 12

MATERIALS
Record 9, *What Do You Hear? 12: Intervals;* spirit master

VOCABULARY
stepwise, leapwise, contour

TEACHER INFORMATION

In *What Do You Hear? 12*, children are asked to identify melodies that move mostly stepwise or mostly leapwise.

You may want to play the recording more than once so that children can feel confident when they make their responses on paper.

MODULE 22

OBJECTIVES, p. xv

THE ARTS: Contour

MATERIALS
Record 3, "All the Pretty Little Horses"; Pupil's Book, pp. 196 and 197; bells, piano, or Autoharp

VOCABULARY
contour, downward direction, upward direction

IDEAS FOR TEACHING
1. Have children sing "All the Pretty Little Horses", p. 49. As they sing, have them trace in the air the movements of the tones in the last two measures of each phrase. (With the exception of the repeated tone at the end of each phrase, the tones move downward by step.)

2. Direct attention to the three contour lines at the top of p. 196 in the Pupil's Book. Question: Which one of the contour lines shows the phrase endings of "All the Pretty Little Horses"? (No. 3 shows the downward movement of the phrase endings.)

3. Have children try singing tones to match the contour of Nos. 1 and 2 at the top of p. 196. They need not be exact. Suggestion: Here is a melody that follows the contour of No. 1:

Which of these lines shows the contour of the phrase endings of "All the Pretty Little Horses?"

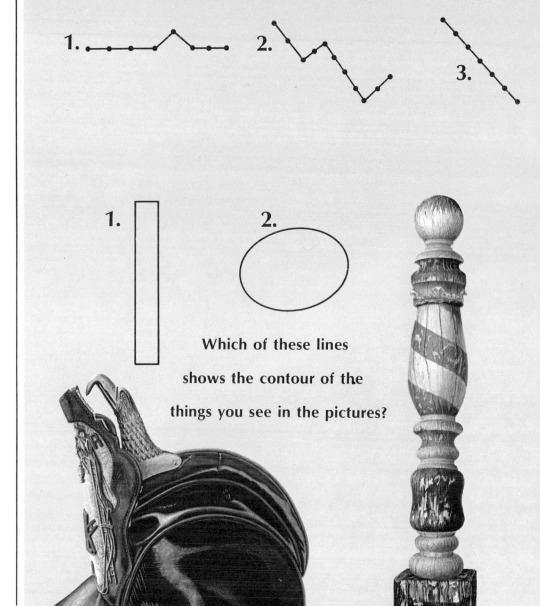

1.

2.

Which of these lines shows the contour of the things you see in the pictures?

196 MODULE 22: The Arts—Contour

REVIEW/REINFORCEMENT

1. There are other graphics in this book that suggest easily recognizable contours that children can draw—for example, instruments, pp. 80, 127, 137, 139; kitten, p. 192; painting, pp. 94 and 95.

2. Fragments of songs with melody contours children can sing and trace are:

(1) A Ram Sam Sam, p. 33

(2) Clover, p. 50

(3) For Health and Strength, p. 132

These lines suggest the contour of a melody.

Sing or play a melody of your own that follows the lines.

SOUND PIECE 6: Sound Contours   JOYCE BOGUSKY REIMER

Make up your own sound piece using some of these ideas.

197

4. Have children look at the two contour drawings on p. 196. Questions: Which of the drawings shows the contour—the general shape—of the fire helmet? Which shows the contour of the barber pole? (Help children discover that the general shape, minus details, is oval for the helmet and rectangular for the pole.)

5. Direct attention to *Sound Piece* 6 on p. 197 in the Pupil's Book. The lines in the Sound Piece suggest the contour of a melody.

6. Have children try improvising a melody that will match the lines in the Sound Piece, using the singing voice and mouth sounds, or bells, piano, or Autoharp. Encourage children to use sounds in an imaginative way. When they are ready, give them an opportunity to perform for the class.

<u>Point out</u>: Some things that can add musical interest to the performances are changes of tempo, changes of dynamics, changes of register, changes of tone color. Let children experiment freely, while keeping the basic idea of upward contour, downward contour, same level contour, and combinations of all three.

TRY THIS

1. Many objects in the environment have an easily recognizable overall shape, or contour. Play a contour guessing game. Children draw the contour they see—tree, book, desk, chair, etc.—and ask the class to guess what it is.

2. A melody contour game can also be played. Each child chooses a fragment of a song, humming it while drawing its contour on the chalkboard. The others must guess the song.

3. Encourage children to create their own contour score like the one on p. 197 in their book.

MODULE 23

OBJECTIVES, p. xv

TEXTURE • Lesson 1

MATERIALS
Record 9, "He's Got the Whole World in His Hands," Versions 1 and 2; Pupil's Book, p. 198; Autoharp

VOCABULARY
melody alone, melody with harmony

IDEAS FOR TEACHING

1. Play the recording of "He's Got the Whole World in His Hands," Versions 1 and 2. Questions: Are the performances the same, or different? (Different) How are they different? (Through questioning and discussion, help children discover that Version 1 is sung as a melody alone; that Version 2 uses an Autoharp accompaniment, which adds harmony to the melody.)

2. When children know the song, have them perform it both ways—first, as a melody alone, then adding harmony to the melody by playing the Autoharp chords as an accompaniment.

The Autoharp player will use two chords—F and C_7 (the chord letters in the music will tell the player when to change from one chord to the other) and will use a rhythm pattern of two strums to a measure throughout.

3. After children have performed the song both ways, point out the symbols at the top of p. 198 in the Pupil's Book.

Sing this song as a melody alone. Then add harmony by playing the Autoharp chords.

HE'S GOT THE WHOLE WORLD IN HIS HANDS

BLACK SPIRITUAL   Piano acc. p. 263

1. He's got the whole world   in his hands,
2. He's got the wind and rain   in his hands,
3. He's got both you and me   in his hands,

He's got the whole world   in his hands,
He's got the wind and rain   in his hands,
He's got both you and me   in his hands,

He's got the whole world   in his hands,
He's got the wind and rain   in his hands,
He's got both you and me   in his hands,

He's got the whole world in his hands.
He's got the whole world in his hands.
He's got the whole world in his hands.

198   MODULE 23: Texture

REVIEW/REINFORCEMENT

1. Play the recording of "A Ram Sam Sam," Versions 1 and 2 (see p. 33 in the Teacher's Edition) and have children listen to hear which version is performed as a melody alone and which is performed as a melody with harmony. Play Version 2 first. (Version 2—melody with harmony; Version 1—melody alone)

2. To reinforce this concept further, play the recording of the two listening selections that are introduced on p. 33.

Smith: *Three Brevities for Solo Flute,* No. 1 (melody alone)
Sor: *Variations on a Theme by Mozart* (melody with harmony)

AN SERENI

FOLK SONG FROM LATIN AMERICA   ENGLISH WORDS BY DELIA RÍOS

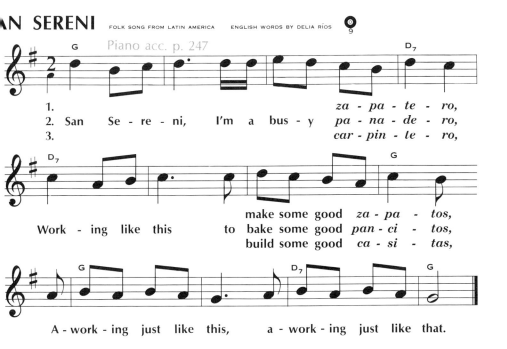

Piano acc. p. 247

1.   za - pa - te - ro,
2. San Se - re - ni,   I'm a bus - y   pa - na - de - ro,
3.   car - pin - te - ro,

make some good za - pa - tos,
Work - ing like this   to bake some good pan - ci - tos,
build some good ca - si - tas,

A - work - ing just like this,   a - work - ing just like that.

Voices or Instruments

Texture 199

MATERIALS
Record 9, "San Serení," Versions 1 and 2; Pupil's Book, p. 199; Autoharp

VOCABULARY
melody alone, melody with harmony, steady beat, contour

IDEAS FOR TEACHING

1. Play the recording of "San Serení," Versions 1 and 2. Through questioning and discussion, help children discover that Version 1 is sung as a melody alone; that Version 2 has an added harmony part.

2. When children know the song, have them perform it both ways—as a melody alone and, by adding an Autoharp accompaniment, as a melody with harmony.

The Autoharp player will use two chords—G and D₇—and will strum the steady beat—two beats per measure—throughout.

3. Play the recording of Version 1 and have children follow the notation of the song to *hear* and *see* how the tones move.

4. Play Version 1 again, but this time have children follow the notation of the instrumental part at the bottom of p. 199. Through questioning and discussion, help children discover that the instrumental part follows the contour of the melody of the song, but a third lower.

TEACHER INFORMATION

Verse 1: *zapatero* (zap-pah-teh-roh) means "shoemaker"; *zapatos* (zah-pah-tohs), "shoes"

Verse 2: *panadero* (pah-nah-deh-roh) means "baker"; *pancitos* (pahn-sée-tohs), "rolls"

Verse 3: *carpintero* (kahr-peen-téh-roh) means "carpenter"; *casitas* (kah-sé-tahs), "little houses"

TRY THIS

The instrumental part for "San Serení" can be played on bells, recorder, or piano. Give children an opportunity to practice the instrumental part on their own. Then, for an ensemble, some children can sing the melody, others can play the Autoharp chords, and those who are able can play the instrumental part.

TEXTURE • Lesson 3

MATERIALS
Record 10, "When I First Came to
This Land"; Pupil's Book, pp. 200 and
201

VOCABULARY
harmony, steps, leaps, repeated
tones, cadence

IDEAS FOR TEACHING
1. Tell children there is a hidden
nursery tune in the melody of
"When I First Came to This Land."
Play the recording and have children
try to identify the nursery tune.
(Some children may notice the simi-
larity between the melody of "When
I First Came to This Land" and
"Twinkle, Twinkle, Little Star"—see p.
166. Experiences such as this will
sharpen children's ears.)

2. Play the recording again and have
children follow the notation of the
song on p. 200 as they listen.
Point out: "When I First Came to
This Land" is a cumulative song. In
each verse a part of the melody is
repeated one more time than in the
preceding verse—the words are different for each repetition.

3. Direct attention to the melody of
the cumulative part of the song
(third staff, measures 1–3) and help
children analyze how the tones
move. (The melody moves by step
and repeated tones.) The last note in
measure 3 is sung on the word *I* in
each cumulative part— ——→

There is a familiar tune hiding in this song.

Can you hear what it is?

WHEN I FIRST CAME TO THIS LAND

WORDS AND MUSIC BY OSCAR BRAND
TRO—© COPYRIGHT 1957 & 1965 LUDLOW MUSIC, INC., NEW YORK, N.Y. USED BY PERMISSION

Repeat these four measures for additional lines in verses 2–5.

2. When I first came to this land,
   I was not a wealthy man.
   Then I bought myself a cow,
   I did what I could.
   I called my cow, *No-milk-now,*
   I called my shack, *Break-my-back.*
   But the land was sweet and good;
   I did what I could.

200 Texture

3. When I first came to this land,
   I was not a wealthy man.
   Then I bought myself a duck,
   I did what I could.
   I called my duck, *Out-of-luck,*
   I called my cow, *No-milk-now,*
   I called my shack, *Break-my-back.*
   But the land . . .

TEACHER INFORMATION

Oscar Brand, who wrote the lyrics for "When I First Came
to This Land," is a scholar, compiler, and performer of
American folk songs. Along with Pete Seeger, Tom Glazer,
and others, Brand played a key role in stimulating interest
in folk music during the thirties, forties, and fifties. He be-
lieves that folk music should be sung in a special folk
style, a spontaneous style he finds easier to recognize than
to describe. Brand can be heard on many recordings and is
the author of *The Ballad Mongers,* a study of folk songs
and American politics.

4. When I first came to this land,

I was not a wealthy man.

Then I got myself a wife,

I did what I could.

I called my wife, *Run-for-your-life,*

I called my duck, *Out-of-luck,*

I called my cow, *No-milk-now,*

I called my shack, *Break-my-back.*

But the land . . .

5. When I first came to this land,

I was not a wealthy man.

Then I got myself a son,

I did what I could.

I called my son, *My-work's-done,*

I called my wife, *Run-for-your-life,*

I called my duck, *Out-of-luck,*

I called my cow, *No-milk-now,*

I called my shack, *Break-my-back.*

But the land . . .

These endings are called *cadences.*

How do the tones move in each one?

Which cadence will you sing to end each verse?

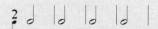

Texture 201

I called my cow, I called my duck. etc. The notation of the cumulative part can be written like this:

4. Direct attention to the notation at the bottom of p. 201. Children will see three endings, called *cadences,* which they can sing for the last three measures of the song. Help children analyze how the tones move in each ending.

R—Repeat; S—Step; L—Leap

5. When children know the melody of the song, have them choose one of the cadences on p. 201 to sing for the final *I did what I could* in each verse.

6. Have a small group of children choose one of the endings to sing while the class sings *I did what I could* as notated in the song. Call attention to the harmony that results when the two endings are sung at the same time.

TRY THIS

Children can add harmony to "When I First Came to This Land" by playing the Autoharp. They will use the chords C, C₇, and F. Children should strum once per measure, using this rhythm:

The chord letter names in the music will tell them when to change from one chord to another.

MATERIALS

Record 10, "This Land Is Your Land"; Pupil's Book, pp. 202 and 203; Auto-harp

VOCABULARY

harmony, no harmony, steady beat, countermelody, thin sound, thicker sound

IDEAS FOR TEACHING

1. Ask children to look at the symbols at the top of p. 198 in their book. Question: What do the symbols mean? (No. 1 means a melody alone; No. 2 means a melody with harmony.)

2. Play the recording of "This Land Is Your Land" and have children show whether they hear harmony or no harmony by pointing to the correct symbol. (Children should point to the symbol that shows a melody with harmony—No. 2.)

3. Play the recording again and, when they can, have children add their voices to those on the recording. <u>Point out</u>: The melody of section B (verse) is like the melody of section A (refrain)—knowing this will make the song easier to learn.

4. When children are able to sing the song independently, they will be able to perform "This Land Is Your Land" two ways—as a melody alone and, by adding an Autoharp accompaniment, as a melody with harmony. <u>Note</u>: The Autoharp player will use three chords—G, D₇, and C. The player will strum the steady beat—two beats per measure.

THIS LAND IS YOUR LAND

Piano acc. p. 24

WORDS AND MUSIC BY WOODY GUTHRIE

TRO—© COPYRIGHT 1956 & 1958 LUDLOW MUSIC, INC. NEW YORK, N.Y. USED BY PERMISSION

REFRAIN

This land is your land,____ This land is my land____

From Cal - i - for - nia____ to the New York is - land;____

From the red wood for - est ____ to the Gulf Stream wa - ters;____

This land was made for you and me.____

VERSE

1. As I was walk - ing____ that rib - bon of high - way,____

I saw a - bove me____ that end - less sky - way.____

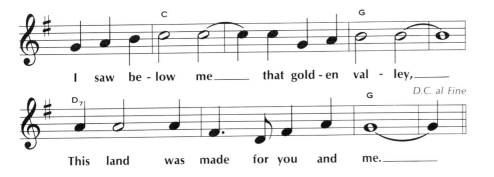

I saw be-low me___ that gold-en val - ley,___

D.C. al Fine

This land was made for you and me.___

2. I've roamed and rambled and I followed my footsteps
   To the sparkling sands of her diamond deserts,
   And all around me a voice was sounding,
   "This land was made for you and me."

3. When the sun comes shining and I was strolling
   And the wheatfields waving and the dust clouds rolling,
   As the fog was lifting a voice was chanting,
   "This land was made for you and me."

Recorder or bells

Texture   203

Note: The chord letter names in the music will tell children when to change from one chord to another. Also, they will begin to strum on the first full measure on the word *your*.

5. If stereo equipment is available, use the Pick-a-Track technique to isolate the accompaniment and the voice parts. Play the accompaniment track alone and have children notice the difference between the accompaniment for the refrains and the accompaniment for the verses. (The accompaniment for the verses is thin; the accompaniment for the refrains is thicker. The addition of the recorder countermelody on p. 203 contributes to the thicker texture in the second and third refrains.)

TRY THIS

Children can perform "This Land Is Your Land" without harmony, then with the harmony added, using the following routine:

Verse 1: Sing melody alone.
Verse 2: Add Autoharp chords.
Verse 3: Add countermelody on recorder or bells.

Point out: As each harmony part is added, the sound of the music becomes thicker.

MATERIALS
Pupil's Book, pp. 204 and 205; bells
or other mallet instruments

VOCABULARY
harmony, ostinato

IDEAS FOR TEACHING
1. The ostinatos (melodic or rhythmic patterns that are repeated over
and over) notated on pp. 204 and
205 in the Pupil's Book can be used
to add harmony parts to songs that
children know. The parts can be
played on the bells or on other mallet instruments.

2. When playing the parts, the notes
with stems going down are played
with a mallet held in the left hand;
the notes with stems going up are
played with a mallet held in the
right hand. Call attention to the
ostinatos in which two bells are
played simultaneously (No. 5 and
No. 10).

3. Use pp. 204 and 205 over a period
of time, having each child play the
pattern she or he chooses while others sing the song. If possible, make
the bells and the Pupil's Book available so that children can practice outside music class time.

Play a harmony part to a song you know.

Play the part all through the song.

The Tree in the Wood, p. 10

1.

Roll an' Rock, p. 12

2.

Michie Banjo, p. 20

3.

Michie Banjo, p. 20

4.

Hey Ho, Hey Lo, p. 42

5.

Skin and Bones, p. 52

6.

204   Texture

To play the patterns on pp. 204 and 205, children will need the following bells:

1. C G C

2. C G G

3. F C

4. F C F

5. A D A

6. E B C D

7. E B C D

8. E B E

9. F C

10. D A

11. F C D

12. F C C

MATERIALS
Record 2, "A Ram Sam Sam," Versions 1, 2, and 3; Pupil's Book, pp. 32, 33, 206, and 207; Autoharp

VOCABULARY
harmony, no harmony

IDEAS FOR TEACHING

1. Write the three diagrams shown on p. 32 in the Pupil's Book (without the explanatory statements) on the chalkboard and ask children to tell what each one represents. (No. 1 shows a melody alone. No. 2 shows a melody with chords. No.3 shows a melody performed as a round.)

2. Ask children to look at the three diagrams on p. 32 in the Pupil's Book. Then play the recording of the three versions of "A Ram Sam Sam" in this order: Version 2, Version 1, Version 3. Ask children to decide which diagram shows what they hear.

3. Reinforce the concept of harmony, no harmony by having children perform "A Ram Sam Sam" three ways. First, have them perform the song (p. 33) as a melody alone. Then call attention to the first diagram on p. 32. Point out: The single wavy line shows a melody sung with no harmony added.

4. Ask a child to play the Autoharp chords as the class sings the melody. The Autoharp player will play two strums per measure, following the chord letters in the music. Then call attention to the second diagram. Point out: The single wavy line plus the short horizontal lines represents a melody with chords—a melody with chords has harmony. ——→

Listen to the recording of "A Ram Sam Sam.

Follow one of the voice parts as you listen.

Will you follow the part for Voice 1, or the part for Voice 2?

A RAM SAM SAM FOLK SONG FROM MOROCCO

206 Texture

Texture 207

5. Have children sing the song as a two-part round. Then call attention to the third diagram. <u>Point out</u>: Sometimes two groups sing the same melody, but don't begin at the same time (a round)—a melody sung as a round has harmony.

6. Ask children to look at the notation of "A Ram Sam Sam" on pp. 206 and 207 in the Pupil's Book. Call attention to the voice parts, Voice I and Voice II. <u>Point out</u>: Each part is written on its own staff and both staffs are connected by a bracket, which means that the music on both staffs is to be performed simultaneously—the song is written out as a two-part round.

7. Play the recording of "A Ram Sam Sam," Version 3, and ask children to choose one of the voice parts to follow as they listen.

TRY THIS

Here is a countermelody that children can play on recorder or bells as others sing the melody of "A Ram Sam Sam." <u>Point out</u>: Adding a countermelody is another way to add harmony to a melody.

TEXTURE • Lesson 7

MATERIALS

Record 9, "America, the Beautiful"; Record 10, Ward: *America, the Beautiful;* Pupil's Book, pp. 208 and 209; bells, recorder

VOCABULARY

texture, density (thick, thin)

IDEAS FOR TEACHING

1. On p. 184, the song "America, the Beautiful" is used primarily to focus on the wide interval in the melody that occurs on the word *A-mer-i-ca* at the beginning of the third phrase. In this lesson, the song is used in different ways to provide an experience in density.

2. Direct attention to the two photographs on p. 209 in the Pupil's Book. Through questioning and discussion, help children discover that the photograph at the bottom has a thicker density than the one at the top. (The bird perching amid a sparse growth of branches suggests a thinner density; the thick blanket of daffodils suggests a thicker density. The photograph at the top has a few things; the photograph at the bottom includes many more things.)

3. Have children sing the first verse of "America, the Beautiful" without the recording.

4. To make the texture a little thicker, have bell or recorder players add the countermelody (p. 185) to the singing.

5. Add the accompaniment on the recording (Record 9) to the singing and playing. ⟶

Sing the melody of "America, the Beautiful" without accompaniment

Follow the notes to help you.

Piano acc. p. 272

AMERICA, THE BEAUTIFUL   MUSIC BY SAMUEL A. WARD   WORDS BY KATHARINE LEE BATES

O beau - ti - ful for spa - cious skies, For am - ber waves of grain,
O beau - ti - ful for pa - triot dream That sees be - yond the years

For pur - ple moun - tain maj - es - ties A - bove the fruit - ed plain!
Thine al - a - bas - ter cit - ies gleam, Un - dimmed by hu - man tears!

A - mer - i - ca! A - mer - i - ca! God shed His grace on thee

And crown thy good with broth - er - hood From sea to shin - ing sea!

Now play the recorder melody on p. 185 to go with

"America, the Beautiful."

This part is called a *countermelody.*

Add the accompaniment on the recording to your

singing and playing.

Notice how the added parts make the music sound thicker.

Listen to another version of "America, the Beautiful."

Is the density *thick,* or *thin?* Why?

 Ward: *America, the Beautiful*

208   Texture

TRY THIS

Ask children to bring in pictures that show (1) one thing, (2) a few things, and (3) many things, so that they can see gradation of density.

TEACHER INFORMATION

For the story of how "America, the Beautiful" was written, see Teacher Information, p. 185.

6. <u>Point out</u>: The added parts make the music sound thicker.

7. Play the recording of Ward's *America, the Beautiful* and ask children to listen for the density. (Most children will hear that it is thick. Some children will be able to express that the use of voices and instruments makes the density thicker. In this experience, the focus should be on *hearing* and *feeling* the difference between thick and thin density. Not all children can be expected to verbalize about what they hear.)

REVIEW/REINFORCEMENT

Throughout this book, children have experienced the textures of melody alone, melody with harmony (Autoharp chords), and melody with other added parts. Review a few of these experiences and encourage children to choose and work on different selections from the following lists:

Autoharp chords
The Tree in the Wood, p. 10
Mama Paquita, p. 18
Lady, Come, p. 22
Ain't Gonna Rain, p. 24
Sweetly Sings the Donkey, p. 25
A Ram Sam Sam, p. 33
Alouette, p. 46
Polly Wolly Doodle, p. 74
Shepherds Came to Bethlehem, p. 120
For Health and Strength, p. 132
Frère Jacques, p. 132
Oh, Susanna, p. 133
Nobody's Business, p. 134
German Instrument Song, p. 136
Hawaiian Rainbows, p. 146
Joyous Chanukah, p. 152
The Mad Man, p. 162
San Sereni, p. 199
(continued below)

Rounds
Lady, Come, p. 22
Sweetly Sings the Donkey, p. 25
Sing Together, p. 32
A Ram Sam Sam, p. 33
Sandy McNab, p. 63
Pray God Bless, p. 78
Valentine Round, p. 78
For Health and Strength, p. 132
Frère Jacques, p. 132
Ol' Clo', p. 164
Kookaburra, p. 189

Added parts
Skin and Bones, p. 52
New Year's Song, p. 60
Love, p. 68
The Ghost of John, p. 71
The Sow Took the Measles, p. 98
Hana ichi momme, p. 128
Nobody's Business, p. 134
German Instrument Song, p. 136
America, p. 183
This Land Is Your Land, p. 202
Ostinatos, pp. 204, 205

MATERIALS

Record 10, *Call Chart 12: Texture;* Pupil's Book, p. 210

VOCABULARY

texture, melody alone, melody accompanied, melody sung as a round

IDEAS FOR TEACHING

1. Write these symbols on the chalkboard and make sure children know what each one means before playing the recording of *Call Chart 12.*

 (1) ‿‿‿ (melody alone)

 (2) (accompanied)

(3) ‿‿‿ (round)

2. Have children listen to *Call Chart 12* to hear the different textures. The drawings in the Call Chart will help them focus attention on this specific musical quality.

Children will hear excerpts from the following:
• *For Thy Gracious Blessing* (round)
• *Little David, Play on Your Harp* (accompanied)
• *Hato Popo* (melody alone)
• *Ringing Bells* (round)
• *Howjido* (accompanied)

Listen to the recording to discover the *texture* in these songs.

The chart will help you by showing a drawing of the texture you hea

CALL CHART 12: TEXTURE

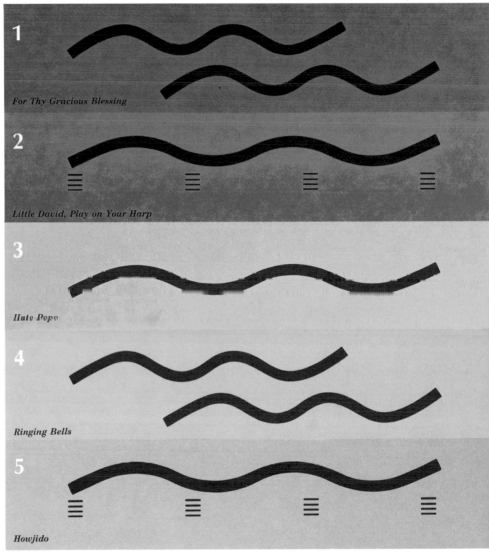

1
For Thy Gracious Blessing

2
Little David, Play on Your Harp

3
Hato Popo

4
Ringing Bells

5
Howjido

210 Texture

TRY THIS

Some children may be able to find other recorded examples throughout the book that show a melody alone, a melody sung as a round, or a melody with chords. Make the recordings available to responsible children, then give them an opportunity to share their discoveries with the class.

When each number is called, decide whether you hear *harmony,* or *no harmony.* Then decide what *tone colors* you hear. Do you hear voices, or instruments, or voices and instruments?

Listen. Then circle everything you hear.

Zynczak: *Love You*

1 HARMONY   (VOICES)
   (NO HARMONY)   INSTRUMENTS
   VOICES AND INSTRUMENTS

2 (HARMONY)   (VOICES)
   NO HARMONY   INSTRUMENTS
   VOICES AND INSTRUMENTS

3 (HARMONY)   VOICES
   NO HARMONY   INSTRUMENTS
   (VOICES AND INSTRUMENTS)

4 (HARMONY)   (VOICES)
   NO HARMONY   INSTRUMENTS
   VOICES AND INSTRUMENTS

5 (HARMONY)   (VOICES)
   NO HARMONY   INSTRUMENTS
   VOICES AND INSTRUMENTS

6 (HARMONY)   VOICES
   NO HARMONY   INSTRUMENTS
   (VOICES AND INSTRUMENTS)

Texture   211

TEXTURE • Lesson 9

MATERIALS
Record 10, *What Do You Hear? 13: Texture;* spirit master

VOCABULARY
harmony, no harmony, tone color

TEACHER INFORMATION

In *What Do You Hear? 13,* children are asked to listen for two things: (a) harmony, or no harmony and (b) tone color—voices, or instruments, or voices and instruments.

It is suggested that this What do You Hear? be given twice. The first time, have children listen for harmony or no harmony only. The second time, have them listen for voices, or instruments, or voices and instruments.

MATERIALS
Record 10, "El Nacimiento"; "El rorro"; Pupil's Book, pp. 212 and 213; Autoharp, bells, recorder

VOCABULARY
harmony, no harmony, texture, countermelody

IDEAS FOR TEACHING
1. Play the recording of "El Nacimiento" and "El rorro" and ask children which one has harmony and which one has no harmony. ("El Nacimiento" has no harmony; "El rorro" has harmony.)

2. After children are able to sing "El Nacimiento" as a melody alone, they can add harmony by playing the Autoharp pattern and the recorder or bell countermelody notated on p. 212 in the Pupil's Book. Suggestion: Assign the added parts to selected children—some have had many experiences playing the Autoharp, others have been working with recorder and bell parts.

Note: It is not necessary for every child to be involved in every activity. The performance can serve as a means of helping the children heighten their musical perception. In this case, they hear how different parts create harmony.

Listen to two songs that children in Mexico sing at Christmastime.

Which one has harmony?
Which one has no harmony?

EL NACIMIENTO

San Jo-sé y Ma-rí-a____ a Be-lén lle-ga-ron,

Pi-die-ron po-sa-da____ y se la ne-ga-ron.

Sing the melody alone.

Add harmony by playing Autoharp chords.

A min. A min. E₇ E₇ throughout

Add a countermelody.

Recorder or Bells

212 Texture

TEACHER INFORMATION

Literal translation for "El Nacimiento": Saint Joseph and Mary arrived in Bethlehem. They asked for lodging and they were refused, (El Nacimiento means "the birth.")

Pronunciation guide:
San Jo-sé y Mar-ri-a a Be-len lle-ga-ron,
sahn hoh-seh ee mah-ree-ah ah beh-lehn yeh-gah-rohn

Pi-die-ron po-sa-da y se la ne-ga-ron.
pee-theyh-rohn poh-sah-thah ee seh lah neh-gah-rohn

L RORRO

CHRISTMAS SONG FROM MEXICO   ENGLISH WORDS BY VERNE MUNOZ   Piano acc. p. 224

A la ru-ru-ru, ni-ño chi-qui-to,

Duer-ma-se ya,___ mi Je-su-si-to.___

1. Now all the an-i-mals their si-lence keep,___

So they will not dis-turb the In-fant's sleep.

The choirs of holy angels from on high,
Foretold the coming of this blessed child.

Oh, night of happiness, oh, night of joy,
Guard well the Mother and Her Little Boy.

Recorder

Recorder, Violin, Bells

Texture 213

TRY THIS

1. Add the tone color of percussion instruments for an "El Nacimiento" ensemble.

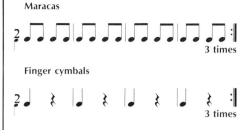

Maracas

3 times

Finger cymbals

3 times

2. The recorder and violin parts for "El rorro" (notated on p. 213 in the Pupil's Book) can also be played on bells or keyboard. However, if possible, stimulate the children's interest in string instruments by inviting older children into the classroom to demonstrate.

<u>Note</u>: There are many countermelodies and ostinato parts throughout the book that can be played on orchestral instruments.

TEACHER INFORMATION

Literal translation for "El rorro": A la ru-ru-ru, dear little child. Sleep now, my little Jesus. (*El rorro* means "the Baby.")

Pronunciation guide:
A la ru-ru-ru, ni-ño chi-qui-to,
ah lah roo-roo-roo nee-nyoh chee-kee-toh

Duer-ma-se ya, mi Je-su-si-to,
dwehr-mah-say yah mee hay-soo-see-toh

MATERIALS

Record 10, "Melchior and Balthazar";
Pupil's Book, p. 214; bells

VOCABULARY

texture, harmony

IDEAS FOR TEACHING

1. Play the recording of "Melchior
and Balthazar" and help children discover that verse 1 is sung in unison,
that verses 2 and 3 are sung as a
two-part round.

2. When children are familiar with
the song, have them sing it as a melody alone. Then have them change
the texture by adding harmony.
• Choose a child to play the bell ostinato (notated on p. 214 in the Pupil's Book) throughout the singing.
• Have the children change the texture again by singing the melody as
a two-part round.

MELCHIOR AND BALTHAZAR

FOLK SONG FROM FRANCE   ENGLISH WORDS BY EMILY VID

1. Mel - chi - or   and   Bal - tha - zar

Went up - on   a   jour - ney, Went up - on   a   jour - ney;

Mel - chi - or   and   Bal - tha - zar

Went up - on   a   jour - ney   far   with   King   Gas - par.

2. When they came to Bethlehem

   They opened up the baskets,

   Opened up the baskets;

   When they came to Bethlehem

   They opened up the baskets

   They had brought with them.

3. Then they ate some cabbage soup.

   They were very hungry,

   Oh, so very hungry;

   Then they ate some cabbage soup.

   They were just as hungry

   As they could be.

Play this bell part all through the song.

Bells

214 Texture

TRY THIS

Have children add the tone color of percussion instruments to the performance of "Melchior and Balthazar."

Drum

Ringing instrument

Woodblock—Play the rhythm of the words.

WHAT DO YOU HEAR? 14: STYLE 🔘

Each time a number is called there will be two pieces played.
Sometimes the two pieces will come from the same
musical family, or style.
Other times the two pieces will be from two different musical
families, or styles.

If you think the two pieces are in the same style, draw a circle
around the word SAME.

If you think the two pieces are in different styles, draw a circle
around the word DIFFERENT.

Listen. Then circle what you hear.

1	SAME	(DIFFERENT)	*Idiophone Solo* Ravosa: *Love*
2	(SAME)	DIFFERENT	*Buying Fish* *'Taters*
3	(SAME)	DIFFERENT	Bach: *Suite No. 3 in D Minor,* "Overture" Bach: *Suite No. 2 in B Minor,* "Overture"
4	SAME	(DIFFERENT)	Debussy: *Children's Corner Suite,* "Golliwog's Cakewalk" Ussachevsky: *Four Miniatures,* No. 1
5	(SAME)	DIFFERENT	Mozart: *Three German Dances,* No. 3 Mozart: *Horn Concerto in E♭ Major*
6	(SAME)	DIFFERENT	Ussachevsky: *Four Miniatures,* No. 1 Hays: *Sound Piece No. 3*
7	SAME	(DIFFERENT)	Vivaldi: *The Four Seasons* (winter) Bartók: *Roumanian Dance No. 6*

215

MODULE 24

OBJECTIVES, p. xv

STYLE: Time Lines

MATERIALS
Record 10, *What Do You Hear? 14:
Styles;* spirit master

VOCABULARY
style

TEACHER INFORMATION

Defer giving this What Do You Hear?
evaluation until children have
worked through the material on pp.
216 and 217 in the Pupil's Book.
What Do You Hear? 14 presents an
opportunity to reinforce the perception of style as the overall effect of
the music. These SAME or DIFFER-
ENT examples are quite easy to identify, but nevertheless encourage care-
ful comparisons.
Make sure the children understand
that when each number is called,
two pieces will be heard for them to
compare.

STYLE: Time Lines

MATERIALS

Record 10, *Style: Time Lines;* Pupil's Book, pp. 216 and 217

VOCABULARY

style

IDEAS FOR TEACHING

1. Direct attention to the time line on p. 216 in the Pupil's Book. Start a trip through history, beginning with Columbus's voyage to America in 1492. Have children follow the dotted line and discuss each event as it is pictured.

- First Thanksgiving celebrated—1621
- George Washington lived—1732-1799
- Abraham Lincoln lived—1809-1865
- Thomas Edison developed the electric light bulb—1879
- Television invented—c. 1927
- Sputnik (first space satellite) launched—1957
- NOW—have children list current happenings.

2. Discussion: As time went on, during the course of history, some important things happened. We remember those times in the past by the important things that occurred. In each time period the style of life was quite different—people dressed differently, ate different things, lived in different kinds of houses, even *talked* differently.

3. Direct attention to the music time line on p. 217 in the Pupil's Book. Play *Dadme Albricias, Hijos d'Eva,* the first selection on the recording *Style: Time Lines.* Tell children that this music comes from around the

→

Find the things that happened very long ago.

Find the things that happened not so long ago.

What is happening now?

Follow the dotted line to help you.

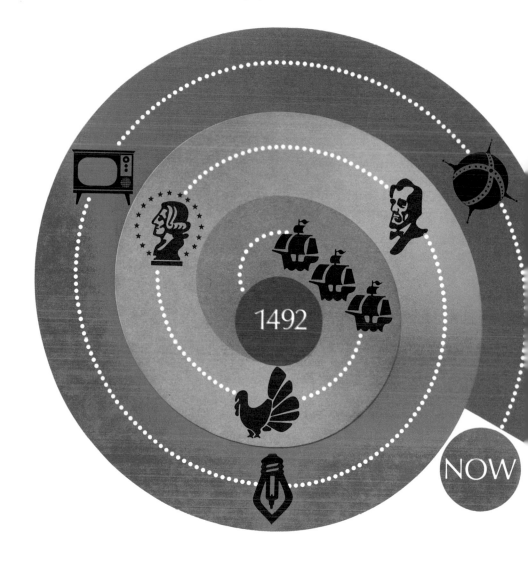

216   Style: Time Lines

You have listened to music in different *styles* composed at different times. Follow the dotted line while you listen. Discover which instruments were used to help create different *styles of music*. Pretend you are a child living at one of these times. What musical style would you listen to? Listen to the piece you have selected.

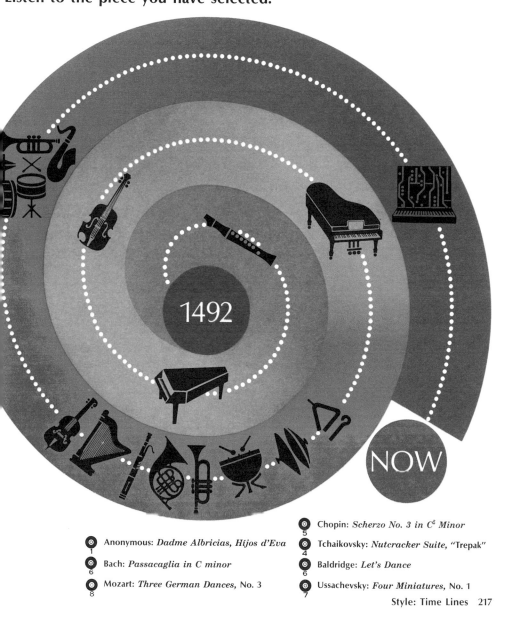

1492

NOW

Anonymous: *Dadme Albricias, Hijos d'Eva*
1

Bach: *Passacaglia in C minor*
6

Mozart: *Three German Dances*, No. 3
8

Chopin: *Scherzo No. 3 in C♯ Minor*
5

Tchaikovsky: *Nutcracker Suite*, "Trepak"
4

Baldridge: *Let's Dance*
6

Ussachevsky: *Four Miniatures*, No. 1
7

Style: Time Lines   217

time that Columbus came to America—it is in the *style* of music that Columbus might have known.

4. Continue playing the selections on the recording *Style: Time Lines*. <u>Point out</u>: Each selection (all from previous lessons) is in a style of music that comes from a particular time.

<u>Suggestion</u>: If interest permits, you may want to draw some parallels be tween the music selections listed on p. 217 and the events pictured in the time line on p. 216.

- Bach (1685-1750)—Washington (1732-1799)
- Mozart (1756-1791)—Washington (1732-1799)
- Chopin (1810-1849)—Lincoln (1809-1865)
- Tchaikovsky (1840-1893)—Edison (1847-1931)
- Baldridge (first half of the 20th century)—Television (c. 1927)
- Ussachevsky (1911-)—Sputnik (1957)

When students complete this lesson, they are ready to take Test 3 for Book 3. Additional information about Silver Burdett Music Competency Tests is found in the introduction of this book.

TEACHER INFORMATION

This lesson attempts to reinforce the children's growing ability to grasp the concept of historical flow. Music has a history, as does every other important aspect of human culture. While details of different styles need not be grasped at this age, the idea that musical styles change in time is an important one.

AMERICA

TRADITIONAL
WORDS BY SAMUEL FRANCIS SMITH

PUPIL'S BOOK, PAGE 183

My coun - try! 'tis of thee, Sweet land of lib - er - ty,
My na - tive coun - try, thee, Land of the no - ble free,
Our fa - thers' God, to Thee, Au - thor of lib - er - ty,

Of thee I sing; Land where my fa - thers died, Land of the
Thy name I love; I love thy rocks and rills, Thy woods and
To Thee we sing; Long may our land be bright With free - dom's

Pil - grims' pride, From ev - 'ry moun - tain - side Let__ free - dom ring!
tem - pled hills, My heart__ with__ rap - ture thrills Like__ that a - bove.
ho - ly light; Pro - tect__ us__ by Thy might, Great__ God, our King!

With spirit

YANKEE DOODLE

TRADITIONAL
ARRANGED BY WILLIAM WARD
WORDS BY DR. RICHARD SHUCKBURGH

PUPIL'S BOOK, PAGE 130

1. Fath'r and I went down to camp, A - long with Cap - tain Good - in', And
2. And there we saw a thou - sand men, As rich as Squire__ Da - vid; And

there we saw the men and boys As thick as hast - y pud - din'.
what they wast - ed ev - 'ry day, I wish it could be sav - ed.

218

Yan - kee Doo - dle, keep it up, Yan - kee Doo - dle dan - dy,

Mind the mu - sic and the step And with the girls be hand - y.

3. And there was Captain Washington
    Upon a slapping stallion,
    A-giving orders to his men;
    I guess there was a million.

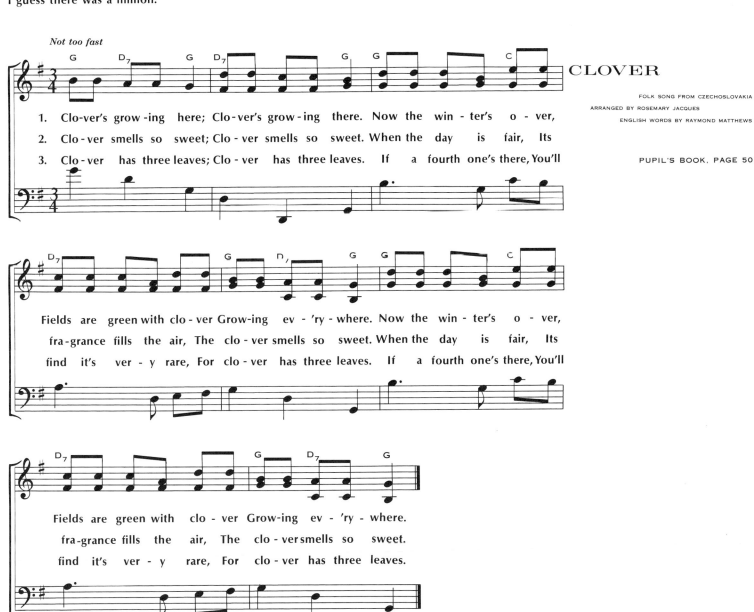

Not too fast

CLOVER

FOLK SONG FROM CZECHOSLOVAKIA
ARRANGED BY ROSEMARY JACQUES
ENGLISH WORDS BY RAYMOND MATTHEWS

PUPIL'S BOOK, PAGE 50

1. Clo-ver's grow-ing here; Clo-ver's grow-ing there. Now the win-ter's o - ver,
2. Clo-ver smells so sweet; Clo-ver smells so sweet. When the day is fair, Its
3. Clo-ver has three leaves; Clo-ver has three leaves. If a fourth one's there, You'll

Fields are green with clo-ver Grow-ing ev - 'ry-where. Now the win-ter's o - ver,
fra-grance fills the air, The clo-ver smells so sweet. When the day is fair, Its
find it's ver - y rare, For clo-ver has three leaves. If a fourth one's there, You'll

Fields are green with clo-ver Grow-ing ev - 'ry-where.
fra-grance fills the air, The clo-ver smells so sweet.
find it's ver - y rare, For clo-ver has three leaves.

ALL THE PRETTY LITTLE HORSES

FOLK SONG FROM SOUTHERN UNITED STATES
ARRANGED BY ROSEMARY JACQUES
COLLECTED, ADAPTED AND ARRANGED BY
JOHN A. LOMAX & ALAN LOMAX
TRO-® COPYRIGHT 1934 AND RENEWED 1962 LUDLOW MUSIC,
INC., NEW YORK, N.Y. USED BY PERMISSION.

PUPIL'S BOOK, PAGE 49

Hush - a - by, don't you cry, Go to sleep - y, lit - tle ba - by.

When you wake, you shall have All the pret - ty lit - tle hors - es:

Blacks and bays, dap - ples and grays, Coach and six - a - lit - tle hors - es.

Hush - a - by, don't you cry, Go to sleep - y, lit - tle ba - by.

CHE CHE KOOLAY

SINGING GAME FROM GHANA
FROM HI, NEIGHBOR (BOOK 2) BY UNITED STATES FOR UNICEF
UNITED NATIONS, N.Y. USED BY PERMISSION.

PUPIL'S BOOK, PAGE 34

SOLO — CHORUS — SOLO — CHORUS

Che - che koo - lay, che - che koo - lay, Che - che Ko - fee sa che - che Ko - fee sa

SOLO — CHORUS — SOLO — CHORUS

Ko - fee sa - lan - ga, Ko - fee sa - lan - ga. Ka - ka - shee lan - ga, ka - ka - shee lan - ga.

SOLO — CHORUS

Koom - ma - dye - day, Koom - ma - dye - day.

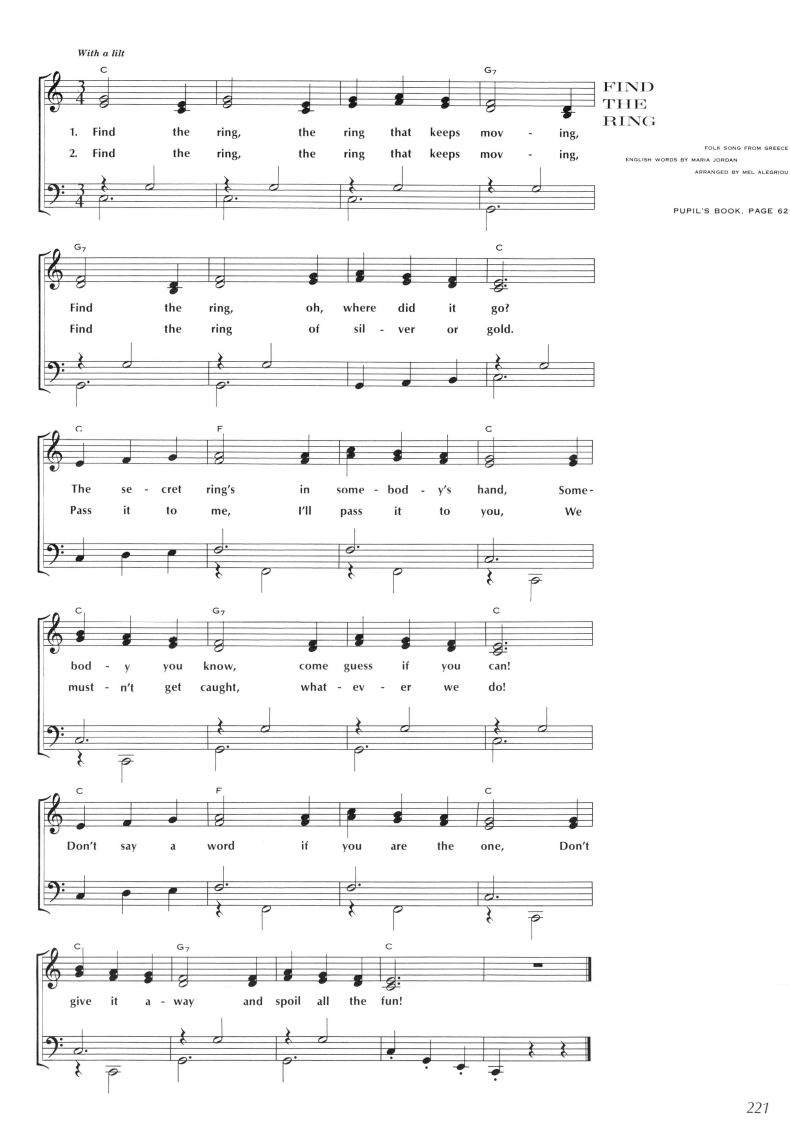

FOLK SONG FROM GREECE

ENGLISH WORDS BY MARIA JORDAN

ARRANGED BY MEL ALEGRIOU

FIND THE RING

PUPIL'S BOOK, PAGE 62

With a lilt

C — G₇

1. Find the ring, the ring that keeps mov - ing,
2. Find the ring, the ring that keeps mov - ing,

G₇ — C

Find the ring, oh, where did it go?
Find the ring of sil - ver or gold.

C — F — C

The se - cret ring's in some - bod - y's hand, Some-
Pass it to me, I'll pass it to you, We

C — G₇ — C

bod - y you know, come guess if you can!
must - n't get caught, what - ev - er we do!

C — F — C

Don't say a word if you are the one, Don't

C — G₇ — C

give it a - way and spoil all the fun!

THE GHOST OF JOHN

WORDS AND MUSIC BY MARTHA GRUBB
ARRANGED BY ROSEMARY JACQUES

PUPIL'S BOOK, PAGE 71

Spookily

Have you seen the ghost of John? Long white bones with the skin all gone, _____

Oo, _____ Oo, _____ Would-n't it be chil-ly with no skin on!

THE BARNYARD

WORDS AND MUSIC BY CARMINO RAVOSA
ARRANGED BY ROSEMARY JACQUES
© 1972 CARMINO RAVOSA

PUPIL'S BOOK, PAGE 118

Brightly

1. Barn-yard, barn-yard, all a-round the barn-yard, Hear the cow go, "Moo, moo."
2. Barn-yard, barn-yard, all a-round the barn-yard, Hear the pig go, "Oink, oink."

Barn-yard, barn-yard, all a-round the barn-yard, Hear the duck go, "Quack, quack."
Barn-yard, barn-yard, all a-round the barn-yard, Hear the sheep go, "Baa, baa."

All a-round the barn-yard, An-i-mals are talk-ing;
All a-round the barn-yard, An-i-mals are talk-ing;

Though it sounds to you like Just a lot of squawk-ing.
Though it sounds to you like Just a lot of squawk-ing.

Barn - yard, barn-yard, all a - round the barn - yard, Hear the goose go, "Honk, honk."
Barn - yard, barn-yard, all a - round the barn - yard, Hear the horse go, "Neigh, neigh."

Barn - yard, barn-yard, all a - round the barn - yard, Hear the chick-en, "Cluck, cluck,
Barn - yard, barn-yard, all a - round the barn - yard, Hear the don-key, "Hee - haw,

Cluck, cluck."
Hee - haw."

U - mi wa hi - ro - i na oh - ki - i na,

Tsu - ki ga no - bo - ru shi hi ga shi - zu - mu.

IMAGINATION OF GRAND SEA

FOLK SONG FROM JAPAN
ARRANGED BY GEORGE DOUGLASS
ENGLISH WORDS BY RICHARD MORRIS

PUPIL'S BOOK, PAGE 129

1. *Grand is the evening sea, majestic and deep;*
   There, as the moon awakes, the sun will go to sleep.

2. *Calm are the mighty waves; the water, so blue;*
   I wonder where the sea and all the waves go to.

3. *Many the tiny ships that float on the sea;*
   Some day to foreign lands those ships will carry me.

EL RORRO

CHRISTMAS SONG FROM MEXICO
ARRANGED BY ROSEMARY JACQUES
ENGLISH WORDS BY VERNE MUÑOZ

PUPIL'S BOOK, PAGE 213

A la ru - ru - ru, ni - ño chi - qui - to, Duer - ma - se ya, ___ mi Je - su -

si - to. ___
1. Now all the an - i - mals their si - lence keep, ___
2. The choirs of ho - ly an - gels from on high, ___
3. Oh, night of hap - pi - ness, oh, night of joy,

So they will not dis - turb the In - fant's sleep.
Fore - told the com - ing of this bless - ed Child. A la ru - ru - ru, ni - ño chi -
Guard well the Moth - er and Her lit - tle Boy.

qui - to, Duer - ma - se ya, ___ mi Je - su - si - to. ___

OLD
DAN
TUCKER

AMERICAN FOLK SONG
ARRANGED BY SCOTT GARRISON

PUPIL'S BOOK, PAGE 15

Old Dan Tuck - er was a might - y man, He washed his face in the fry - ing pan,

Combed his hair with a wag - on wheel, Had a tooth - ache in his heel;

So get out the way, Old Dan Tuck-er; Get out the way, Old Dan Tuck-er;

Get out the way, Old Dan Tuck-er, You're too late to get your sup-per.

Simply

Twin-kle, twin-kle, lit-tle star, How I won-der what you are.

Up a-bove the world so high, like a dia-mond in the sky.

TWINKLE, TWINKLE, LITTLE STAR

TRADITIONAL
ARRANGED BY BERNARD HEIDEN

PUPIL'S BOOK, PAGE 166

Lyrically

Twin-kle, twin-kle, lit-tle star, How I won-der what you are,

Up a-bove the world so high, Like a dia-mond in the sky.

TWINKLE, TWINKLE, LITTLE STAR

MUSIC BY DAVID EDDLEMAN
WORDS TRADITIONAL

PUPIL'S BOOK, PAGE 166

HEY HO, HEY LO

SLOVAKIAN FOLK TUNE
ARRANGED BY ROSEMARY JACQUES
ENGLISH WORDS BY RAYMOND MATTHEWS

PUPIL'S BOOK, PAGE 42

Hey ho, hey lo, tam-bou-rines are ring-ing; Hey ho, hey lo, ring-ing all a-round.

Lis-ten, lis-ten, hear them jin-gle jan-gle, Mak-ing mu-sic with a hap-py sound.

Fast-er, fast-er, how they jin-gle jan-gle, Mak-ing mu-sic with a hap-py sound.

BUT THE CAT CAME BACK

WORDS AND MUSIC BY JOSEF MARAIS (ASCAP)
ARRANGED BY EDWARD PAYNTER
COPYRIGHT 1956. FIDEREE MUSIC CO. USED BY PERMISSION

PUPIL'S BOOK, PAGE 20

1. Fred-die Wil-son had a cat that he did-n't want to keep. He
2. Fred-die put him on a ship and they head-ed for Cey-lon. The
3. Then he put the cat a-board with a man in a bal-loon, Who would

of-fered him for free and he tried to sell him cheap. He called up-on the
ship was o-ver-loaded more than twen-ty thou-sand ton. Not far a-way from
give the cat a-way to the man in the moon. The bal-loon it did-n't

preach-er one Sun-day for ad-vice; The preach-er said, "Yes, leave him here, it
shore___ the car-go ship went down, There was-n't an-y doubt a-bout it:
rise, ___ it burst in bits in-stead, And ten miles from the spot, they found the

REFRAIN

B

would be so nice!"
ev-'ry-body drowned. But the cat came back, he would-n't stay a-way, He was
man___ stone dead.

sit-ting on the porch on the ver-y next day. The cat came back, he

did-n't want to roam, The ver-y next day it was "Home, Sweet Home."

Gaily

ALOUETTE

FOLK SONG FROM CANADA
ARRANGED BY W. W. SCHMIDT

A - lou-et - te, gen - tille A - lou-et - te, A - lou-et - te

PUPIL'S BOOK, PAGE 46

Fine

je te plu - me - rai. 1. Je te plu - me - rai la tête, Je te plu - me - rai la tête,
2. Je te plu - me - rai la bec, Je te plu - me - rai la bec,

1. Et la tête, et la tête.

2. Et la bec, et la bec. A - lou -ette, A - lou -ette. Oh!
   Et la tête, et la tête.

3. Le nez   4. Le dos   5. Les pattes   6. Le cou

LOVE

WORDS AND MUSIC BY CARMINO RAVOSA
ARRANGED BY JAMES ROOKER
© 1971 CARMINO RAVOSA

PUPIL'S BOOK, PAGE 68

Gaily

1. Love can charm the birds____ right out of the trees,
2. Love can turn a hur - ri - cane in - to a breeze,
3. Love can bring a gi - ant right down to his knees,

Love can take the hon - ey a - way from the bees;
Love can get a her - mit to smile and say, "Cheese";
Love can make the North and the South Poles un - freeze;

Love can make a li - on stand up and say, "Please."____
Love can make a dog learn to live with his fleas.____
Love can make a kid learn to eat all his peas.____

LEMONS

FOLK SONG FROM PUERTO RICO
ARRANGED BY ROSEMARY JACQUES
ENGLISH WORDS BY ELIZABETH S. BACHMAN

PUPIL'S BOOK, PAGE 170

1. A sil - ly old bird in a lem - on tree Just sat the whole day through; A
2. He grabbed __ a lem - on and took a bite, Then made an aw - ful face. He

sil - ly old bird in a lem - on tree Just sat the whole day through. Ah, 'tis
grabbed __ a lem - on and took a bite, Then made an aw - ful face. Ah, 'tis

true! Ah, 'tis true!
A sil - ly old bird in a lem - on tree Just
He bit ___ the lem - on and made a face, I

sat, and all that he could see Were yel - low lem - ons hang - ing on the
guess he did - n't like the taste Of the yel - low lem - ons hang - ing on the

tree.
tree. Ah, 'tis true!

3. That silly old bird was very mad, } (2 times)
   He shook the lemon tree.
   Ah, 'tis true! Ah, 'tis true!
   That silly old bird was mad, you see,
   With all his might he shook the tree,
   And sent the lemons crashing down on me.

229

CALYPSO FROM JAMAICA
ARRANGED BY WILLIAM SIMON
ENGLISH WORDS BY MARGARET MARKS

PUPIL'S BOOK, PAGE 180

HILL AN' GULLY

Moderately

REFRAIN

Hill an' gul-ly rid-er, Hill an' gul-ly.

Hill an' gul-ly rid-er, Hill an' gul-ly.

VERSE

1. Took my horse an' come down, Hill an' gul-ly. But my horse done stum-ble down, Hill an' gul-ly. An' the night-time come an' tum-ble down, Hill an' gul-ly.

2. Oh, the moon shine bright down, Hill an' gul-ly. Ain't no place to hide in down, Hill an' gul-ly. An' a zom-bie come a rid-in' down, Hill an' gul-ly.

3. Oh, my knees they shake down,
   Hill an' gully.
   An' my heart starts quakin' down,
   Hill an' gully.
   An' I run till daylight breakin' down,
   Hill an' gully.

4. That's the last I set down,
   Hill an' gully.
   Pray the Lord don' let me down,
   Hill an' gully.
   Ain't nobody goin' to get me down,
   Hill an' gully.

OH, SUSANNA

WORDS AND MUSIC BY STEPHEN FOSTER
ARRANGED BY ALBERT DEVITO

PUPIL'S BOOK, PAGE 133

1. I__ came from Al - a - ba - ma With my ban - jo on my knee, I'm__
2. I__ had a dream the oth - er night, When ev - 'ry -thing was still. I__

going to Loui - si - an - a, My____ true love for to see; It__
thought I saw Su-san - na A-com - ing down the hill. The __

rained all night the day I left, The weath-er it was dry; The__
buck-wheat cake was in her mouth, The tear was in her eye. Says__

sun so hot I froze to death; Su - san na, don't you cry.
I, "I'm com - ing from the South, Su-san - na, don't you cry."

REFRAIN

Oh, Su - san-na, Oh, don't you cry for me, I've__

come from Al - a - ba - ma With my ban - jo on my knee.

Smoothly

HAWAIIAN RAINBOWS

HAWAIIAN FOLK SONG
ARRANGED BY BRUCE SIMPSON

PUPIL'S BOOK, PAGE 146

Ha - wai - ian rain - bows, White clouds roll by;

You show your col - ors A - gainst the sky.

Ha - wai - ian rain - bows, It seems to me,

Reach from the moun - tain Down to the sea.

Merrily

WONDERS NEVER CEASE

YIDDISH FOLK SONG
ARRANGED BY ROSEMARY JACQUES
ENGLISH WORDS BY ELIZABETH S. BACHMAN

"HOB ICH A POR OKSN" FROM A TREASURY OF JEWISH
FOLKSONG EDITED BY RUTH RUBIN COPYRIGHT © 1950 BY
SCHOCKEN BOOKS INC. REPRINTED BY PERMISSION OF SCHOCKEN
BOOKS INC.

PUPIL'S BOOK, PAGE 186

1. I've a pair of ox - en, ox - en, Ox - en who cut noo - dles, noo - dles,
2. I've a pair of bears, bears, Bears who sweep the rooms, rooms.

Do you mean you've nev - er seen An ox cut noo - dles by the oo - dles?
Do you mean you've nev - er seen A
bear sweep rooms with - out a broom? An ox cut noo - dles by the oo - dles?

232

*Repeat these two measures for additional lines in verses 2-6.

3. I've a pair of goats, goats,
   Goats who wheel the children, children.
   Do you mean you've never seen
   A goat so glad to wheel a lad?
   A bear sweep rooms without a broom?
   An ox cut noodles by the oodles?
   Wonders . . .

4. I've a pair of dogs, dogs,
   Dogs who write with ink, ink.
   Do you mean you've never seen
   A dog who'd think to write with ink?
   A goat so glad to wheel a lad?
   A bear sweep rooms without a broom?
   An ox cut noodles by the oodles?
   Wonders . . .

5. I've a pair of hens, hens,
   Hens who gather wood, wood.
   Do you mean you've never seen
   A hen so good at gath'ring wood?
   A dog who'd think to write with ink?
   A goat so glad to wheel a lad?
   A bear sweep rooms without a broom?
   An ox cut noodles by the oodles?
   Wonders . . .

6. I've a pair of birds, birds,
   Birds who like to bake, bake.
   Do you mean you've never seen
   A bird who baked a layer cake?
   A hen so good at gath'ring wood?
   A dog who'd think to write with ink?
   A goat so glad to wheel a lad?
   A bear sweep rooms without a broom?
   An ox cut noodles by the oodles?
   Wonders . . .

THE MAD MAN

AMERICAN FOLK TUNE
ARRANGED BY GEORGE DOUGLASS
WORDS BY JEANNE WILHELMS

PUPIL'S BOOK, PAGE 162

3. The bag of ice it turned to slush
   And he fell in a pan of mush.

4. The pan of mush it was so cold
   And he fell in a pot of gold.

5. The pot of gold it was so rich
   And he fell in a muddy ditch.

6. The muddy ditch it was so deep
   And he fell in a flock of sheep.

7. The flock of sheep did moan and groan
   And he fell in an ice-cream cone.

8. The ice-cream cone it was so sweet
   And he fell on his own two feet.

GERMAN
INSTRUMENT
SONG

FOLK SONG FROM GERMANY
ARRANGED BY LURA SNELL
ENGLISH WORDS BY TRILLA STATLER

PUPIL'S BOOK, PAGE 136

1. If I had a bell to play a tune on, If I had a bell, oh, how I'd *ring.*
(Instrumental)

2. If I had a fiddle, fiddle, fiddle,
   If I had a fiddle, how I'd *bow.*

3. If I had a pipe to play a tune on,
   If I had a pipe, oh, how I'd *blow.*

4. If I had an Autoharp to play on,
   If I had an Autoharp, I'd *strum.*

5. If I had a drum that I could play on,
   If I had a drum, oh, how I'd *beat.*

6. Now we have a tune to play together,
   Now we have a tune, oh, how we'll *play.*

I
CLAP
MY
HANDS

WORDS AND MUSIC BY CHRIS DEDRICK
© 1972 ALMITRA MUSIC COMPANY, INC.

PUPIL'S BOOK, PAGE 2

1. Ev-'ry time I hear some mu-sic play-in' in time,—
2. Ev-'ry time I see some-bod-y win-nin' a race,—

I clap my hands. ___

Ev - 'ry time I no - tice that the
Ev - 'ry time a pup - py comes a -

weath - er is fine, ___
lick - in' my face, ___

I clap my hands. ___

f

Clap your hands. ___

Clap your hands. ___

Clap your hands. ___

Clap your hands. ___

3. Ev-'ry time I see some-bod-y smil-in' at me,____ I clap my hands.

Ev-'ry time I think a-bout how good life can be,____

I clap my hands.____ Clap your hands.____

Clap your hands. ____

Clap your hands. ____

Clap your hands. ____

< Yeah!

Vigorously

SOLO CHORUS SOLO CHORUS

OLD HOUSE

AMERICAN FOLK SONG
COLLECTED BY JOHN W. WORK
ARRANGED BY CAMERON MCGRAW

PUPIL'S BOOK. PAGE 181

1. Old house. Tear it down! Who's going to help me? Tear it down!
2. New house. Build it up! Who's going to help me? Build it up!

SOLO CHORUS SOLO CHORUS

Bring me a ham-mer. Tear it down! Bring me a saw. ___ Tear it down!
Build it up! Build it up!

SOLO CHORUS SOLO CHORUS

Next thing you bring me, Tear it down! Is a wreck-ing ma-chine. Tear it down!
Build it up! Is a car-pen-ter man. Build it up!

GING
GONG
GOOLI

FOLK SONG FROM BRITISH GUIANA
ARRANGED BY LAURA S. WENDEL

PUPIL'S BOOK, PAGE 67

OLD
JOE
CLARK

AMERICAN FOLK SONG
ARRANGED BY DARRELL PETER
WORDS BY RAYMOND MATTHEWS

PUPIL'S BOOK, PAGE 8

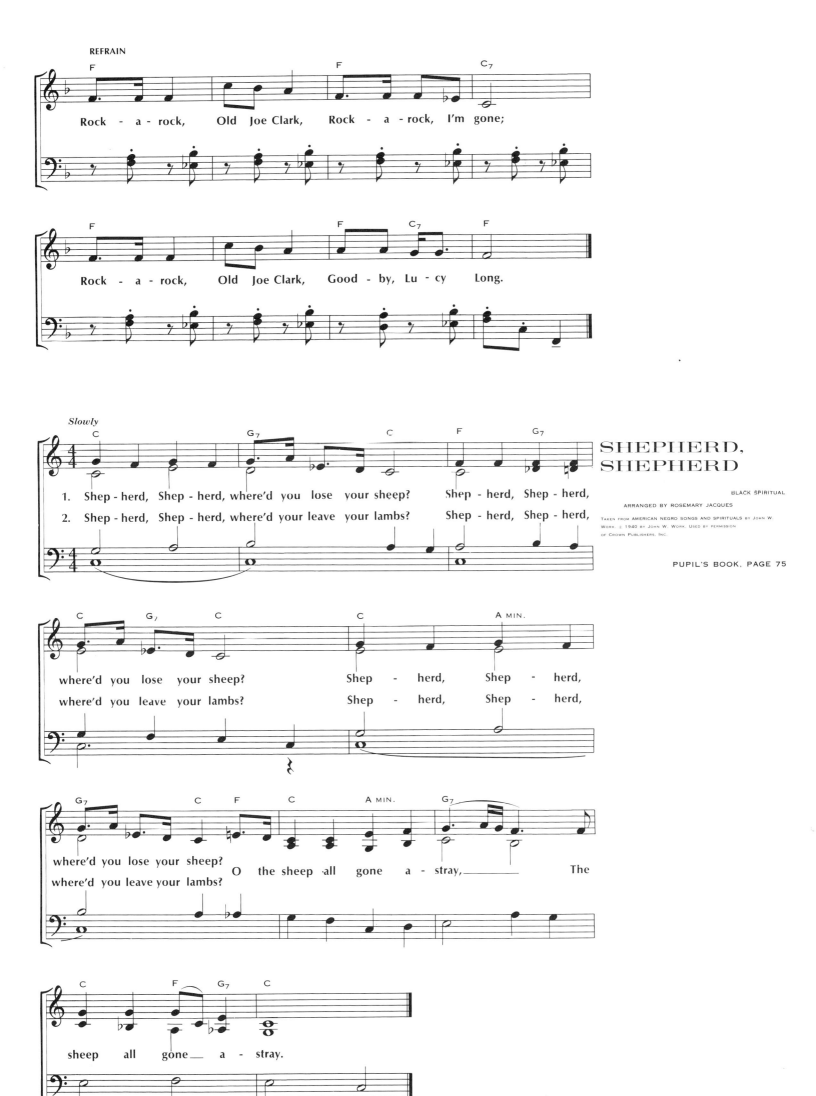

SHEPHERD, SHEPHERD

BLACK SPIRITUAL

ARRANGED BY ROSEMARY JACQUES

Taken from American Negro Songs and Spirituals by John W. Work. © 1940 by John W. Work. Used by permission of Crown Publishers, Inc.

PUPIL'S BOOK, PAGE 75

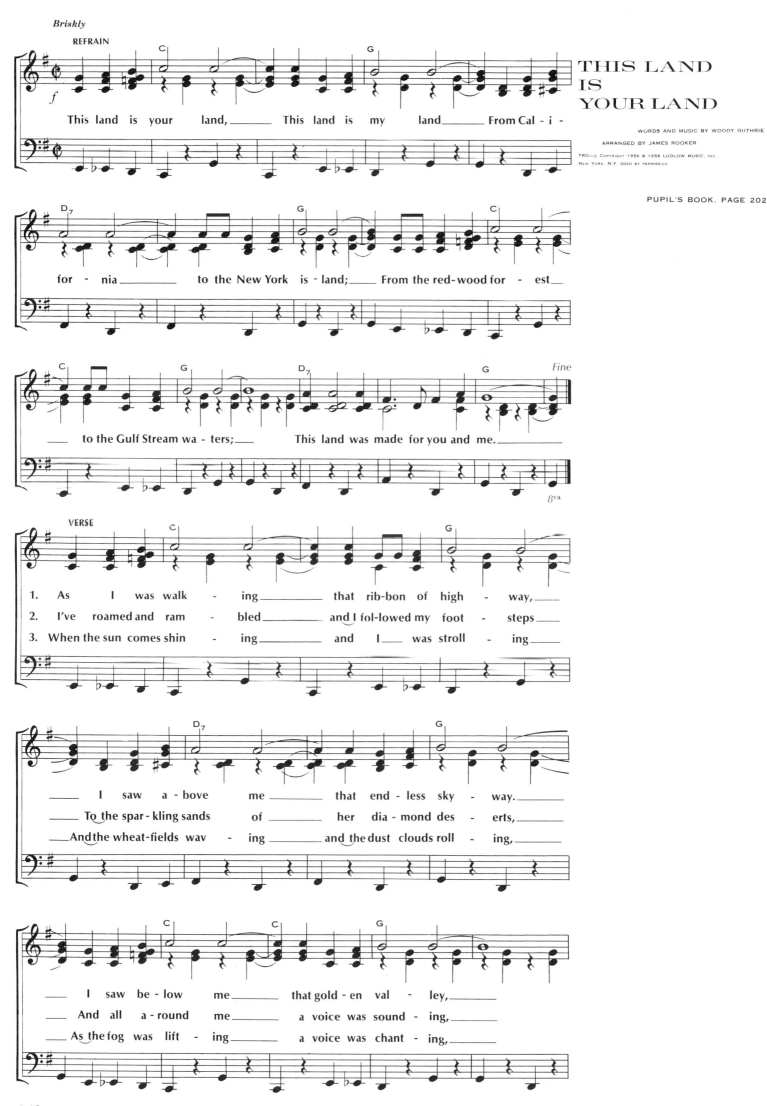

THIS LAND IS YOUR LAND

WORDS AND MUSIC BY WOODY GUTHRIE
ARRANGED BY JAMES ROOKER

TRO—© Copyright 1956 & 1958 Ludlow Music, Inc.
New York, N.Y. Used by permission.

PUPIL'S BOOK, PAGE 202

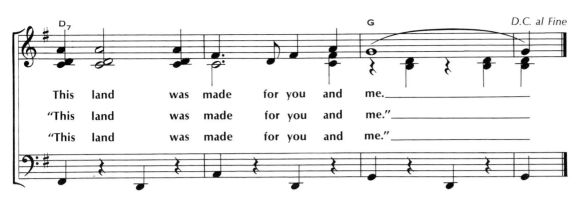

D.C. al Fine

This land was made for you and me._____

"This land was made for you and me."_____

"This land was made for you and me."_____

Gaily

REFRAIN

BELLA
BIMBA

FOLK SONG FROM ITALY

ARRANGED BY JAMES HARRIS

ENGLISH WORDS BY RICHARD MORRIS

PUPIL'S BOOK, PAGE 101

How well you dance, my bel - la bim - ba, bel - la bim - ba, bel - la bim - ba. How

Fine

well you dance, my bel - la bim - ba, bel - la bim - ba, how you dance!

VERSE

1. Bright as a sun - beam, Grace - ful and fair,_____
2. Whirl - ing and twirl - ing, Round and a - round,_____

D.C. al Fine

Light as a feath - er, Float - ing on air.
Feet al - ways mov - ing When mu - sic sounds.

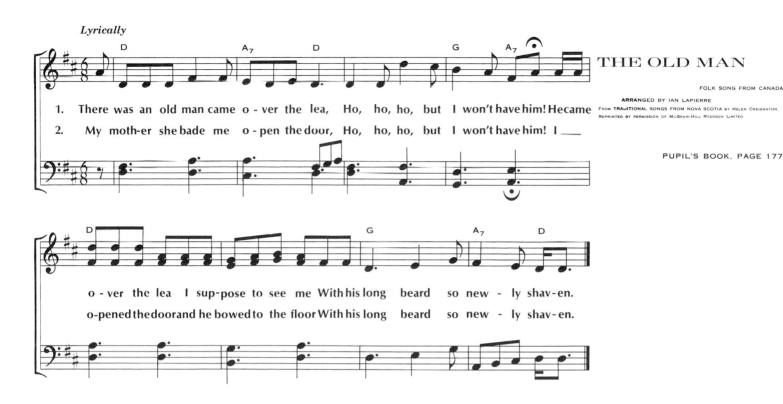

THE OLD MAN

FOLK SONG FROM CANADA

ARRANGED BY IAN LAPIERRE

From TRADITIONAL SONGS FROM NOVA SCOTIA by Helen Creighton. Reprinted by permission of McGraw-Hill Ryerson Limited.

PUPIL'S BOOK, PAGE 177

3. My mother she bade me set him a chair,
   Ho, ho, ho, but I won't have him!
   I set him a chair, but I didn't care
   For his long beard so newly shaven.

4. My mother, she bade me give him some meat,
   Ho, ho, ho, but I won't have him!
   I gave him some meat, but he wouldn't eat
   With his long beard so newly shaven.

5. My mother she bade me sit on his knee,
   Ho, ho, ho, but I won't have him!
   For I sat on his knee and he tried to kiss me
   With his long beard so newly shaven.

MARCHING TO PRETORIA

DUTCH FOLK SONG FROM SOUTH AFRICA

ARRANGED BY DARRELL PETER

ENGLISH WORDS BY JOSEF MARAIS

From SONGS FROM THE VELD. © 1942. G. Schirmer, Inc. Used by permission.

242

PUPIL'S BOOK, PAGE 4

THE
WEE
FALORIE
MAN

FOLK SONG FROM IRELAND
COLLECTED BY DAVID HAMMOND
ARRANGED BY SEAN O'MEARA

PUPIL'S BOOK, PAGE 176

1. I am the wee Fa-lo-rie man, A rat-tlin', rov-in' Irish-man, I can do all that ev-er you can, For
2. I am a good old work-in' man, Each day I carry my wee tin can, A large pen-ny bap and a clipe___ of ham,

3. I am the wee Falorie man,
   A rattlin', rovin' Irishman,
   I can do all that ever you can,
   For I am the wee Falorie man.

I am the wee Fa-lo-rie man.
I am a good old work-in' man.

OH, WON'T YOU
SIT DOWN?

BLACK SPIRITUAL
ARRANGED BY JAMES ROOKER

PUPIL'S BOOK, PAGE 90

REFRAIN

Oh, won't you sit down?___ Lord, I can't sit down.___ Oh, won't you sit down?___ Lord, I can't sit down.___ Oh, won't you

244

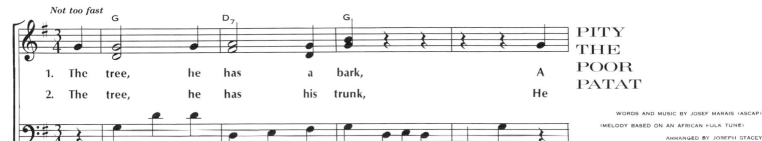

PITY
THE
POOR
PATAT

WORDS AND MUSIC BY JOSEF MARAIS (ASCAP)
(MELODY BASED ON AN AFRICAN FOLK TUNE)
ARRANGED BY JOSEPH STACEY
Copyright 1946, 1958 Fideree Music Co. Used by permission

PUPIL'S BOOK, PAGE 9

Not too fast

1. The tree, he has a bark, A
2. The tree, he has his trunk, He

bark that's thick or thin.
stares up in the sky.

Pit - y___ the poor pa - tat, He's
Pit - y___ the poor pa - tat, He

on - ly got a skin.
can't see with his eye.

3. The tree, he has his leaves,
They're waving all around.
Pity the poor patat,
For he lives in the ground.

4. Although the tree is proud,
He only gives us wood,
But from the poor patat
We get our daily food.

OL' CLO'

MUSIC BY DORIS HAYS

PUPIL'S BOOK, PAGE 165

♩ = 104 – 108

My___ un - cle he sells ol' clo', He's a

246

dealer in___ chi-na, you know; And wher - ev - er you go, when you hear

"Ol'___ clo'," My un-cle's there, you know.

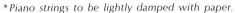

*Piano strings to be lightly damped with paper.

SAN SERENI

FOLK SONG FROM LATIN AMERICA

ARRANGED BY MARTIN QUARLES

ENGLISH WORDS BY DELIA RIOS

PUPIL'S BOOK, PAGE 199

1.
2. San Se - re - ni, I'm a bu - sy pa - na - de - ro,
3.

za - pa - te - ro,
car - pin - te - ro,

make some good za - pa - tos,
Work - ing like this to bake some good pan - ci - tos, A -
build some good ca - si - tas,

work - ing just like this, a - work - ing just like that.

247

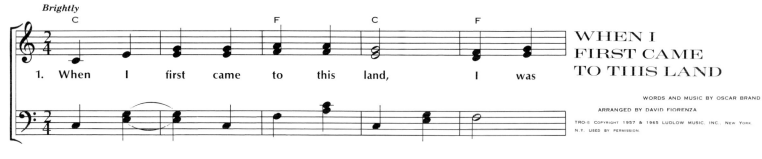

WORDS AND MUSIC BY OSCAR BRAND
ARRANGED BY DAVID FIORENZA
TRO-© Copyright 1957 & 1965 LUDLOW MUSIC, INC., New York,
N.Y. Used by Permission.

PUPIL'S BOOK, PAGE 200

*Repeat these four measures for additional lines in verses 2–5.

2. When I first came to this land,
   I was not a wealthy man.
   Then I bought myself a cow,
   I did what I could.
   I called my cow, *No-milk-now,*
   I called my shack, *Break-my-back.*
   But the land was sweet and good;
   I did what I could.

3. When I first came to this land,
   I was not a wealthy man.
   Then I bought myself a duck,
   I did what I could.
   I called my duck, *Out-of-luck,*
   I called my cow, *No-milk-now,*
   I called my shack, *Break-my-back.*
   But the land . . .

4. When I first came to this land,
   I was not a wealthy man.
   Then I got myself a wife,
   I did what I could.
   I called my wife, *Run-for-your-life*,
   I called my duck, *Out-of-luck*,
   I called my cow, *No-milk-now*,
   I called my shack, *Break-my-back*.
   But the land . . .

5. When I first came to this land,
   I was not a wealthy man.
   Then I got myself a son,
   I did what I could.
   I called my son, *My-work's-done*,
   I called my wife, *Run-for-your-life*,
   I called my duck, *Out-of-luck*,
   I called my cow, *No-milk-now*,
   I called my shack, *Break-my-back*.
   But the land . . .

BUYING FISH

YIDDISH FOLK SONG

ARRANGED BY FRANCIS GIRARD

ENGLISH WORDS BY ELIZABETH S. BACHMAN

"FISHELECH KOYFN" REPRINTED BY PERMISSION OF SCHOCKEN BOOKS INC. FROM A TREASURY OF JEWISH FOLKSONG EDITED BY RUTH RUBIN. COPYRIGHT © 1950 BY SCHOCKEN BOOKS INC.

PUPIL'S BOOK, PAGE 65

1. One day his moth - er sent him to mar - ket To buy some fish to fry. But when he got there he could - n't re - mem - ber What kind she want - ed him to buy.

2. Moth - er had said, "Go straight to the mar - ket; Don't lin - ger on the way." But he stopped to watch a game in the park, And now — oh, dear! What will Moth - er say?

REFRAIN

Day, day, day, day, day, day, Day, day, day, day, day day,

Day, day, day, day, day, day, Day, day, day, day.

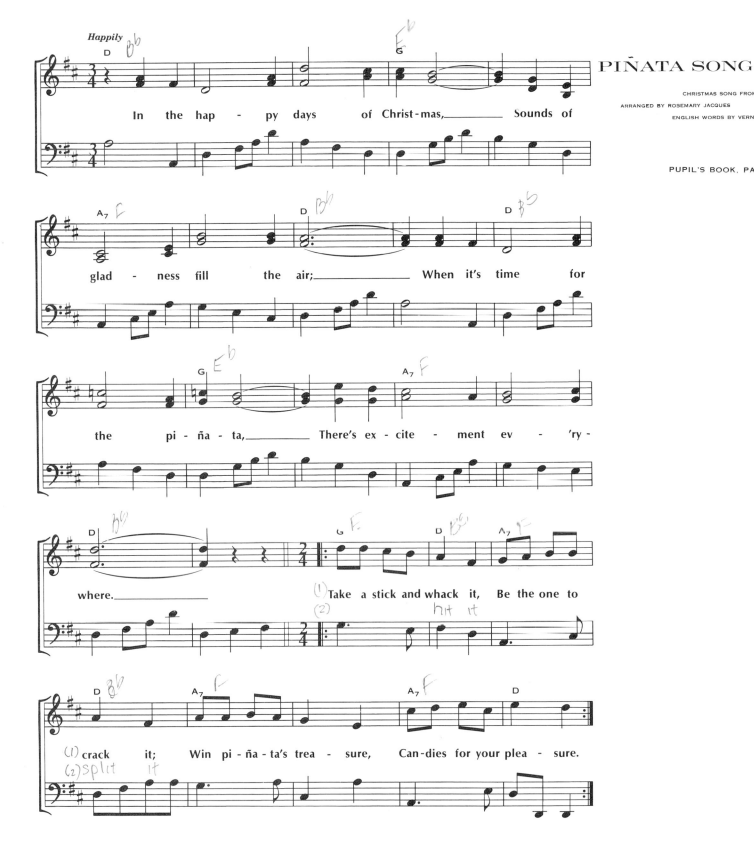

PIÑATA SONG

CHRISTMAS SONG FROM MEXICO
ARRANGED BY ROSEMARY JACQUES
ENGLISH WORDS BY VERNE MUÑOZ

PUPIL'S BOOK, PAGE 92

In the hap - py days of Christ-mas,_____ Sounds of glad - ness fill the air;_____ When it's time for the pi - ña - ta,_____ There's ex - cite - ment ev - 'ry - where._____ Take a stick and whack it, Be the one to crack it; Win pi - ña - ta's trea - sure, Can-dies for your plea - sure.

(2) hit it
(2) split it

Not too fast

(A)

ROLL AN' ROCK

BLACK SPIRITUAL
ARRANGED BY DAVID McHUGH

PUPIL'S BOOK, PAGE 12

Oh, tell me,___ Mar-tha,___ Mar-tha, won't you tell me, Where have___ you been so

CARROT STEW

WORDS AND MUSIC BY LARRY GROCE
ARRANGED BY GEORGE WINSTON
© 1976 WALT DISNEY MUSIC COMPANY. REPRINTED BY PERMISSION.

PUPIL'S BOOK, PAGE 44

Brightly

VERSE Ⓐ

1. When-ev-er we have a friend for lunch, There's just one thing to do.___ We pick some ber-ries and catch some fish, And we make a car-rot stew.

REFRAIN Ⓑ

Car-rot stew, car-rot stew, It's our fav'-rite thing to do. Get a pot and a car-rot or two, And cook up a car-rot stew.

2. Nothing makes our tummies so full
   And keeps us happy too
   As a great big pot or a little bitty bowl
   Or a spoonful of carrot stew. *Refrain*

3. So when you come to our little house,
   Bring a carrot if you have a few.
   We'll put it in a pot 'til it's nice and hot,
   And make some carrot stew. *Refrain*

POLLY WOLLY DOODLE

AMERICAN FOLK SONG
ARRANGED BY DONALD KALBACH

PUPIL'S BOOK, PAGE 74

Lively

1. Oh, I went down South for to see my Sal, Sing-ing
2. Oh, my Sal, she is a___ maid-en fair, Sing-ing

3. The partridge is a pretty bird,
   It has a speckled breast,
   It steals away the farmer's grain,
   And totes it to its nest! *Refrain*

4. The raccoon's tail is ringed around,
   The 'possum's tail is bare,
   The rabbit's got no tail at all,
   Just a little bitty bunch of hair! *Refrain*

BATTLE HYMN OF THE REPUBLIC

MUSIC BY WILLIAM STEFFE

WORDS BY JULIA WARD HOWE

PUPIL'S BOOK, PAGE 131

Glo - ry, glo - ry, hal - le - lu - jah! Glo - ry, glo - ry, hal - le - lu - jah!

Glo - ry, glo - ry, hal - le - lu - jah! His truth is march - ing on.

Brightly

HOW D' YE DO AND SHAKE HANDS

MUSIC BY OLIVER WALLACE

WORDS BY CY COBEN

ARRANGED BY HARRIET SINGER

© 1951 WALT DISNEY MUSIC COMPANY. REPRINTED BY PERMISSION.

PUPIL'S BOOK, PAGE 144

You go through life and nev - er know the day when fate may bring A

sit - u - a - tion that will prove to be em - bar - rass - ing. Your

face gets red, you hide your head, and wish that you could die, _____ But

that's old - fash - ioned, here's a new thing you should real - ly try. Say

254

"How d' ye do" and shake hands, Shake hands, shake hands, Say

"How d' ye do" and shake hands, State your name and bus' - ness.

Gently
8va throughout

1. Shep-herds, bring can-dy and milk to the Child. See lit-tle Je - sus

2. Mar - y and an-gels are sing-ing a song, There in the sta - ble

MELODY

cry - ing there. Hang up your coats to keep out the wind.

shab - by and bare. Jo-seph so wea - ry comes from the stream.

Jo - seph is rock-ing the Ba - by so mild.

He washed the swad-dling clothes all the day long.

SHEPHERDS, BRING CANDY AND MILK

17TH-CENTURY CHRISTMAS SONGS FROM BELGIUM

ENGLISH WORDS BY SALLI TERRI

FROM BELGIAN CHRISTMAS SONGS, SET I © 1971 BY LAWSON-GOULD MUSIC PUBLISHERS, INC. USED BY PERMISSION.

PUPIL'S BOOK, PAGE 154

3. Mary and Jesus are lying there.

Joseph is gath'ring wood for the fire.

See how he tends to all of the chores.

He loves the Baby and Mary fair.

NOBODY'S
BUSINESS

AMERICAN FOLK SONG
ARRANGED BY ROSEMARY JACQUES

PUPIL'S BOOK, PAGE 134

1. I went to town in a lit-tle red wag-on, Come back home with the
2. I've got a wife and she's a dai-sy, She won't work and

hub a-drag-gin', It's no-bod-y's busi-ness what I
I'm too la-zy, It's no-bod-y's busi-ness what I

REFRAIN

do.
do. It's no-bod-y's busi-ness, busi-ness, No-bod-y's

busi-ness, busi-ness, No-bod-y's busi-ness what I do.

OLD BLUE

Moderately

VERSE

SOUTHERN MOUNTAIN SONG
ARRANGED BY MERLE BUFORD

PUPIL'S BOOK, PAGE 112

1. I had an old dog, And his name was Blue,

REFRAIN

And I bet-cha five dol-lars he's a good dog, too. Come on, Blue,

you good dog,— you;_____ Come on, Blue,_____

you good dog,— you._____

2. I grabbed my axe and I tooted my horn,
   Gonna git me a 'possum in the new-ground corn. *Refrain*

3. Chased that ol' 'possum up a 'simmon tree,
   Blue looked at the 'possum, 'possum looked at me. *Refrain*

4. Blue grinned at me, I grinned at him,
   I shook out the 'possum, Blue took him in. *Refrain*

5. Baked that 'possum all good and brown,
   And I laid them sweet potatoes 'round and 'round. *Refrain*

6. Well, Old Blue died, and he died so hard,
   That he shook the ground in my back yard. *Refrain*

7. I dug his grave with a silver spade,
   I let him down with a golden chain. *Refrain*

8. When I get to heaven, first thing I'll do,
   Grab me a horn and blow for Old Blue. *Refrain*

AY, DI, DI, DI

HASIDIC MELODY

ARRANGED BY ROSEMARY JACQUES

PUPIL'S BOOK, PAGE 129

Ay, di, di, di, ay, di, di, di, di; Ay, di, di, di, di,

ay, di, di, di, di. Ay, di, di, di, ay, di, di, di, di;

Ay, di, di, di, di, ay, di, di, di, di.

THE SOW TOOK THE MEASLES

AMERICAN FRONTIER SONG
ARRANGED BY DAVID FIORENZA

PUPIL'S BOOK, PAGE 98

REFRAIN

How do you think I be-gan in the world? I got me a sow and sev-'ral oth-er thing. The sow took the mea-sles and she died in the spring. *Fine*

VERSE

1. What do you think I made of her hide? The ver-y best sad-dle that you ev-er did ride. Sad-dle or bri-dle or an-y such thing, The sow took the mea-sles and she died in the spring.

D.C. al Fine after verse 4

2. What do you think I made of her nose?
The very best thimble that ever sewed clothes.
Thimble or thread or any such thing,
The sow took the measles and she died in the spring.

3. What do you think I made of her tail?
The very best whup that ever sought sail.
Whup or whupsocket, or any such thing,
The sow took the measles and she died in the spring.

4. What do you think I made for her feet?
The very best pickles that you ever did eat.
Pickles or glue or any such thing,
The sow took the measles and she dies in the spring. *Refrain*

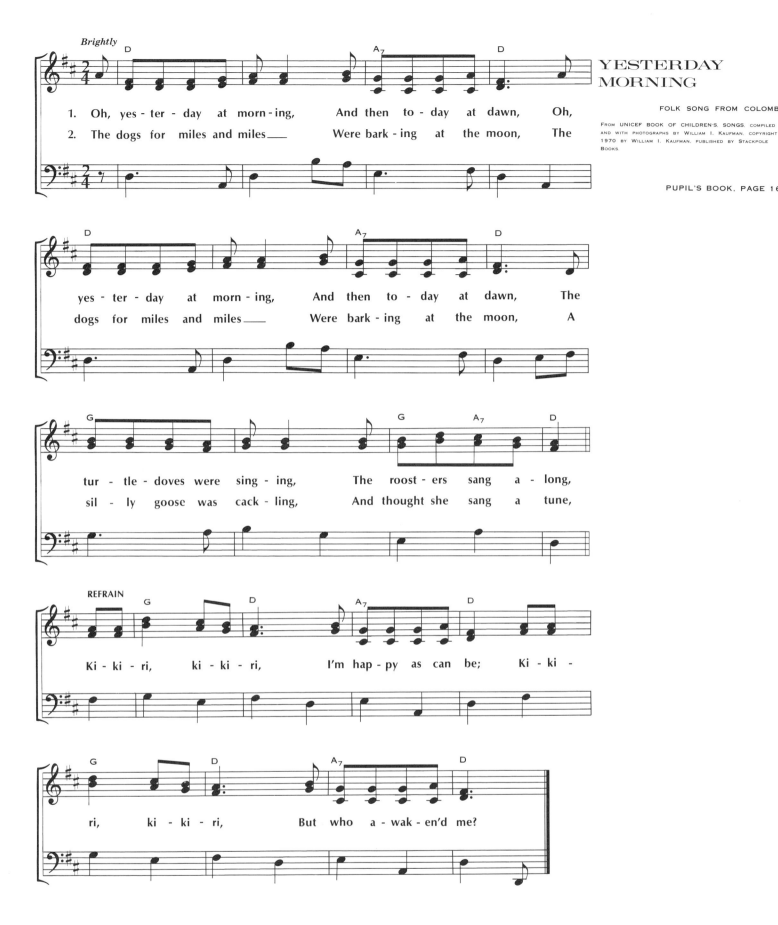

YESTERDAY MORNING

FOLK SONG FROM COLOMBIA

FROM UNICEF BOOK OF CHILDREN'S SONGS, COMPILED AND WITH PHOTOGRAPHS BY WILLIAM I. KAUFMAN, COPYRIGHT 1970 BY WILLIAM I. KAUFMAN, PUBLISHED BY STACKPOLE BOOKS.

PUPIL'S BOOK, PAGE 168

1. Oh, yes-ter-day at morn-ing, And then to-day at dawn, Oh,
2. The dogs for miles and miles___ Were bark-ing at the moon, The

yes-ter-day at morn-ing, And then to-day at dawn, The
dogs for miles and miles___ Were bark-ing at the moon, A

tur-tle-doves were sing-ing, The roost-ers sang a-long,
sil-ly goose was cack-ling, And thought she sang a tune,

REFRAIN

Ki-ki-ri, ki-ki-ri, I'm hap-py as can be; Ki-ki-

ri, ki-ki-ri, But who a-wak-en'd me?

3. A heavy rain was falling, }
   And when it rains it pours, } *(2 times)*
   With thunder, wind and lightning,
   I wish I had some oars, *Refrain*

259

MAMA
PAQUITA

CARNIVAL SONG FROM BRAZIL
ARRANGED BY ROSEMARY JACQUES
ENGLISH WORDS BY MARGARET MARKS

PUPIL'S BOOK, PAGE 18

2. Mama Paquita, Mama Paquita,
    Mama Paquita, buy your baby some pajamas,
    Some new pajamas, and a sombrero,
    A new sombrero that your baby will enjoy, ma-ma-ma-ma,
    Mama Paquita, Mama Paquita,
    Mama Paquita says, "I haven't any money
    To buy pajamas and a sombrero,
    Let's go to Carnival and dance the night away!"

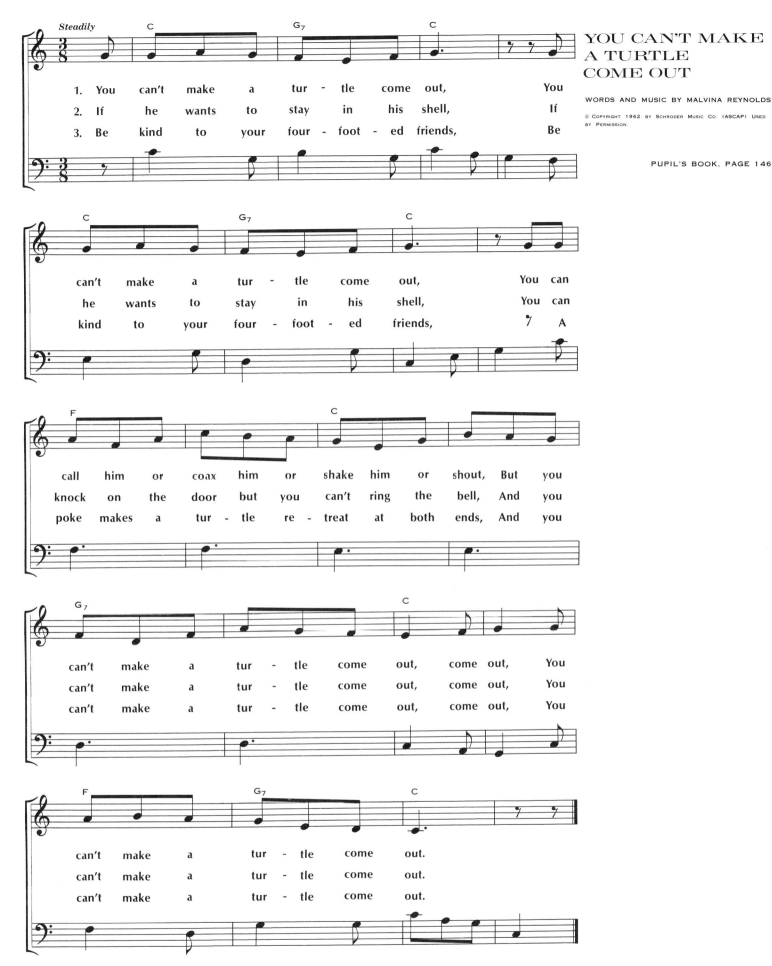

YOU CAN'T MAKE A TURTLE COME OUT

WORDS AND MUSIC BY MALVINA REYNOLDS

© Copyright 1962 by Schroder Music Co. (ASCAP) Used by Permission.

PUPIL'S BOOK, PAGE 146

1. You can't make a tur - tle come out, You can't make a tur - tle come out, You can call him or coax him or shake him or shout, But you can't make a tur - tle come out, come out, You can't make a tur - tle come out.

2. If he wants to stay in his shell, If he wants to stay in his shell, You can knock on the door but you can't ring the bell, And you can't make a tur - tle come out, come out, You can't make a tur - tle come out.

3. Be kind to your four - foot - ed friends, Be kind to your four - foot - ed friends, A poke makes a tur - tle re - treat at both ends, And you can't make a tur - tle come out, come out, You can't make a tur - tle come out.

4. So you'll have to patiently wait, (*2 times*)
And when he gets ready he'll open the gate,
But you can't make a turtle come out, come out,
You can't make a turtle come out.

5. And when you forget that he's there, (*2 times*)
He'll be walking around with his head in the air,
But you can't make a turtle come out, come out,
You can't make a turtle come out.

JOIN INTO THE GAME

WORDS AND MUSIC BY PAUL CAMPBELL
ARRANGED BY ROSEMARY JACQUES

"(COME ON AND) JOIN INTO THE GAME" TRO—© COPYRIGHT 1951
FOLKWAYS MUSIC PUBLISHERS, INC. NEW YORK, N.Y. USED BY
PERMISSION.

PUPIL'S BOOK, PAGE 11

1. Let ev - 'ry-one clap hands like me, (*clap hands*)   Let ev - 'ry-one
2. Let ev - 'ry one whis - tle like me, (*whistle*)   Let ev - 'ry-one

REFRAIN

clap hands like me. (*clap hands*)   Come on   and join in - to the
whis - tle like me. (*whistle*)   Come on   and join in - to the

game; _____   You'll find   that it's al - ways the same. (*clap hands*)
game; _____   You'll find   that it's al - ways the same. (*whistle*)

3.   Let ev'ryone laugh like me, (*laugh*)   5.   Let ev'ryone yawn like me, (*yawn*)

4.   Let ev'ryone sneeze like me, (*sneeze*)   6.   Let ev'ryone do what he wants, (*various sounds*)

ON THE FIRST THANKSGIVING DAY

TRADITIONAL AMERICAN HYMN
ARRANGED BY THERON HAITHWAITE

PUPIL'S BOOK, PAGE 56

On   the   first Thanks-giv - ing Day,   Pil - grims went   to church to   pray,

Thanked the Lord for   sun   and rain,   Thanked him   for   the   fields of   grain.

Now Thanks-giv - ing comes a - gain: Praise the Lord as they did then.

Thank him for the sun and rain, Thank him for the fields of grain.

HE'S GOT THE WHOLE WORLD IN HIS HANDS

BLACK SPIRITUAL

ARRANGED BY GEORGE WINSTON

PUPIL'S BOOK, PAGE 198

1. He's got the whole world __ in his hands, __ He's got the whole world __ in his hands, __ He's got the whole world __ in his hands, __ He's got the whole world in his hands. _____

2. He's got the wind and rain . . .

3. He's got both you and me . . .

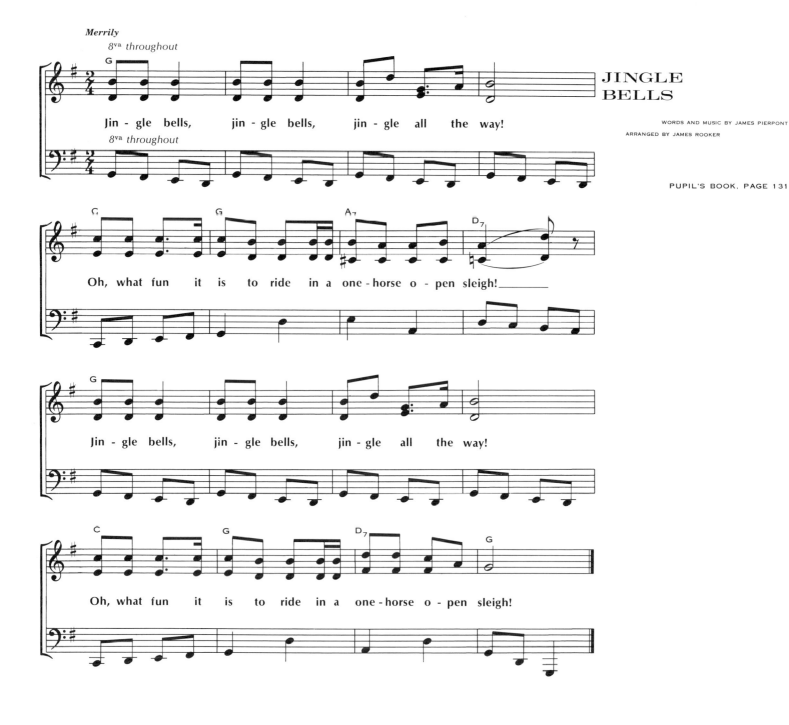

JINGLE
BELLS

WORDS AND MUSIC BY JAMES PIERPONT
ARRANGED BY JAMES ROOKER

PUPIL'S BOOK, PAGE 131

Jin - gle bells, jin - gle bells, jin - gle all the way!

Oh, what fun it is to ride in a one - horse o - pen sleigh!_____

Jin - gle bells, jin - gle bells, jin - gle all the way!

Oh, what fun it is to ride in a one - horse o - pen sleigh!

JOYOUS
CHANUKAH

HEBREW FOLK SONG
ARRANGED BY ROSEMARY JACQUES
ENGLISH WORDS BY PHYLLIS RESNICK

PUPIL'S BOOK, PAGE 152

Cha - nu - kah, Cha - nu - kah, hol - i - day so fair,

Glow - ing light, can - dles bright, hap - pi - ness we share.

264

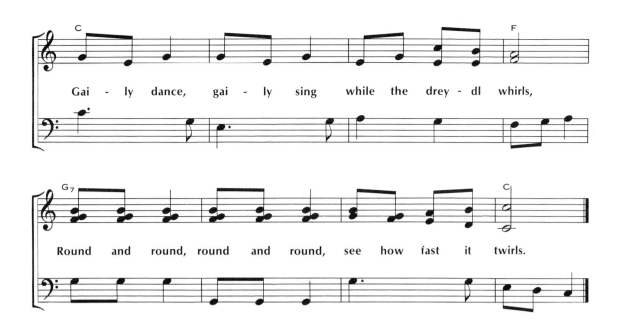

Gai - ly dance, gai - ly sing while the drey - dl whirls,

Round and round, round and round, see how fast it twirls.

THE PIG

FOLK TUNE FROM MEXICO
ARRANGED BY LAURA S. WENDEL
ENGLISH WORDS BY MARGARET MARKS

PUPIL'S BOOK, PAGE 114

Mis - sus Tor - res had a pi - hig, Ver - y fat and ver - y bi - hig,

Dressed him in a fun - ny wi - hig, Tried to make him dance a ji - hig.

But the pig, whose name was Sa - ham, Said, "I'm ver - y sor - ry, Ma - ham,

Can't you leave me as I a - ham? I don't want to be a ha - ham!"

AIN'T
GONNA
RAIN

AMERICAN FOLK SONG
ARRANGED BY ROSEMARY JACQUES

PUPIL'S BOOK, PAGE 24

1. The wood-chuck, he's a-chop-pin' wood, The pos-sum, he's a-haul-in'. My

2. Just bake them bis-cuits good and brown, It ain't gonna rain no more. _____

poor old dog fell off a log And killed him-self a-bawl-in'.

Swing your la-dies round and round, It ain't gonna rain no more. _____

REFRAIN

It ain't gon-na rain, it ain't gon-na rain, It ain't gon-na rain no more.

Come on down, ev-'ry-bod-y sing. It ain't gon-na rain no more. more.

3. I'll tune the fiddle, you get the bow,

It ain't gonna rain no more.

The weatherman just told me so,

It ain't gonna rain no more. *Refrain*

4. Oh, what did the blackbird say to the crow?

"It ain't gonna rain no more.

It ain't gonna hail, it ain't gonna snow,

It ain't gonna rain no more." *Refrain*

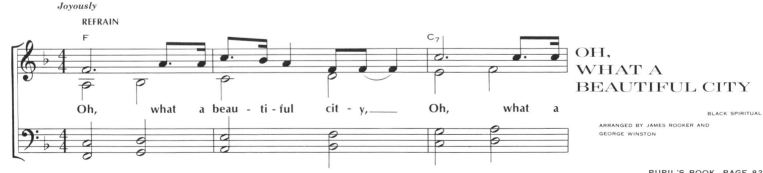

Joyously

REFRAIN

Oh, what a beau-ti-ful cit-y, _____ Oh, what a

OH,
WHAT A
BEAUTIFUL CITY

BLACK SPIRITUAL
ARRANGED BY JAMES ROOKER AND
GEORGE WINSTON

PUPIL'S BOOK, PAGE 82

*End here for the version of "Oh, What A Beautiful City" on page 40.

WHAT IS LOVE?

WORDS AND MUSIC BY CHRIS DEDRICK

© 1972 ALMITRA MUSIC COMPANY, INC.

PUPIL'S BOOK, PAGE 109

I know a ver-y hard ques - tion:

What is love? Ver-y wise peo-ple can't find the words to

say what love is. I fig-ured out that there can't be words for

some-thing quite that good. If you stop, If you stop to think a-bout your

friends, your folks, your pup-py, your cat, the sun-shine, the trees and e-ven your-self__

You know all a-bout love; Al - most ev-'ry-one does.

Love, love, I know all a-bout love, but I can't

tell. Love, love, Words can't tell a-bout

Ped. *Ped.* *Ped.* *
rall.(2nd time) *Ped.* *Ped.* *

love, it's just as well.

rall. (2nd time)

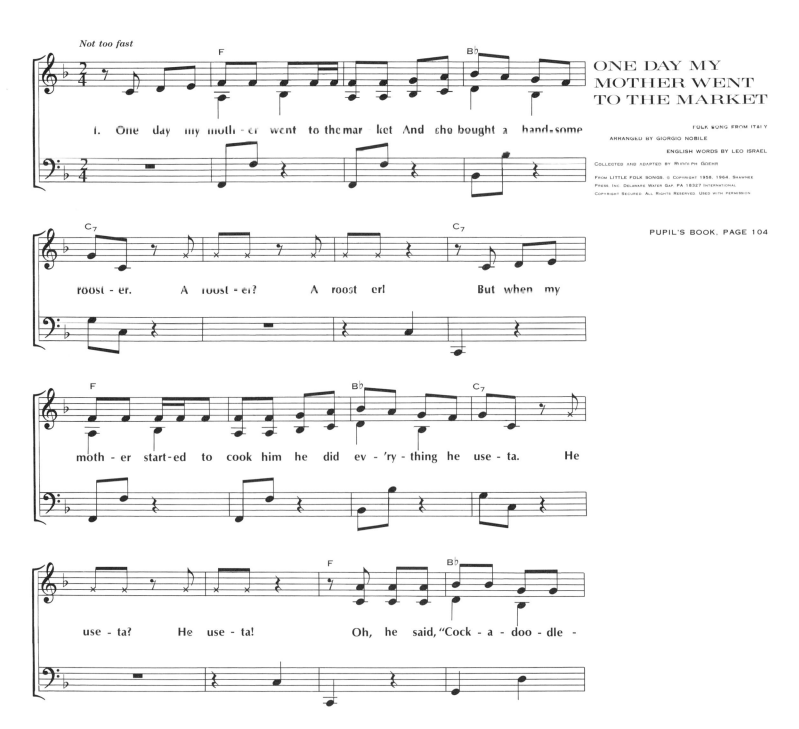

ONE DAY MY MOTHER WENT TO THE MARKET

Not too fast

1. One day my moth-er went to the mar-ket And she bought a hand-some roost-er. A roost-er? A roost-er! But when my moth-er start-ed to cook him he did ev-'ry-thing he use-ta. He use-ta? He use-ta! Oh, he said, "Cock-a-doo-dle-

FOLK SONG FROM ITALY
ARRANGED BY GIORGIO NOBILE

ENGLISH WORDS BY LEO ISRAEL

COLLECTED AND ADAPTED BY RUDOLPH GOEHR

FROM LITTLE FOLK SONGS. © COPYRIGHT 1958, 1964, SHAWNEE
PRESS, INC. DELAWARE WATER GAP, PA 18327 INTERNATIONAL
COPYRIGHT SECURED. ALL RIGHTS RESERVED. USED WITH PERMISSION

PUPIL'S BOOK, PAGE 104

doo, How I love you, how I love you." Oh, he said, "Cock - a - doo - dle-

doo," And a - way he flew, and a - way he flew.

2. . . . and she bought a little pig . . .
    But when my mother started to cook him,
    He got up and danced a jig . . .
    Oh, he said, "Oink, oink, oink,
    Though I'd like to stay, though I'd like to stay."
    Oh, he said, "Oink, oink, oink,"
    And he ran away, and he ran away.

3. . . . and she bought a pretty lamb . . .
    But when my mother started to cook him,
    He said, "Who do you think I am?" . . .
    Oh, he said, "Baa, baa, baa,
    I'm silly, it's true, I'm silly, it's true."
    Oh, he said, "Baa, baa, baa,
    Not as silly as you, not as silly as you."

4. . . . and she bought a lovely hen . . .
    But when my mother started to cook her,
    She began to cluck again . . .
    Oh, she said, "Cluck, cluck, cluck, cluck, cluck."
    But she forgot, but she forgot,
    Oh, she said, "Cluck, cluck, cluck, cluck, cluck,"
    And fell into the pot, and fell into the pot.

Easily

Ka - te u - re - shii___ ha - na i - chi mom - me.

Mu - ka - i no da - re ka san chot - to o - i - de.

HANA ICHI MOMME

FOLK SONG FROM JAPAN
ARRANGED BY FRANCIS GIRARD

PUPIL'S BOOK, PAGE 128

AMERICA, THE BEAUTIFUL

MUSIC BY SAMUEL A. WARD

WORDS BY KATHARINE LEE BATES

PUPIL'S BOOK, PAGE 184

O beau-ti-ful for spa-cious skies, For am-ber waves of grain, For
O beau-ti-ful for pa-triot dream That sees be-yond the years Thine

pur-ple moun-tain maj-es-ties A-bove the fruit-ed plain! A-
al-a-bas-ter cit-ies gleam, Un-dimmed by hu-man tears!

mer-i-ca! A-mer-i-ca! God shed His grace on thee And

crown thy good with broth-er-hood From sea to shin-ing sea!

RAIN SONG

WORDS AND MUSIC BY DAVID McHUGH

© 1972 David McHugh

PUPIL'S BOOK, PAGE 59

Lightly   8va throughout

The rain   just keeps on
clouds   keep pass-ing

fall-ing, And the sky is col-ored grey; The
o-ver, Bring-in' rain to flow'rs be-low; While the

birds don't stop their sing-ing__ 'Cause it's just an-oth-er
sun keeps wait-ing pa-tient-ly To un-veil its gold-en

day; And the
glow; Some - times sun shines, and oth-er times it

rains; ____ But to me it's all the same, ____ To

me it's all the same. ____

AMERICAN PIONEER SONG
ARRANGED BY ROSEMARY JACQUES
FROM MORE SONGS OF THE NEW WORLD BY DESMOND MacMAHON,
PUBLISHED BY HOLMES McDOUGALL LIMITED

PUPIL'S BOOK, PAGE 85

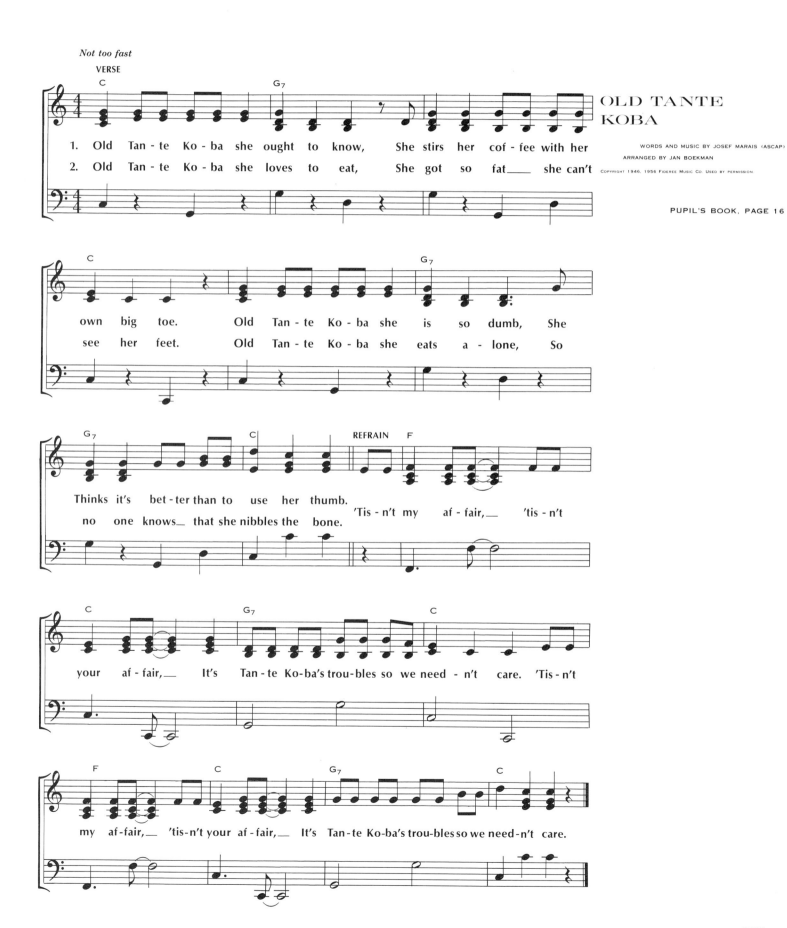

OLD TANTE
KOBA

WORDS AND MUSIC BY JOSEF MARAIS (ASCAP)
ARRANGED BY JAN BOEKMAN
Copyright 1946, 1956 Fideree Music Co. Used by permission.

PUPIL'S BOOK, PAGE 16

SCRATCH, SCRATCH

WORDS AND MUSIC BY HARRY BELAFONTE AND
LORD BURGESS
ARRANGED BY LAURA S. WENDEL

"SCRATCH, SCRATCH ME BACK" BY HARRY BELAFONTE AND LORD BURGESS
© COPYRIGHT 1957 BY CLARA MUSIC PUBLISHING CORPORATION
ALL RIGHTS RESERVED USED BY PERMISSION

PUPIL'S BOOK, PAGE 116

Not too fast

1. Oh, we went out to a par - ty, It was me and Ben and

I was quite em - bar-rassed, Till my two friends I did

scratch-ing was con - ta - gious, And it didn't take ver - y

Mac, And be - fore I knew what hap-pened, I got an

see, Well,___ they were mad - ly itch - ing, And they were

long, Ev'ry - body there was itch - ing, As they

REFRAIN

itch - in' on my back.

scream - ing louder than me.

joined me in this song.

Scratch, scratch me back,

Scratch, scratch me back. It real - ly is a fact,___ The less I

1., 2. **3.**

itch, the more I scratch. 3. Now, this

2. Well,___

scratch.

ORFF-INSTRUMENT ACCOMPANIMENTS

The accompaniments on the following pages are arranged for pitched and nonpitched instruments. The names of the instruments are abbreviated at the beginning of each line of music.

Sop. Gl.	Soprano Glockenspiel	Timp.	Timpani
Alto Gl.	Alto Glockenspiel	Cast.	Castanets
Sop. Xyl.	Soprano Xylophone	Cym.	Cymbal
Alto Xyl.	Alto Xylophone	F.C.	Finger Cymbals
Bass Xyl.	Bass Xylophone	Tam.	Tambourine
Sop. Met.	Soprano Metallophone	Tri.	Triangle
Alto Met.	Alto Metallophone	W.B.	Woodblock
Bass Met.	Bass Metallophone		

The pitches to be played on each pitched percussion instrument are indicated at the beginning of the score. (If the instrumentation is changed within a composition, the new instrument is listed and pitches are indicated at the appropriate entrance.) Capital letters are used for the pitches in the lower octave of the instrument; small letters for the upper octave. Bars that are not used may be removed from the instrument.

All instrument parts (except timpani) are notated in the treble clef. This allows greater flexibility in substituting one instrument for another if necessary.

Notes with a down-stem are played with the mallet in the left hand; notes with an up-stem are played with the mallet in the right hand. When two instruments are notated on one staff, one is indicated by up-stems, the other by down-stems.

USING THE TEACHING SUGGESTIONS

The teaching suggestions at the top of each page are designed as ways to "get to" the instruments. These suggestions are not the only method possible, but offer one approach to the music.

The first step in learning each accompaniment is to *know the song*. Do not attempt to add instruments until the children are confident with at least one verse of the song. Whenever possible, all children should practice the chants and rhythm exercises so that they are involved in the music, whether or not they are playing an instrument.

Allow portions of several class sessions to learn each accompaniment. Some may be mastered in two or three sessions; some may require several.

Although learning the accompaniments is primarily an aural experience, notation may be helpful. When appropriate, notate or have children notate the rhythm and melody patterns as they learn them.

The recordings of these Orff arrangements are literal reproductions of the notation. As children work with the accompaniments, they should be encouraged to improvise introductions, interludes, and melodies of their own.

MALLET TECHNIQUES FOR ORFF INSTRUMENTS

1. Sit or stand with good posture. Hold the arms slightly away from the body. Bend the elbows so the forearms are several inches above the instrument keyboard.

2. The correct feel of holding the mallets is like holding bicycle handle bars. Hold the mallets between the thumbs and curved index fingers, lightly wrapping the other fingers around each handle. The ends of the handles should be visible. Thumbnails face each other; palms "look at" the floor. *Note:* Don't let the index fingers straighten to point down the mallet.

3. To avoid hitting the mallet sticks against each other, hold one mallet slightly farther away from the body than the other. Also, the mallet sticks should slant toward each other at a 45° angle. This helps keep the arms and hands in position for good wrist action.

4. Whenever possible, alternate left and right hands. This helps coordination, playing fast passages, and playing both hands simultaneously.

5. Play in the center of the bar.

6. Play with a flexible wrist, Begin from a "ready" position above the bar and return to this position after each stroke. Think of pulling the tone out of the bar, not beating it in.

NEW YEAR'S SONG

1. Bass Xyl: Pat legs.

Side of R. Leg
R. Leg
L. Leg

New Year's mu sic

(a) Practice the chant alone, then with the song. (b) Transfer to the instrument. (c) Have the children notate the pattern on the board.

2. Alto Met., Alto Gl., Sop. Gl.: Snap / Clap / Pat

(a) Practice the pattern alone, then with the song. (b) Divide the pattern among three groups, each group performing one note. (c) Notate the rhythm. (d) Step the rhythm while singing the song. (e) Transfer to the instruments.

3. Woodblock: Play a circle game with a ball. The first person bounces the ball on beat one, catches it on beat two, and passes it to the next person in two beats:

Bounce and catch! Pass it on!

NEW YEAR'S SONG *Kazoe-uta*

FOLK SONG FROM JAPAN

ARRANGED BY MARILYN COPELAND DAVIDSON

ENGLISH VERSION BY ROSEMARY JACQUES

(Alternative piano acc., p. 298)

278

Transfer to the instrument, alternating one measure of sound, one measure of silence.

4. Finger Cymbals: Have children snap at the proper time while singing.

5. Gong: Two one-note solos—at the beginning and at the end.

6. During verse 3, the children may improvise on the Sop. Xyl. using the pitches E, F♯, G, B, c, e.

'TATERS

To reinforce the concept of beat, children should aim for rhythmic precision. After they know the song well, add the accompaniment. Each number below represents a repetition of the first verse of "'Taters." Numbers 1–5 are to be used to teach the xylophone parts, 6 and 7 with the

Dec - o - rate the bam-boo trees to cel - e - brate the day,_____ Cel - e - brate the day.
O - ka - za - ri ta - te - ta - ru ma - tsu - ka - za - ri,_____ Ma - tsu - ka - za - ri.

2. On the eve of New Year's,
Paper streamers, fresh plum blossoms
Hang above the door,
Hang above the door,
Telling all who pass by to have a happy day,
Have a happy day.

3. On the day of New Year's,
Games are played and songs are sung
To celebrate the day,
Celebrate the day.
People come to wish each other Happy New Year's Day,
Happy New Year's Day.

TATERS YIDDISH FOLK SONG ARRANGED BY MARILYN COPELAND DAVIDSON ENGLISH WORDS BY JACOB SLOAN

"ZUNTIG-BULBE" REPRINTED BY PERMISSION OF SCHOCKEN BOOKS INC. FROM A TREASURY OF JEWISH FOLKSONG BY RUTH RUBIN. COPYRIGHT © 1950 BY SCHOCKEN BOOKS INC. COPYRIGHT RENEWED © 1978 BY RUTH RUBIN.

(Alternative piano acc., p. 293)

1. Sun - day, 'ta - ters, Mon - day, 'ta - ters, Tues - day and Wednes - day,_ 'ta - ters,

tambourine part. Some steps may take several repetitions before the class masters them. Allow portions of three or four sessions to learn the accompaniment. As children sing:

1. Snap the fingers of both hands on "TUES-day and WEDNES-day", "THURS-day and FRI-day", and "SUN-day STARTS with." (quarter notes)

2. On the second snap in each set, move both hands to the left.

3. For the other measures of the song, start with the left hand and alternate left-right leg patting. Pat eighth notes, chanting "baked po-ta-to" if desired.

4. Pat the last syllable ("-to") of the "baked potato" ostinato slightly to the right of the right leg—on a desk, chair, etc.

5. Transfer these movements to the correct bars on the xylophones. Introduce notation as desired.

6. Play the tambourine on the beat (quarter notes)

7. Substitute ♫♫♩♪ in measures 4, 6, and 10.

Chant the words *there's a 'tater pudding.*

2. Bread and 'taters,
    Meat and 'taters,
    Lunch and dinner, 'taters.
    Over and over, 'taters.
    Once, for a special treat, there's a 'tater pudding!
    Sunday starts with 'taters.

3. Still, 'taters,
    Ever, 'taters,
    Always, always, 'taters!
    Today and tomorrow, 'taters!
    After Sabbath pot roasts there's a 'tater pudding!
    Sunday starts with 'taters.

LITTLE DAVID, PLAY ON YOUR HARP

Section A

1. Sop. Xyl.: (a) Practice the rhythm by patting legs.

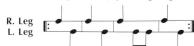

(b) Transfer this rhythm to bongo drums (smaller drum on the child's right) to emphasize the high-low pattern. (c) Play the pattern on the xylophone.

2. Alto Xyl.: (a) Practice the rhythm by patting legs.

(b) Transfer this rhythm to bongo drums to emphasize the low-high pattern. (c) Play the pattern on the xylophone.

To reinforce the high-low and low-high patterns in Section A, divide the class into two groups. One group will stand on the high notes and sit on the low notes with the Soprano Xylophone, one group with the Alto Xylophone.

Section B

Alto Met. and Bass Met.: Play a tremolo as written with a crescendo to the accented note in the last measure.

LITTLE DAVID, PLAY ON YOUR HARP

BLACK SPIRITUAL

(Alternative piano acc., p. 292)

ARRANGED BY MARILYN COPELAND DAVIDSON

MICHIE BANJO

Practice the rhythms below, saying the chants. All children should learn all the chants. Divide the class into six groups. Let each group perform one chant; then combine them, one at a time, until all six are sounding at once. Transfer the patterns, one at a time, to the instruments. Work the patterns in the following order:

1. Bass Xyl.: Pat legs.

Mich - ie Ban - jo Look! Look!

2. Alto Xyl.: Pat legs.

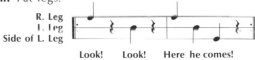

Look! Look! Here he comes!

MICHIE BANJO
CREOLE BAMBOULA ARRANGED BY MARILYN COPELAND DAVIDSON
(Alternative piano acc., p. 299)

(whisper) He's gone!

SHEPHERDS CAME TO BETHLEHEM
POLISH CAROL

ARRANGED BY MARILYN COPELAND DAVIDSON   ENGLISH WORDS BY ROSEMARY JACQUES   (Alternative piano acc., p. 294)

Bass Xylophone, Drum, and Finger Cymbals play the first four measures as an introduction.   (Teaching notes, p. 284)

1. Shep-herds came to Beth - le - hem on Christ - mas Day.   How the Ba - by smiled as they their pipes did play.

3. Tambourine: Clap.

Mich - ie Ban - jo Here he comes!

4. Sop. Xyl.: Pat legs.

R. Leg
L. Leg

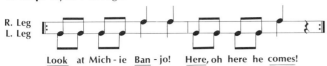

<u>Look</u> at Mich - ie Ban - jo! <u>Here</u>, oh here he <u>comes</u>!

5. Woodblock: Clap.

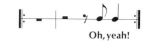

Oh, yeah!

6. Alto Gl. and Sop. Gl.: Snap on underlined syllables of chant **4** above.

Snap to right
Snap to center
Snap to left

To play "Michie Banjo," begin with four measures of the Bass Xylophone. Add one instrument every four measures

Voice: Glo - ry, sing glo - ry to God in the high - est, And peace on earth, Peace on earth.

2. Then a shepherd beat upon a little drum.
   How it pleased the Baby with its rum-tum-tum.
   Glory, . . .

3. As the shepherds bowed before the blessed Boy,
   All the heavens rang with sounds of wondrous joy.
   Glory, . . .

SKIN AND BONES

FOLK SONG FROM KENTUCKY   COLLECTED BY JEAN RITCHIE   ARRANGED BY MARILYN COPELAND DAVIDSON

© 1952 Jean Ritchie Geordie Music Publishing, Inc.

(Teaching notes, p. 284) (Alternative piano acc., p. 292)

Mysteriously

Voice:
1. { There was an old wom - an all skin and bones,
   { She lived down by the old grave - yard,

until all the instruments are playing. Then add the singing. Take out the instruments in reverse order from the way they were introduced. Finish with the two-measure coda.

SHEPHERDS CAME TO BETHLEHEM

In all instrument parts for this song, emphasize the combinations of long and short sounds and the accented notes. Have the children say "long" and "short" for each note as they practice the rhythm patterns. Use leg patting for all notes except for the accented notes, which should be clapped. Children may step the patterns and notate them as they learn the accompaniment.

SKIN AND BONES

1. Bass Xyl.: Pat legs.

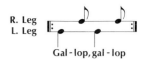

2. Sop. Gl. and Alto Gl.: As the class sings the song, have them clap on the words *skin*, *ooh*, and *old*. Continue clapping at the same places throughout the song.

3. Sound Effect: As the children sing the song, have them snap on the dotted quarter rests in the melody.

Divide the class into three groups to practice one of the parts as they sing. To reinforce the rhythm patterns have

2. One night she thought she'd take a walk,
    Oo-oo-oo-ooh!
    She walked down by the old graveyard,
    Oo-oo-oo-oh! *(To verse 3)*

3. She saw the bones a-layin' around,
    Oo-oo-oo-ooh!
    She went to the closet to get a broom,
    Oo-oo-oo-ooh! *(To coda)*

THE TREE IN THE WOOD

FOLK SONG FROM ENGLAND   ARRANGED BY MARILYN COPELAND DAVIDSON
(Alternative piano acc., p. 298)

the Bass Xyl. group tap their desk with a pencil in their left hand; have the middle group slam books shut instead of clapping; assign each child in the last group (six children) one place for an improvised sound.

Transfer the rhythms to the instruments.

THE TREE IN THE WOOD

Practice the rhythm of each instrumental part. Have the children sing the pitch names before transferring the rhythms to the instruments.

1. Bass Xyl.: Practice the first pattern; then the second.

2. Alto Xyl.: Pat legs

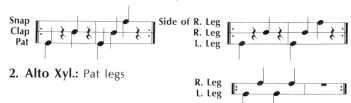

2.	And on this tree there grew a limb,
	The finest limb you ever did see;
	The limb was on the tree.
	The tree was in the wood,
	And the green leaves grew . . .

3.	And on this limb there was a branch, . . .

4.	And on this branch there was a nest, . . .

5.	And in this nest there was an egg, . . .

6.	And in this egg there was a bird, . . .

7.	And on this bird there was a wing, . . .

8.	And on this wing there was a feather, . . .

* Eliminate for verse 1. Perform for additional lines in verses 2–8, repeating as necessary. Children may choose a different instrument

to play (x) for each verse, 2–8.

3. Alto Gl.:

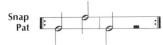

4. Sop. Gl.: Pat legs, keeping the right hand farther away from the body to prevent mallets hitting each other.

To practice the repeated section, play a leg "tremelo" for two counts, rest one count, and snap one count. Then substitute a different nonpitched instrument or sound effect for the snap in each verse (except verse 1).

WHAT YOU GONNA CALL YOUR PRETTY LITTLE BABY?

Section A

1. Sop. Gl. and Alto Gl.: While singing the song, have children pat both hands on the first beat of each measure for six measures. (They will pat on the words *what* and *pretty*.) Clap softly the rhythm of *Born, . . . Bethlehem*.

2. Bass Met.: Help the children discover the repeated tones and downward motion in the lower part. (They should first hear the part, then see the notation.) Have children learn the upper part and combine the parts for measures 1–6. The rhythm of measure 8 is the same as the word *Bethlehem*.

3. Alto Met.: Put the notation on the board. Have the children pat the rhythm, one hand at a time. The pattern is played three times. The rhythm of measure 8 is the same as the word, *Bethlehem*.

WHAT YOU GONNA CALL YOUR PRETTY LITTLE BABY?

BLACK SPIRITUAL   ARRANGED BY MARILYN COPELAND DAVIDSON   (Alternative piano acc., p. 295)

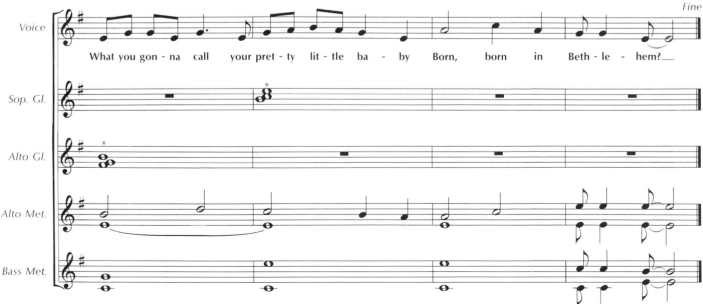

Section B

1. Have glockenspiel players practice changing from bars to mallets and back to bars. They will play the half-note rhythm with mallets.

2. The metallophone parts are the same as in measures 7 and 8 of Section A.

FORTY-NINE ANGELS

Section A

1. Bass Xyl.: Pat legs.

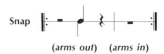

2. Sop. Gl.: Add a finger snap while singing the song. During the whole rest, the children may bring their elbows closer to their bodies to feel the silence.

3. Sop. Met. and Triangle: Pat legs.

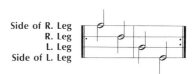

Section B

1. Alto Gl.: Pat legs.

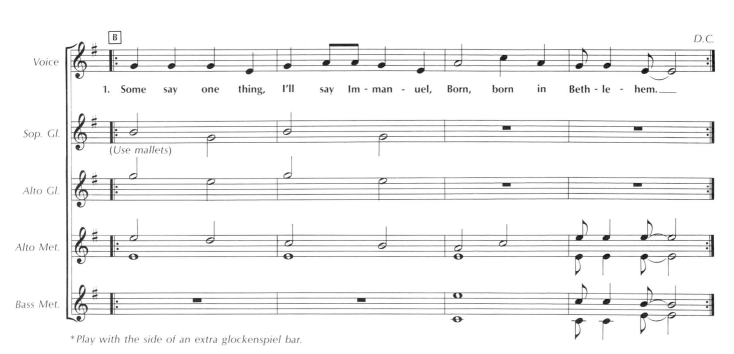

*Play with the side of an extra glockenspiel bar.

2. Some call Him one thing,
I'll call Him Jesus,
Born, born in Bethlehem.

3. Sweet little baby,
Born in a manger,
Born, born in Bethlehem.

FORTY-NINE ANGELS

WORDS AND MUSIC BY ROBERT SCHMERTZ   ARRANGED BY MARILYN COPELAND DAVIDSON

FROM A PICTURE BOOK OF SONGS AND BALLADS BY ROBERT SCHMERTZ. USED BY PERMISSION.

(Alternative piano acc., p. 296)

Keep the right hand farther away from the body. Play four patterns with the hands several inches apart, then move the left hand closer to the right to play the last three patterns.

2. Bass Met. and Alto Met.: As someone plays the Alto Gl., have half the children snap each part.

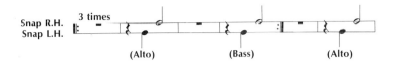

3. Sop. Gl.: Add the cluster on the last note. A light, delicate touch is necessary for a beautiful sound.

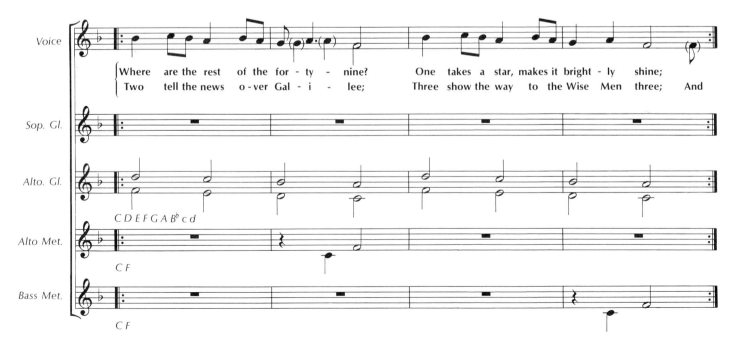

MY TWENTY PENNIES

As the children sing the song, have them accent the first beat of each measure. The feeling of a flowing meter in three is important for learning the instrument parts. Also notice the two measures that are repeated for the cumulative verses.

1. Bass Xyl.: Pat legs.

To learn where the changes are, extend the chant:

Practice the entire song, notating the sequence of patterns if necessary. Transfer to the instrument and sing.

2. Alto Xyl.: Sing the xylophone part with letter names and word patterns:

3. Alto Gl.: Snap fingers of both hands on the first beat of each measure.

*Play with the side of an extra glockenspiel bar.

MY TWENTY PENNIES

FOLK SONG FROM VENEZUELA   TRANSLATION BY J. OLCUTT SANDERS

ARRANGED BY MARILYN COPELAND DAVIDSON

COPYRIGHT © 1948 BY COOPERATIVE RECREATION SERVICE. RENEWED 1976. USED BY PERMISSION.

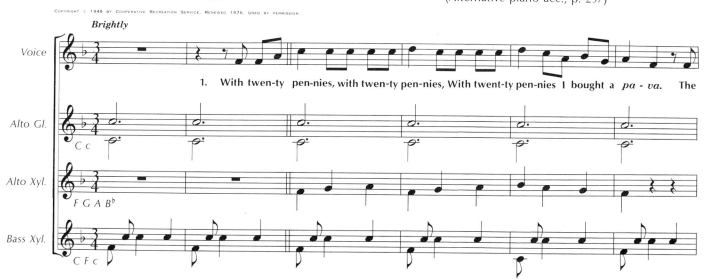

BROTHER NOAH

This accompaniment is made up of stepwise melodic segments that emphasize the upward/downward concept. Teach the instrument parts in this order: Sop. Gl. (upward); Alto Xyl. (upward); Sop. Xyl. (upward and downward); Bass Xyl. (repeated tones, downward and upward, upward); Woodblock and Cymbal.

For each melodic segment, help the children discover:

1. The melodic direction

2. The direction to play (left/right) and the number of notes to play in each direction
3. Any repeated tones
4. Any rests
5. The rhythm pattern

Add one part at a time, over several lessons. To help the children find their starting pitch, have the Sop. Gl. play the rhythm of the cymbal part on the introduction. Play D and d on the two quarter notes. The woodblock rhythm is the same as the word *Halleloo*.

*Repeat for additional lines in verses 2–6.

2. With twenty pennies, with twenty pennies,
   With twenty pennies I bought a *gata*.
   The *gata* had a *gatito*,
   I have the *gata* and the *gatito*;
   I have the *pava* and the *pavito*;
   And so I still have my twenty pennies.

3. . . . *chiva* . . . *chivito* . . .

4. . . . *mona* . . . *monito* . . .

5. . . . *lora* . . . *lorito* . . .

6. . . . *vaca* . . . *vaquito* . . .

BROTHER NOAH

AMERICAN SEA SONG   ARRANGED BY MARILYN COPELAND DAVIDSON

REPRINTED FROM AMERICAN SEA SONGS AND CHANTEYS. COMPILED BY FRANK SHAY AND ILLUSTRATED BY EDWARD A. WILSON. BY PERMISSION OF W. W. NORTON & COMPANY, INC. COPYRIGHT 1948 BY FRANK SHAY AND EDWARD A. WILSON. COPYRIGHT RENEWED 1976.

(Alternative piano acc., p. 294)

2. No, you can't sir, No, you can't sir,
   You can't come into the Ark of the Lord,
   Though it's growing very dark and it's raining very hard.
   Halleloo, halleloo, halleloo-oo-oo-oo-ia!

SKIN AND BONES

Mysteriously

1. There was an old wom-an all skin and bones, Oo - oo - oo - ooh! 2. She
3. One night she thought she'd take a walk, Oo - oo - oo - ooh! 4. She
5. She saw the bones a-layin' a-round, Oo - oo - oo - ooh! 6. She

FOLK SONG FROM KENTUCKY
COLLECTED BY JEAN RITCHIE
ARRANGED BY MARJORIE AMES
© 1952 JEAN RITCHIE GEORDIE MUSIC PUBLISHING, INC.

PUPIL'S BOOK, PAGE 52

lived down by the old grave-yard, Oo - oo - oo - ooh!
walked down by the old grave-yard, Oo - oo - oo - ooh!
went to the closet to get a broom, Oo - oo - oo - ooh!

7. She o-pened the door and BOO!!

LITTLE DAVID, PLAY ON YOUR HARP

Brightly

REFRAIN

BLACK SPIRITUAL
ARRANGED BY HANNAH TORAIN

PUPIL'S BOOK, PAGE 88

Lit-tle Dav - id, play on your harp, Hal - le - lu, hal - le -

lu, Lit-tle Dav - id, play on your harp, Hal - le - lu.

292

VERSE

Lit - tle Dav - id was a shep - herd boy, ____ He killed Go - li - ath and shout - ed for joy.

D.C. al Fine

'TATERS

YIDDISH FOLK SONG
ARRANGED BY ROSEMARY JACQUES
ENGLISH WORDS BY JACOB SLOAN

"ZUNTIG-BULBE" REPRINTED BY PERMISSION OF SCHOCKEN BOOKS INC. FROM
A TREASURY OF JEWISH FOLKSONG EDITED BY RUTH RUBIN. COPYRIGHT
© 1950 BY SCHOCKEN BOOKS' INC. COPYRIGHT RENEWED © 1978 BY
RUTH RUBIN.

Monotonously

1. Sun - day, 'ta - ters, Mon - day, 'ta - ters, Tues - day and Wednes - day, ___
2. Bread and 'ta - ters, Meat and 'ta - ters, Lunch and __ din - ner, ___
3. Still, ___ 'ta - ters, Ev - er, 'ta - ters, Al - ways, ___ al - ways, ___

PUPIL'S BOOK, PAGE 66

'ta - ters, Thurs - day and Fri - day, ___ 'ta - ters, Sab - bath, for a spe - cial treat,
'ta - ters. O - ver and o - ver, ___ 'ta - ters. Once, __ for a spe - cial treat,
'ta - ters! To - day and to - mor - row, ___ 'ta - ters! Af - ter Sab - bath pot __ roasts

there's a 'ta - ter pud - ding! Sun - day ___ starts with ___ 'ta - ters.
there's a 'ta - ter pud - ding! Sun - day ___ starts with ___ 'ta - ters.
there's a 'ta - ter pud - ding! Sun - day ___ starts with ___ 'ta - ters.

BROTHER NOAH

AMERICAN SEA SONG

ARRANGED BY LAURA S. WENDEL

Reprinted from American Sea Songs and Chanteys. Compiled by Frank Shay and illustrated by Edward A. Wilson, by permission of W. W. Norton & Company, Inc. Copyright 1948 by Frank Shay and Edward A. Wilson. Copyright renewed 1976.

PUPIL'S BOOK, PAGE 6

1. Broth-er No-ah, Broth-er No-ah, May I come in-to the
2. No, you can't, sir, No, you can't, sir, You can't come in-to the

Ark of the Lord, For it's grow-ing ver-y dark and it's rain-ing ver-y hard?
Ark of the Lord, Though it's grow-ing ver-y dark and it's rain-ing ver-y hard.

REFRAIN

Hal-le-loo, hal-le-loo, hal-le-loo-oo-oo-oo-ia!

SHEPHERDS CAME TO BETHLEHEM

POLISH CAROL

ARRANGED BY FRANCIS GIRARD

ENGLISH WORDS BY ROSEMARY JACQUES

PUPIL'S BOOK, PAGE 120

1. Shep-herds came to Beth-le-hem on Christ-mas Day.
2. Then a shep-herd beat up-on a lit-tle drum.
3. As the shep-herds bowed be-fore the bless-ed Boy,

How the Ba-by smiled as they their pipes did play.
How it pleased the Ba-by with its rum-tum-tum.
All the heav-ens rang with sounds of won-drous joy.

WHAT YOU
GONNA CALL
YOUR PRETTY
LITTLE BABY?

BLACK SPIRITUAL
Arranged by LURA SNELL

PUPIL'S BOOK, PAGE 77

FORTY-NINE ANGELS

WORDS AND MUSIC BY ROBERT SCHMERTZ
ARRANGED BY JAMES ROOKER
FROM A PICTURE BOOK OF SONGS AND BALLADS BY ROBERT
SCHMERTZ. USED BY PERMISSION.

PUPIL'S BOOK, PAGE 140

MY TWENTY PENNIES

FOLK SONG FROM VENEZUELA

ARRANGED BY WALLACE SCHMIDT

TRANSLATION BY J. OLCOTT SANDERS

COPYRIGHT © 1948 BY COOPERATIVE RECREATION SERVICE. RENEWED 1976. USED BY PERMISSION.

PUPIL'S BOOK, PAGE 194

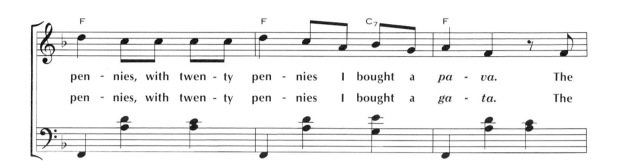

*Repeat for additional lines in verses 3–6.

3.   . . . chiva . . . chivito . . .

4.   . . . mona . . . monito . . .

5.   . . . lora . . . lorito . . .

6.   . . . vaca . . . vaquito . . .

NEW
YEAR'S
SONG

Kazoe-uta

FOLK SONG FROM JAPAN
ARRANGED BY JAMES ROOKER
ENGLISH VERSION BY ROSEMARY JACQUES

PUPIL'S BOOK, PAGE 60

2. On the eve of New Year's,
    Paper streamers, fresh plum blossoms
    Hang above the door,
    Hang above the door,
    Telling all who pass by
      to have a happy day,
    Have a happy day.

3. On the day of New Year's,
    Games are played and songs are sung
    To celebrate the day,
    Celebrate the day.
    People come to wish each other
      Happy New Year's Day,
    Happy New Year's Day.

THE TREE
IN THE WOOD

FOLK SONG FROM ENGLAND
ARRANGED BY JAMES ROOKER

PUPIL'S BOOK, PAGE 10

green leaves grew all a-round, a-round, a-round, And the green leaves grew all a-round.

*Repeat for additional lines in verses 3–8.

3. And on this limb there was a branch,
   The finest branch you ever did see;
   The branch was on the limb,
   The limb was on the tree,
   The tree was in the wood,
   And the green leaves grew . . .

4. And on this branch there was a nest, . . .

5. And in this nest there was an egg, . . .

6. And in this egg there was a bird, . . .

7. And on this bird there was a wing, . . .

8. And on this wing there was a feather, . . .

MICHIE BANJO

CREOLE BAMBOULA
ARRANGED BY WILLIAM SIMON
ENGLISH WORDS BY MARGARET MARKS

PUPIL'S BOOK, PAGE 20

Look at Mich-ie Ban-jo, Fan-cy Mich-ie Ban-jo, Strut-tin'___ down the street.

1. Cha-peau ___ cocked on one side, Mich-ie Ban-jo, High but-ton shoes that squeak,
2. Dia-mond ___ pin in his tie, Mich-ie Ban-jo, Bright yel-low gloves so neat,

Walk-in' stick a-swing-in' wide, Mich-ie Ban-jo, Ev-'ry-thing's all com-plete.
Trou-sers pleat-ed way up high, Mich-ie Ban-jo, Ev-'ry-thing's all com-plete.

TUNING THE AUTOHARP

It is essential to keep the Autoharp in tune. Factors such as weather and
frequency of use may necessitate tuning the Autoharp occasionally. Unless
you have had a great deal of experience in hearing chords, you may need to
request the help of your music teacher or a local music store.

SUGGESTED TUNING PROCEDURE

Since the Autoharp is a chording instrument, it should be tuned by chords rather
than by consecutive tones of the scale.

1. Start with the F-major chord. Press the F button and check all F, A, and C
strings with the corresponding tones on a well-tuned piano or a set of tuned
bells. (Tighten the string to raise its pitch; loosen it to lower its pitch. To be
certain that you are tuning the correct string, trace your finger along the
string to its tuning peg.)

2. Press the C-major button and tune the C chord (C—E—G). If you have tuned
all C's carefully (in the F chords), you have only the E and G strings to tune.

3. Continue, as above, tuning chords in the following order:

—*G-major chord* (G—B—D). Only the B and D strings remain to be tuned as
the G strings were tuned in the C chord.

—*G_7 chord* (G—B—D—F) should now be in tune as the F strings were tuned
earlier.

—*D_7 chord* (D—F$^\sharp$—A—C). Only the F$^\sharp$ strings remain to be tuned.

—*B$^\flat$ chord* (B$^\flat$—D—F). Only the B$^\flat$ (A$^\sharp$) strings remain to be tuned.

—*E_7 chord* (E—G$^\sharp$—B—D). Only the G$^\sharp$ strings remain to be tuned.

—*A_7 chord* (A—C$^\sharp$—E—G). Only the C$^\sharp$ strings remain to be tuned.

—*E$^\flat$ chord* (E$^\flat$—G—B$^\flat$). Only the E$^\flat$ strings remain to be tuned.

4. All members of the following chords belong to other chords which have
already been tuned: C_7, A min., D min., G min., D, F_7.

DO ✍ RE ✍ MI ✍ FA ✍ SOL ✍ LA ✍ TI ✍ DO¹ ✍

KODALY GUIDE

Listed below are basic melody patterns found in the song materials in SILVER BURDETT MUSIC, Book 3. The list is intended as a resource for teachers who incorporate Kodály techniques in their teaching. The headings (S, M, M, S, etc.) indicate the melody patterns. The numbers in

parentheses indicate the measures that contain the patterns. The letter *u* before a number means that the pattern begins with the upbeat to the measure.
To give children experience with reading rhythm, see Note-Reading Index, Reading Rhythm (p. 302).

S-M
A Ram Sam Sam, 33 (u 5, u 6)
America, the Beautiful, 184 (u 1, u 5)
Kookaburra, 189 (2)
What Is Love? 109 (23-24, 28-29)
Wonders Never Cease, 186 (2, 3, 5, 6)

M-S
El rorro, 213 (u 1, u 3)
Sow Took the Measles, The, 98 (2, 8)

S-M-S
Joyous Chanukah, 152 (1, 2, 9, 10)

S-L-S-M
Hill an' Gully, 180 (1, 3)

S-L
Love, 68 (1, 5, 9)

S-L-S
Shepherds Came to Bethlehem, 120 (3-4, 7-8)
You Can't Make a Turtle Come Out, 146 (u 1, u 5)

L-S
Roll an' Rock, 12 (10, 12, 14)

S-M-L
Clover, 50 (3, 6)

L-M
Hey Ho, Hey Lo, 42 (1, 3, 7, 11)

M-D
Barnyard, The, 118 (1, 3, 5, 7, 17, 19)
But the Cat Came Back, 20 (9, 16)
Kookaburra, 189 (4, 7)
Oh, Won't You Sit Down? 90 (9-10, 13-14)
Sow Took the Measles, The, 98 (1, 7, 11)

M-D-M
Little David, Play on Your Harp, 88 (1, 5)

S-M-D
He's Got the Whole World in His Hands, 198 (u 1, u 5)
Mama Paquita, 18 (u 1, u 3, u 17, u 19)
Piñata Song, 92 (1-2, 9-10)

S-D
Sweetly Sings the Donkey, 25 (u 5-6)

D-M-S-L-S
When I First Came to This Land, 200 (1-4, 9-12, 20-23)

M-R-D
Clover, 50 (1, 5, 8)
Hop, Old Squirrel, 31 (2, 6)
Lullaby, 31 (1-2, 5-6)

D-R-M
Polly Wolly Doodle, 74 (u 17, u 19)

D-R-M-D
Frère Jacques, 132 (1, 2)
Hill an' Gully, 180 (u 5, u 7, u 9)
Melchior and Balthazar, 214 (1, 5)
Polly Wolly Doodle, 74 (u 1-2, u 3-4)

R-M-D
Forty-Nine Angels, 140 (13, 15, 17, 19)

D-M-S
Ging Gong Gooli, 67 (u 1)
Oh, What a Beautiful City, 40 (1-2, 5-6)

D-R-M-S
Oh, Susanna, 133 (u 1, u 5, u 9, u 13, u 21)

S-L-D¹
Love, 68 (1-2, 5-6)

S₁-D
A Ram Sam Sam, (u 1, u 2)
Mad Man, The, 162 (u 1, u 3)
Sing Together, 32 (9-10, 11-12)
Yankee Doodle, 130 (u i, u 3, u 5)

S₁-L-S₁-D
Oh, Won't You Sit Down? 90 (u 1, u 3, u 5)

S-D¹
Brother Noah, 6 (u 7, u 8, u 9)
Yesterday Morning, 168 (u 13, u 17)

S-L-S-M-D
Oh, Susanna, 133 (u 2, u 6, u 10, u 14, u 22)
Wee Falorie Man, The, 176 (1-2, 5-6)

S₁-D-R-M
Lemons, 170 (u 1-2, u 5-6, u 11-12)

D-S₁
Wind Up the Apple Tree, 43 (5, 6)

D-S₁-D
Frère Jacques, 132 (7, 8)

D-L₁
Hey Ho, Hey Lo, 42 (5, 9)
Old Dan Tucker, 15 (1, 5)
Skin and Bones, 52 (1, 5, 9)

D-L₁-S₁
Little David, Play on Your Harp, 88 (2-3, 6-7)
Wind Up the Apple Tree, 43 (1, 3)

NOTE-READING INDEX

The following information is intended for teachers who wish to develop a music-reading program using materials in SILVER BURDETT MUSIC, Book 3. It is divided into two sections as follows.

Reading Rhythm: This section lists songs according to the note values that make up the rhythm, and (beginning with the heading (♪ ♩ ♪) according to specific note combinations (patterns) that occur in the songs. When the note values or rhythm patterns apply only to part of a song, specific measures are identified in parentheses. The letter *u* before a measure number means that the upbeat to the measure is included. Note: The numeral before each song title indicates the meter of the song (6 equals $\frac{6}{8}$ meter).

Reading Melody: This section lists songs according to the pitches they use. When the pitches apply to only part of a song, specific measures are identified in parentheses. The letter *u* before a measure number means that the upbeat to the measure is included. Note: The headings are organized according to scale degrees, from lowest to highest—e.g., D, R, M; D, R, M, F; D, M; R, M, F, S. Some teachers may wish to use numbers instead of the pitch syllables (do, re, mi, etc.) to designate scale degrees—D-1, R-2, M-3, etc.

READING RHYTHM

♩ ₹
4 Pray God Bless (1-2), 78

♩ ₹ ♫
3 Bella Bimba (refrain), 101
4 Wind Up the Apple Tree (1-4), 43

♩ ♫
4 A Ram Sam Sam (u 1-4), 33
3 Clover, 50
4 Frère Jacques (5-6), 132
4 Hill an' Gully (1, 3, u 5, u 7, u 9), 180
2 Jingle Bells (1-2; 9-10), 131
4 Kookaburra (1-4), 189
2 Melchior and Balthazar (1-2; 5-6), 214
2 Piñata Song (18-25), 92
2 Valentine Round (1-4), 78
4 What You Gonna Call Your Pretty Little Baby? (9-10), 77
2 Wonders Never Cease (1-12), 186

♩ ♫ ♪
3 El rorro (u 1-2), 213
3 My Twenty Pennies (u 1-2; u 5-8), 194

♫ ♪
2 Mad Man, The, 162

♩ ₹ ♫ ♩
4 Ay di, di, di, 129
3 Bella Bimba, 101
4 Hop, Old Squirrel, 31
3 Imagination of Grand Sea, 129
2 Polly Wolly Doodle (verse), 74

♩ ₹ ♩
3 Lullaby, 31
3 Pity the Poor Patat (u 1-7; u 13-16), 9

♩ ♫ ♩
4 A Ram Sam Sam, 33
4 Forty-Nine Angels (5-10; 14-17; 22-25), 140
4 Frère Jacques, 132
4 Ghost of John, The (7-8), 71
4 Hey Ho, Hey Lo, 42
2 Joyous Chanukah, 152
4 On the First Thanksgiving Day (9-10), 56
4 Pray God Bless (3-4), 78

3 Sandy McNab, 63
2 Shepherds Came to Bethlehem, 120
2 Wonders Never Cease, 186

♩ ♩
3 Buying Fish (1-4); u 9-12), 65
4 Frère Jacques (1-4; 7-8), 132
4 Lady, Come, 22
4 On the First Thanksgiving Day (3-4; 7-8; 13-16), 56
4 Twinkle, Twinkle, Little Star (traditional), 166
2 When I First Came to This Land (1-12; 20-23), 200

♩ ₹ ♫ ♩ ○
4 What Is Love? (1-22), 109

♩ ♫ ♩ ○
4 Kookaburra, 189

♩ ₹ ♫ ♩ ♩
4 Ol' Clo', 164

♩ ♫ ♩ ♩
4 Ghost of John, The, 71
3 Love (u 13-16), 68

♩ ♩ ♩
3 Find the Ring, 62

♩ ♫ ♪ ₹
4 Tree in the Wood, The (u 1-4), 10
2 Yankee Doodle (verse), 130

♩ ♪ ♫ ♩
6 How D'ye Do and Shake Hands (u 18-25), 144
6 Shepherds, Bring Candy and Milk, 154
6 Wee Falorie Man, The, 176

♪ ♩ ♪
2 Ain't Gonna Rain (verse), 24
2 Little David, Play on Your Harp (2-5); 6-8), 88
2 Nobody's Business (refrain), 134
4 Old Dan Tucker (9-14), 15

♫ ♩
4 Hill an' Gully, 180
4 Oh, What a Beautiful City (11-14; 17-18), 82

♩ ♩ ♩
4 Chicka Hanka (1-8; 13-16), 54

♬
2 Ging Gong Gooli (1-9), 67
2 Melchior and Balthazar, 214

♩. ♪
3 America, 183
4 America, the Beautiful, 184
3 Buying Fish (refrain), 65
3 Join into the Game, 11
3 Love, 68
4 Old Tante Koba (verse), 16
4 On the First Thanksgiving Day, 56
2 San Sereni (5-12), 199
4 Twinkle, Twinkle, Little Star (Eddleman), 166
4 What Is Love? (23-32), 109
4 What You Gonna Call Your Pretty Little Baby? (1-6), 77
2 Yesterday Morning, 186

♫♪
2 Ain't Gonna Rain (refrain), 24
2 Debka hora, 153
2 One Day My Mother Went to the Market (1-5; u 20-23), 104
2 'Taters (1-6; 9-10), 66

♫
2 All the Pretty Little Horses, 49
4 Allouette, 46
4 Battle Hymn of the Republic, 131
4 Brother Noah, 6
2 Jingle Bells, 131
2 Mama Paquita, 18
2 Marching to Pretoria (verse), 4
2 Oh, Susanna, 133
4 Oh, What a Beautiful City (1-6), 40, 82
2 Old Joe Clark (1-14), 8
3 Pig, The, 114
4 Shepherd, Shepherd (1-6), 75
4 Sweetly Sings the Donkey (1-4), 25
4 Tree in the Wood, The (u 5-10), 10
2 Yankee Doodle (refrain), 130

♪ ♩.
4 Carrot Stew (u 7-10), 44
4 Chicka Hanka (9-12), 54
4 Rain Song (u 1-16), 59

♪♪♪
2 Rabbit Hash, 117

302

READING MELODY

D, R, M
Clover (1, 5, 8), 50
Frère Jacques (1-2), 132
Hop, Old Squirrel, 31
Lullaby, 31
Oh, Won't You Sit Down? (section B), 90
San Sereni (u 9-12), 199

D, R, M, F
Polly Wolly Doodle (u 1-7; u 17-24), 74
This Land Is Your Land (u 1-4; u 9-12;
    u 17-20; u 25-28), 202

D, R, M, F, S
Forty-Nine Angels (u 12-19), 140
German Instrument Song (1-4), 136
How D'ye Do and Shake Hands
    (1-5; u 10-13),
Jingle Bells, 131
Lady, Come, 22
Marching to Pretoria (1-16; u 29-32), 4
Michie Banjo (1-4), 20
Old Tante Koba (u 9-14), 16
Pity the Poor Patat, 9

D, R, M, F, S, L
Clover, 50
Ging Gong Gooli (10-25), 67
He's Got the Whole World in His
    Hands, 198
Join into the Game (u 1-8; u 13-16), 11
My Twenty Pennies (u 1-6), 194
Nobody's Business, 134
Oh, Susanna, 133
San Sereni, 199
Shepherd, Shepherd (u 7-10), 75
Tree in the Wood, The, 10
Twinkle, Twinkle, Little Star (tradi-
    tional), 166
What Is Love? 109
Wonders Never Cease, 186

D, R, M, F, S, L, D¹
On the First Thanksgiving Day (1-8), 56
Roll an' Rock, 12
Shepherds Came to Bethlehem
    (9-16), 120

D, R, M, S
Forty-Nine Angels (9-10; 24-25), 140
Jingle Bells (1-4; 9-12), 131
Old Blue (refrain), 112
Old Man, The (u 1-2), 177
Old Tante Koba (1-6), 16
What Is Love? (1-4; 23-32), 109

D, R, M, S, L
Oh, Susanna (u 1-16; u 21-24), 133
Wee Falorie Man, The (5-8), 176

D, R, M, S, L, D'
Carrot Stew (refrain), 44
Little David, Play on Your Harp
    (verse), 88
Love (1-8), 68

D, M
Barnyard, The (1, 3, 5, 7, 17, 19, 21,
    23), 118
Oh, Won't You Sit Down? (9-10;
    13-14), 90
Sing Together (1-2), 32

D, M, F, S
Oh, What a Beautiful City (1-6), 40, 82
Old Joe Clark (9-10; 13-14), 8

D, M, F, S, L
Oh, What a Beautiful City (11-18), 82

D, M, S
Mama Paquita (u 1-3; u 17-19), 18
Piñata Song (1-2; 9-10), 92
Scratch, Scratch (u 1-2), 116
Sow Took the Measles, The (1-2; 7-8), 98

D, M, S, L
Hill an' Gully (1-4), 180
My Twenty Pennies (u 1-2), 194
Wee Falorie Man, The (1-2; 5-6), 176
When I First Came to This Land (1-4;
    9-12; 20-23), 200

D, S
Sweetly Sings the Donkey (u 5-6), 25

R, M, F, S
El rorro (u 1-5), 213

R, M, F, S, L
Find the Ring (1-8), 62

R, M, S
America, the Beautiful (u 1-2;
    u 5-6), 184

M, F, S, L
You Can't Make a Turtle Come Out
    (u 1-8), 146

M, S
A Ram Sam Sam (u 5-6), 33
Joyous Chanukah (1-2; 9-10), 152
Sing Together (5-6), 32

M, S, L
Clover (3, 6), 50
Hana ichi momme (3-4; 7-8), 128
Kookaburra (1-2), 189
Little David, Play on Your Harp (9-13), 88

M, L
Hey Ho, Hey Lo (1, 3, 7, 11), 42

M₁, L₁
'Taters (1-2), 66

S, L, T, D¹
Yesterday Morning (u 13-14;
    u 17-18), 168

TEACHER'S NOTES

TEACHER'S NOTES

TEACHER'S NOTES

TEACHER'S NOTES

CLASSIFIED INDEX

CONCEPTS

PLAYING INSTRUMENTS

INDEX

PICTURE CREDITS

Cover: Victoria Beller-Smith

Instruments: courtesy of Dorn & Kirschner Band Instrument Co., Union, N.J. 2: *t.* Silver Burdett Photos; *b.* Victoria Beller-Smith for Silver Burdett. 3: Victoria Beller-Smith for Silver Burdett. 5: Silver Burdett Photo. 6: Victoria Beller-Smith for Silver Burdett. 7: Silver Burdett Photo. 12: Victoria Beller-Smith for Silver Burdett. 13, 14: Silver Burdett Photos. 18: John Bacchus for Silver Burdett. 22: Silver Burdett Photo. 26: *t.* Cornell Capa from Magnum; *b.* Victoria Beller-Smith for Silver Burdett. 27: Victoria Beller-Smith for Silver Burdett. 28, 29: Silver Burdett Photos. 34, 35: Victoria Beller-Smith for Silver Burdett. 38: *t.* Susan Johns from Rapho Guillumette; *m.* William Carter; *b. l.* Joel Gordon from Photo Trends; *b. r.* Victoria Beller-Smith for Silver Burdett. 39: D. Kateley from DeWys, Inc. 40, 41: Al Freni. 48: Tim Eagan from Woodfin Camp. 53: Silver Burdett Photo. 58: Victoria Beller-Smith for Silver Burdett. 61, 63: John Bacchus for Silver Burdett. 70: *t.* Norman Owen Tomalin from Bruce Coleman; *b.* Neville Fox-Davies from Bruce Coleman. 71, 72: Victoria Beller-Smith for Silver Burdett. 80: *t. r., b. l.* Courtesy, Sheldon Jackson College, Sitka, Alaska; *m. r., t. l., b. r.* Museum of the American Indian. 80, 81: John Running. 82: *l.* John Running; *r.* Belzeaux from Rapho Guillumette. 84, 86: Silver Burdett Photos. 86: *b. l.* Victoria Beller-Smith for Silver Burdett. 89: Silver Burdett Photo. 96: John Bacchus for Silver Burdett. 97, 100: Victoria Beller-Smith for Silver Burdett. 108: Doug Bates. 111: Victoria Beller-Smith for Silver Burdett. 127, 137: John Bacchus for Silver Burdett. 139: *t. l.* Baldwin Piano and Organ Company; *t. r.* Hal McKusick from D. P. I.; *m. l., m.* Photo Media Ltd.; *m. r., b.* John Bacchus for Silver Burdett. 142: Silver Burdett Photos. 148, 149: Victoria Beller-Smith for Silver Burdett. 158, 159: Silver Burdett Photos. 162–164, 172, 173: Victoria Beller-Smith for Silver Burdett. 178: W. Bryant from Camera 5. 178, 179: Victoria Beller-Smith for Silver Burdett. 179: *t.* Silver Burdett Photo; *b.* Jim Eversole. 184, 185: Victoria Beller-Smith for Silver Burdett. 192, 193: DeWys, Inc. 209: *t.* John Running; *b.* Tim Eagan.

1 2 3 4 5 6 7 8 9 10–RRD–85 84 83 82 81 80